# MIGRATION TO THE ARAB WORLD

## DATE DUE

| | | | |
|---|---|---|---|
| | | | |
| | | | |
| | | | |
| | | | |
| | | | |
| | | | |
| | | | |
| | | | |
| | | | |
| | | | |
| | | | |
| | | | |
| | | | |
| | | | |
| | | | |
| | | | |
| | | | |
| | | | |

DEMCO 38-296

## Note to the Reader from the UNU

In 1983, the United Nations University launched a project on the Global Impact of Human Migration, with a major focus on migration caused by uneven industrialization in different countries and regions of the world. The impact of large-scale migration is not limited to economic effects, but has social and cultural dimensions as well, in both the sending and the receiving countries. The first phase of the project was concerned with surveying the migration flows from seven Asian countries to the Arab region and was published in *Migration of Asian Workers to the Arab World* (1986).

*Migration to the Arab World: Experience of Returning Migrants* reports the results of a unique empirical and cross-cultural study of migrant workers in the pre-, during, and post-migration phases in the seven Asian countries. The data and information were collected primarily through open-ended interviews with some 500 returned migrants in each country on the basis of a common research framework to enable comparison on a regional level. The study makes a series of recommendations to the governments, the private sectors, and NGOs to improve the situation of the returned migrants.

# MIGRATION TO THE ARAB WORLD: EXPERIENCE OF RETURNING MIGRANTS

Edited by Godfrey Gunatilleke

 UNITED NATIONS UNIVERSITY PRESS

The views expressed in this publication are those of the authors and do not necessarily represent the views of the United Nations University.

United Nations University Press
The United Nations University, Toho Seimei Building, 15-1 Shibuya 2-chome, Shibuya-ku,
Tokyo 150, Japan
Tel.: (03) 3499-2811   Fax: (03) 3499-2828   Telex: J25442   Cable: UNATUNIV TOKYO

Typeset by Asco Trade Typesetting Limited, Hong Kong
Printed by Permanent Typesetting and Printing Co., Ltd., Hong Kong
Cover design by Takashi Suzuki

HSDB-47/UNUP-745
ISBN 92-808-0745-5
United Nations Sales No. E.90.III.A.11
03500 C

# CONTENTS

# INTRODUCTION

**Godfrey Gunatilleke**
Marga Institute, Colombo, Sri Lanka

The present volume is a sequel to *Migration of Asian Workers to the Arab World*, which surveyed the experiences of the migration in seven Asian countries on the basis of the information and data available from existing secondary sources. The countries that participated in the project were: Bangladesh, India (State of Kerala), Republic of Korea, Pakistan, Philippines, Sri Lanka, and Thailand. The state-of-the-art survey in the previous volume was the first phase of a research project sponsored by the United Nations University to examine the global impact of human migration. The Asian migration to Arab countries was selected as one important component of that project.

In its second phase the project organized studies in the seven countries that had originally participated in the research. In these studies the project aimed to verify and further explore some of the general conclusions that emerged from the state-of-the-art survey by means of a comprehensive survey and analysis of the experience of a representative group of about 500 migrants who had returned after the migration. The project thereby expected to gather a body of reliable primary data for itself, within a framework which facilitated inter-country comparisons and which provided the scope for further in-depth inquiry into selected aspects of the migration.

## The Scope of the Study

The survey covered all three phases of the migration: the pre-migration phase during which migrants seek employment, are recruited and make preparations for the migration; the period of their employment abroad when households as well as migrants adjust to the new circumstances and manage the new flows of income they receive; and the period after return, with the process of reintegration and readjustment that follows. The survey selected migrants who had returned after employment abroad because these migrants were able to speak for the entire process of migration, from the time they seek employment abroad, through their sojourn in the host country, to their final return and reabsorption in the home

1

country. The survey sought answers to a wide range of questions in each phase of the migration.

First, it gathered detailed information on the social and demographic characteristics of the migrants, their motivation in seeking employment, and the goals and objectives they had set for themselves.

Next, the survey examined how the migrants were recruited and what problems they encountered in the process of recruitment; how they prepared for the migration, in terms of training and orientation as well as seeking knowledge and information about the host country. The survey inquired in some depth into the manner in which the prevalent system and existing government machinery functioned to regulate and facilitate the migration. It obtained information on the costs that were incurred and the incidence of fraud and irregularity committed by agents and intermediaries.

Third, the survey dealt with the conditions of employment in the host country and how the migrants adjusted to their foreign environment and their separation from home. It also covered the situation of the family that had been left behind, and the impact the migration had on spouse, children, and intra-family relations.

Fourth, the data were gathered in such a way as to facilitate comparison between the condition of households prior to migration and their condition after employment abroad. Therefore, one of the central components of the survey was the impact of the migration on the material well-being of the migrant and his family in terms of wealth, income, and quality of life. This included their nutrition, housing, and education.

Fifth, the survey dealt with the migrant's return and examined how he had re-entered the workforce, and whether the migration had helped him to achieve a sustained improvement in his standard of living.

The survey also examined the impact of the migration on human resource development in its widest sense – the acquisition of new skills and aptitudes, attitudinal and ideological changes, and the effect on the relationship between the migrant and his family and the community in which they lived.

These were some of the main questions explored in the survey. The project thus aimed to evaluate the impact of the migration both on the economic well-being of the migrant and his family and on their total human development.

Before the survey was undertaken, the researchers met at a workshop in which the research design, the interview schedule, and the methodology for the selection of the sample were discussed at length and a comparative framework was accepted for the study as a whole. The methodology for selecting the sample varied according to the needs of the different countries. The task of identifying the migrants for inclusion in the sample posed a variety of problems and revealed the serious deficiencies in the systems of information that were available regarding the migration. There was no readily available source in any of the countries from which the researchers could prepare a reliable sample frame. In most cases the migrants had to be selected purposively either from locations which were known to have supplied migrants on a large scale, as in the case of Bangladesh or the Philippines, or from institutions and firms, as in the case of the Republic of Korea. The Sri Lankan researchers first compiled a list of 5,000 migrants through visits and field investigations, and used this as the frame from which they drew the final sample. While the sample designs employed by the researchers could not ensure a statistically representative sample for the migration as a whole, they were able to select a sample which corresponded to the composition of the migrant flow in terms of the mix of skills and their regional distribution. This they were able to do on the basis of the information that had already been gathered in previous surveys and studies. As a result of these problems, there was some variation in the size of the sample. While Sri Lanka, the Philippines, Thailand, and the Republic of Korea selected samples ranging between 480 and 510, the sample in Bangladesh covered 368 migrants, and the Kerala sample included 696.

As this survey was confined to migrants who had returned after employment abroad, the sample comprised persons who, by and large, were successful in obtaining employment in the Arab countries. As a result, the survey sample did not adequately represent those persons who had failed in their attempts to migrate for a variety of reasons, such as fraud and malpractices relating to the recruitment process. Therefore, the deficiencies in the prevailing system and the extent of victimization are not fully revealed in the survey, except through the experiences of the migrants who succeeded in migrating.

There were other inherent constraints and limitations in the type of survey that was undertaken, and the authors have drawn attention to these in their analysis. One problem with the methodology that had been adopted was that of recall. Most researchers were not able to obtain accurate and firm data on various aspects of the migration, such as incomes earned by the household prior to migration, the exact amounts that were earned, spent, and saved abroad and remitted home, and the nature and intensity of the adjustments faced by both the migrant in the host country and the families that were left behind. These problems of exactitude, however, do not seriously affect the reliability of the data for the purpose of making reasonable estimates and assessments. In most cases the estimates of earnings, savings, and investments were related to the assets that had been acquired, or the improvements that had been made, or the savings that had been accumulated and were still available. Very often, these were demonstrable aids to recall and were adequate for the purpose of the evaluation attempted in the study. Similarly, some of the main events in the different phases of migration, as they related to the recruitment, the nature of the contract, the procedures followed for remittances, and the mode of communication with the family, seldom presented serious problems of recall.

Another problem to which the researchers draw attention is the subjective bias in the responses made by the migrants. It is likely that some migrants suppress certain of the unpleasant and negative experiences that they may have had, and are boastful of their achievements. On the other hand, migrants who were not particularly successful may tend to exaggerate the negative features of the migration and present them as an experience that should be avoided. There is no doubt that the account of the migration is coloured by the character traits of the migrants themselves, and to that extent distorts both the positive and the negative aspects of the migration. This is particularly applicable to the questions relating to the impact of the migration on the personal lives and relationships of the migrants and their families. Any conclusions regarding the extent of the distortion that subjective biases introduced into the responses of migrants must, however, remain speculative.

It is without doubt difficult to ascertain the human cost of the migration through

3

a single "question-and-answer" type of inquiry. The researcher would have to probe beneath what is apparent to the migrant, or even what is consciously accepted by him, and observe his life and relationships over a period of time. The project did not provide for such participant observation. It also did not test the migrant's responses against those of the household and family, although in many of the studies the interview took place in the home, very often in the presence of other members of the household. As a result, there was sufficient interaction to reflect the situation of the household as a whole in areas where the spouse and the children might be involved.

The project, as it was designed, confined the scope of its inquiry to an intensive examination of the individual experiences of the migrants. It did not attempt to place the migration within the context of the larger political and social structures in each country, or to examine the "political economy" of the migration to the Arab countries. In a few of the studies some of these larger constraints, which are inherent in the ongoing socio-economic and political processes in the different countries, are reflected in the individual experiences of the migrants. The Kerala study refers to the inordinate cost of the migration to the individual migrant, and attributes this to the unregulated character of the migration, where the state has been unable to enforce the required norms and where the recruiting agencies form a powerful interest group. The Pakistan study refers to the proliferation of private investment banks, which attracted the savings of expatriates and then managed these resources in a manner disadvantageous to the migrants. The Bangladesh study describes in some detail the way in which the migration has forged links with the economy through the various new services and activities that it has generated.

In each case the migration has become a multifaceted, profitable economic activity. The way, therefore, in which the benefits of the migration accrue to the migrant himself will depend to a great extent on the prevailing economic system and how it functions. This applies to all phases of the migration, but it is most evident in the recruitment phase, where the businesses dealing with the migration itself are most active, and in the return phase, where the savings skills and other capacities are put to use in the domestic economy. In both these stages, intermediaries and entrepreneurs of various types enter the scene and exploit the conditions that enable them to appropriate a large share of the economic benefits of the migration. This distribution of benefits is often influenced by political processes as well. Those in positions of power that are linked to the regulation and management of the migration find ready-made opportunities to acquire an interest in this new market.

As noted later, most studies reveal that a significant proportion of the migrants showed a strong preference for self-employment. The extent to which the aspirations of the migrants in this category are realized will depend essentially on the place given to the small entrepreneur and the small investor in the national system, and this in turn is largely determined by the political character of the ruling élites and the way in which it balances the interests of big business with the promotion of small enterprise and self-employment. The studies were unable to undertake serious examination of many of these politico-economic aspects and have had to confine themselves to the observations that arise from the specific experience of migrants. While an inter-country comparison of these factors in the seven countries would provide valuable insights as regards our total understanding of the migration, it would have to form part of a separate study.

**Table 1.** Skill composition of migrants (percentages)

| Country | Unskilled[a,b] | Skilled[a] | Mid-level[c] | High-level[c] |
|---|---|---|---|---|
| Republic of Korea | 8.5 | 70 | 13.1 | 8.5 |
| Bangladesh | 35 | 50 | 15 | 15 |
| Philippines | — | 78 | 22 | 22 |
| Pakistan | 45 | 37 | 18 | 18 |
| Thailand | 28 | 60 | 12 | 12 |
| Sri Lanka | 74 | 21 | 5 | 5 |
| State of Kerala (India) | 48 | 24 | 25 | 25 |

a. Skilled and unskilled include all manual labour, such as construction labour, operators of equipment, house workers, caretakers, and service workers of all types.
b. The distinction between semi-skilled and unskilled is not always clear. The semi-skilled have been classified among the unskilled in some samples and among the skilled in others.
c. Mid-level and high-level workers include white-collar jobs and supervisory, technical, and professional grades.

## The Demographic and Socio-economic Characteristics of Migrants: An Inter-country Comparison

The seven country studies also have special value in that they provide a fairly comprehensive survey of the experience of migration as it occurs in a broad spectrum of development in the developing countries of Asia. The migrant samples, which, as stated earlier, are broadly representative of the migration to the Middle East from each of these countries, show considerable variation in their profiles of skill, age, gender, educational level, and other socio-economic characteristics.

There are distinct differences between the level of skill of the migrants from the South Asian countries and those of the three countries from South-East and East Asia. The four South Asian countries have a much larger proportion of unskilled jobs, whereas this category accounts for less than 10 per cent of the migrants from the Republic of Korea and none from the Philippines. The proportion of unskilled from Thailand, at 28 per cent, is still considerably lower than that from Pakistan, Kerala, or Sri Lanka. The sample for Bangladesh is not altogether representative of the skill composition in the national outflow; even so, the proportion of unskilled in the Bangladesh sample is also higher, at 35 per cent. Other more representative surveys have indicated that the proportion of unskilled in the migrant outflow from Bangladesh is as high as 50 per cent. Several factors seem to combine to produce this regional distribution of skills. In a market in which the supply of unskilled and semi-skilled labour is abundant, host countries are able to bid down wages to levels which give the low-wage countries of South Asia a competitive edge in this labour category over the other sending countries.

The distribution of skills of migrants among the different sending countries and the proportions of the different skills in each sample bears some relationship to the differentials between the foreign and domestic wages for the different skills and grades. The differentials for unskilled wages in the case of the Republic of Korea, the Philippines, and Thailand do not appear to attract these grades in the same proportions as in the South Asian countries. Other costs, such as travel, are likely to be lower for South Asian migrants, as they come from closer destinations. In the

5

case of skilled labour, however, the situation tends to be different, as the supply is less elastic and the relatively scarce skills have to be recruited from various countries depending on their availability. However, there are special characteristics in the labour market of the host countries which cannot be explained entirely in terms of supply and demand. These include preferences based on religious, social, and cultural grounds as well as other distortions, such as those introduced by the processes of recruitment and the appropriations made by the intermediaries in both the host and the labour-supplying countries. There is also some differentiation in wage payments to migrants depending on the country of origin, and to this extent the labour supply is segmented. This differentiation is related in part to the host country's perception of varying proficiency and competence, such as literacy or the average level of performance of workers from each country based on past experience. These, among other factors, influence the distribution of skills in the migrant workforce among the countries of the region.

All country samples contain a small component of middle and higher level skills in clerical, supervisory, and professional grades. This proportion was highest in the Republic of Korea, the Philippines and Kerala, rising to over 20 per cent of the total sample. It was much lower for the other four countries, ranging from around 5 to 12 per cent. The managerial and supervisory component in the case of Korea is linked to the special nature of migration, which results in the transfer to the host country of a full working unit, including workers of all grades, from unskilled labour to management. In the case of the Philippines and Kerala, the supply of middle- and high-level workers reflects the relatively high rates of national participation in the upper levels of education. Kerala in particular presents an interesting case in its composition of skills, with sizeable components in the unskilled as well as in the middle and higher categories.

The educational profile of the migrants from the seven countries does not reveal the same comparative pattern as the skill profile. The Sri Lankan and Kerala samples, which have high proportions of unskilled labour, have also relatively high educational levels, comparing favourably with those of the three countries that had larger proportions of skilled labour in their samples. The Philippines sample shows the highest educational level, and correspondingly its skill composition of migrants does not include unskilled labour. Over 16 per cent of the migrants in both Bangladesh and Pakistan have no formal education. When the educational levels of the migrants are compared with the average educational levels for the population as a whole, it would appear that for most of the countries the average educational level of migrants is higher than the national average. The better-educated appear to have had greater access to the opportunities for employment abroad, even in the case of the unskilled category. This is clearly reflected in, for example, the data for Bangladesh and Pakistan, where the proportion with no formal education is much lower than the national average and the proportion with secondary-school education considerably higher.

Although there are noticeable differences in the age composition of the workforce, on the whole the large majority of the workers are under 35 years. The youngest workforce in the sample is from Pakistan, where approximately 37 per cent of the migrants are less than 25 years of age at the time of migration. Kerala and Bangladesh come next, with 32 per cent and 30 per cent respectively in this

**Table 2.** Educational level of migrants (percentages)

| Country | No formal education | Primary | Secondary | | Tertiary |
|---|---|---|---|---|---|
| | | | Lower | Upper | |
| Bangladesh | 17 | 26 | 29 | 19 | 9 |
| Kerala (India) | 7 | 47 | 22 | 18 | 6 |
| Republic of Korea | 1 | 19 | 24 | 41 | 15 |
| Pakistan | 16 | 16 | 54 | 12 | 2 |
| Philippines | | | | 88 | 12 |
| Sri Lanka | 2 | 22 | 75 | 75 | 1 |
| Thailand | | 88 | 12 | 12 | |

age-group. The other countries have relatively older migrant workers. Korea had only 20 per cent of its workforce below the age of 25, Sri Lanka 10, and the Philippines 6. In the case of Korea and the Philippines, the higher skill composition is likely to be related to the somewhat older workforce with longer work experience. No such relationship, however, can be observed in the case of Sri Lanka, where the large majority of the workers are in the unskilled category.

As might be expected, the share of married workers in the migrant workforce is larger for the migrant samples which have an older age composition. About two-thirds of the migrant workers or more are married in the case of Sri Lanka, the Philippines, Thailand, and Korea. The data for Bangladesh are not comparable, as they refer to marital status after return; most of the unmarried migrants who had returned with earnings from abroad would have married and set up new households. The number of heads of households should normally bear a fairly close relationship to marital status. The proportion of heads of households for Korea, the Philippines, and Thailand does not differ very much from the number married. The situation is, however, very different for Pakistan, Sri Lanka, and Kerala. In the case of Kerala and Sri Lanka, the proportion of heads of households is in the region of 20 per cent of the total sample, although the number married amounts to a much larger share. In the case of Pakistan, the number of heads of households is double that of married workers. Sri Lanka sends as housemaids a large number of married females, who do not enjoy the position of head of household. The circumstances that have contributed to the very sharp difference between the situations of Pakistan and Kerala are not clear from the data gathered in the studies. In one case, migrants had married at a very young age prior to migration, but have not assumed the responsibilities of heads of households. In the other case, young workers remained unmarried but had already moved into the position of head of household.

The married state and responsibility as head of household are important factors, affecting first the nature of the adjustments that have to be made by both families as well as migrants and, second, the performance in terms of savings and the use of the incomes earned. Migration imposes stresses on the migrant and the household through separation. It places new responsibilities on the family. At the same time the married condition provides stronger motivation to maximize the benefits of the migration. On these criteria, both the problems of adjustment and the

**Table 3.** Distribution of migrants by age and gender (percentages)

| Country | Age | | | Gender | |
|---|---|---|---|---|---|
| | Under 25 | 25–34 | Over 35 | Male | Female |
| Bangladesh | 30 | 34 (25–30 yrs)[a] | 36 (over 30 yrs) | 100 | — |
| Kerala (India) | 32 | 38 | 30 | 100 | — |
| Republic of Korea | 20 | 60 | 20 | 100 | — |
| Pakistan | 37 | 45 | 18 | 100 | — |
| Philippines | 6 | 44 | 50 | 93 | 7 |
| Sri Lanka | 10 | 51 | 39 | 38 | 62 |
| Thailand | 30 (21–30 yrs) | 43 (31–40 yrs) | 27 (over 40 yrs) | 100 | — |

a. The figures in parentheses refer to the age-groups for these countries, which deviate slightly from those given in the columns.

motivation to derive the full benefit from the migration have been present to a high degree in countries such as Korea, the Philippines and Thailand, which had the largest proportions of married household heads.

Family size and the number of working members, factors that are closely related to the economic status of the households from which workers migrate, vary from country to country. The size of households was much larger for the four South Asian countries than for the three countries in South-East Asia and East Asia. At the same time the number of working members per household was less. For example, the average household size in Kerala was approximately 8, with one working member per household. In Pakistan it was 7 with 1.68 working members. In contrast, Thailand had a family size of 5.1 with three working members, and Korea 4 to 4.5 for the different categories of workers with approximately 1.75 working members. The smaller family with more working members provided a stronger resource base for the migrant, and would have normally given greater scope for savings and for maximization of the benefits of the migration.

Sri Lanka and Kerala included a large number of migrants who were unemployed at the time of migration. The figures were as high as 30 per cent for Kerala and 24 per cent for Sri Lanka. At the other end, the Korean migrants were almost all employed prior to the migration. In-between are the other countries, containing 10 to 12 per cent of unemployed as well as a few students who had not yet entered the workforce. For both Sri Lanka and Kerala, the migration, which included a significant component of unemployed workers, helped to mitigate the problems of high unemployment both by absorbing some of the unemployed and by creating employment opportunities through the outflow of those already employed. From the evidence available through other studies of the migration, the outflow of labour does not appear to have created any major problems in the domestic labour market, in regard to the supply; what problems there were, for example in the case of construction labour in Sri Lanka, were soon overcome through accelerated training and other supply measures.

The migrants from South Asian countries come from households that are more disadvantaged socio-economically and have lower levels of income than those from other countries. On the whole, the nature of the incremental benefits that the migration brings to households in the South Asian situation would be higher, and any national economic loss in terms of the migration of skills that are needed domestically would be lower, than for the other countries. The inter-country comparison of the socio-economic status of the households in the seven samples would not be significantly different from the comparison of the per capita incomes of these countries for the population as a whole. Bangladesh, Kerala, Sri Lanka, and Pakistan are all in the category of low-income countries as defined in the World Development Report, with per capita incomes ranging from US$150 for Bangladesh to US$380 for Sri Lanka. The Philippines and Thailand are in the middle-income category, with per capita incomes of US$580 and US$800 respectively, while Korea is in the upper-middle-income group, with a much higher per capita income of US$2,150. As might be expected, the inter-country sample reflected these large regional disparities of income.

From the samples that have been studied, it can be said that the migration to the Arab countries has included the lower-income strata and the manual workers of the sending countries as no other migration flow from these countries has ever done before. To the question of whether the migration reached the poorest segments of these societies, the answer is less clear. From the socio-economic characteristics of the migrants in the samples, such as their educational levels and locations, it would appear that the migration did not include a significant component of the segments that were most deprived or in absolute poverty; most came from social layers that were above this segment. It was those migrants who had had some years of schooling, and who were close to urban centres, who were able to seize the opportunities that emerged. The migrant samples that have been studied, however, refer to the early and middle phases of the migration. As the demonstration effects of the migration and the information regarding the opportunities spread, it is likely that some of the segments which had previously been excluded would begin to take part. The extent to which this happened would depend on a number of factors. At the national level the processes of recruitment would have to function more equitably and efficiently; and in the host countries the demand for foreign labour would have to be sustained without significant contraction if new social layers were to participate in the migration.

The disparities in income between employment abroad and employment at home become progressively narrower as we move from the lowest-income countries to the highest – that is, the Republic of Korea. Whereas for the lowest-paid migrant from Sri Lanka – the housemaid – the difference may be as much as tenfold, in Korea it has narrowed down to two-and-a-half times. As can be observed from table 4, a significant number of the migrants, particularly from the South Asian countries, are unemployed and have no earned income prior to the migration. This, of course, has a variety of implications for the push-and-pull factors of the migration. In the case of the migrants from the poor countries, their entire orientation to the migration and their perspective regarding the benefits that it might bring will be influenced by one compelling motive – the desire to escape their present dire poverty and, in many instances, a situation of long-term unemployment. In such a situation, the better future life that has to be realized, and the specific nature of the improvements and investments, financial and human, that are required for that better life, are seldom clearly articulated in the minds of migrants; the changes that they desire are seen mainly in terms of moving out of

**Table 4.** Distribution of migrants by marital, household, and activity status (percentages)

| Country | Married | Single | Heads of households | Unemployed |
|---|---|---|---|---|
| Bangladesh | — | — | — | 12 |
| Kerala (India) | 49 | 51 | 21 | 38 |
| Republic of Korea | 64 | 36 | 67 | — |
| Pakistan | 24 | 76 | 50 | 11 |
| Philippines | 77 | 23 | — | 10 |
| Sri Lanka | 66 | 32 | 22 | 24 |
| Thailand | 88 | 12 | 83 | — |

present hardship, and a generalized radical change and improvement. In the case of the migrants from Korea what is desired is an incremental improvement. The quality of life already enjoyed provides some basis on which future improvements can be clearly identified, defined, and planned as a part of the goals of the migration. Similarly, the management of the migration becomes an easier task when the increment to the income is not inordinately higher than the current income. The Korean household, with an income that is regular and of a reasonable size, would be much better equipped to plan, budget, and manage the twofold increment that it receives than a poor household in Sri Lanka, which, after barely having enough money to satisfy basic needs, is now receiving a five- to tenfold increase in income. It is, therefore, not surprising that in terms of most criteria, such as savings, achievement of the specific economic objectives of the migration, and improvement in economic status, the outcome for the majority of Korean migrants was positive.

## An Overview of Costs and Benefits

The process of recruitment is one of the most decisive factors of migration. The studies show that the channel of recruitment and the type of intermediary often determines the costs of migration and the nature of the contract the migrant receives, and the reliability of the contractual arrangements that are made. With the exception of Korea, migrants had recourse to informal channels and unlicensed recruiting agents in varying proportions. For example, in Kerala, licensed recruiting agencies accounted for only a small proportion, of less than 8 per cent. In Pakistan, illegal private agencies and friends and relatives were the channels of recruitment for nearly 37 per cent of the migrants. In Bangladesh, Sri Lanka, and the Philippines, the informal channels of friends, relatives, and unlicensed agencies accounted for smaller proportions, ranging from about 20 per cent in Bangladesh to approximately 11 per cent in the Philippines.

When the cost of migration is estimated as a proportion of the earnings of migrants abroad, the migrants from Kerala appear to be faring the worst. The average cost to a Kerala migrant is reported to be approximately Rs. 9,000 in the sample that was interviewed. This compares with the average monthly earnings of migrants, which for approximately 77 per cent were below Rs. 3,000 in the first job they held abroad. It would appear that the migrant has to use approximately four to five months' earnings abroad to offset the cost of migration. The next highest costs per migrant were observed in Thailand, where the payments made by migrants averaged approximately 30,000 to 40,000 baht, or three to four times their monthly earnings. Costs begin to fall significantly with the other countries: according to the surveys in Bangladesh and Pakistan, they come to approximately two to two-and-a-half months' earnings; in Sri Lanka and the Philippines, they are less than a month's earnings; and in Korea, less than half a month's earnings. These, however, were the average figures for the samples surveyed. They masked significant variations. The unskilled migrants and those who were illiterate or had low educational attainments appear to have fared the worst while being also the ones who could afford least. In Bangladesh the average cost for the professional was in the region of 22,000 taka, the equivalent of about a month's salary; the unskilled worker incurred nearly five times his month's salary – an average of 35,000 taka. In Kerala, the college-educated or degree-holding migrant incurred approximately Rs. 20,000 as migration costs, while 20 per cent of illiterate migrants spent more than this amount on average.

On the whole, migrants appear to have learnt from the experience of other migrants who were known to them, or from their own experience abroad, or from cases of malpractice and irregularity that had been reported in the media. In Thailand, although the role of the state in the recruitment process and in its regulation was relatively weak, the average migrant appears to have had enough information and knowledge to avoid being defrauded or cheated. The contract agents who had set themselves up in the business of supplying labour to the Arab countries were either from the location in which they were recruiting the labour or were migrants themselves. The Thai study reports that over time the incidence of fraud and irregularity seems to have declined. But on the whole it appears that where the state was active in enforcing norms and regulating the recruitment process, the costs of migration were comparatively low and the incidence of irregularity as reported in the surveys was also low. This is seen in the surveys in Korea, the Philippines, and Sri Lanka.

Recent information indicates that the situation has deteriorated in Sri Lanka and the Philippines and that payments made by migrants to intermediaries have risen substantially, often reaching the equivalent of three to four months' salary earned abroad. Certain features that are inherent in the labour market for migration appear to be contributing to these conditions. On the one hand, the gap between domestic wages and wages earned abroad continues to be very wide for most of the countries participating in the migration, particularly the South Asian countries. On the other hand, there is a considerable over-supply of prospective migrants seeking employment abroad. These factors combine to create market conditions in which the distribution of the benefits of the migration become weighted heavily in favour of the intermediaries. Migrants appear to be competing among themselves for employment abroad, and are willing to part with a substantial share of their earnings to secure such employment, provided what remains for them is still significantly more than they can hope to earn at home. Among the intermediaries, however, there appears to be less competition, even though the capital required for establishing a recruiting agency is small; but establishing the right links and gaining access to the labour market in host countries will operate as a limiting

**Table 5.** Costs of migration, income and savings of Asian migrants to Arab countries[a]

| Country | Cost of migration | Monthly income abroad | Average savings (%) |
|---|---|---|---|
| Republic of Korea | Less than 200,000 won | 542,000 won | 80 |
| Philippines | 4,200–6,000 pesos | (Total income) above 80,000 pesos | 55 |
| Thailand | 30,000–40,000 baht | 8,000–10,000 baht | 80 |
| Pakistan | Rs. 9,000 | Rs. 4,000–6,500 | 65 |
| Kerala (India) | Rs. 9,000 | Below Rs. 3,000 (77%) Rs. 3,000–5,000 (18%) | 46 |
| Bangladesh | 26,000 taka | 11,000 taka (av.) 7,000 taka (unskilled) | 70 |
| Sri Lanka | Rs. 1,500 (females)[b] Rs. 3,000 (males) | Rs. 2,600 (females) Rs. 7,000 (males) | 76 |

a. Estimates derived from country studies.
b. Mainly housemaids.

factor. Furthermore, there is evidence that with slower growth of demand for imported labour in the Arab countries, the principal recruiting agents in those countries either reduce their commissions to local agents, impose new levies, or are not willing to defray travel costs, all of which are transmitted to the migrants as costs to be borne by them. State interventions to improve the conditions for the migrants so as to ensure that they retain the major share of their earnings need to be carefully designed. However, state regulation and bureaucratic controls of the migration, by themselves, can create bottlenecks and produce their own forms of corruption, resulting in a reduction of the total outflow. What might produce better results is a mix of policies in which more effective monitoring of recruiting agencies is combined with the promotion of healthier competition among the agencies, which can also include a state agency.

Table 5 presents a comparison of the costs, monthly earnings and savings of the migrants surveyed in the seven countries. As stated earlier, most of the samples correspond to the skill composition of the national migrant flow to the Arab countries as used in the available national data. The only exception is probably the Bangladesh sample, where the weight of the skilled and the higher-level migrants appears to be significantly higher in the sample than in the national figures. As a result, the average earnings and savings derived from the data in the Bangladeshi study are higher than the national averages. However, the study presents the data on the various categories of migrants, from which conclusions can be drawn about the situation of each category. With the exception of Kerala and the Philippines, the remittances of migrants as a proportion of their earnings are quite high, ranging from approximately 75 per cent for Sri Lanka to over 80 per cent for Korea. Although, in the cases of Kerala and the Philippines, the aggregate savings of migrants taken by themselves are quite substantial, the significantly lower rate in comparison to the other countries deserves closer examination. It is difficult to explain why their rate of savings should have been considerably lower. The possible explanations are that they either retained their savings abroad or transferred them illegally and were not willing to disclose information on such savings or transfers. The prevailing exchange rate and the lack of incentives for transfers may well have contributed to this situation. The surveys, however, do not throw light on either of these alternative explanations.

All the studies show that on a straightforward financial cost–benefit evaluation of the migration, the average migrant benefitted substantially. The financial benefits, taken as a whole, far outweigh the costs, including both the expenditure actually incurred on the migration and the earnings forgone. This general conclusion, however, obscures many of the significant deviations from the average; it also evades a much more fundamental issue, concerning the gap between potential and actual performance. Finally, the evaluation in terms of financial costs and benefits does not take into account some of the other costs and benefits that have a significant and durable impact on the lives of migrants and their households.

The surveys in the seven countries clearly show that the majority of migrants have been able to make some addition to their assets. A significant number improved their housing conditions, purchased some consumer durables, and made some income-earning investments. It is only a minority of migrants who suffered a decline in their economic status and who regard the outcome of the migration as unsatisfactory. But the proportion of migrants who have improved their income earning capacity in a sustained and durable way, and whose savings have not been mostly absorbed in economically unproductive assets, such as housing, consumer durables, and jewellery, remains a minority for most of the countries, with perhaps the exception of Korea and Thailand.

The Sri Lankan study estimates this proportion at around 30 to 40 per cent. In Kerala, while the assets of the average household of the migrant showed an increase of about 32 per cent, only 25 to 30 per cent had been invested in productive assets such as machinery and equipment, vehicles, and business investments. In Bangladesh, the proportions that had acquired assets that could be considered productive or income-earning, including fixed deposits, investments in business, and purchase of vehicles, amounted to approximately 40 per cent; but this, as stated earlier, might be better than the national average for Bangladeshi migrants to the Arab countries, as the sample appears to be weighted in favour of the skilled and the higher-level migrants. Using a more representative sample, the Thai study revealed a higher percentage of migrants in the category who had relatively successful outcomes. In a comparison of the asset position before and after migration, 20 per cent of the Thai households had more cultivable land, 18 per cent owned more farm equipment in the form of water pumps, and 33 per cent more in the form of trucks. The pattern of savings and investments revealed in the Thai study is more positive than that emerging from the other country studies, with the exception of Korea. Four-fifths of the families had settled their debts, most of which were incurred to finance the migration; over 70 per cent held savings in the form of fixed deposits, and significant proportions had invested in agricultural land, farm equipment, vehicles, and other productive assets. In Korea, most of the returned migrants put their remittances to the uses they had planned for prior to the migration. About 42 per cent had already invested in the purchase of a house, and about one-fourth invested substantial amounts in their own business. In about two-thirds of the migrant households, the income after the migration was higher than that enjoyed before.

The Thai and Korean performance indicates that the households which participated in the migration have demonstrated a better capacity to manage their enhanced resources prudently, and to achieve a sustained improvement in their incomes. In the other countries the large majority of migrants have failed to raise their income-earning capacity or significantly add to their productive assets. Such a performance cannot be regarded as entirely successful, despite the increase in well-being these migrants may have temporarily enjoyed or the additions they have made to their non-productive assets, such as housing and consumer durables. While it is true that most of these migrants could not have hoped to own these assets without migrating, they return to real incomes that are not significantly different from, and are at times lower than, those they enjoyed prior to migration. Some of them are unemployed and live on the capital they have accumulated. Within this relatively unsuccessful majority, there are migrant groups who are specially vulnerable. This vulnerability is already seen at the time of recruitment and migration. As mentioned earlier, the cost of migration seems to be highest for the migrants who belong to unskilled categories and who are the poorest. This is partly attributable to poor educational level, which makes these people heavily dependent on recruiting agents and intermediaries, who are ready to exploit their ignorance and helplessness. These disadvantaged categories of migrants require special forms of assistance that will enhance their capacity to manage the migration to their greater benefit.

The gap between actual and potential is quite large for most countries. The performance of the successful minority of migrants indicates the extent to which the benefits of the migration could be enhanced, both for the national economy and for the individual migrant and his household. While the experience across countries shows that the higher the income level and the earnings of migrants, the better the average performance, the frequent deviations from this norm within countries suggest that, irrespective of income, there is a great deal that can be done to increase the level of productive investments and make very much better use of the resources which the migration brings.

However, the conditions which underlie the successful performance, whether it be in Korea or some of the poorer countries, are much more complex than can be explained by the income levels. In the case of Korea, the inherent capacity of households at a higher economic level, combined with an extremely well-regulated system which ordered the migration from recruitment to return, ensured a high level of savings. Therefore, both the external system and the capacity of the households play an equally important role. The fact that income alone is not a decisive factor is illustrated in numerous individual cases of migrants who have been included in the sample surveys. For example, the Sri Lankan case-study includes, on the one hand, the housemaids who, after a two-year contract on a modest monthly salary of US$100, have been able to liquidate their debts, lay by some money in interest-earning deposits, make modest improvements to their houses, and acquire a few items of furniture and other appliances, which have improved the quality of the home while maintaining a stable family relationship. On the other hand, there are employees at the skilled level who have earned large incomes, made substantial savings and frittered these away in risky ventures or wasteful and ostentatious consumption, and were not able to make the required adjustments in their family relationships during their stay abroad. Some of these migrants, on account of the high level of earnings, might enjoy an economic position superior to what they had prior to the migration. Nevertheless, the second case is not an unmixed success. It contains a number of elements that reflect the negative aspects of the migration, resulting in less than an optimal use of resources. In contrast, the housemaids referred to earlier have been able to manage their migration with modest expectations appropriate to their level of earnings, to keep their consumption within reasonable limits, and to graduate to a slightly better economic level that has the virtue of durability and sustained improvement. It is these cases which demonstrate the potential for managing the migration in a manner appropriate to each level, so as to minimize the costs and maximize the benefits, as explained in the concluding sections of this chapter. The third phase of the UNU project will explore some of these aspects that are related to the capacity of households for managing the migration.

In several countries a high proportion of the migrants who have returned remain unemployed and are not able to use their skills productively. In the countries where the economy is expanding and where employment is being generated at a satisfactory rate, the re-absorption of the migrants into the workforce and the appropriate use of their productive capacities pose no serious problem. It is where economic growth and employment generation are sluggish that the return migration compounds the already existing problems. When the scale of the return migration is as high as it is in Pakistan, these problems begin to manifest themselves in an increasingly acute form. Yet, it is in this very situation that the human and the financial resources of the migration and the potential they offer for both growth and employment creation require special policy initiatives. A sizeable proportion of migrants seek opportunities for self-employment and for small-scale business enterprises of their own. They need to be supported with appropriate policies and institutions that create the right economic environment for small-scale enterprise and assist them with extension services and development finance.

The human costs of migration are easily ignored amidst the more quantifiable economic gains and losses. Each study draws attention to the major problems of personal and social adjustment that face the migrants and their families. For example, in Pakistan, the patriarchal nature of the family and the structure of authority is easily disturbed when the chief householder migrates abroad. The impact on spouses and children is very different from the impact of the migration on families in Thailand, or Sri Lanka, or the Philippines, where family structures are different and where the allocation of responsibilities between spouses, as well as intergenerational adjustments, are more easily managed. The Sri Lankan migration has special features, in that it contains a large proportion of married females. The strains of adjustment on both spouses and children are more pronounced in those circumstances. But in all these situations there are various alleviating factors which intervene. Most migrant households have substantial family support from elders and relations. In some countries, such as the Philippines, the experience of migration was already fairly common prior to the migration to the Arab countries.

What is particularly noteworthy, however, is the widely prevailing view among the migrants that the experience of the migration had a positive effect on their relationships with their family. Many reported that they had come closer to their children, that they were more ready to share responsibilities with their spouses, that they were more progressive and liberal in their attitudes towards the women, and that they rendered more material assistance to their relations. For many, the separation had made them more conscious of the value of their personal relations. The migration and the stresses that it brought were hardships which had to be endured once for all, for the common good of the family. In that sense, employment abroad was a family enterprise where the household resources had to be mobilized in support. There is no doubt that in the modern context in which the migration takes place, the facilities for regular communication, the opportunity to return home after a given period of service, and the consciousness that modern transport and communication could bring the family together without inordinate delay have all helped to mitigate the austerities of the migration. These positive human aspects of the migration emerged clearly in almost all the studies. There is no evidence in any of them that the separation caused by the migration had resulted in a more frequent disruption of family and marital relations, or in more separation and divorce, than is observed in these societies as a whole. Nevertheless, it can be argued that the inquiries made in the survey will not elicit the negative residue of the migration which lies beneath the surface. The psychological strains and the trauma of unfamiliar separation, particularly in the case of children, may have effects which will find expression in the long term. Certainly, this possibility cannot be dismissed. It will require, however, more studies, in depth and over longer periods, before one can make any definite judgements.

But apart from family relationships, the human costs are perhaps seen most clearly in the experience of many migrants who return from employment abroad hoping to lead a productive life that can maintain the standard of living made possible by the migration, but are unsuccessful in their efforts. One of the most painful processes of adjustment is obviously the one caused by a sudden rise and fall in income. Households are elevated suddenly to a level of income which is very much higher than that to which they were accustomed. With the termination of the contract, the resource flow immediately dries up. Depending on the way in which the income flows were managed, this steep rise in income followed by a sharp decline can be one of the most frustrating experiences for migrant households.

## Conclusion

In an overall assessment of the migration, it would appear that, in terms of economic well-being and human development, the migration has brought benefits to a significant proportion of the migrants. The large majority of migrants made some improvement in terms of wealth and quality of life. In many countries the systems that are in place have been capable of an average performance in which the process of recruitment and placement has taken place without inordinate delay or excessive cost to the migrant, and with no high incidence of fraud or malpractice.

The average migrant and his family have been able to adjust to the separation without serious human cost. Indeed, many migrants have reported that the migration has resulted in a heightened awareness of the value of family relationships and that family members have experienced a stronger need for closer communication with children and spouse. The surveys provide insights into the diverse ways in which migrant and family have developed through the exposure to this experience; these include attitudinal changes regarding the role of women, intergenerational relations and the expectations relating to children, and a wider international awareness. In most of the labour-supplying countries, these new elements are introduced into rural settings that have traditional value systems which change very slowly. The socio-cultural impact of the migration on such communities is bound to be far-reaching. The successful migrants often become leaders and pace-setters of change. The studies, while they refer to these aspects, are not able to reflect their full impact, first because these effects will only become clearly identifiable over time and, second, because it is not easy to isolate the impact of the migration from other influences without much more intensive observation and study.

There are several aspects of the migration which require more purposeful action from governments, the private sector, and non-governmental agencies.

1. Despite the fact that the performance of the majority of migrants indicates that the systems are operating with a fair degree of efficiency and acceptance, there is a sizeable group of migrants for whom the deficiencies in the system have entailed high economic and human costs. These are generally the disadvantaged migrants who are unskilled and illiterate or have low educational attainments.

2. The large gaps between domestic wages and the wages in host countries, combined with the high demand for foreign employment in the labour-supplying countries, have created a market in which a disproportionate share of the income earned by migrants tends to be appropriated by intermediaries. There has to be better monitoring and regulation of the private recruiting system, together with greater competition among recruiting agents.

3. The studies identify problems which are country- specific and require policies and corrective measures that have to be designed to suit the national context. The ratio of savings to incomes earned is low in Kerala and the Philippines – a situation that calls for incentives directed at increasing transfers. The capacity for maximizing the benefits of the migration is least in the poorer households, who are suddenly required to manage flows of income very much larger than those they are accustomed to. This situation is most evident in the South Asian countries. Problems of family adjustment to the migration vary from country to country. Where the majority of migrants are household heads, as in the case of Korea, the Philippines, Thailand, and Pakistan, the problems are of one kind. Where they are married mothers who are not household heads, as in the case of Sri Lanka, the consequences of separation are of a different order. In the patriarchal structure of the Pakistan household, the removal of the household head creates new demands and stresses, which do not occur for the household in Thailand or the Philippines. Any programmes for household support during the migration will need to be different for each of these situations.

4. Although the majority of migrants have in one way or another benefitted economically and socially from the migration and evaluate its outcome as positive, a large proportion of them – the majority in five of the seven countries studied – have not been successful in raising their income-earning capacity on a durable basis after their return. The failure or the relative lack of success of these migrants is due to a wide variety of reasons, some of them originating in the character of the migrants themselves, in their family circumstances or in some especially unfavourable

17

conditions in the host country which led to early termination of their contract. But, in many of these cases, the migration has not yielded its full benefits owing to the failure of the migrants to set well-defined goals for themselves and to plan ahead. As a result, expenditures during the period of increased income have not been contained within reasonable limits so as to build up income-earning capacity and thus sustain and improve standards of living after the migration.

5. Surveys reveal that there is a considerable degree of variation in the performance of migrants with the same level of earnings abroad. Some have made substantial and durable gains while others have failed to do so. Studies, therefore, point to the significant gap between what has been actually achieved and the potential for better utilization of resources and higher benefits from the migration. The task of enhancing the capacity of these migrants and their households to manage the resource flows more efficiently and productively should command high priority in the national policies and programmes dealing with migration. Some of these issues are examined in the third phase of the UNU project which follows the present study.

6. At the same time it has to be emphasized that the best efforts of migrants may be insufficient to overcome external conditions, such as continued unemployment after return and rapid inflation that erodes the savings of migrants, reducing them to a situation perhaps worse than the one they faced before the migration. Therefore, the macro-economic policies, the institutional arrangements and the economic environment as a whole have to be conducive to the reabsorption of the migrants, after their return, in economic activities that provide the opportunity for the productive use of their resources.

7. In most of the countries, a considerable number of returning migrants sought opportunities for self-employment. Migrants report that, in diverse ways, their experiences had given them a better attitude to work. The migration brought them in contact with new forms of management and discipline, and more advanced technology and its applications. Several migrants with substantial savings aspired to be entrepreneurs on a small scale. In most countries, special programmes are needed to cater to this group.

8. Most countries did not have the institutional framework to make best use of the human capital that was built up through the migration. Apart from the major area of employment and enterprise, migrants can make a useful contribution in a wide variety of activities – in terms of work ethos and productivity, technological and other improvements in their specific trade, management of households, and family adjustments to change. A more conscious and systematic national effort is needed to identify the different types of human assets that have been created and provide opportunities for migrants to perform more meaningful economic and social roles after their return.

1

# ASIAN MIGRATION TO THE ARAB WORLD: KERALA (INDIA)

## P.R. Gopinathan Nair

Centre for Development Studies, Trivandrum, Kerala, India

## Introduction

India has experienced a substantial expansion of international migration during the post-Second World War period. The migration flows are of different patterns and magnitudes. Differences in patterns are reflected in the directions of the flows as well as in the ethnic, occupational, and skill compositions of the different streams. Differences exist also in the conditions under which migration flows take place. Two distinct streams of migration usually identified are, first, the outflow of skilled manpower to developed countries and, second, the circulatory flows of less skilled and unskilled manpower to other developing countries and back. Migration of the first type takes place from India mostly to countries in Europe and to the United States. In the second category, the most important and the largest has been that to the Arab World, which comprises regions such as the UAE, Saudi Arabia, Oman, Kuwait, Qatar and Bahrain. This type of migration from India had been going on for several decades, but only on a small scale. In the past decade it has acquired massive dimensions owing to the growth in demand for foreign labour in construction activities initiated by Arab countries in the wake of the oil price hike of 1973 and the consequent increase in oil revenues and accumulation of massive surpluses.

The Arab migration is of a purely temporary nature, for several reasons – religious, ethnic, and political. The rules of access to foreign nationals are quite strictly defined, giving them rights only to short-duration stay and employment. No immigrant of non-Arab origin and non-Islamic faith can expect to acquire rights of domicile and citizenship in any country of the Arab world. Immigrants' social and economic freedom also tends to be severely circumscribed by the rules and regulations in these countries. The temporary character of the migration seems to have had some influence in deciding the socio-economic composition of migrants, their earning, spending, and saving behaviour, and the manner of disposition of their savings.

It is likely that the urge to transfer incomes to the country of origin is greater for temporary than for permanent migrants. Not only are the average amounts of the

19

remittances likely to be higher, but the pattern of disposition of savings is also different. For instance, migrants to the Arab countries were presumed to be of low educational, training, and experience levels, and to come, in general, from households of low economic and social status. That being the case, provision for the essential, basic needs of life such as food, housing, clothing and education of the members of the household, as well as support for marriages and formation of new households, could be expected to take precedence over the satisfaction of other growth-promoting activities such as accumulation and investment. One would also expect greater efforts on the part of this category of migrants to minimize their own consumer spending while in employment in the host country, and to maximize remittances for the purpose of raising the standard of living of their families and discharging household liabilities and obligations.

However, the demand on their savings for the provision of food, housing, clothing, etc., and the discharge of liabilities would not remain undiminished for extended periods. Once adequate arrangements have been made for meeting such demands, they will cease to be a drain on the migrants' savings. The migrants and their households will then turn to other less immediate but more growth-promoting lines of disposition of savings. With the prospects of unexpected and abrupt termination of employment and compulsory repatriation looming large as a constant reminder of the transient nature of their jobs, the migrants will tend to be circumspect in the way they use their foreign-earned incomes.

Little reliable information is available yet regarding the spending habits of Indian migrants and their households. The information base is weak not only in respect of the disposition of savings, but also with regard to almost every other dimension of the migration phenomenon, such as: (1) composition of the migrants judged in terms of age, sex, education, work experience, and earning and marital status; (2) economic status of the households from which migrants come; (3) social and economic compulsions underlying migration to the Arab World; (4) the sources of information, agencies of assistance, and processes of recruitment; (5) terms and conditions of living and working abroad; (6) the adjustment problems; (7) the changes that exposure to and experience acquired from foreign countries have brought about in the habits and attitudes of the migrants; and (8) institutional arrangements both for mobilizing and channelling the savings of the migrants for optimum use, and for migrants' rehabilitation on return. In India such questions have remained almost entirely unanswered, even unasked, except in a few village studies.

A different set of dimensions related to the migration phenomenon also exists. They are the macro-dimensions, such as the size of the stock of migrants abroad, the size of their annual outflows and return flows, the magnitudes of annual remittances, and the macro-impact of migration on commodity and factor prices, employment, and income distribution. Information is available, from a few village studies made in Kerala, on some of these aspects.

In the present chapter we address ourselves primarily to the first set of micro-issues, even though references to the macro-dimensions will also be made on occasion.

The migration process seems to have begun in an almost free-market situation. Official intervention in the process, either by the migrant-sending or by the migrant-receiving countries, was minimal, at least during the early phase. Efforts made by the migrant-receiving countries to streamline the process, for instance by insisting on residence or work permits for the immigrant workers, or those made by the migrant-sending countries in insisting on valid passports, employment agreements, and travel documents, must have come later; but the intensity of such efforts and the degree of their success are not clearly documented. It is not likely that they met with much success. Since the bargaining power of the unorganized migrants from Asian countries was in general quite weak, the terms and conditions of living and work were probably the ones dictated to them by the host countries. The host countries were apparently able to employ Asian workers at rates of remuneration much lower than those paid to local workers in comparable jobs, but even such low rates were probably quite acceptable because they were much higher than the prevailing rates in the immigrants' countries of origin.

One cannot a priori know whether the effects of migration have been, on balance, favourable to the migrant-sending households, localities, and countries. Among the possible favourable results at the level of the migrants and their households are a reduction in unemployment, an improvement in income and standard of living, and the acquisition of progressive attitudes. The negative outcomes may include hardships undergone by the migrants during their stay abroad, problems of adjustment experienced by members of the household, misuse of incomes, and acquisition by the migrants and their households of unhealthy habits and attitudes. Problems of rehabilitation and readjustment may also have been present.

The balance-of-payments support that the migration-sending countries have enjoyed from the remittances made by the migrants is one of the favourable macro-results to be noted. In addition, the opportunities that the manpower connection opens up for the development of more sustained economic, social, and cultural relationships between the Asian and the Arab countries should also be considered a major positive contribution. Despite the importance of the Arab migration from several points of view, little effort has been made in India to study either the micro- or the macro-dimensions of this phenomenon.

In the present chapter, the attempt will be, as already indicated, to focus attention on the micro-dimensions. It is hoped that the study will also be of help in identifying shortcomings in the process, and thus in helping to rectify them by appropriate policy interventions.


## Area of Study, Sample Size, and Collection of Data

Ideally, the study should have attempted to cover the migration process that takes place to the Arab World from India as a whole. It is known that there is migration from several states in the country – Kerala, Tamil Nadu, Karnataka, Andra Pradesh, Maharashtra, Gujarat, and Punjab. Given the resources of time and finances at our disposal, the scope of the study could not be enlarged to include the whole of India: we had to select one state from among those mentioned above. The choice was naturally Kerala, since it is from this small state (which accounts for less than 4 per cent of the population and a little more than 1 per cent of the geographical area of India) that more than 50 per cent of the migrants to the Arab countries re-

**Table 1.** Age distribution of migrants at the time of first migration

| Age-group (years) | Proportion of migrants (%) |
|---|---|
| Less than 20 | 9.2 |
| 20–25 | 31.7 |
| 25–35 | 37.5 |
| 35–45 | 17.4 |
| 45–60 | 4.2 |
| Total | 100.0 |

portedly originate. In addition, Kerala is the only state in India which has some information on the spatial distribution of the migrants. This study is therefore confined to the state of Kerala.

The study was undertaken at a time when reports of the declining opportunities of employment in the Arab countries for Asian expatriate labour had begun to appear. The suspicion that prevailed in the state was that net migration had turned negative. Since the unemployment situation in the state was alarming, and worsening day by day, there was little hope for the migrants returning home to find jobs unless they had been previously employed and had retained a right to those jobs during their absence. The alternatives were to remain unemployed, to find means of self-employment, or to return to the Arab countries. It was therefore deemed important to look into the question of the rehabilitation of the migrants as a part of the enquiry. Naturally, the information to be collected was from the returned migrants. There was also an added advantage to selecting the returned migrants as the respondents, since this made it possible to collect information relating to all phases of the migration from persons who have actually gone through the process.

The problem that had to be faced at the outset was that of identifying the returned migrants. No information was available from any agency, official or private, about the return of migrants. The only source of information about migration to the Arab countries available on a state-wide basis was the Report on Housing and Employment, which shows the spatial distribution of migrants by village, *taluk*, and district.

Selection of the sample was carried out in several stages. The first stage involved the selection of districts on the basis of migration intensity rate (i.e. number of migrants per 1,000 population). From the eleven districts (in existence at the time of the survey), five were identified as those with the highest intensity of migration. At the second stage, one *taluk* (subdistrict) with the highest migration intensity was identified from each district. At the third stage, the intensity rate was calculated in the different villages and towns in each of the selcted *taluks*. Finally, from among the different villages and towns with the highest migration intensity rate, eleven localities, eight rural areas and three town areas were chosen for the study.

The next problem was to identify the *panchayats* (the lowest local self-government unit) in the rural areas and the wards in the town areas. This was done by local enquiry.

In each of these *panchayats* and town wards, an intensive tracer survey was made to identify the households of returned migrants. After tracing 5,906 households, we were able to identify 2,749 households from which migration had taken place to the Arab countries; among these, migrants from as many as 866 households had returned home from foreign employment. In order to survey a sample of 700 respondents, it was decided to select about 75 respondents from each rural area and 50 respondents from each of the town areas. In all we were able to collect information from 696 migrants.

The survey was conducted during October–December 1984 using trained field investigators.

## Migrants and Their Households: A Profile

It has been estimated that in 1983 the stock of Indian migrant workers in the Gulf countries was of the order of about 1 million, of which nearly 50 per cent were from Kerala. The peak levels of migration were presumably reached by 1981. There exists some evidence to suggest that the annual outflow of migrants has been steadily on the decline. According to the Protector General of Emigrants in India, the total number of emigration clearances granted in 1981 was 276,000; the corresponding numbers for the subsequent years were progressively smaller: 239,500 in 1982, 225,000 in 1983, and 205,000 in 1984. During the first nine months of 1985, only 134,000 emigration clearances were granted. While emigration was thus declining, return migration was reportedly rising. Reliable information on return migration is however not available in India.

The present survey showed that of the 4,039 migrants (belonging to 2,749 households), 948 (866 households) had already returned. The ratio of returned migrants to the total number of migrants was thus 23.5 per cent. Approximately, therefore, there was one returned migrant for every 4.25 migrants still abroad. There are indications that this proportion has gone up since the time of the survey.

The few earlier village studies mapped out the broad features of the migration phenomenon from Kerala. According to them, the migrants were relatively young persons, almost entirely males, mainly from rural areas, possessing low-level educational qualifications and relatively little vocational training and experience, and coming from low-income and low-middle-income groups. Our present study reinforces these findings.

### Migrants

In Kerala, community considerations are important in deciding a person's assets, income, educational and employment status, and degree of mobility. This has been the result mostly of historical factors. There are three important religious groups in this region, the Hindus (60 per cent), Christians (20 per cent), and Muslims (20 per cent). Among the Hindus, there are a large number of castes and subcastes. Though caste factor has lost much of its earlier influence in deciding a person's socio-economic status, the lowest caste groups, the erstwhile agricultural slave castes and hill tribes, still remain educationally and economically much more backward than the other groups, and are seldom in a position to raise resources, establish contacts and get employment allowing them to migrate into other regions in India or other countries of the world; they do not, therefore, figure at all among the migrants. Hindus, even though they are the single largest community group in the state, are not in a majority among the migrants. Nor do the Christians account for a large share, even though they have a fairly long tradition of migration to other parts of the world, particularly to the West. In the migration to the Arab countries, it is the Muslims who predominate. In spite of the fact that they account for only one-fifth of the total population of the state, they represent as much as 78 per cent of the migrants, Hindus and Christians accounting for only about 12 and 10 per cent respectively.

The Muslims have an edge over the others in migration to the Arab countries for several reasons — historical, cultural and economic — besides the obvious religious factor. The proportion of very young and illiterate/less-educated persons among Muslim migrants is higher than among the Hindu or Christian migrants, a fact that is a reflection of the low educational status of the Muslim community as a whole in the state. In respect of professional/technical education and vocational training, the status of Muslim migrants was also lower than that of the others. However, in respect of work experience and earning status, the Muslims were marginally better off. This can be partly attributed to the fact that Muslims in general drop out from school at a relatively early age and engage in various economic activities such as fishing, trading, and other petty business.

In our sample there were no women respondents; all the returned migrants were men. To what extent this applies to the state as a whole cannot be ascertained. However, it appears that women from Kerala in employment in the Arab countries — mostly as nurses and other paramedical personnel—are quite few in number and have yet to be repatriated.

The data show that more than two-fifths of the migrants were, at the time of migration, very young, below the age of 25. The largest proportion, 37.5 per cent, was however from the 25–35 age-group. The average age of migrants from Kerala was 29 years.

The educational levels of the migrants were on the whole low, even though the proportion of illiterates among them was less than 7 per cent. Illiteracy was highest among migrants in the 25–35 age-group. The distribution of migrants according to educational level is shown in table 2. Among the literates, the below-matriculates predominated, accounting for nearly 70 per cent.

Half the number of migrants were married at the time of first migration. Three out of every four in the 35–45 age-group and more than nine out of every ten in the 45–60 age-group were already married. Naturally, the proportions of unmarried persons were lower in the under-25 age-group.

Among those with higher education, the proportion of unmarried persons was higher. Thus, while the proportion of unmarried persons was only slightly over one-third among the illiterates, it was as high as four-fifths among the college-educated. Similarly, the proportion of younger migrants was also higher the higher the educational qualification, up to and including the level of the college-educated

**Table 2.** Distribution of migrants by general education

| Level of general education | Proportion of migrants (%) |
|---|---|
| Illiterate | 6.6 |
| Literate (primary level) | 47.6 |
| Literate (secondary level) | 21.7 |
| Matriculate | 18.1 |
| College-educated (with no degree) | 3.3 |
| Degree-holder (1st degree) | 2.4 |
| Degree-holder (2nd degree) | 0.3 |
| Total | 100.0 |

(with no degree). These findings suggest that unmarried status and younger age were factors favourable to migration.

Professional or technical education was not an important prerequisite for migration. In the majority of cases, the migrants possessed no such education. Even among those who did, the proportion of those who held low-level technical education, such as certificate courses, was the highest. Vocational training played a more important role than technical/professional education. More than one in every five migrants possessed some vocational training at the time of first migration.

Still more useful for migration was work experience. The proportion of migrants who had some work experience (as artisan or technical workers, or even as unskilled workers) came to approximately 60 per cent of the total number of migrants. About 30 per cent of the migrants had no employment prior to migration and another 1.8 per cent were students.

Clearly, therefore, migrants contained a larger proportion of employed than of totally unemployed. The educational levels – general or technical – of the unemployed were on average low. However, the fact that they were mostly young unmarried persons was to their advantage. Their mobility was higher than that of the older, married, and employed persons.

Older persons also have other constraints, since they are often married and have become heads of households. Push-and-pull factors are much stronger for such people than for the young and unmarried. The data show that, of the total, only one in five was a head of household and that almost all the heads of households (92 per cent) were married. Over the years, the proportions of employed persons and heads of households among migrants have been declining.

More than employment status, the most important factor influencing migration was earning status. There were earners among the unemployed (from non-wage sources) and non-earners among the employed (self-employment in family farm or other enterprise). Nearly 50 per cent had no earnings at all. Another 20 per cent had very low monthly earnings of less than Rs. 200 per month. The proportion of migrants with monthly earnings of Rs. 1,000 and above was quite small, less than 4 per cent. The majority of non-earners were unmarried persons and belonged to the younger age-groups.

The most important destination for migrants was the UAE region, accounting for 68 per cent of the sample. Other important countries were Saudi Arabia (12.4 per

**Table 3.** Ever-married persons by age-group at the time of first migration

| Age-group (years) | Proportion of ever-married persons (%) |
|---|---|
| Less than 20 | 9.4 |
| 20–35 | 16.3 |
| 35–45 | 75.1 |
| 45–60 | 91.7 |
| All age-groups | 50.0 |

cent), Qatar (7.5 per cent), Bahrain (5.6 per cent), Oman (3.6 per cent), and Kuwait (2.7 per cent).

## Households

An interesting observation pertains to the size of households. In general, migration has taken place from relatively large households: the average was 8.05 members, much larger than the average for the state as a whole, which was between 5 and 6. Among the three religious groups, those of the Muslims had the largest average size (8.38 members), followed by Hindus (7.94) and Christians (5.57). While 57.4 per cent of the households of the Christians had only five members or less, the corresponding proportions among the households of Hindus and Muslims were much lower, 23 and 20.5 per cent respectively.

Low economic status and low educational levels are associated with high birth-rates and large household size. Since the Christians in Kerala are economically and educationally in advance of the rest of the communities, their average household size is smaller.

In the migrants' households, the number of male members was higher than that of females. The proportion of children below the age of 15 was also smaller. The households had a lower work participation rate than for the general population, only 21.5 per cent for males and 2.3 for females. Thus we find that the households had large number of members, more men than women, low employment rates, and a higher proportion of members of the working age.

The economic status of the households is revealed by their assets and income levels. Four-fifths of the households had only small areas of less than one acre of landed property. Among them there were about 9 per cent which did not possess any land at all. In respect of landed property the Christian households were much better placed than the others: the proportion that possessed more than one acre came to about 44 per cent, as against 20 per cent for the Hindus and 16 per cent for the Muslims. On the whole, the picture that emerges from the data is that of households of relatively low landed property levels. However, it is also necessary to examine the status of migrants in relation to their total asset position on the eve of migration.

In the evaluation of assets, both physical and financial assets have been taken into account. These comprise land, livestock and poultry, buildings, ornaments and jewellery, vehicles, agricultural and other machinery, consumer durables, and

**Table 4.** Migrants by occupation status on the eve of first migration

| Occupational status | No. | % |
|---|---|---|
| Engineer/scientist/doctor/administrator/ business executive/manager | 11 | 1.6 |
| Nurse/midwife | 2 | 0.3 |
| Schoolteacher | 9 | 1.3 |
| Draughtsman/overseer/other related technical personnel | 3 | 0.4 |
| Clerk/typist/stenographer/accountant/cashier | 16 | 2.3 |
| | 41 | 5.9 |
| Machine operator (office) | 4 | 0.6 |
| Salesman/insurance agent | 20 | 2.9 |
| Farmer/farm worker/landowner | 12 | 1.7 |
| Fisherman/quarryman/hunter/logger/gardener | 71 | 10.2 |
| Driver | 17 | 2.4 |
| Other transportation/communication worker | 5 | 0.7 |
| Spinner/weaver/tailor | 14 | 2.0 |
| Goldsmith/carpenter | 4 | 0.6 |
| Electrician/plumber/packer/printer | 15 | 2.2 |
| Fireman/policeman | 1 | 0.1 |
| Housekeeper/cook/barber/launderer | 35 | 5.0 |
| Priest or other religious worker | 2 | 0.3 |
| Petty producer | 3 | 0.4 |
| Petty trader | 81 | 11.6 |
| Receptionist or other service personnel | 26 | 3.7 |
| Painter/photographer | 6 | 0.9 |
| | 316 | 45.4 |
| Other workers, including unskilled labour | 103 | 14.8 |
| Unemployed | 265 | 38.0 |
| Student | 12 | 1.8 |
| Total | 696 | 100.0 |

financial assets. The value taken was the present value as reported by the respondents and checked by the investigators. In spite of the care taken, the figures reported may be very reliable for several reasons: the tendency of the respondent to report a higher economic status at the time of first migration, so that the difference between then and now would look much smaller than it in fact would be; the differences in value that could arise from the differences in quality and year of production of the assets (except in the case of land and ornaments); the inability of the investigator to verify the quality of the assets; the differences that exist in the value of land between one plot and another, depending on advantages of location and fertility; and so on. Since the study has not attempted to quantify precisely the value of assets, but only to obtain a broad picture of the economic level of the migrants, a few general observations could be made on the basis of table 6.

About three-fifths of the sample households belonged, on the eve of first migra-

**Table 5a.** Migrants by earnings and marital status on the eve of first migration (percentages)

| Earnings per month (Rs.) | Single | Married (including separated) |
|---|---|---|
| No earnings | 69.3 | 28.4 |
| Less than 100 | 3.2 | 2.3 |
| 100–200 | 10.1 | 23.3 |
| 200–500 | 12.1 | 30.5 |
| 500–1,000 | 5.2 | 10.3 |
| 1,000–2,000 | 1.7 | 4.9 |
| 2,000 and above | 0.3 | 0.3 |
| Total | 100.0 | 100.0 |

**Table 5b.** Migrants by earnings and age on the eve of first migration (percentages)

| Earnings per month (Rs.) | Age-group (years) | | | | | |
|---|---|---|---|---|---|---|
| | Below 20 | 20–25 | 25–35 | 35–45 | 45–60 yrs | Total |
| No earnings | 82.5 | 66.1 | 39.7 | 24.8 | 31.0 | 49.0 |
| Less than 100 | 4.8 | 2.3 | 2.7 | 2.5 | 3.4 | 2.7 |
| 100–200 | 7.9 | 9.5 | 22.5 | 22.3 | 13.8 | 16.7 |
| 200–500 | 4.8 | 14.0 | 28.2 | 28.9 | 17.2 | 21.2 |
| 500–1,000 | — | 5.9 | 4.6 | 14.0 | 17.2 | 6.8 |
| 1,000–2,000 | — | 1.8 | 1.9 | 7.4 | 17.2 | 3.3 |
| 2,000 and above | — | 0.5 | 0.4 | — | — | 0.3 |
| Total | 100.0 | 100.0 | 100.0 | 100.0 | 100.0 | 100.0 |

**Table 6.** Households classified by value of assets and religious group (percentages)

| Size group by value of assets | Religious group | | | Total |
|---|---|---|---|---|
| | Hindu | Muslim | Christian | |
| Low | 25.2 | 20.3 | 14.8 | 20.4 |
| Lower-middle | 23.0 | 20.9 | 5.9 | 19.7 |
| Upper-middle | 20.7 | 35.9 | 17.6 | 12.2 |
| High | 31.0 | 22.9 | 61.7 | 47.7 |
| Total | 100.0 | 100.0 | 100.0 | 100.0 |

tion of their members, to the upper-middle and high asset groups. In this respect, a similar pattern to that observed earlier becomes clear, showing a preponderance of Christian households in the higher asset groups.

In order to draw conclusions on the economic status of the households, it was necessary also to look into their income levels. In contrast to the picture that emerges from the asset inquiry, the income status of households, as in the case of the income status of individual migrants, is on the average quite low. Nearly 85 per

**Table 7.** Classification of households by range of annual income on the eve of migration, according to religious group (percentages)

| Households by annual income group (Rs.) | Religious group | | | Total |
|---|---|---|---|---|
| | Hindu | Muslim | Christian | |
| Low: less than 5,000 | 78.2 | 54.0 | 67.6 | 58.3 |
| Lower-middle: 5,000–15,000 | 17.2 | 29.9 | 20.6 | 27.4 |
| Upper-middle: 15,000–30,000 | 4.6 | 11.7 | 11.8 | 10.8 |
| High: 30,000 and above | — | 4.4 | — | 3.5 |
| Total | 100.0 | 100.0 | 100.0 | 100.0 |

**Table 8.** Classification of households by numbers of members working in the Arab countries, according to religious group

| Number of members working in the Arab countries | Number of households | Religious group (%) | | | Total (%) |
|---|---|---|---|---|---|
| | | Hindu | Muslim | Christian | |
| 0 | 484 | 81.6 | 66.5 | 77.9 | 69.5 |
| 1 | 153 | 12.6 | 24.4 | 14.7 | 22.0 |
| 2 | 44 | 3.4 | 6.7 | 7.4 | 6.3 |
| 3 | 9 | 2.3 | 1.3 | — | 1.3 |
| 4 | 5 | — | 0.9 | — | 0.7 |
| 5 | 1 | — | 0.2 | — | 0.1 |
| Total | 696 | 100.0 | 100.0 | 100.0 | 100.0 |

cent of the households came under the categories of low, or lower-middle, income groups. In this respect, there did not exist significant differences between the religious groups.

The conclusion that emerges is therefore that the migrants' households had in general some assets to rely upon, while their income levels were low. Perhaps it was this particular situation, along with the large household size, large number of male members of working age, and high unemployment rates, that provided the optimum conditions for migration once opportunities revealed themselves. Households without assets would have stayed behind, however much they desired to partake in the migratory process, since migration involves financial costs.

## Factors of Migration: The Pre-migration Phase

One of the puzzles related to the migration from India is its extreme regional concentration. A region such as Kerala, which accounts for less than 4 per cent of India's population, is sending half the total number of migrants. What are the features of Kerala which give it such a unique position? Before seeking answers to this question from the survey data, we may also briefly mention the demographic, employment, and economic features of Kerala.

**Table 9.** Selected socio-economic indicators, Kerala and India, 1981

| Indicator | Kerala | India | Rank of Kerala among the 22 states in India |
|---|---|---|---|
| Density of population | 655 | 254 | 1 |
| Literacy rate | 70 | 36 | 1 |
| Proportion of unemployed to total population | 10 | 3 | 1 |
| Person–land ratio (hectares per person) | 0.14 | 0.44 | 22 |
| Work participation rate (%) | 31 | 38 | 22 |
| Per capita income, 1983–1984 (Rs.) | 1,760 | 2,201 | 10 |

Kerala is the mostly densely populated region in India. In 1981, the density of population per square kilometre was 655 in Kerala as against 254 in the country as a whole. The people of Kerala are far ahead of the rest of the population in literacy and general education levels, the literacy rate being more than twice that of India. But the work participation rates in the state are the lowest, with unemployment levels high and rising. About 2.6 million persons out of a total population of 26 million are on the registers of the employment exchanges. The man–land ratio (0.14 hectares per person) is one of the lowest in India. Owing to the extremely low rate of growth of the productive economic sectors – agriculture and industry – the per capita income in Kerala lags behind that of all India, which itself is one of the lowest among the nations of the world (see table 4).

Such a situation, with high unemployment, low income, and high education, favoured the growth of migratory processes. In fact, Kerala has had a net outflow of migrants to other parts of the country for the past half-century. In addition, people of Kerala, particularly of the coastal belt, have a rich tradition and experience of migration to other countries such as Sri Lanka, Malaysia, Singapore, Mauritius, and the West Indies. The trading and matrimonial relationship that the Muslims of Kerala have maintained with the Arab world for several centuries have also provided an additional impetus to migration.

In the migration to the Arab world, the sections of the population involved were thus of different types: communities that had long traditions of trading, religious, and matrimonial relationships with the Middle East (the Muslims); communities that had higher educational levels, higher standards of living and stronger economic contacts with the rest of the world (the Christians); and socio-economic groups with some asset base but only poor income levels. In general, it was only the sections without any asset base and therefore little command over funds, or the most affluent, who did not take to foreign employment. The most ignorant and the least mobile neither aspired nor had the capacity to participate in the process of migration. If all the aspirants were not able to migrate, much of the reason for it may be traceable to the lack of opportunities to do so.

Since the majority of the migrants came from low-income households, were of low educational status, were unemployed or employed in low-income jobs, and had no professional education, technical skills or vocational training, the most im-

**Table 10.** Distribution of migrants by most important reason for seeking employment abroad

| Category | To get a job | To get a higher income in order to live better | To earn enough for redemption of financial liabilities | To earn enough to discharge family responsibilities | To accumulate savings for investment | To travel and go places | Other |
|---|---|---|---|---|---|---|---|
| *Religion* | | | | | | | |
| Hindu | 54.0 | 23.0 | 5.7 | 14.9 | — | 1.2 | 1.2 |
| Muslim | 43.4 | 22.0 | 2.2 | 29.9 | 0.6 | 0.4 | 1.5 |
| Christian | 47.0 | 32.4 | 5.9 | 14.7 | — | — | — |
| *Education* | | | | | | | |
| Illiterate | 19.6 | 17.4 | 4.3 | 54.4 | — | — | 4.3 |
| Literate (primary level) | 39.3 | 23.9 | 3.9 | 31.1 | — | 0.6 | 1.2 |
| Literate (secondary level) | 55.0 | 17.2 | 3.3 | 21.9 | 1.3 | — | 1.3 |
| Matriculate | 60.3 | 22.2 | 0.8 | 14.3 | 0.8 | 0.8 | 0.8 |
| College-educated (with no degree) | 52.2 | 43.5 | — | 4.3 | — | — | — |
| Degree-holder | 21.1 | 52.6 | — | 26.3 | — | — | — |
| *Monthly earnings* | | | | | | | |
| No earnings | 68.3 | 17.3 | 1.5 | 10.6 | 0.6 | 0.6 | 1.1 |
| Less than Rs. 100 | 26.3 | 31.6 | 5.3 | 36.8 | — | — | — |
| Rs. 100–Rs. 250 | 26.7 | 19.8 | 4.3 | 48.3 | — | — | 0.9 |
| Rs. 250–Rs. 500 | 20.9 | 25.7 | 6.1 | 44.6 | — | — | 2.7 |
| Rs. 500–Rs. 1,000 | 17.0 | 55.3 | 2.1 | 25.5 | — | — | — |
| Rs. 1000 and above | 24.0 | 36.0 | — | 32.0 | 4.0 | 4.0 | — |
| *Annual income (in thousands of rupees)* | | | | | | | |
| Low: less than 5 | 47.3 | 23.9 | 2.7 | 24.4 | — | 0.2 | 1.5 |
| Lower-middle: 5–15 | 36.7 | 20.4 | 4.7 | 35.6 | 0.5 | 0.5 | 1.6 |
| Upper-middle: 15–30 | 53.3 | 28.0 | 1.3 | 17.3 | — | — | — |
| High: 30 and above | 50.0 | 16.7 | — | 20.8 | 8.3 | 4.2 | — |
| All | 45.1 | 23.1 | 3.0 | 26.6 | 0.4 | 0.4 | 1.3 |

portant consideration for them in their decision to migrate was the need to overcome their pressing economic difficulties rather than to accumulate economic power. The distribution of migrants, by the most important reason for migration, is given in table 10.

The main reason as stated by 45 per cent of the respondents is lack of job opportunities in Kerala. To get a job was the prime motive underlying their migration. For 27 per cent, the discharge of family obligations was the consideration which weighed with them most. The next important reason was the augmentation of income for raising the standard of living of the household.

The objective of accumulation of savings for investment and economic growth was not in the minds of the migrants, except for a tiny proportion of 0.4 per cent. Thus, the motives that dominated their decision-making were consumption and maintenance rather than savings and growth.

Differences are observed between the reasons given by the various religious, educational, earnings and income groups. There are, moreover, large differences in the order of importance of the reasons. In general it was found that securing a job was the most important reason for migration for the better-educated and the non-earners. The objective of earning enough to discharge family responsibilities was more important among those with little or no education, who belonged to low or lower-middle income groups. The desire to raise standards of living was the most important reason among a fairly high proportion of college-educated non-degree-holders, those with more than average earning levels and those who belonged to the upper-middle income groups. In short, unemployment was the major push factor for the educated; the desire to improve living standards was also high among them. As a person moves along the educational ladder, his aspirations for a better life also increase. For the illiterate and the poorly educated, poverty at home was the major driving force: while a person's income remained low, his obligations and liabilities grew over the years regardless of his economic situation. No wonder, therefore, that, more than the desire to get a job, the prime objective for most was the discharge of responsibilities and liabilities. However, the data also suggest that the income levels of the households did not influence to any significant extent the decisions on migration. More significant were the variables relating to the persons themselves.

### Sources of Information

We find that in Kerala information about opportunities for jobs in the Arab countries reached the migrants, not through any official or institutional agency, but through personal contacts with friends, relatives and neighbours already in employment in countries in the Middle East.

### Recruitment

Most of the migrants from Kerala went abroad for jobs, not as regular workers recruited by employers or their agents, or by authorized recruiting agencies, but with the help of friends and relatives. Licensed recruiting agencies accounted for only a small proportion, less than 8 per cent. A few highly qualified persons or those with professional or technical education were able to get jobs by making direct applications to employers; however, these came to only about 4 per cent of the total number.

## Waiting Period between Enquiry and Enlisting

Since much of the migration took place outside the official channels and through unauthorized agencies, most migrants had to wait for months on end after making the first enquiries and establishing contacts in order actually to enlist for migration. Here, it would not be appropriate to use the term recruitment, since most migrants migrated without being selected for specific jobs under agreed terms and conditions of work.

On average, the waiting period came to about 15 months, though in nearly 45 per cent of cases it was less than 6 months.

The length of the waiting period has however been steadily on the increase over the years. Prior to 1970, 84 per cent of the migrants were able to enlist within six months of first enquiry; the corresponding proportions declined to 60 per cent during 1970–1972, 51 per cent during 1973–1975 and 34 per cent during 1975–1984. This was due to the swelling of the ranks of applicants and the growth of the links in the chain of intermediaries connected with the selection of migrants for transhipment. The length of the waiting period was less for the better-educated than for the illiterates and the less-educated, since the former had a greater ability as regards communication, mobility, and bargaining.

Between selection and migration, there was another waiting period involved, but not as long. Nearly 50 per cent of the migrants were able to proceed abroad immediately after selection or the granting of a visa. Another 40 per cent went abroad within two months. Only in the case of 10 per cent was the waiting period three months or longer.

## Employment Contract

Since the process of selection and recruitment was mostly informal and arranged through friends and relatives, employment contracts specifying terms and conditions of work, remuneration, and living existed only in a minority of cases, about a quarter of the total number of migrants (see table 11).

**Table 11.** Migrants by type of contract of employment (percentages)

| Type of contract | Proportion of migrants |
| --- | --- |
| Formal contract specifying terms and conditions | 24.3 |
| Letter and other communications mentioning some of the main terms and conditions | 5.2 |
| Informal arrangement | 66.7 |
| No conditions stipulated | 3.8 |
| Total | 100.0 |

### Employment Counselling

Since recruitment of migrants took place mainly through informal channels, the government's involvement in the process was nominal. There did not exist any formal arrangements for advising the prospective migrants on the socio-economic, political, and cultural environment to which they were going or on the working and living conditions, the labour laws, and the grievance settlement procedures in the countries of their destination. Whatever information the migrants received was from friends and relatives, and only 7 per cent received such information.

The counselling services have improved to some extent in recent years. The various agencies who act as intermediaries in the migration process distribute pamphlets on these matters to intending migrants who approach them for emigration clearance. Besides distribution of such pamphlets, little else takes place in the way of counselling. For the respondents in our survey, even this source was non-existent. For the large majority of them, migration was a leap in the dark.

### Bargaining for Better Terms and Conditions of Work

As most migrants did not have employment contracts or even any idea of the employers under whom they would be working, the question of bargaining for better terms and conditions of work did not arise at all.

Only 39 (5.6 per cent) returned migrants reported that they had made some attempt at bargaining at the time of recruitment for better terms and conditions. The majority had thought it injudicious. The proportion that thought that the terms and conditions stipulated were satisfactory was a mere 13 per cent (90 migrants). Sixty-five persons (9.3 per cent) made no attempt at bargaining for fear of loss of the job opportunity at hand. For a small number of about 2 per cent, the reason for acquiescence was reportedly lack of knowledge or skills, or assistance from others. The overall impression that one gets is that the migrants had been on the receiving end, and were in no position to bargain for better terms and conditions of employment.

### Migration Expenses

Migrants incurred expenses on various items in connection with their travel abroad, such as passport and visa fees, charges for medical check-ups, and air fares. A few of the migrants did not have to spend much on visas or No Objection Certificates (NOCs) because they were procured for them by relatives or close friends. But the majority had to buy visas or NOCs at exorbitant prices from recruiting agencies or other sources which themselves had bought them from Arab employers. On average, the cost of migration came to a little over Rs. 9,000. About 42 per cent of the migrants had incurred less than Rs. 5,000 and another 22 per cent between Rs. 5,000 and 10,000. There was, however, a significant proportion, approximately one-fifth, who incurred expenditures above Rs. 15,000.

There is no reason why the average cost of migration should have been as high as Rs. 9,000, rising to between Rs. 15,000 and Rs. 50,000 for a significant number of migrants. This would not have occurred had the recruitment been done entirely through approved channels and the payments made according to rates recognized and approved by government. However, migration from Kerala has remained by and large an uncontrolled and unregulated process. Migrants would have paid according to both their ability to pay at the time of migration and their earning potential abroad.

Owing to the absence of effective control of the recruitment process and the massive demand for visas, fraudulent agencies and individuals have proliferated. The number of persons who fall victim to them is large. The media report cases in which unwary individuals seeking to migrate have become victims of fraud and lost large sums of money. Efforts to streamline the process of migration have not succeeded in eliminating irregularities and reducing opportunities for fraud and exploitation.

## Financing

The mobilization of finances to meet the cost of migration presents a mixed situation in which savings and borrowings are of relatively equal importance. About 43 per cent relied on savings – nearly one-fourth on their own savings and one-fifth on the savings of their parents. Borrowing accounted for approximately 40 per cent, with friends and relatives providing the bulk of it. The role that friends and relatives played in financing migration, by giving loans interest-free or at very low rates of interest, was also significant. Nearly one-third of the total number received such help. For the others, the most important method of financing was sale of assets. The part played by banks or governmental agencies in this respect was negligible.

The respondents faced very few problems on arrival in the host countries with regard to passports, visas, work permits, etc. Only 10 per cent made mention of any such problem.

On arrival, the migrants did not make any effort to contact their employers or the Indian embassy; first, they contacted their friends and relatives. This is not surprising, since friends and relatives were the source of information and assistance for migration in the majority of cases. Besides, there did not exist, for a large proportion, any employer to contact; they had with them only residence or work permits.

## Waiting Period between Arrival and Placement

Although most of the migrants went abroad without any firm offer of employment, they were absorbed into jobs without long periods of waiting. It is reported that for 40 per cent there was no waiting period at all. The average waiting period for the entire group of respondents was as short as 2.3 months. However, the fact that, even for those who were recruited by licensed agencies and construction firms, varying periods of waiting were involved shows that the practice of securing visas and recruiting without prior job placement was not uncommon.

Though absorption into employment did not present serious difficulties, the type of employment received and the wages and salaries fixed posed problems. Only one-third of the total number of migrants received the type of employment that was promised to them earlier. For a larger proportion, the question did not arise,

**Table 12.** Costs of migration

| Cost (hundreds of rupees) | Proportion of migrants (%) |
|---|---|
| 0.5 | 4.7 |
| 5–10 | 7.0 |
| 10–50 | 29.0 |
| 50–100 | 22.6 |
| 100–150 | 15.2 |
| 150–200 | 12.5 |
| 200–250 | 5.9 |
| 250–500 | 2.9 |
| 500 or more | 0.1 |
| Total | 100.0 |

since no employment at all had been promised to them. In such a situation, there was little reason for the majority of the migrants to complain about the jobs received.

## Working Conditions

Most migrants, whether recruited by employers, migrating with work permits, or smuggling themselves without valid documents, had expectations about working and living conditions in the host countries which were of a general character and not clearly defined. Only 509 of the 696 respondents (i.e. 75 per cent) replied to the question. Those who had a specific understanding of such conditions formed only a small proportion, about one-fifth. But proportions varied from item to item. For example, in respect of job description and salary and allowances, more than one-third had specific ideas; with regard to hours of work and living conditions, 29 and 25 per cent respectively said that they had had specific knowledge. In regard to terms of employment, such as compensation for accidents, termination benefits, and travel facilities within the countries of employment, the proportions with a clear understanding were lower – only 11 to 14 per cent. In the vast majority of cases, the terms and conditions of work were, however, unspecified and unknown.

Since a large proportion (about 75 per cent) of the migrants had proceeded without formal contracts, without specific jobs in mind, and without hopes of comfortable working conditions, there was little disappointment among most of them about the terms and conditions of work they eventually received. A small proportion of less than 10 per cent felt that they got more than they had expected; one-third stated that what they did receive was not significantly different from what they had hoped for; another one-fourth felt, however, that things did not live up to expectations. But the typical response came from about 30 per cent who stated that they were ready to accept whatever they received as they did not have any norms of working terms and conditions with which they could make comparisons.

The respondents did not in general harbour the feeling that the conditions were less favourable to them than to expatriate workers from other Asian countries. In fact, more than two-thirds of those who responded to this question thought that their conditions were better.

There was of course a small minority that was dissatisfied and made complaints before labour courts in the countries of employment, but to no avail except in one case. It was not the lack of awareness of the legal procedure for grievance settlement but lack of optimism about the fairness of the outcome, as well as fear of losing their job, that kept migrants from lodging complaints or seeking redress in the courts of law.

## Living Conditions

The term living conditions takes in housing, food, facilities for entertainment, recreation, and travel, medical care, and education.

As regards housing, nearly four-fifths were more than satisfied, though for those employed in the lower strata of the occupational hierarchy housing conditions were not as good as for the others. But the proportion of migrants who were dissatisfied with housing conditions formed less than one-fifth of the total number. The proportion was higher among persons in employment under private sector agencies than those who worked for the government. The housing facilities were satisfactory or very good for more than four-fifths. Among them were a large proportion of persons employed in professional, technical and administrative, teaching, and ministerial jobs. Those who were dissatisfied with the housing conditions were mostly artisans and unskilled workers. The overall impression that the data provide is therefore that, in the host countries, housing conditions for expatriate workers from India were satisfactory.

Most migrants were satisfied with the quality of food available during their stay. Only one-eighth of the total number considered it poor. Similarly, the proportion of migrants who reported adequate facilites for entertainment was much higher than those who reported otherwise. With regard to opportunities for listening to the radio, watching television, or going to the cinema, only half the total number were satisfied. Facilities for travel, medical care, and education were reported to be adequate or very good by the majority. The facilities that were found inadequate by most were sports, picnics, and tours. One can hardly conclude from this that living conditions were poor or unsatisfactory, since most other, more basic, facilities were available to the majority, and most migrants had never before enjoyed such facilities, even at home. The Muslim migrants from Kerala had little difficulty as regards religious practice and observance, but for the non-Muslims opportunities for worship were almost non-existent. However, this cannot be considered a serious problem, since it is well known that the Islamic countries of the Middle East do not allow, except in very exceptional cases, facilities for the practice of non-Islamic faiths.

Expatriate workers from Kerala did not lead an enclave life while in employment in the host countries. At least one-fourth of the total number maintained close contacts with the citizens of the countries of their employment; for another 47 per cent, there were contacts, but only very distant ones. The migrants had relationships not only with fellow Indians but also with the migrant workers from the different countries of South and South-East Asia. The harrowing tales about the ill-treatment of Indian expatriate workers by Arab employers, and of the walls of silence that separate workers from different Asian countries, are thus found to be exaggerated, at least in so far as our sample respondents are concerned. If

**Table 13.** Migrants by most important source of financing

| Source | Proportion of migrants (%) |
|---|---|
| Personal savings | 24.7 |
| Parents' savings | 18.5 |
| Borrowing from friends | 11.8 |
| Borrowing from relatives | 20.0 |
| Borrowing from moneylenders | 4.9 |
| Borrowing from banks | 3.4 |
| Sales of assets (land, buildings, etc.) | 6.6 |
| Sales of assets (ornaments, jewellery, etc.) | 8.2 |
| Government assistance | 1.9 |
| Total | 100.0 |

our findings are any guide, it is possible to conclude that the migration of Asian workers to Arab countries has served to promote international understanding between peoples of Asia and the Arab world on a scale that would have been impossible through the conventional diplomatic economic channels.

Migrants in our sample had the impression that the embassies of India in the Arab countries are not effective in helping them solve problems regarding employment, wages and salaries, or settlement of other grievances. Because of the lack of confidence in their effectiveness, the migrants did not make contact with the embassies, neither on arrival, nor during their stay, nor on departure. However, the respondents admitted that the embassies came to their assistance in emergency and crisis situations, for example in cases of compulsory termination of work permit and repatriation.

## Adjustment Problems

Migration raises adjustment problems, first for the migrant dealing with a foreign, unfamiliar environment and with separation from his family, and second for the migrant's family, who must cope with the new set of problems arising from the absence of the migrant from home. Such problems have physical, psychological, and financial aspects. We first look at the adjustment problems for the households.

### Households

The adjustment problems encountered by households varied in character and intensity. They were more severe in homes where the migrant was the household head, or where he was married and had left his wife and children behind. When the migrant was not the head of the household, or was unmarried or unemployed, migration seldom caused any severe problems, at least of a physical and financial nature.

The physical and financial problems that households had to face included those of management of the household and of landed property, business, and finances.

**Table 14.** Migrants' actual terms and conditions of work in comparison with those expected/specified in contract (percentages)

| Item | Whether terms and conditions specified or not | | | | Terms and conditions according to expectations | | | | |
|---|---|---|---|---|---|---|---|---|---|
| | Specified | Not specified | Not applicable | Total | Better | Same | Worse | Not applicable | Total |
| Job description | 35.6 | 4.5 | 59.9 | 100.0 | 9.3 | 46.1 | 27.2 | 17.4 | 100.0 |
| Salary and allowance | 34.1 | 4.9 | 61.0 | 100.0 | 6.6 | 35.2 | 42.8 | 15.4 | 100.0 |
| Hours of work | 29.0 | 9.2 | 61.8 | 100.0 | 27.3 | 40.0 | 14.7 | 18.0 | 100.0 |
| Overtime | 16.4 | 16.9 | 66.7 | 100.0 | 7.6 | 23.3 | 27.0 | 42.1 | 100.0 |
| Living accommodation | 23.4 | 13.4 | 63.2 | 100.0 | 9.6 | 36.1 | 30.5 | 23.8 | 100.0 |
| Travel facilities | 13.9 | 20.0 | 66.1 | 100.0 | 7.0 | 31.2 | 26.7 | 35.1 | 100.0 |
| Casual leave | 17.5 | 17.3 | 64.9 | 100.0 | 4.0 | 32.2 | 33.5 | 30.5 | 100.0 |
| Medical leave | 20.4 | 15.4 | 64.2 | 100.0 | 10.6 | 41.1 | 21.8 | 26.4 | 100.0 |
| Compensation for accident | 13.6 | 18.1 | 68.3 | 100.0 | 4.2 | 32.6 | 17.0 | 46.3 | 100.0 |
| Food | 18.2 | 17.1 | 64.7 | 100.0 | 10.2 | 34.6 | 28.3 | 26.9 | 100.0 |
| Home leave | 18.8 | 16.1 | 65.1 | 100.0 | 4.5 | 34.5 | 27.9 | 33.2 | 100.0 |
| Termination of contract | 18.8 | 15.8 | 65.4 | 100.0 | 9.5 | 30.7 | 22.6 | 37.2 | 100.0 |
| Return travel | 17.4 | 17.0 | 63.6 | 100.0 | 6.8 | 33.3 | 29.4 | 30.3 | 100.0 |
| Termination of benefits | 11.2 | 16.4 | 72.4 | 100.0 | 1.9 | 24.7 | 25.4 | 48.0 | 100.0 |
| Total | 20.6 | 14.4 | 63.0 | 100.0 | 8.5 | 34.0 | 26.8 | 30.7 | 100.0 |

Management of household affairs passed into the hands of wives in a quarter of all cases, even though the proportion of married persons among the migrants was one-half. But all the married persons were not heads of households at the time of migration: in fact, household heads formed only 8 per cent of the total number. In the households in which management did not pass to the wives, the responsibility was vested in parents or near relatives. The absence of migrants, therefore, did not present serious problems of household management in the majority of cases, and no substitute arrangements were necessary.

Management of landed property was not a major problem either, since the size of property was small in the majority of cases. No household sold off landed property owing to management difficulties. In the management, wives, parents or relatives were in charge, but in a few cases wives and parents also sought help from relatives.

In contrast to the situation with landed property, not all business establishments run by the migrants' households continued in existence after the migrants had left. A few had to be wound up. A few others passed to the management of friends and relatives. New arrangements for financial management were necessary only in about 10 per cent of the households, the majority being those from which the head or the major earning member had migrated.

In the matter of adjustment, the households had to depend entirely on their own resources, or on friends and relatives. There were no other aid agencies, whether official or private, voluntary or statutory. Even in the absence of outside sources of help, most households adjusted to the new problems with efficiency and courage. Only 11 per cent considered that they were unable to make satisfactory adjustments.

The psychological problems of separation are the staple diet of reports on the consequences of migration. Among such problems, the deviant behaviour of children is considered important. It is usually alleged that in the households from which heads have migrated, the children become wayward and unruly. The responses that we received from the survey show that the dismal picture that is usually drawn is a gross distortion. Unruly behaviour there certainly was, but it was confined to a tiny minority; further, it cannot be attributed, by any logic, entirely to migration. Such unruly behaviour may not be uncommon in the other households as well. The causes for such behaviour should be traced more to the social, political, and economic ills of the society than to the psychological problems that supposedly emerge from the absence of the breadwinner from home. In the majority of the migrants' households the children are studious, disciplined, and healthy. However, the fact remains that about 10 to 15 per cent of the households experienced behavioural problems on the part of the children. It is essential that some responsible agency – governmental, religious, or social – take care of these and similar problems. Unfortunately, no agency in Kerala has so far assumed this responsibility.

In households from which the head and the main bread winner had migrated, the responsibility for management of the household and household finances often fell on the shoulders of wives. For most of them it imposed new burdens. Yet, the majority faced the challenges successfully and acquired the mental strength and ability to cope with the new responsibilities. There were, however, a few who were less resourceful and courageous. About 10 per cent of the wives, who had broken

**Table 15.** Effect of separation on marital and family relationship

| Relationship | Greater (%) |
|---|---|
| Sharing of responsibility of household and family | 78.2 |
| Affection among members | 97.7 |
| Faithfulness on the part of the spouses | 99.2 |
| Strengthening of family relationship | 96.1 |

down under stress, managed to surmount their problems only with the assistance of other members of the household or relatives.

In Kerala, stories abound about the infidelity of the wives of migrants. It is true that physical separation for long periods is a factor that might strain marital ties, particularly in the case of spouses who are young and newly wed. The affluence that remittances bring to the migrants' households is considered a factor that induces the young wives of hasty "Gulf marriages" to commit adultery. Our data show that, in contradiction to the widely held impression, marital relations have remained intact in about four-fifths of the total number of households. Migrants during their stay abroad have also remained faithful and considerate to their wives. In fact, there was a greater degree of understanding and sharing of responsibilities between husband and wife after migration than before. Table 15 presents the respondents' views on the effect of the migration on family relationships.

**Migrants**

The migrants, in general, adjusted admirably well to the foreign environment. But the adjustment had its psychological costs. For instance, three out of every five migrants developed signs of withdrawal from social contacts and kept themselves exclusively to the routine of work and rest. Only one-fourth of the total really enjoyed their lives in the host country by cultivating friendships with fellow Indians and other nationals and spending off-work hours in their company. About one-eighth started smoking after migration; among those who were already smokers, the habit became stronger in about 25 per cent. About one-eighth started drinking. It was also observed that life in the host countries adversely affected both the physical and the mental health of about 10 to 20 per cent.

The migrants did not in general take their spouses to the countries of employment, for several reasons. Host countries granted permission to bring families only to certain categories with high levels of income. Lack of accommodation facilities was another constraint, as was the desire to save as much as possible. Another reason was the family problems that would be caused by wives moving away from home.

Among the positive aspects related to the adjustment problem were the new household skills the migrants had perforce to acquire during the period of separation from their wives.

There is no doubt that the psychological problems of adjustment could have been mitigated if there had existed effective counselling agencies at home and in the host countries. The positive effects could also have been reinforced. Unfortunately no such agencies existed in either location. In this respect, government

41

as well as religious and other voluntary agencies could have made significant contributions.

## Communication

The most common means used by the migrants for communication with members of their households, friends, and relatives was the postal service. About 98 per cent used this means only. Telephones and telegrams were also used, but only by a very small proportion. Taped conversations were hardly used at all.

Communication was on the whole quite regular and frequent, though there were wide inter-migrant variations. Communication between spouses was the most frequent and regular, while that with others – children, parents, relatives, and friends – was less so.

In the majority of households, no major problem, personal, familial, or financial, arose during the period the migrant was away. About three-fifths of the households fell into this category. The rest of the households reported serious problems of various types, the most important among them being illness and death, which afflicted 37 per cent. The other problems included threat to personal safety, disputes, and marital problems, but they were reported only by about 3 per cent of the total. In general, the households appear to have coped with these problems satisfactorily, despite the migration.

## Earnings and Remittances

### Earnings and Expenditure

Among the migrants, there were a few who had held as many as five different jobs in succession before returning home. The number who had held more than three jobs was, however, very small. While information on the first job was supplied by 610 persons, only 242 reported that they had got a second job; the number that reported a third job was still smaller, only 89 (12.8 per cent).

Analysis of earnings and expenditure while in the first job shows that, in the case of about 98 per cent, expenditure was less than earnings, though about 2 per cent spent more than they reportedly earned. Excess of expenditure over earnings is seen mainly in the case of persons who reported very low levels of earnings, i.e. of less than Rs. 3,000 per month. Whether expenditure was in fact really in excess of earnings or whether the finding is the result of the underreporting of incomes is not known. This category may include both. Among the lowest earning group a few may have been net borrowers.

The data show that the proportion of persons in the lowest expenditure group far exceeded that in the lowest earning group. In the higher earning groups, the reverse was true, that is, the proportion in each earnings group was higher than the proportion in each expenditure group (see table 16). Not all the earnings groups were savers, and expenditure did not increase in step with the increase in earnings.

In the second job, the average earnings levels were higher, presumably owing to the experience and job skills acquired from the first job. However, it was observed that no workers were found in the high-earning brackets of Rs. 20,000 and above. It

**Table 16.** Migrants by monthly earnings and expenditure classes: 1st job

| Monthly earnings/ expenditure class (thousands of rupees) | Proportion of migrants according to earnings (%) | Proportion of migrants according to expenditure (%) |
|---|---|---|
| Less than 1 | 16.5 | 67.0 |
| 1–2 | 36.4 | 26.5 |
| 2–3 | 23.1 | 3.0 |
| 3–5 | 18.2 | 1.5 |
| 5–10 | 4.1 | 1.7 |
| 10–15 | 1.0 | 0.2 |
| 15–20 | 0.2 | — |
| 20–25 | 0.3 | — |
| 25 and above | 0.3 | 0.2 |
| Total | 100.0 | 100.0 |

is likely that the highly paid employees did not, or were not able, to stay on for the second and successive jobs, owing to the time-specific and non-renewable nature of the official contracts which they had entered into with their employers. As we have already observed, a large proportion of the migrants who stayed on after their first contract were also in the two lowest expenditure groups. Levels of expenditure did not increase in line with increases in earnings. When it came to the third job, a further improvement is observed in the earnings levels. The proportion in the lowest earnings groups declined, but the proportions in the lowest expenditure groups remained almost unchanged.

## Savings

The proportion of annual savings to annual income was fairly high for the migrants as a whole. There were savers in every income group. About 54 per cent of the migrants had annual savings of less than Rs. 10,000 each while on the first job; another 33 per cent were in the range of Rs. 10,000–25,000. Only about 13 of the migrants had annual savings of more than Rs. 25,000. The upper limit of annual savings from the first job was Rs. 200,000. The proportions of savers in the higher annual savings groups were higher in the second and the third jobs (see table 10).

The average income-saving ratio of the saving migrants was 0.46 for the first job, and 0.55 for the second and third jobs. The corresponding income-remittance ratios were a little lower; 0.43 for the first and second jobs and 0.41 for the third job. These figures suggest that the migrants who worked for longer periods retained an increasing proportion of their savings. These savings were probably taken home with them, either in cash or in kind, when they went on leave or after termination of their job.

## Frequency and Mode of Remittance

Most migrants used to make remittances in regular instalments, either once a month or once every two months. Migrants who made remittances at very irregu-

**Table 17.** Migrants by monthly earnings and expenditure classes: 2nd job

| Monthly earnings/expenditure class (thousands of rupees) | Proportion of migrants according to earnings (%) | Proportion of migrants according to expenditure (%) |
|---|---|---|
| Less than 1 | 8.3 | 59.5 |
| 1–2 | 31.0 | 32.6 |
| 2–3 | 28.5 | 4.5 |
| 3–5 | 20.2 | 2.1 |
| 5–10 | 10.7 | 0.4 |
| 10–15 | 1.2 | 0.8 |
| 15–20 | — | — |
| 20–25 | — | — |
| 25 and above | — | — |
| Total | 100.0 | 100.0 |

**Table 18.** Migrants by monthly earnings and expenditure classes: 3rd job

| Monthly earnings/expenditure class (thousands of rupees) | Proportion of migrants according to earnings (%) | Proportion of migrants according to expenditure (%) |
|---|---|---|
| Less than 1 | 7.9 | 52.8 |
| 1–2 | 24.7 | 37.1 |
| 2–3 | 28.1 | 5.6 |
| 3–5 | 23.6 | 2.2 |
| 5–10 | 12.4 | 2.2 |
| 10–15 | 3.4 | — |
| 15–20 | — | — |
| 20–25 | — | — |
| 25 and above | — | — |
| Total | 100.0 | 100.0 |

**Table 19.** Migrants by annual savings classes: 1st, 2nd, and 3rd jobs

| Annual savings class (thousands of rupees) | Proportion of migrants (%) | | |
|---|---|---|---|
| | 1st job | 2nd job | 3rd job |
| Less than 5 | 33.3 | 26.8 | 28.1 |
| 5–10 | 20.3 | 18.2 | 14.6 |
| 10–15 | 14.6 | 15.7 | 16.9 |
| 15–25 | 18.9 | 21.9 | 11.2 |
| 25–50 | 10.6 | 7.9 | 24.7 |
| 50–75 | 1.3 | 5.0 | 4.5 |
| 75–100 | 0.3 | 3.3 | — |
| 100–200 | 0.7 | 0.8 | — |
| 200 and above | — | 0.4 | — |
| Total | 100.0 | 100.0 | 100.0 |

lar intervals formed about one-third of the total number. Bank drafts were the principal mode of remittance for about four-fifths of the migrants. Less than one-fifth of them had opened non-resident external accounts.

The bulk of the amounts that the households received was kept in the form of cash in hand and was used for various routine expenses. The balances, if any, were kept in bank accounts. However, only about one-third of the households had bank balances. The amounts kept in bank accounts were more often in the names of spouses, parents, or other members of the households than in those of friends or relatives.

The incidence of fraud in the matter of remittance was minimal: 96 per cent of the migrants reported that they had no such experience at all. But it is unfortunate that about 4 per cent did have such an experience, where monies were lost in transit or misappropriated by the recipients of remittances.

On average it took about 1.5 weeks for remittances to reach their destination. The migrants were on the whole satisfied with the banking facilities in the host countries. Most dissatisfaction existed about banking facilities in Kerala. The complaints were not only about inadequate facilities but also about the poor quality of service rendered. Normally, it took less than four weeks for the encashment of bank drafts once they had reached the recipients.

### Disposition of Savings made from Remittances

The bulk of the remittances was used by the households on routine consumption items, though a substantial balance remained after these had been purchased. Such balances were used for a variety of purposes, such as construction and repair of buildings, repayment of loans, arrangement of marriages, purchase and improvement of land, purchase of ornaments and jewellery, acquisition of vehicles,

**Table 20.** Percentage disposition of savings according to items of expenditure

| Item | Proportion of savings spent | Proportion of households reporting expenditure |
|------|------------------------------|------------------------------------------------|
| Construction and repair of buildings | 27.0 | 40.8 |
| Marriage | 22.8 | 29.6 |
| Purchase and improvement of land | 14.9 | 20.8 |
| Purchase of vehicles | 8.0 | 8.0 |
| Investment in business | 6.0 | 9.5 |
| Repayment of loans | 4.7 | 38.1 |
| Purchase of ornaments and jewellery | 3.7 | 20.7 |
| Purchase of consumer durables | 3.2 | 26.9 |
| Gifts and donations | 2.7 | 24.3 |
| Financing migration of others | 2.6 | 10.8 |
| Education and medical treatment | 2.2 | 17.1 |
| Investment in financial assets | 1.6 | 2.0 |
| Festivals | 0.6 | 5.6 |
| Total | 100.0 | |

livestock, and financial assets, education and medical treatment, and investment in business. The items of expenditure and the proportions of savings spent on them are shown in table 20.

The average savings disposed of per household on the various items came to Rs. 79,900. Among these items, only a few may be considered productive: investment in business and in financial assets, and a part of the investment in vehicles. These three items of expenditure together accounted for less than one-sixth of the total savings disposed of by the households. Given that the migrants were obliged to spend money on the repayment of loans and on the migration of other members of the household, as well as on education and medical treatment (which together accounted for less than 10 per cent of the savings disposed of), about 75 per cent was still left. A significant proportion of this balance, particularly the amounts devoted to items such as ornaments and jewellery, marriages, festivals, consumer durables, and gifts and donations, could have been tapped, if adequate institutional arrangements had existed for the purpose, for productive investment. The funds thus mobilized would have been quite substantial. Unfortunately, such arrangements did not, and still do not, exist in Kerala.

## Costs and Benefits

Labour migration involves both costs and benefits, and these have several dimensions: economic, social, psychological, and cultural. Economic costs for the households concerned include mainly expenditure incurred in the financing of migration, and loss of income in cases in which the migrant had been in employment before migration. For the economy in general, costs should also include expenditure required to replace migrants who were members of the workforce. Here we discuss only the money costs incurred by the households to finance migration: costs in the way of income forgone and social costs are not dealt with.

### Costs

Some dimensions of the money costs of migration were indicated earlier. Here we discuss the trends in money costs over the years and the distribution of money costs among the households, classified on the basis of education.

The average cost per person of migration was Rs. 8,730, and this has been steadily increasing year by year (see table 21). While, during 1973–1975, the initial years of migration after the oil hike, 55 per cent of the migrants paid out less than Rs. 5,000 each, in 1981–1984 only 12 per cent belonged to this expenditure group. Similarly, while no migrant in 1973–1975 had spent more than Rs. 25,000, there were nearly 8 per cent in this category in 1983–1984. It is thus obvious that the per migrant cost of migration was rapidly rising owing to the increasing pressure of aspirants and the increasing exploitation of them by intermediaries.

The costs of migration were, on average, higher for the less educated. The highest average costs are seen to have been incurred by the illiterate – approximately 6.6 per cent of the total sample. Among them, more than 60 per cent had spent Rs. 10,000 or more. For the literate with primary-level education, the costs were slightly lower, the proportion that spent more than Rs. 10,000 being only about 30 per

**Table 21.** Cumulative distribution of households according to money costs incurred per migrant by period of migration (percentages)

| Period of migration | Money costs less than | | | | | | | | | Total |
| | Rs. 500 | Rs. 1,000 | Rs. 5,000 | Rs. 10,000 | Rs. 15,000 | Rs. 20,000 | Rs. 25,000 | Rs. 50,000 | |
|---|---|---|---|---|---|---|---|---|---|
| Before 1970 | 21.3 | 46.6 | 89.3 | 97.3 | 97.3 | 98.6 | 100.0 | — | 100.0 |
| 1970–1972 | 7.5 | 23.9 | 80.6 | 97.0 | 98.5 | 98.5 | 98.5 | 100.0 | 100.0 |
| 1973–1975 | 4.6 | 13.8 | 55.1 | 82.6 | 97.3 | 98.2 | 100.0 | — | 100.0 |
| 1976–1980 | 1.9 | 4.4 | 28.0 | 53.8 | 76.4 | 91.4 | 96.8 | 100.0 | 100.0 |
| 1981–1984 | 0.8 | 1.6 | 11.5 | 33.6 | 47.3 | 76.3 | 92.3 | 99.2 | 100.0 |
| Average | 4.7 | 11.7 | 40.7 | 63.3 | 78.5 | 91.0 | 96.9 | 99.9 | 100.0 |

cent. Interestingly, the corresponding proportions were higher for the literates with secondary schooling and for the matriculates than for the literates with primary-level schooling. However, costs of migration were lowest for the degree-holders. The illiterates were perhaps the most easily exploited group. For the literates with secondary-school education and for the matriculates, average costs were higher because the demand for persons of their educational level was relatively small while their supply was very large. It was the unskilled and those with little work experience belonging to these groups who had to incur heavy costs, rather than the skilled and semi-skilled and the experienced.

One can see from table 22 that while only about 20 per cent of the degree-holders spent Rs. 10,000 or more, the corresponding proportion among the illiterate was more than 60 per cent. Similarly, while none of the degree-holders and the college-educated spent more than Rs. 20,000, 20 per cent of the illiterates had to do so.

### Benefits

Benefits of migration may be examined in terms of improvement in income and asset status, consumption level, and housing and other household amenities.

Income

On average, migrants stayed and/or worked in the host countries for about 5.5 years. The average annual income of the household of a migrant increased by about Rs. 4,936 (from Rs. 7,154 to Rs. 12,090). In addition, the proportion of households that depended mainly on incomes earned from employment in the Arab countries nearly doubled (from 14 to 27 per cent).

Assets

The asset position of the households has also registered a marked improvement consequent on the receipt of foreign-earned incomes. This improvement is reflected in all the important types of assets held by households, such as (a) physical assets including land, buildings, livestock, tools and equipment, vehicles, ornaments and jewellery, and durable consumer goods, and (b) financial assets. Thus, in all, the assets of an average migrant household have shown an increase of about 32 per cent. Making allowance for the liabilities of the households on both dates (Rs. 3,930 prior to migration and Rs. 6,474 afterwards) does not alter the proportionate size of the increase.

Consumption

Comparison of consumption levels of the households between the two dates is not attempted on a quantitative basis since data on consumption levels prior to migration were not collected. However, it is possible to arrive at certain conclusions on the basis of the respondents' views. The majority of them (about 57 per cent) thought that consumption levels in their households had increased; for 16 per cent of them the increase was of a very high order.

Thus we may conclude that the households of the migrants had improved, on the whole, their economic status, judged on the basis of income, assets, and consumption levels. The costs incurred by them for the purpose of financing migration

**Table 22.** Cumulative distribution of households by money costs incurred per migrant according to level of general education (percentages)

| Level of general education | Money costs less than | | | | | | | | | Total |
|---|---|---|---|---|---|---|---|---|---|---|
| | Rs. 500 | Rs. 1,000 | Rs. 5,000 | Rs. 10,000 | Rs. 15,000 | Rs. 20,000 | Rs. 25,000 | Rs. 50,000 | | |
| Illiterate | 6.5 | 10.9 | 23.9 | 39.1 | 54.3 | 80.4 | 100.0 | — | | 100.0 |
| Literate (primary level) | 4.8 | 12.4 | 45.6 | 69.5 | 82.3 | 92.8 | 97.6 | 99.7 | | 100.0 |
| Literate (secondary level) | 6.0 | 10.6 | 37.1 | 61.6 | 76.8 | 89.4 | 96.0 | 100.0 | | 100.0 |
| Matriculate | 1.6 | 11.1 | 36.5 | 56.3 | 75.4 | 89.7 | 94.4 | 100.0 | | 100.0 |
| College-educated (with no degree) | 4.4 | 13.1 | 47.9 | 60.9 | 87.0 | 100.0 | — | — | | 100.0 |
| Degree-holder | 10.5 | 15.8 | 47.4 | 79.0 | 89.5 | 100.0 | — | — | | 100.0 |
| Average | 4.7 | 11.7 | 40.7 | 63.3 | 78.5 | 91.0 | 96.9 | 96.8 | | 100.0 |

**Table 23.** Value of assets per household prior to and after migration

| Type of asset | Value of assets | |
|---|---|---|
| | Before | After |
| Land | 187,818 | 206,292 |
| Livestock | 400 | 669 |
| Buildings | 41,028 | 72,591 |
| Ornaments and jewellery | 12,680 | 16,958 |
| Vehicles | 2,260 | 7,524 |
| Implements, tools, and equipment | 185 | 526 |
| Durable consumer goods | 2,678 | 7,667 |
| Financial assets | 20,266 | 41,594 |
| Total | 267,315 | 353,821 |

were more than covered by the remittances (and other types of transfer of income). Housing conditions also improved significantly for the majority.

A word of caution is however necessary in this context. The fact that the economic status of the migrants and their households have improved overall should not blind us to the fact that there were cases of dismal failure, where households had lost in terms of income, wealth, and consumption. Even housing conditions and other amenities deteriorated for a few.

In respect of all these variables, households have moved along the scale in both directions; for instance, with regard to annual income 14.4 per cent of households moved down the scale, 43.8 per cent remained in the income groups to which they had earlier belonged, and only 43.8 per cent went up the scale. The decline was precipitous in a few cases, with households who earlier were well-to-do falling to the bottom. Similar falls have occurred in terms of the value of particular assets; 8.2 per cent of the households suffered in respect of the value of land owned, 4.9 per cent in livestock, 2.4 per cent in buildings, 11.4 per cent in ornaments and jewellery, 3.2 per cent in vehicles, and 1.9 per cent in financial assets.

## Return and Rehabilitation

### Reasons for Return

The reasons for return were several, but the major ones were expiry or termination of contract. These two reasons together accounted for about 56 per cent of the cases. The next most important reason was compulsory repatriation by the host government (17.2 per cent). Other reasons, such as difficult living conditions (6.5 per cent), difficult working conditions (8.1 per cent), repatriation for illegal entry (2.6 per cent), and family problems (9.5 per cent), were much less important. The relative importance of these various reasons has not undergone any significant change over the years.

Among the persons who returned for personal reasons, such as difficult living or working conditions or family problems, the majority were relatively well-qualified, for instance those belonging to professional, technical, and administrative categories.

## Rehabilitation

There does not exist in Kerala, or any other part of India, any agency – governmental, institutional, or voluntary – to deal with the problem of the rehabilitation of returned migrants. There is no agency or arrangement to help with the retraining or placement of these persons, and they have to fall back on friends and relatives, though in the majority of cases even this source was not of great help. The assistance rendered by friends and relatives included advice about employment (including self-employment) opportunities and sources of finance.

## Activity Status

A small proportion of the returned migrants (less than 2 per cent) have permanently retired from active work, either voluntarily or because they have become incapacitated. The vast majority, about 60 per cent, remained unemployed. Of the employed, about 39 per cent, nearly 25 per cent were self-employed.

The proportion of unemployed is much higher among the respondents after return than was the case prior to migration. This is because the proportions of the employed and the self-employed have declined from 33 to 14 per cent, and from 28 to 25 per cent respectively.

The large majority of the self-employed were engaged in trade and transport. The unemployed migrants were not, on the whole, of the view that the skills and work experience they gained abroad were of much help in securing employment in Kerala, even though they did not doubt the usefulness of such skills and experience.

Earlier, the returned migrants were not very enthusiastic about approaching the government for assistance in finding employment or other help in their rehabilitation. However, they have formed, in recent months, organizations to pressurize the government either to help them in starting business ventures or to provide employment. Unfortunately, their activities have until now been almost entirely ineffective.

The average period of unemployment among the unemployed returned migrants was, at the time of the survey, about 2 years and 2 months. It was clear that, for those who remained unemployed, the chances of securing employment in Kerala were remote. Nor were the chances of their returning to the Arab countries any brighter, though the majority of them entertained hopes of remigration. Most of them were willing to accept any job that came their way. It is interesting to note that not only the unemployed, but even some of those already employed (or self-employed), were seeking opportunities for remigration.

Nevertheless, of the 441 persons who reportedly desired to return, only 252 (or 57 per cent) were willing to bribe the intermediaries to secure the documents necessary for re-entry. But of those who were willing, there were a sizeable number prepared to spend huge amounts (Rs. 15,000 and above) for the purpose. A few were even prepared to spend over Rs. 50,000.

Paradoxically, even among the unemployed not everyone wanted to remigrate.

They had several reasons: according to some, living and working conditions were poor and levels of wages/salaries were falling. Others, who were more realistic, realized that there no longer existed employment opportunities for them. The number of persons who were disinclined to remigrate for reasons of ill-health and family problems was extremely small.

The unemployed migrants were not very interested in the idea of making investments in industry or other businesses in Kerala. For most of them the major reason was lack of finance. Even those who had financial resources were generally reluctant for various reasons, including fear of labour troubles, raw material shortages, dearth of technical competence, fear of undue government intervention, and marketing problems.

The marital and dependency status of the migrants have undergone changes during the period of employment abroad. A large proportion of them are now married and heads of households. The proportion of married persons increased from 50 to 84 per cent, and the proportion of heads of households from 21 to 39 per cent.

## Changes in Value System and Attitudes

This discussion may be concluded with a few observations on changes in value system and attitudes as perceived by the returned migrants themselves. These changes are related to questions of socio-economic status, attitudes to and of neighbours, and aspirations and life-styles.

### Economic and Social Status

On the question of economic standing, the respondents were not unanimous in their views. There was a large majority (62 per cent) which thought that their economic standing has remained unchanged; about 31 per cent was of the view that it has improved; but the rest, about 6 per cent, considered that migration has ruined their economic status. However, since a larger number reported improvement, the overall effect has been positive. The distribution of migrants, according to their own views of the changes in their economic standing, is shown in table 24.

The distributional pattern of change in social status follows broadly that of economic status.

### Attitudes

A large proportion now was of the view that they were held in great esteem by friends and relatives. They were also sought after for advice and help. Persons who held this view came to about 80 per cent of the sample. On the other hand, nearly 17 per cent thought that they had fallen in the esteem of relatives and friends. The net effect was thus towards an enhancement of the prestige of the migrants. The fact of migration by itself does not seem to have made any significant change in the attitudes of local people towards the respondents, nor have the attitudes of the migrants towards the local people undergone any remarkable change. The

**Table 24.** Distribution of migrants according to own views of change in economic status (percentages)

| Categories of status | Prior to migration | After migration |
|---|---|---|
| High | 3.2 | 8.6 |
| Upper-middle | 32.5 | 43.5 |
| Lower-middle | 41.2 | 35.7 |
| Low | 23.1 | 12.2 |
| Total | 100.0 | 100.0 |

local communities have not alienated the migrants, nor have the migrants tended to keep away from them, except in every rare cases.

This is not to deny that migrants have undergone an attitudinal change. But most changes that have taken place are of a positive and desirable type. For example, migrants have become more positively inclined than earlier towards the education of children, both boys and girls. Their aspirations regarding the employment and social status of their children have also gone up. Now they are willing to grant more freedom to them in the matter of choosing a career. However, in the question of choosing a marriage partner, they are unwilling to grant their children as much freedom as they would in other matters. It is also noted that the freedom granted to daughters in matters of education, career, and marriage is much more limited than that granted to sons.

The foreign experience and exposure to diverse cultures and civilizations has broadened the vision of the respondents in respect of the sharing of household duties and responsibilities, and financial management, with spouses and other members of the household. The migrants have also become more receptive to ideas of family limitation; but in these matters, changes have taken place in both directions, in favour and against, and all such changes cannot be attributed entirely to the migration experience alone.

Their religious and political attitudes have remained, in general, unchanged. The small changes that did occur were not fundamental and were confined to a tiny proportion of the respondents. On the whole, the conclusion that emerged from an inquiry into the influence of exposure to foreign peoples, ideas, cultures, habits, and beliefs was that the impact was quite insignificant. Political attitudes and economic ideology have also remained almost entirely unaffected.

More significant have been changes in attitudes to work. Migrants now value more the importance of hard work, work discipline, and the scientific approach. The influence of migration on the widening of interests and the broadening of perspectives has also been significant and positive.

Involvement in social activities has remained, by and large, unchanged by the migration experience. So also were ideas about the prestige and status of different types of occupations. Most respondents would like, or had already returned to, the jobs they were engaged in prior to migration.

With respect to employment prospects in the Arab countries, the assessment of the majority was realistic. They were of the opinion that the employment prospects in those countries for expatriate labour were on the decline and that the skill-composition and educational level required for the jobs that were still available were quite different. For instance, they were aware that the demand for unskilled and semi-skilled workers has gone down and the demand is rising for skilled and professional workers.

Taking into account all the positive and negative aspects of the migration experience, the migrants were satisfied that they were net gainers. But the gains that they were quite sure of were the economic ones. In other matters – political, sociological, religious, and cultural – the respondents did not consider the effects of migration important. Even in the matter of economic gains, not all the respondents or households were net gainers. However, the proportion of losers was much smaller than that of gainers.

## Policy Issues

The major objective of the foregoing discussion was to bring out the socio-economic characteristics of migrants to the Arab countries and their households in Kerala. The discussion has indicated the causes and consequences of migration at the level of the household economy. It has also looked into the different phases of the migration cycle – the process of recruitment, the adjustment problems while in employment in foreign countries, earnings, remittances and disposition of savings, and post-return problems of rehabilitation.

The overall conclusion that emerged from the discussion has been that, even though the process was one that involved tens of thousands of persons and households, substantial economic and psychological costs, and large net flows of foreign exchange, the institutional and organizational support rendered by the government or other agencies in counselling, financing, protecting, and rehabilitating the migrants has been small.

Yet, the net benefits of migration to the household economy on the whole have been positive and significant. They could have been much larger had there been a greater degree of systematization, monitoring and follow-up at each stage of the migration process. If adequate and effective governmental control and supervision had existed, much of the cheating, bribery, underpayment, and wastage of funds could have been eliminated.

In India, a major handicap for the analysis of the dimensions and impact of migration is the paucity of data. No reliable statistics exist on the size of the annual outflows and return flows of migrants, the stock of expatriate workers in the different countries, their occupational and income status, the flow of remittances, the countries of origin, the channels used, the pattern of utilization of remittances, and the demand for expatriate labour. For the formulation of any meaningful policy and its effective implementation, the basic prerequisite is information.

As our discussion has shown, the migrants and their households are exposed at different stages in the migration cycle to a variety of problems – financial, psychological, and technical. No agency exists in India to take care of such problems. It is surprising that, where we have a surfeit of voluntary agencies (religious, cultural, and social), such wanton disregard of the problems of large numbers of persons has continued to exist.

The role that the Indian embassies have played in protecting the legitimate interests of Indian workers in the Arab countries is reportedly minimal. There exists a strong impression in the minds of the respondents that the embassies are of little help in settling grievances. It should be possible, with better liaison with the host countries and the proper streamlining of operations, for the Indian embassies to play a more effective role in safeguarding the working and living conditions of Indian workers abroad.

Most workers from Kerala are satisfied that the levels of wages/salaries that they received in the Arab countries were much higher than the levels prevailing at home for comparable jobs. They were also satisfied that, in comparison with workers from other Asian countries, they did not suffer from discrimination. However, the fact remains that they were paid much less than Arab workers and workers from countries in the West. It should be the endeavour of the migrant-sending countries to see that they are compensated, through appropriate credit-funding, for the underpayment of their nationals.

Even though migration to the Gulf countries has raised the income, consumption, and asset levels of large numbers of households, it has also ruined a few thousands. Our analysis has shown that nearly 15 per cent of the migrants have suffered a fall in economic status. The reasons for this are the huge costs incurred by way of the illegal gratification of recruiters and their agents, failure to get job placement in the host countries, or loss of income due to fraud, cheating, or wasteful expenditure. As yet there has been no systematic effort to check the proliferation of unlicensed recruitment agencies and the practice of taking huge sums of money from intending migrants for the securing of visas.

The survey data show that a sizeable proportion of remittances, which went on unproductive or wasteful expenditure, could have been mobilized and invested if effective machinery had existed for the purpose. The efforts made by the Kerala government for mobilization of the funds of migrants or their households have until now been largely unsuccessful. It seems, however, that in the area in which the government has been inactive, the private financiers have begun operating. The spate of investment funds in Kerala (popularly known as "blade companies," since their activities are razor-sharp and cut both ways, cheating the depositor and the borrower simultaneously) is a typical case in point. The activities of such institutions are fuelling the inflationary process and further reducing the benefits which the migration might have brought to the poor and middle-income groups. Steps taken to bring to book such institutions have so far been successfully resisted by the interest groups concerned.

Rehabilitation of the returnees has not engaged the serious attention of the government. As many as 60 per cent of the returned migrants remain unemployed. Although the unemployed migrants have been calling the attention of the government to their plight, the government machinery has yet to move effectively to deal with them. With the prospects of the Gulf exodus coming to an end and of an increasing flow of returnees, the situation that prevails in Kerala, and probably in the rest of the migrant-sending states of India, with regard to the rehabilitation and re-employment of migrants, as well as to the overall generation of work opportunities for the unemployed, is a cause for serious concern.

# 2

# KOREAN MIGRANT WORKERS TO THE MIDDLE EAST

**Hyunho Seok**

Department of Sociology, Sung Kyun Kwan University, Seoul, Republic of Korea

## Introduction

This study examines the characteristics of the migrants, the process of migration, work and living conditions in the host country, the adjustment of the migrant and his family, the motives for migration and the use to which remittances are put. It also assesses the impact of migration on the household and the economy as a whole.

The study was based on a sample of 480 return migrants, of whom 376 were hired by Korean construction firms specifically for work in the Middle East, while the remaining 104 were transferred temporarily to that area. The former were sampled primarily from construction sites in metropolitan Seoul and the latter were drawn from six construction firms in the city. Available data indicate that the ratio of temporary to permanent workers from the Republic of Korea in the West Asian region was about nine to one; the sample has been weighted in favour of the temporary workers.

The causes that led to the development of the Middle Eastern migrant labour markets have been well documented and analysed (Ecevit, 1981; Shaw, 1979; Birks and Sinclair, 1979, 1980; Berouti, 1976). Korean firms responded quickly to the large demand for construction know-how and manpower that was created in the region following the sudden and very large increase in oil revenues. In 1974, the first Korean firm won a contract for highway construction in Saudi Arabia, and took along 218 Korean workers. This was the start of an important process of migration for construction work in the region.

Korean migrant workers in the Middle East were almost exclusively in the construction sector. During the period 1974–1985, the total value of contracted work, and the flow of migrants, had experienced a steady increase followed by a decline. This follows the pattern of oil revenues and construction investments in the region. Between 1974 and 1977 the total value of Korean construction (contract awards) averaged US$1.67 billion (US$6.7 billion for the period). In the subsequent four years the annual awards to Korean construction companies increased at an annual average of US$8.6 billion (US$34.4 for the period). Thereafter awards fell to an

**Table 1.** Annual number of Korean migrant workers to the Middle East by country of destination, 1974–1985

| Destination | 1974 | 1975 | 1976 | 1977 | 1978 | 1979 | 1980 | 1981 | 1982 | 1983 | 1984 | 1985 |
|---|---|---|---|---|---|---|---|---|---|---|---|---|
| Saudi Arabia | 218 (55.2)[a] | 3,593 (55.6) | 15,855 (74.5) | 32,748 (62.2) | 56,161 (68.5) | 80,787 (81.5) | 99,441 (78.1) | 112,963 (73.5) | 122,606 (70.9) | 122,443 (71.8) | 88,534 (64.2) | 58,924 (54.8) |
| Iraq | — | 9 (0.1) | 84 (0.4) | 213 (0.4) | 428 (0.6) | 1,063 (1.1) | 161 (0.1) | 6,265 (4.1) | 19,920 (11.5) | 15,424 (9.0) | 14,449 (10.5) | 10,607 (9.9) |
| Libya | — | — | — | 677 (1.3) | 1,018 (1.2) | 2,046 (2.6) | 3,757 (3.0) | 15,264 (9.9) | 16,788 (9.7) | 19,504 (11.4) | 21,761 (15.8) | 23,138 (21.5) |
| Kuwait | — | 48 (0.7) | 462 (2.2) | 4,657 (8.9) | 8,646 (10.5) | 7,155 (7.2) | 10,927 (8.6) | 9,060 (5.9) | 5,644 (3.3) | 4,722 (2.8) | 4,335 (3.1) | 4,127 (3.8) |
| Jordan | — | 90 (1.4) | 486 (2.3) | 1,651 (3.2) | 1,418 (1.7) | 902 (0.9) | 2,404 (1.9) | 1,840 (1.2) | 1,354 (0.9) | 1,365 (0.8) | 587 (0.4) | 447 (0.4) |
| Qatar | — | — | 636 (3.0) | 1,491 (2.8) | 1,915 (2.3) | 1,854 (1.9) | 1,356 (1.0) | 1,980 (1.3) | 1,309 (0.8) | 859 (0.5) | 717 (0.5) | 699 (0.7) |
| UAE | — | 39 (0.6) | 155 (0.7) | 804 (1.5) | 2,689 (3.3) | 3,503 (3.5) | 6,758 (5.3) | 2,957 (1.9) | 1,414 (0.8) | 1,110 (0.7) | 1,491 (1.1) | 1,268 (1.2) |
| Iran | 177 (44.8) | 2,402 (37.2) | 1,630 (17.1) | 6,264 (12.0) | 7,418 (9.1) | 64 (0.1) | 30 (0.0) | 198 (0.1) | 455 (0.3) | 1,263 (0.7) | 1,995 (1.4) | 3,669 (3.4) |
| Others[b] | — | 285 (4.4) | 1,961 (9.2) | 3,717 (7.1) | 2,116 (3.0) | 1,540 (1.6) | 2,489 (2.0) | 3,174 (2.1) | 3,478 (2.0) | 3,811 (2.2) | 4,114 (3.0) | 4,621 (4.3) |
| Total | 395 (100.0) | 6,466 (100.0) | 21,269 (100.0) | 52,247 (100.0) | 81,987 (100.0) | 99,141 (100.0) | 127,323 (100.0) | 153,699 (100.0) | 172,968 (100.0) | 170,501 (100.0) | 137,983 (100.0) | 107,500 (100.0) |

a. Percentages in parentheses.
b. Included are Egypt, Yemen, Bahrain, Oman, and Sudan.

average annual total of US$7.7 billion for the period 1982-1985. In 1981, when the Korean construction work in the region reached a peak, the value of work was US$13 billion, with more than 100 firms engaging over 150,000 Korean workers. Thereafter the value of work to Korean firms declined, to US$4 billion in 1985.

The Korean workforce in West Asia contained two types of workers – first there were regular workers who were permanently employed in a Korean firm and were assigned to the Middle East on work undertaken by that firm; second, temporary workers were recruited on contracts of limited duration solely for work in the Middle East. The regular workers normally belonged to the professional, managerial, and supervisory grades and included clerical and similar support staff. The temporary workers were generally engaged for the operative and manual occupations, both skilled and unskilled.

## Characteristics of Migrants and Motives for Migration

Nearly all Korean migrant workers in the Middle East have been engaged by Korean construction firms operating in the region. The migrants fall into two categories, employees of firms who are relocated and those hired by the firms specifically for work in West Asia. The former are in the managerial, administrative, and engineering grades, and include support staff such as clerks. The latter are the skilled and unskilled construction workers, on contract only for the duration of the work. The socio-economic background and the reasons for migration are somewhat different for the workers in the two categories.

### Family and Socio-economic Background

All Korean migrants are males. Nearly three-quarters (73 per cent) of both groups fall into the 25-40 age-group. However, the regular employees are on average younger than the temporary contract workers. A large proportion of the regular workers are younger, unmarried, and non-household heads. About half of the regular workers (48 per cent) were married, compared with more than three-quarters (69 per cent) of the temporary workers. About half of the former (51 per cent) were household heads compared with more than three-quarters of the latter category (71 per cent). Although a significant proportion of the migrants were neither married nor household heads, most were family members with a responsible role, owing to their improved financial position brought about by the migration. The survey data indicate that a majority of those who were not married before migration got married on their return and became the head of a household (see table 2). The size of the migrants' families (4.5 for temporary workers and 4.1 for the regular workers) remained unchanged before and after migration.

The migrants have a high average level of education. The temporary workers have a high-school education (44 per cent), while of the regular employees all have a high-school education and three-quarters have a college-level education. More than half (53 per cent) of the temporary workers with high-school education had obtained vocational training. About 70 per cent of the regular employees with college degrees had graduated in engineering or business. However, less than one-

58

**Table 2.** Familial status of migrant workers to the Middle East, before migration and current, by overseas working status

| | Before migration | | | | Current | | | |
|---|---|---|---|---|---|---|---|---|
| Familial status | Temporary workers | | Regular employees | | Temporary workers | | Regular employees | |
| Marital status | | | | | | | | |
| Married | 258 | | 50 | (48.1) | 336 | (89.4) | 76 | (73.7) |
| Unmarried | 118 | (31.4) | 54 | (51.9) | 40 | (10.6) | 28 | (26.3) |
| Total | 376 | (100.0) | 104 | (100.0) | 376 | (100.0) | 104 | (100.0) |
| Head of household | | | | | | | | |
| Head | 269 | (71.5) | 53 | (51.0) | 337 | (89.6) | 75 | (72.1) |
| Non-head | 107 | (28.5) | 51 | (49.0) | 39 | (10.4) | 29 | (27.9) |
| Total | 376 | (100.0) | 104 | (100.0) | 376 | (100.0) | 104 | (100.0) |

a. Percentages in parentheses.

fifth (19 per cent) of the temporary workers and one-quarter of the regular workers had received training other than their formal education.

Most of the workers in the temporary category were selected from among those with experience: with the exception of two persons, all had more than five years of work experience. The regular workers, however, are primarily those with high levels of education, and their previous employment experience is relatively low. Only four persons in the sample had no previous employment, being new entrants to the workforce.

The survey data indicate that about one-quarter of the migrants in the temporary category had been in stable occupations, regular wage employment or self-employment, before migration. The majority, however, had been in temporary or non-permanent employment. The regular workers, on the other hand, were only shifting locations; almost all had therefore been in regular employment before migration.

### Motives for Migration

The primary motive for migration for most workers was an economic one. However, it is possible to differentiate between workers according to the type of investment or purchases they hoped to make. More than one-quarter of the temporary workers (28 per cent) had migrated in order to generate the funds to purchase a home. About one-fifth intended to invest in a business. About one out of ten migrants in the temporary category intended to invest in their children's education. However, more than one-quarter (27 per cent) had a target sum which they expected to raise; these persons had not identified an avenue for investment of their earnings. About one in ten of the temporary workers stated that the primary reason for migration was to pay off debts or supplement family income. The reasons for migration for the regular workers were different from those of the temporary work-

**Table 3.** Educational level of migrant workers to the Middle East by overseas working status

| Educational status | Temporary workers | | Regular employees | |
|---|---|---|---|---|
| No formal education | 4 | (1.1)[a] | — | |
| Primary school | 91 | (24.2) | — | |
| Middle school | 117 | (31.1) | — | |
| High school | 156 | (41.5) | 22 | (21.2) |
| Junior college | 2 | (0.5) | 15 | (14.4) |
| College or more | 7 | (1.9) | 67 | (64.4) |
| Total | 376 | (100.0) | 104 | (100.0) |

a. Percentages in parentheses.

**Table 4.** Duration of employment before migration to the Middle East by occupational status in overseas employment

| Duration of employment (years) | Temporary workers | | | Regular employees[a] | | |
|---|---|---|---|---|---|---|
| | Unskilled | Skilled | Total | Low-level | High-level | Total |
| Less than 5 | — | 2 | 2 | 2 | 19 | 21 |
| | | (0.6)[b] | (0.5) | (3.2) | (46.3) | (20.2) |
| 5–9 | 9 | 56 | 65 | 48 | 14 | 62 |
| | (22.6) | (16.7) | (17.3) | (76.2) | (34.1) | (59.6) |
| 10–14 | 13 | 110 | 123 | 11 | 8 | 19 |
| | (31.7) | (32.8) | (32.7) | (17.5) | (19.5) | (18.3) |
| 15–19 | 10 | 81 | 91 | 2 | — | 2 |
| | (24.4) | (24.2) | (24.2) | (3.2) | | (1.9) |
| 20–24 | 6 | 60 | 66 | — | — | — |
| | (14.9) | (17.9) | (17.6) | | | |
| 25–29 | 2 | 16 | 18 | — | — | — |
| | (4.9) | (4.8) | (4.8) | | | |
| 30 or more | 1 | 10 | 11 | — | — | — |
| | (2.4) | (3.0) | (2.9) | | | |
| Total | 41 | 335 | 376 | 63 | 41 | 104 |
| | (100.0) | (100.0) | (100.0) | (100.0) | (100.0) | (100.0) |

a. High-level employees include assistant directors and directors, and low-level ones are those below the assistant director level.
b. Percentages in parentheses.

ers. The regulars migrated primarily as a result of job assignment (44 per cent); nevertheless, financial incentives were important for a significant proportion (one-third). Also, experience and skill development were given as important reasons by 10 and 5 per cent of the regular workers respectively. Although a large proportion of the regular employees stated that job assignment was the primary reason for migration, there is a strong underlying economic reason even for these migrants, as the move is a voluntary one.

**Table 5.** Last working status of migrant workers before migration by their first working status

| Last status | First working status | | | | |
|---|---|---|---|---|---|
| | Regularly employed | Temporarily employed | Self-employed | Family worker | Total |
| Regular | 139 | 2 | — | 5 | 146 |
| Temporary | 29 | 186 | 24 | 36 | 226 |
| Self-employed | 10 | 13 | 17 | 7 | 47 |
| Family worker | — | — | — | 9 | 9 |
| Total | 169 | 201 | 41 | 57 | 468 |

**Table 6.** Last working status of migrant workers before migration by overseas working and occupational status (percentages)

| Last working status before migration | Overseas working status | | | | | |
|---|---|---|---|---|---|---|
| | Temporary workers | | | Regular employee | | |
| | Unskilled | Skilled | Total | Low-level | High-level | Total |
| Family worker | 1 | 8 | 9 | — | — | — |
| | (2.4) | (2.4) | (2.4) | | | |
| Self-employed | 10 | 36 | 46 | 1 | — | 1 |
| | (24.4) | (10.8) | (12.3) | (1.7) | | (1.0) |
| Temporarily employed | 26 | 245 | 271 | — | — | — |
| | (63.4) | (73.8) | (72.7) | | | |
| Regularly employed | 4 | 43 | 47 | 58 | 40 | 98 |
| | (9.8) | (13.0) | (12.6) | (98.3) | (100.0) | (99.0) |
| Total[a] | 41 | 332 | 373 | 59 | 40 | 99 |
| | (100.0) | (100.0) | (100.0) | (100.0) | (100.0) | (100.0) |

a. Excluded are never employed (6 cases) and last working status not classifiable (1 case).

Only one person among those surveyed stated that the primary reason for migration was because there was no employment at home. During the years of high West Asian migration the Republic of Korea enjoyed economic prosperity, and the employment situation, especially in construction, was good (Park, 1983).

The primary reason for migration varies among migrants according to age, marital status, education, and previous occupational status. The variation is greater among the temporary workers. For them, the younger the migrant the stronger the motive to save for investment in self-employment. Those who are married are more likely to save to purchase a home, while those with children save for their education. Among the regular workers, the older and the higher the level of education, the more likely it is that the move is for career objectives. Among the temporary workers, the lower the occupational status the stronger the economic motive for migration, and the higher the status the more likely it is that the move is related to career objectives.

**Table 7.** Last occupation of migrant workers before migration by overseas occupation (percentages)

| Last occupation before migration | Overseas occupation | | | | |
|---|---|---|---|---|---|
| | Service | Production | Clerical | Professional | Total |
| Farmer | — | 15 | 1 | — | 16 |
| | | (4.0) | (2.0) | | (3.4) |
| Sales and service | 3 | 30 | 2 | — | 35 |
| | (60.0) | (8.1) | (3.9) | | (7.3) |
| Production | 1 | 317 | 1 | 1 | 320 |
| | (20.0) | (85.2) | (2.0) | (2.0) | (67.5) |
| Clerical | 1 | 8 | 44 | 1 | 54 |
| | (20.0) | (2.2) | (86.3) | (2.0) | (11.4) |
| Professional | — | 2 | 3 | 44 | 49 |
| | | (0.5) | (5.9) | (96.0) | (10.3) |
| Total[a] | 5 | 372 | 51 | 46 | 474 |
| | (100.0) | (100.0) | (100.0) | (100.0) | (100.0) |

a. Excluded are never employed before migration.

**Table 8a.** Main reasons for migration to the Middle East by order of move, temporary workers

| Main reasons | Order of move | | | Total moves |
|---|---|---|---|---|
| | 1st move | 2nd move | 3rd–6th move | |
| Purchasing own house | 96 | 64 | 29 | 189 |
| | (25.5)[a] | (32.2) | (29.3) | (28.0) |
| Investing in business | 68 | 44 | 20 | 132 |
| | (18.1) | (22.1) | (20.2) | (19.6) |
| Fund for children's education | 28 | 21 | 15 | 64 |
| | (7.4) | (10.6) | (15.2) | (9.5) |
| A round sum of money | 115 | 47 | 17 | 179 |
| | (30.6) | (23.6) | (17.2) | (26.6) |
| Insufficient earnings | 29 | 13 | 8 | 50 |
| | (7.7) | (6.5) | (8.1) | (7.4) |
| Redeeming debts | 16 | 3 | 2 | 21 |
| | (4.3) | (1.5) | (2.0) | (3.1) |
| Cannot find a job | 1 | — | — | 1 |
| | (0.3) | | | (0.1) |
| Overseas experience | 17 | 4 | 3 | 24 |
| | (4.5) | (2.0) | (3.0) | (3.6) |
| Skill improvement | — | 1 | — | 1 |
| | | (0.5) | | (0.1) |
| Other reasons | 6 | 2 | 5 | 13 |
| | (1.5) | (1.0) | (5.0) | (1.9) |
| Total | 376 | 199 | 99 | 674 |
| | (100.0) | (100.0) | (100.0) | (100.0) |

a. Percentages in parentheses.

**Table 8b.** Main reasons for migration to the Middle East by order of move, regular employees

| Main reasons | Order of move | | | Total moves |
|---|---|---|---|---|
| | 1st move | 2nd move | 3rd–6th move | |
| Purchasing own house | 19 | 4 | 7 | 30 |
| | (18.3)[a] | (9.5) | (25.0) | (17.2) |
| Investing in business | 2 | 2 | 4 | 8 |
| | (1.9) | (4.8) | (14.8) | (4.6) |
| A round sum of money | 11 | 5 | 3 | 19 |
| | (10.6) | (11.9) | (10.7) | (10.9) |
| Insufficient earnings | 4 | 2 | 1 | 7 |
| | (3.8) | (4.8) | (3.6) | (4.0) |
| Redeeming debts | 2 | 1 | — | 3 |
| | (1.9) | (2.4) | | (1.7) |
| Overseas experience | 14 | 3 | 1 | 18 |
| | (13.5) | (7.1) | (3.6) | (10.3) |
| Skill improvement | 6 | 2 | — | 8 |
| | (5.8) | (4.8) | | (4.6) |
| Job assignment | 43 | 21 | 12 | 76 |
| | (41.3) | (50.0) | (42.9) | (43.7) |
| Other reasons | 3 | 2 | — | 5 |
| | (2.9) | (4.8) | | (2.9) |
| | 104 | 42 | 28 | 174 |
| Total | (100.0) | (100.0) | (100.0) | (100.0) |

a. Percentages in parentheses.

## Preparation for Migration

Korean labour migration to the Middle East takes place within a well-established sytem of recruitment. However, like any other voluntary type of migration, it involves a series of problems at the pre-migration stage, especially those related to inadequate information about the overseas move.

### Information on Overseas Employment

Information on employment opportunities and living and working conditions in the Middle East is an important factor affecting not only the decision to move but also the adjustment to the host country. The study examined sources of information about opportunities and conditions as well as the adequacy of the information on the situation at the destination.

Table 9 presents sources of information on the employment situation and on the application procedures. Sources of information differ between categories of workers. Neither government organizations nor private recruitment agencies played a significant role in providing information. The temporary workers tend to obtain information on employment opportunities from diverse sources: close

**Table 9.** Sources of information on employment opportunities, working and living conditions in the Middle East, application procedures, and contents of employment contract by overseas occupational status (percentages)

| Sources of information | Temporary workers | | | Regular employee | | |
|---|---|---|---|---|---|---|
| | Unskilled | Skilled | Total | Low-level | High-level | Total |
| *Employment opportunities* | | | | | | |
| Boss or fellow workers | 2 | 70 | 72 | 36 | 22 | 58 |
| | (4.9) | (20.9) | (19.1) | (57.1) | (53.7) | (55.8) |
| Friends | 26 | 111 | 137 | 3 | 1 | 4 |
| | (63.4) | (33.1) | (36.4) | (4.8) | (2.4) | (3.8) |
| Recruitment officers | 2 | 87 | 89 | 20 | 18 | 38 |
| | (4.9) | (26.0) | (23.7) | (31.7) | (43.9) | (36.5) |
| Government agencies | — | 8 | 8 | — | 1 | 1 |
| | | (2.4) | (2.1) | | (2.4) | (1.0) |
| Private agencies | 1 | 2 | 3 | — | — | — |
| | (2.4) | (0.6) | (0.8) | | | |
| Newspaper advertisement | 10 | 65 | 75 | 1 | | 1 |
| | (24.4) | (19.4) | (19.9) | (1.6) | | (1.0) |
| Other sources | — | 2 | 2 | 3 | | 3 |
| | | (0.6) | (0.5) | (4.8) | | (2.9) |
| Total | 41 | 335 | 376 | 63 | 41 | 104 |
| | (100.0) | (100.0) | (100.0) | (100.0) | (100.0) | (100.0) |
| *Working and living conditions* | | | | | | |
| Boss or fellow workers | 2 | 37 | 39 | 38 | 26 | 64 |
| | (5.0) | (11.5) | (10.6) | (60.3) | (66.7) | (64.6) |
| Friends | 18 | 75 | 93 | — | — | — |
| | (45.0) | (22.9) | (25.3) | | | |
| Recruitment officers | 17 | 187 | 204 | 24 | 11 | 35 |
| | (42.5) | (57.2) | (55.6) | (38.1) | (28.2) | (35.4) |
| Government agencies | 2 | 20 | 22 | — | 2 | 2 |
| | (5.0) | (6.1) | (6.0) | | (5.1) | (2.0) |
| Newspaper advertisement | 1 | 3 | 4 | 1 | — | — |
| | (2.5) | (0.9) | (1.1) | (1.6) | | |
| Other sources | — | 5 | 5 | — | — | 1 |
| | | (1.5) | (1.4) | | | (1.0) |
| Total[a] | 40 | 327 | 367 | 63 | 39 | 99 |
| | (100.0) | (100.0) | (100.0) | (100.0) | (100.0) | (100.0) |
| *Application procedures* | | | | | | |
| Boss or fellow workers | 1 | 29 | 30 | 23 | 14 | 37 |
| | (2.4) | (8.7) | (8.0) | (36.5) | (34.1) | (35.6) |
| Friends | 9 | 41 | 50 | — | — | — |
| | (22.0) | (12.2) | (13.3) | | | |
| Recruitment officers | 28 | 246 | 274 | 39 | 26 | 65 |
| | (68.3) | (73.4) | (72.9) | (61.9) | (63.4) | (62.5) |
| Government agencies | 1 | 11 | 12 | — | 1 | 1 |
| | (2.4) | (3.3) | (3.2) | | (2.4) | (1.0) |
| Private agencies | 1 | — | 1 | — | — | — |
| | (2.4) | | (0.3) | | | |

**Table 9.** (*continued*)

| Sources of information | Temporary workers | | | Regular employee | | |
|---|---|---|---|---|---|---|
| | Unskilled | Skilled | Total | Low-level | High-level | Total |
| Newspaper advertisement | 1 (2.4) | 8 (2.4) | 9 (2.4) | — | — | — |
| Other sources | — | — | — | 1 (1.6) | — | 1 (1.0) |
| Total | 41 (100.0) | 335 (100.0) | 376 (100.0) | 63 (100.0) | 41 (100.0) | 104 (100.0) |
| *Contents of employment contract* | | | | | | |
| Boss or fellow workers | 1 (2.4) | 15 (4.5) | 16 (4.3) | 24 (38.1) | 17 (41.5) | 41 (39.4) |
| Friends | 5 (12.2) | 23 (6.9) | 28 (7.4) | — | — | — |
| Recruitment officers | 34 (82.9) | 278 (83.0) | 312 (83.0) | 39 (61.9) | 24 (58.5) | 63 (40.6) |
| Private agencies | 1 (2.4) | 14 (4.2) | 15 (4.0) | — | — | — |
| Newspaper advertisement | — | 4 (1.2) | 4 (1.1) | — | — | — |
| Other sources | — | 1 (0.3) | 1 (0.3) | — | — | — |
| Total | 41 (100.0) | 335 (100.0) | 376 (100.0) | 63 (100.0) | 41 (100.0) | 104 (100.0) |

a. Excluded are those who did not obtain any information on working and living conditions in the host countries.

friends (36 per cent), recruitment officers of employing companies (24 per cent), advertisements in newspapers (20 per cent), and fellow workers or superiors (19 per cent). Information on conditions at the destination, application procedures, and the contents of contracts are most likely to be obtained from the recruitment officers of the employing company. It was also found that temporary workers are more likely than skilled workers to rely on their friends for information.

The main sources of information for the regular employees are, without exception, either their work associates (bosses or colleagues) or the recruitment officers. However, information on employment opportunities and on working and living conditions are more likely to be obtained from work associates, while information on application procedures and contracts comes from the company recruitment officers.

A considerable proportion of the migrant workers leave for the Middle East without sufficient information either on the physical and social conditions of the host country or on living and working conditions at the work camp (table 10). The least information is on the social customs of the host country. The regular employees generally get more information than the temporary workers, while among the temporary workers the skilled workers tend to have more information than the

**Table 10.** Sufficiency of information on climate, native customs, living conditions, and working conditions in the Middle East before migration by overseas occupational status (percentages)

| Kind of information and sufficiency | Temporary workers | | | Regular employees | | |
| --- | --- | --- | --- | --- | --- | --- |
| | Unskilled | Skilled | Total | Low-level | High-level | Total |
| **Climate** | | | | | | |
| Sufficient | 11 | 128 | 139 | 30 | 17 | 47 |
| | (26.8) | (38.2) | (37.0) | (47.6) | (4.15) | (45.2) |
| Insufficient | 21 | 163 | 184 | 26 | 22 | 48 |
| | (51.2) | (48.7) | (48.9) | (41.3) | (53.7) | (46.2) |
| Very insufficient | 9 | 44 | 53 | 7 | 2 | 9 |
| | (22.0) | (13.1) | (14.1) | (11.1) | (4.9) | (8.7) |
| Total | 41 | 335 | 376 | 63 | 41 | 104 |
| | (100.0) | (100.0) | (100.0) | (100.0) | (100.0) | (100.0) |
| **Native customs** | | | | | | |
| Sufficient | 3 | 75 | 78 | 19 | 12 | 31 |
| | (7.3) | (22.4) | (20.7) | (39.2) | (29.3) | (29.8) |
| Insufficient | 25 | 166 | 191 | 33 | 21 | 54 |
| | (61.0) | (49.6) | (50.8) | (52.4) | (51.2) | (51.9) |
| Very insufficient | 13 | 94 | 107 | 11 | 8 | 19 |
| | (31.7) | (28.1) | (28.5) | (17.5) | (19.5) | (18.3) |
| Total | 41 | 335 | 376 | 63 | 41 | 104 |
| | (100.0) | (100.0) | (100.0) | (100.0) | (100.0) | (100.0) |
| **Living conditions** | | | | | | |
| Sufficient | 9 | 128 | 137 | 35 | 25 | 60 |
| | (22.0) | (38.2) | (36.4) | (55.6) | (61.0) | (57.7) |
| Insufficient | 21 | 152 | 173 | 23 | 12 | 35 |
| | (51.2) | (45.4) | (46.0) | (36.5) | (29.3) | (33.7) |
| Very insufficient | 11 | 55 | 66 | 5 | 4 | 9 |
| | (26.8) | (16.4) | (17.6) | (7.9) | (9.8) | (8.7) |
| Total | 41 | 335 | 376 | 63 | 41 | 104 |
| | (100.0) | (100.0) | (100.0) | (100.0) | (100.0) | (100.0) |
| **Working conditions** | | | | | | |
| Sufficient | 9 | 108 | 117 | 38 | 20 | 58 |
| | (22.0) | (32.2) | (31.1) | (60.3) | (48.8) | (55.8) |
| Insufficient | 20 | 160 | 180 | 19 | 16 | 35 |
| | (48.8) | (47.8) | (47.9) | (30.2) | (39.2) | (33.7) |
| Very insufficient | 12 | 67 | 89 | 6 | 5 | 11 |
| | (29.3) | (20.0) | (23.7) | (9.5) | (12.2) | (10.6) |
| Total | 41 | 335 | 376 | 63 | 41 | 104 |
| | (100.0) | (100.0) | (100.0) | (100.0) | (100.0) | (100.0) |

unskilled workers. There is no significant difference in the level of information obtained by different levels of regular employees, except for information on working conditions. The high-level regular employees may have more information than the low-level ones, but many seem to feel that the information they had before migration was not sufficient and that more was needed for them to carry out their jobs.

## Costs of Migration

The costs of Korean labour migration to the Middle East can be separated into two components, monetary and non-monetary. Monetary costs include direct costs such as preparation expenses for migration, travel expenses, and living costs at destination, as well as opportunity costs incurred while seeking an overseas job and costs of re-employment on return. The non-monetary or psychological costs are those related to the adjustment of the migrant and his family. Living costs, and the cost of travel to and from the destination, are excluded since they are borne by the company employing the migrant workers.

Preparation expenses for most of the migrant workers are moderate (table 11). The temporary workers spent an average of about 150,000 won and the regular employees about 70,000 won in preparing to migrate. About two-thirds (64 per cent) of the temporary workers spent more than 100,000 won (about $172 at the 1980 exchange rate) for the preparation, while only a quarter (26 per cent) of the regular workers spent a similar amount. The preparation expenses of the regular

**Table 11**. Total expenses for preparation of migration to the Middle East by overseas occupational status

| Total expenses (thousands of won) | Temporary workers | | | Regular employees | | |
| --- | --- | --- | --- | --- | --- | --- |
| | Unskilled | Skilled | Total | Low-level | High-level | Total |
| None | 1 | 2 | 3 | 18 | 16 | 34 |
| | (2.4)[a] | (0.6) | (0.8) | (28.6) | (39.0) | (32.7) |
| Less than 100 | 15 | 121 | 136 | 27 | 16 | 43 |
| | (36.6) | (36.1) | (36.2) | (42.9) | (39.0) | (41.3) |
| 100–199 | 15 | 143 | 158 | 14 | 8 | 22 |
| | (36.6) | (42.7) | (42.0) | (22.2) | (19.5) | (21.2) |
| 200–299 | 6 | 33 | 39 | 2 | 1 | 3 |
| | (14.6) | (9.9) | (10.4) | (3.2) | (2.4) | (2.9) |
| 300–399 | 2 | 19 | 21 | 1 | — | 1 |
| | (4.9) | (5.7) | (5.6) | (1.6) | | (1.0) |
| 400–499 | 1 | 11 | 12 | 1 | — | 1 |
| | (2.4) | (3.3) | (3.2) | (1.6) | | (1.0) |
| More than 500 | 1 | 6 | 7 | — | — | — |
| | (2.4) | (1.8) | (1.9) | | | |
| | 41 | 355 | 376 | 63 | 41 | 104 |
| Total | (100.0) | (100.0) | (100.0) | (100.0) | (100.0) | (100.0) |

a. Percentages in parentheses.

employees are smaller than those of the temporary workers. This is not only because they usually pay no application fee for admission to overseas employment, but also because most of them live in Seoul, the port of departure for the Middle East, and therefore have few expenses for domestic transportation or room and board during the preparation for overseas employment. All the temporary workers, on the other hand, have to pay an application fee, and those from outside Seoul spend a considerable sum of money on transportation and room and board. A small proportion (4 per cent) of the temporary workers spent over 200,000 won in bribes to recruiting officers to obtain employment abroad. However, it should be noted that the incidence of bribery is low.

In order to finance the migration, some migrants received help from their parents or borrowed money, though the majority bore the costs themselves. A significant proportion of the temporary workers (15 per cent, or 55 persons) had difficulty in meeting the expenses. Of them, 20 were aided by their parents, 29 took out loans, and six sold their property. Of the regular employees, only four persons needed outside help to cover the expenses.

Before departure, the migrant is unemployed for a short period, and as a result income is forgone or lost. This constitutes a cost of migration. Regular employees do not have to bear this cost, as they are transferred by their firms and do not have a period of unemployment. Table 12 thus shows the duration of unemployment for the temporary workers only. The average duration of unemployment for unskilled workers is longer than for the skilled workers, indicating that the former find it more difficult to get an overseas job and tend to waste more time searching for it. About one-quarter (24 per cent) of the unskilled workers spent more than a month looking for an overseas job, while among the skilled workers the proportion was about 18 per cent. A considerable number of temporary workers were unemployed owing to their preparation for the Middle East migration, and their average duration of unemployment due to this reason is estimated at about one month. As a result, the average income forgone, on the basis of monthly income before migration, is about 350,000 won (US$600).

For the temporary workers, the average money costs of migration, including the direct costs for preparation and the income forgone due to unemployment, amount to about 500,000 won (about $860). This corresponds to their average monthly earnings in West Asia. Since the number of those who had training is relatively small, the income forgone due to the skills training for overseas employment is not included in this calculation. The temporary workers are unemployed for an average of about 2.5 months after overseas migration, and if the opportunity cost of unemployment is added to the money costs, it increases to about 1.4 million won (about $2,400).

Finally, the human and psychological costs of migration must be taken into consideration. The survey data indicate that waiting for employment in the Middle East or admission is the most frequent problem for about two-thirds (63 per cent) of the temporary workers. Anxiety about families left behind and adjustment to the conditions in West Asia were problems for about one quarter of the regular workers, while about 10 per cent encountered hardship owing to delays in the job assignment. About three-quarters of the temporary workers wait more than two months for admission to West Asia while the corresponding proportion for regular workers is substantially lower, 13 per cent. The long waiting period adds to the

**Table 12.** Duration of unemployment for those seeking employment in the Middle East, unskilled and skilled workers

| Duration | Unskilled | Skilled | Total |
|---|---|---|---|
| Less than one month | 31 | 275 | 306 |
| | (75.6)[a] | (82.1) | (18.4) |
| 1 month | 4 | 16 | 20 |
| | (9.8) | (4.8) | (5.3) |
| 2 months | 2 | 17 | 19 |
| | (4.9) | (5.1) | (5.1) |
| 3 months | 1 | 12 | 13 |
| | (2.4) | (3.6) | (3.5) |
| 4 months or more | 2 | 15 | 17 |
| | (4.9) | (4.5) | (4.5) |
| Total | 41 | 335 | 376 |
| | (100.0) | (100.0) | (100.0) |

a. Percentages in parentheses.

**Table 13.** Most difficult problems faced by migrants before departing for the Middle East by overseas occupational status

| Difficult problems | Temporary workers | | | Regular employees | | |
|---|---|---|---|---|---|---|
| | Unskilled | Skilled | Total | Low-level | High-level | Total |
| Waiting for admission | 19 | 96 | 107 | 8 | 5 | 13 |
| | (57.9)[a] | (59.6) | (62.9) | (34.8) | (25.0) | (30.2) |
| Overcoming anxiety about family | 5 | 40 | 45 | 8 | 9 | 17 |
| | (26.3) | (24.8) | (26.5) | (34.8) | (45.0) | (39.5) |
| Overcoming anxiety about adjustment to destination | 1 | 12 | 13 | 4 | 2 | 6 |
| | (5.3) | (7.5) | (7.6) | (17.4) | (10.0) | (14.0) |
| Overcoming other anxieties | 2 | 13 | 15 | 3 | 4 | 7 |
| | (10.5) | (8.1) | (8.8) | (13.0) | (20.0) | (16.3) |
| Total[b] | 19 | 161 | 170 | 23 | 23 | 43 |
| | (100.0) | (100.0) | (100.0) | (100.0) | (100.0) | (100.0) |

a. Percentages in parentheses.
b. Excluded are those who did not face any difficult problems.

anxiety workers experience about separation from homes and family. Some of the temporary workers have economic difficulties because of unemployment during this period.

Not only many migrants, but also their family members, were anxious primarily because of family problems and hardship anticipated as a result of the migration. About 15 per cent of temporary workers and 31 per cent of regular employees indicated that they had received strong encouragement to migrate, mostly from non-family members. But about 31 per cent of the former and 40 per cent of the latter had met with strong objections, mostly from family members, because of possible hardships related to overseas work or anticipated stress on the family due to separation. The data indicate strong apprehension regarding migration among a significant proportion of the families. This is a "cost" associated with migration.

## Working and Living Conditions at Destination

The duration of overseas employment coincides with the term of the contract, which is usually one year for both temporary and regular workers. However, contracts can be extended or renewed one or more times. According to the survey, the average total duration of employment was about two years. Some of the migrants return before completing their contract, while others remain for five or more years. While abroad they are housed in a work camp, which is a "total institution," organizing and regulating all aspects of everyday life according to tight "house rules" and insulating workers from the outside world.

### Performance of Contract

Problems with the contract are perhaps one of the most important issues concerning the Middle East employment. The form of the contract for Korean labour migration is standardized and there is little variation in content. The main provisions in a written contract are: job specification; regular working hours per week and the duration of contract; wages; overtime allowance; pay day and ways of payment; the proportion of the wages paid at the workplace; and paid vacation and holidays.

The employers often violate the provisions of the contract. More than one-fifth (22 per cent) of temporary workers and 14 per cent of regular employees reported that actual conditions were different in at least one item out of the seven listed above. Violation of more than one item was encountered by only a small proportion of migrants, 6 per cent of temporary workers and 3 per cent of the regular employees. Most contract violations are related to working hours and wages. About half of those who encountered violations appealed to either senior officers or fellow workers in the work camp, or the labour attaché in the Korean embassy in the host country. Of those who appealed, less than half obtained positive results. However, most breaches of contract were accepted because migrants felt that appealing against them would bring no redress. On the other hand, there were cases where both temporary and regular migrants were often unable to perform contracted duty for various reasons such as illness, injury, and disciplinary punishment. About 31 per cent of both temporary workers and regular employees took at least one leave of absence from work, while about 12 per cent of temporary workers and 7 per cent of regular employees took at least one leave of absence due to injury. The regular employees are more prone to get sick than the temporary workers, perhaps because before migration most of them worked in much more congenial conditions than the temporary workers, who were constantly exposed to changing weather conditions. However, the injury rate is greater among the temporary workers, because nearly all of them are engaged in manual work and are exposed to the risk of accidental injury. The third reason for absenteeism, disciplinary punishment resulting in suspension from work, is due to violation of

**Table 14.** Months waited for admission after application for employment in the Middle East by overseas occupational status (percentages)

| Waiting period (months) | Temporary workers | | | Regular employees | | |
|---|---|---|---|---|---|---|
| | Unskilled | Skilled | Total | Low-level | High-level | Total |
| Less than 2 | 12 | 114 | 126 | 39 | 32 | 71 |
| | (29.3) | (34.1) | (33.6) | (30.0) | (86.5) | (73.2) |
| 2–3 | 13 | 119 | 132 | 18 | 3 | 21 |
| | (31.7) | (25.6) | (35.2) | (30.0) | (8.1) | (21.6) |
| 4–5 | 9 | 44 | 53 | 2 | 1 | 3 |
| | (22.0) | (13.2) | (14.1) | (3.3) | (2.7) | (3.1) |
| 6–7 | 4 | 36 | 40 | — | — | — |
| | (9.8) | (10.8) | (10.7) | | | |
| 8+ | 3 | 21 | 24 | 1 | 1 | 2 |
| | (7.3) | (6.3) | (6.4) | (1.7) | (2.7) | (2.1) |
| Total[a] | 41 | 334 | 375 | 60 | 37 | 97 |
| | (100.0) | (100.0) | (100.0) | (100.0) | (100.0) | (100.0) |

a. Unknown cases are excluded.

rules and regulations. For this reason eight temporary workers out of 380 and one regular employee out of 104 were suspended from work at least once. It should be noted, however, that this figure does not include those who returned prematurely for various reasons. In our sample, three temporary workers were deported.

In the survey, 47 persons, or 12 per cent, out of 380 temporary workers, and six persons out of 104 regular employees, returned to Korea before completing their contract. The main reasons for the premature termination were: ill-health, including illness and injury; hardship; family problems; deportation due to violation of rules; and problems with employers (four out of six premature returnees among regular employees had to return for the last reason). Among the temporary workers, return was due primarily to personal problems such as ill-health (2), hardship (4), family problems (3), deportation (3), and others (9), while the number returning because of problems with employers (8) is not negligible. As these figures indicate, Middle East employment is not an easy assignment, especially for the temporary workers.

The migrant workers in the Middle East are by no means inferior to their counterparts in Korea in terms of physical strength or psychological resilience. The significant differences in living and working conditions in West Asia account for a large part of the personal problems, illness, and injury that results in loss of work days.

### Labour–Management Relationships

A significant proportion of the temporary workers were of the opinion that labour–management relations were either worse or better while in Korea (38 per cent). One-quarter saw no difference. More than half the regular employees (57 per cent)

**Table 15.** Evaluation of labour–management relationship at work camp as compared to the relationship in the Republic of Korea

| Comparison | Temporary workers | | Regular employees | |
|---|---|---|---|---|
| Much better | 29 | (7.7)[a] | 23 | (22.1) |
| Better | 114 | (30.3) | 39 | (37.5) |
| Same | 94 | (25.0) | 29 | (27.9) |
| Worse | 102 | (27.1) | 8 | (7.7) |
| Much worse | 37 | (9.8) | 5 | (4.8) |
| Total | 367 | (100.0) | 104 | (100.0) |

a. Percentages in parentheses.

felt the relationship was better during migration, while 10 per cent thought it was worse. Among the temporary workers, the authoritarian control and discrimination regarding such matters as overtime allocations were among the main considerations leading to the judgement that management was worse in the migratory setting. Nearly one-quarter who indicated that management was worse than in Korea did so because they felt it was authoritarian. About 10 per cent felt there was favouritism and a similar proportion cited unfair overtime allocation.

Disputes between workers and management over such matters are supposed to be resolved by a labour–management council, which is a mandatory organization in every major work camp. However, in many cases, the council did not exist or did not function properly. About 5 per cent of the respondents reported that they did not even know of the existence of such an organization. Among the 314 temporary workers who evaluated the performance of the council, about 40 per cent expressed satisfaction, while 33 per cent were dissatisfied (table 16). As expected, the satisfaction rate is higher among the regular employees (only 15 per cent indicated dissatisfaction, compared with 33 per cent of the temporary workers). This is directly related to the higher proportion of regular workers in managerial and supervisory positions. The major reasons for dissatisfaction with the councils were that they did not function or were unsympathetic to workers and favoured management. Almost half of the dissatisfied respondents (51 per cent) considered the council to be prejudiced against labour. No serious problems were encountered by 15 per cent of the temporary workers and 19 per cent of the regular employees. Lack of adequate safety was one of the most important problems both for the temporary workers who responded (46 per cent of 321) and for the regular employees as well (62 per cent of 841). As mentioned at the start, most Korean workers in West Asia are engaged in construction projects, and safety is an important concern. A surprisingly high proportion of the temporary workers (38 per cent) considered that their superiors were "inhumane" in their treatment of workers, and indicated that this was a serious problem in the workplace. More than a few (12 per cent) of the 84 regular workers who responded were of the same opinion. Conflicts among workers were considered a serious problem by 10 per cent of the temporary and 17 per cent of the regular workers. In summary, the serious problems at the workplace, as perceived by the Korean migrant workers, are safety measures, the vertical relationship between labour and management, and the horizontal relationship among the workers.

**Table 16.** Satisfaction with labour–management council

| Satisfaction | Temporary workers | | Regular employees | |
|---|---|---|---|---|
| Very satisfied | 31 | (9.9)[a] | 6 | (7.1) |
| Satisfied | 93 | (29.6) | 39 | (46.4) |
| Indifferent | 88 | (28.0) | 26 | (31.0) |
| Dissatisfied | 55 | (17.5) | 9 | (10.7) |
| Very dissatisfied | 47 | (15.0) | 4 | (4.8) |
| Total | 314 | (100.0) | 84 | (100.0) |

a. Percentages in parentheses.

## Life in the Work Camp

Almost all of the Korean workers hired by a Korean company in the Middle East stay in one of the work camps established by the company. A camp is usually located near the workplace, and is insulated from local villages by distance and by man-made barriers, such as fences, or by natural barriers. It is a self-sufficient unit of housing similar to a military barracks. A typical camp is equipped with living quarters for the staff and the temporary workers, a meeting hall, a first-aid station, and other service and recreational facilities. The residential unit for the temporary workers is usually divided into two to four large rooms, each of which is shared by 10 to 40 workers.

The social organization of the work camp can be characterized by the previously mentioned "total institution." As in a typical total institution, there is a separation between the regular employees (the staff, in total institution terms) and the temporary workers (the inmates). The staff comprises a director and a number of white-collar workers in both managerial and technical grades. At the workplace an engineer (a member of the staff) directs a few working units, each of which is supervised by a foreman. In the camp an executive manager controls all spheres of the workers' lives and a few selected workers assist the manager. An appointed worker plays a dual role as the conveyor of the orders of management and as a head of the workers' pseudo-voluntary association, called "Saemaul-chachi-hoe." In each work camp there are "house rules" to regulate the workers' conduct and a system of rewards and punishments to enforce the rules. Some important rules are laid down by the Ministry of Labour of the Korean Government and apply to every Korean contract worker in the Middle East; violation of these may be punished by reprimand, reduction of salary or wages, or termination of employment.[1] Besides these government-imposed rules, each camp has a number of additional rules, mostly designed to regulate the daily life of the workers.

The workers' everyday life is tightly scheduled. They start to work at around 6 a.m., take a siesta for two or three hours after lunch, and then return to work, which continues until about 6 or 7 p.m. Since the overtime premium is 50 per cent, almost all work extra hours. Sunday is a rest day, which is usually spent within the camp. When workers go out of the camp, they usually shop at local stores. They are also provided with recreational facilities, and on holidays are occasionally entertained with movies. Yet during the working days they have little leisure time, primarily because they choose to work long hours.

**Table 17.** Number of illnesses suffered during employment in the Middle East

| Number | Temporary workers | | Regular employees | |
|---|---|---|---|---|
| 0 | 159 | (44.3) | 48 | (46.2) |
| 1 | 82 | (21.8) | 19 | (18.3) |
| 2 | 76 | (20.2) | 21 | (20.2) |
| 3 | 40 | (10.6) | 14 | (13.5) |
| 4 | 14 | (3.7) | 1 | (1.0) |
| 5 | 5 | (1.3) | 1 | (1.0) |
| Total | 376 | (99.9) | 104 | (100.2) |

A majority of the workers was satisfied with living conditions in the camp, though a significant minority indicated their dissatisfaction. The facilities and provision for use of leisure time were considered to be inadequate. There was a clear difference between the two groups of workers in their perception of living conditions in the camp, the regular employees generally being more satisfied than the temporary workers.

Workers had relatively little time for leisure. Since the camp is isolated from surrounding areas, the quality of free time within the camp is an important issue for the workers. They took part in sports, watched TV, played cards, or spent time reading. Besides these individual activities, the management occasionally provided group recreation and entertainment such as talent shows, sports, oriental chess or *go* contests, thanks-for-service entertainment, movies, and group sight-seeing tours. Workers were overwhelmingly satisfied with the quality of the group recreation; there were no differences in satisfaction levels between the two categories of workers.

The individual and group recreational activities prevalent in the work camp are not incompatible with local laws and customs, so that they pose few, if any, problems to the management or to the local authorities. However, owing to sharp differences between Korean and Arab culture, some habits or hobbies favoured by Koreans are not allowed in the Middle East. Drinking and gambling are prohibited in most Arab countries, and in the work camp. However, a substantial proportion of Korean workers in the Middle East have secretly enjoyed drinking and gambling: about 140 persons, or 37 per cent of the temporary workers, indicated that they drank while employed in the region; 24, or 17 per cent, said that they drank frequently. A greater proportion of the regular employees answered that they drank occasionally (46 per cent) or frequently (15 per cent) in the Middle East. Fifty-nine per cent of the 63 regular employees said that they drank less in the Middle East in contrast to 13 per cent who drank more. A similar pattern was observed among the temporary workers; of the 140 respondents who had consumed alcohol, more than two-thirds drank less (47 per cent much less). Only 11 per cent said they drank more during their overseas employment.

Gambling was not as prevalent as the consumption of alcohol. A little more than one in ten (12 per cent) of the temporary workers had gambled during the period of migration; only a small proportion of them gambled frequently (nine persons out of 44). A large proportion of the regular workers indicated that they gambled (43

**Table 18.** Number of psychological disorders (percentages)

| Number | Temporary workers | | Regular employees | |
|---|---|---|---|---|
| None | 50 | (13.3) | 10 | (9.6) |
| 1 | 42 | (11.2) | 10 | (9.6) |
| 2 | 66 | (17.6) | 11 | (10.6) |
| 3 | 59 | (15.7) | 20 | (19.2) |
| 4 | 51 | (13.6) | 9 | (8.7) |
| 5 | 35 | (9.3) | 9 | (6.7) |
| 6 | 31 | (8.2) | 11 | (10.6) |
| 7 | 19 | (5.1) | 10 | (9.6) |
| 8 | 10 | (2.7) | 8 | (7.7) |
| 9 | 10 | (2.7) | 8 | (7.7) |
| 10 | 3 | (0.8) | | — |
| Total | 376 | (100.2) | 104 | (100.0) |

per cent). Unlike drinking, gambling was more prevalent among the regular employees in the Middle East than those in Korea. Of 38 regular employees who gambled, 16 said that they gambled more often during their overseas employment than in Korea; 13 said it was the same and nine less. Since they had more money to spend and few things to do in their free time, gambling had become a favoured pastime for some workers.

Gambling was considered a serious problem by significant number of the workers (23 per cent of temporary and 32 per cent of regular workers). However, about one of every five of the Korean migrants seemed to enjoy gambling after work. For a few it interfered with their work. Gambling could lead to grave consequences for the involved workers: some of them were caught by the authorities and punished by imprisonment or deportation.

The inadequate or poor quality of medical care was considered to be one of the most serious inadequacies of the work camp (35 per cent of temporary and 29 per cent of regular employees). Every work camp has a medical station, but it is usually manned by a male nurse or a paramedic. No regular staff are attached to some of these stations. It is rather rare for a camp to have a doctor on call. The rate of illness and injury is very high among the migrant workers and medical facilities seem to be insufficient for the needs of the camp.

Problems with food were considered to be serious by about 15 per cent of the workers (mostly in terms of taste, not quantity). Dormitory conditions, crime, and others were also mentioned as serious problems by less than 10 per cent of the samples. However, 31 temporary workers (8 per cent) and 14 regular employees (14 per cent) said that there was no serious problem at all in their life in the Middle East.

**Social Life**

The hard and prolonged daily work schedules, the radically different culture of the host country, and the physical as well as the social isolation of the camp from the local society discourage workers' contacts with local people. Within the camp the

75

workers can interact with a few Koreans and with foreigners. But no formal social clubs or associations, except for the semi-official Saemaul-chachi-hoe, are allowed. Even religious services other than Islamic ones are officially restricted. Letters are probably the only means for Korean migrant workers to maintain human relationships with those outside the camp, especially with their families in Korea.

The conditions under which the Korean migrants lived and worked did not seem to encourage strong associations and friendships. Nevertheless, most workers made new friends, with both fellow Koreans and foreign workers; a significant proportion, however, only associated with those they knew in Korea. The conditions of work led to contact with construction workers from foreign countries, and a sizeable number of Koreans formed friendships with foreigners. The regular employees tended to have more interactions with foreign workers, who came from many different countries and who held positions similar to the jobs held by the regular workers. The friends and acquaintances of the temporary workers, on the other hand, were mostly from South and South-East Asia – the origin of most skilled and semi-skilled construction workers.

The opportunities for forming social clubs or friendship associations were limited. Formal organizations among the workers are not allowed for these purposes. Thus, about two-thirds (65 per cent) of the temporary workers and more than four-fifths (87 per cent) of the regular employees had not participated in any such association while working in the Middle East. The rest had been members of various social associations, which are mainly informal clubs formed solely for promoting friendship. More temporary than regular workers were members of these associations (35 compared with 13 per cent). Among the associations, "Chiupdongki-hoe" seemed to be most prevalent, drawing about 14 per cent of temporary and 3 per cent of regular employees as members. The membership usually comprised those who started overseas work at around the same time. The organization is normally confined to a single camp and a work camp may have more than one such club if it is large. In some cases, the club collects a small membership fee to finance its meetings or to assist members in need; it usually meets once a month. Another type of friendship club in the camp is called *kye*, a revolving credit club where the members (usually between 10 and 30) contribute money on a monthly basis with one member receiving the entire monthly collection each month; it is a popular method of savings for Koreans. There were other types of social association based on members' home town, hobbies, or school, but these were not prevalent. The members were generally enthusiastic about such organizations, and in the case of the Chiupdongki-hoe the overwhelming majority of the participants (51 of 57) considered themselves to be active members.

Owing to the special characteristics of the work camp, the workers' religious activities are severely restricted. A small proportion, 75 temporary workers (20 per cent) and 18 regular employees (17 per cent), practised their religion during their employment in the Middle East. Of them, 70 temporary workers and 18 regular employees were Christian, three were Buddhist, and two Muslims.

The familial relationship is certainly the most important one for the migrant workers. However, it is a difficult one to maintain closely during migratory work, since the workers cannot bring their family members with them. The separation between the workers and their family members for a prolonged period causes some serious emotional problems to both the workers and their families. Exchanging letters with families is not the sole means of contact, but it occupies much of their time and concern.

Writing letters was one of the major ways of spending free time. Indeed, more than half the sampled workers (52 per cent of the temporary and 56 per cent of regular employees) indicated that they wrote home at least once a week and received letters from home with the same frequency. Only a very small proportion wrote no letters home. Correspondence was primarily with spouses. Most wrote at least once a month.

## Adjustment of Migrant Workers and Their Families

Adjustment depends on the nature of the migration and the characteristics of the destination. Adjustment problems are related to the special features of the Korean migration. The workers usually migrate as a group but without their families; they intend to stay at the destination temporarily and return after a year or so; they migrate primarily for economic reasons; they are a relatively homogeneous group in terms of their demographic and socio-economic background. These characteristics may be regarded as factors that will make adjustment easy. However, the destination and living in camp throughout their stay in the Middle East tend to make adjustment more difficult than in other types of migration; the environment with which they have to cope during migration is different in every respect from what they are used to. The cultural and social differences do not pose serious problems compared with those related to the natural environment, because the Korean migrant has few contacts with the local culture and people. The real social environment to which the workers have to adjust is the camp, which has been compared to the "total institution."

Upon entrance to such an institution, the individual is immediately stripped of the support provided by the social arrangements in his home country. The barrier that the total institution places between the individual and the outside world marks the first curtailment of self. In such institutions there is a process of mortification from the time of admission and individuals are "trimmed" or "programmed." However, the Korean work camp, while sharing some of the features of the total institution, does not include "mortification" procedures that seriously affect the workers.

The first adjustment the migrant must make is to the physical environment, the harsh climate of Middle Eastern countries; this takes a few months. However, adjusting to the environment and organization of the camp is more difficult. Individuals have to get accustomed to the reward system, the rules and regulations of the camp institution. This is a period of learning, experimentation, and adjustment. In order to assess the dimensions of physical adjustment, the survey inquired about specific ailments and ill-health.

The study does not examine the possible relationship between ill-health and adjustment. The hard work appears to take its toll: the workers become susceptible to influenza and the camp conditions promote its spread. Cases of severe fatigue were relatively high, though morbidity due to other causes was low. Incidence of injury also seemed to be low. Workers suffered from occasional physical disorders, but very few experienced frequent health problems. There is a significant differ-

**Table 19.** Overall satisfaction by number of physical disorders

| | Temporary workers[a] | | | | Regular employees[b] | | | |
|---|---|---|---|---|---|---|---|---|
| | 0 | 1–2 | 3–5 | Total | 0 | 1–2 | 3–5 | Total |
| Satisfied | 123 (77.4)[c] | 106 (67.1) | 31 (52.5) | 260 (69.1) | 40 (83.8) | 32 (80.0) | 8 (50.0) | 80 (76.9) |
| Dissatisfied | 36 (22.6) | 52 (32.9) | 28 (47.5) | 116 (30.9) | 8 (16.7) | 8 (20.0) | 8 (50.0) | 24 (23.1) |
| Total | 159 (100.0) | 158 (100.0) | 59 (100.0) | 376 (100.0) | 48 (100.0) | 40 (100.0) | 16 (100.0) | 104 (100.0) |

a. $X^2 = 12.9646$; $P = < 0.01$.
b. $X^2 = 7.8578$; $P = < 0.05$.
c. Percentages in parentheses.

ence between the temporary workers and the regular employees in the rates of two job-related symptoms, neuralgia and injury. The temporary workers who perform physical work are more vulnerable to such ailments than the regular employees, who are mostly white-collar workers. The physical troubles which plagued many of the workers, especially in the earlier period of their overseas employment, were soon overcome. A small proportion had to return to Korea before completing their contract due to ill-health.

However, the incidence of psychological disorders among the Korean migrant workers seemed to be very high compared with physical disorders. About nine out of ten workers in both categories, temporary and regular, suffered from some form of psychological disorder. The survey used common symptoms to measure such disorders, among them sleeplessness, loss of appetite, and nervousness. For most workers the symptoms were new and closely associated with the new setting. Nearly half, 45 per cent of temporary and 37 per cent of regular employees, showed between one and three of the symptoms, while another 31 per cent of temporary and 26 per cent of regular employees showed between four and six. The proportion of the workers who suffered more than six symptoms was higher among the regular employees (25 per cent) than among the temporary workers (11 per cent).

An overwhelming majority of workers, 60 per cent of temporary and 77 per cent of regular workers, expressed satisfaction with the overseas work. As expected, those with adjustment or psychological problems expressed lower satisfaction. Three classes of variables affecting worker adjustment were examined; those associated with individual characteristics, those related to life in the camp, and those related to the adjustment of the family at home. Statistical analysis confirms that the physical and social conditions of the camp were primary factors in determining worker satisfaction; other factors were less significant. A major conclusion drawn from this analysis is that the social organization of the camp, which is more or less a total institution, created the most important adjustment problems for the migrant workers.

### Family Adjustment Problems

Most migrants are married and their temporary absence creates adjustment problems which in some cases are serious. Roles and responsibility have to be reorganized, and in the process capacities are strained, leading to crises. This can result either in dissolution of the family or in a renewal and strengthening of the unit.

Adjustment problems are largely dependent upon the composition of the family. More than three-quarters (76 per cent) of the married temporary workers belonged to nuclear families. A significant proportion of the remainder (19 per cent of the total) were multi-generation extended families. The proportion of nuclear families among married regular employees is much lower than that for the temporary workers: 28 out of 50 families were nuclear. Twenty of the remaining 22 families included one or both of the workers' parents.

The most immediate and greatest impact of a worker's migration is upon his spouse, who bears the burden of family care. The burden may sometimes be shared with other close relatives, such as the worker's parents or brothers, or the wife's parents or brothers. Spouses were, without exception, charged with taking

**Table 20.** Overall satisfaction by number of psychological disorders

| | Temporary workers[a] | | | | Regular employees[b] | | | |
|---|---|---|---|---|---|---|---|---|
| | 0 | 1–3 | 4–10 | Total | 0 | 1–3 | 4–10 | Total |
| Satisfied | 42 (84.0)[c] | 129 (77.2) | 89 (56.0) | 260 (69.1) | 9 (90.0) | 37 (90.2) | 34 (64.2) | 80 (76.9) |
| Dissatisfied | 8 (16.0) | 38 (22.8) | 70 (44.0) | 116 (30.9) | 1 (10.0) | 4 (9.9) | 19 (35.8) | 24 (23.1) |
| Total | 50 (100.0) | 167 (100.0) | 150 (100.0) | 376 (100.0) | 10 (100.0) | 41 (100.0) | 53 (100.0) | 104 (100.0) |

a. $X^2 = 23.2365$; $P = <0.01$.
b. $X^2 = 9.9321$; $P < 0.01$.
c. Percentages in parentheses.

care of the aged members of the family and children during their husband's overseas employment. They were also partly responsible for such matters as the use of
the remittance and property management. Since the latter is a new responsibility
normally handled by the husband, the wife must make an important readjustment.
This can lead to both beneficial as well as negative effects. She may gain new skills
in management of the household and its finances, form new productive relationships, and change attitudes and values. Five areas of impact of the migration
on spouses were examined; health, vitality, sociability, anxiety, and incidence of
infidelity. The first four aspects were compared before and during employment in
the Middle East. According to the comparison, more regular than temporary workers (47 v. 20 per cent) reported that their wives' health became worse during their
overseas employment than before, but for a majority of both samples it was the
same (49 per cent). Wives seem to have become more sociable and active during
the period. However, there were signs of anxiety about wives among the workers,
the temporary workers showing greater concern (88 per cent) than the regular
workers (69 per cent). Although in general the wives seemed to have coped well
during the husbands' absence, a significant proportion of them developed symptoms of acute anxiety. The incidence of reported infidelity was very low: only nine
cases were encountered, all among temporary workers. The low incidence perhaps
related to the fact that cases would not be readily reported.

The worker's overseas employment affects the attitudes and behaviour of his
children. The findings are based on the temporary worker families with children,
since only six regular workers had children of schoolgoing age. Four aspects related to the adjustment of children were examined; trouble with friends, loneliness, problems with school work, and disobedience. The migrants indicated that
about a third of the children had suffered from loneliness. Disobedience and problems at school were not widespread, less than one-fifth of children being affected.
In a majority of cases, the way in which the spouse managed the family seems to
have ensured that children adjusted suitably to the absence of the father.

## Readjustment after Return

On return the migrants face two types of major readjustment. The migrant leaves
the total institution of the work camp and re-enters normal civilian life. He has to
cope with changes that have taken place at home during his absence and make
economic adjustment until new employment is found.

## Physical Readjustment

Long working hours in hot weather, separation from family, and the unfamiliar
surroundings and conditions of the camp contribute to ill-health. Because of ill-
health a considerable number of workers have to return home before completing
their term of contract. Even among those who have completed their contracts,
many cannot start work after their return without resting or undergoing medical
treatment.

About 43 per cent, or 209 persons, out of the 480 sampled returnees stated that
their state of health became worse owing to their overseas work, while only 7 per

**Table 21.** Behavioural changes toward children after employment in the Middle East (compared with before)

| Aspects of change | Much more | More | Same | Less | Much less | Total |
|---|---|---|---|---|---|---|
| Helping with study | 7 (4.6)[a] | 67 (44.4) | 63 (41.7) | 12 (7.9) | 2 (1.3) | 151 (100.0) |
| Playing with children | 8 (5.1) | 58 (36.9) | 69 (43.9) | 20 (12.7) | 2 (1.3) | 157 (100.0) |
| Listening to children | 9 (5.7) | 76 (48.4) | 66 (40.2) | 9 (5.7) | 1 (0.6) | 161 (100.0) |
| Giving presents | 6 (3.9) | 61 (40.0) | 72 (47.4) | 12 (7.9) | 1 (0.6) | 152 (100.0) |
| Punishing | 5 (3.3) | 31 (20.7) | 84 (56.0) | 30 (20.0) | — | 150 (100.0) |
| Considering their future | 54 (33.5) | 88 (54.7) | 19 (11.8) | — | — | 161 (100.0) |

a. Percentages in parentheses.

cent said their health improved. A significant proportion of the temporary workers (10 per cent) were unable to continue work on their return because of ill-health.

About one in every twenty migrants encounters problems of adjustment to environmental conditions upon return. Because of ill-health, a small proportion of the migrants, primarily temporary workers, were unable to work for more than a month after their return; all regular workers returned to work within a month. The long work hours over an extended period during migration seem to have had a noticeable effect on a small but significant proportion of the temporary workers.

### Family Readjustment

Many households had serious problems in dealing with the situation during migration. However, as expected, most household problems were resolved upon the return of the husband and father. The separation seemed to have beneficial effects on marital relationships in more than half of the cases. Most migrants felt that the relationships with their children had improved significantly (7 per cent). Only a small proportion indicated that their relationships with wives and children had deteriorated (3 and 4 per cent respectively).

The family relationships had improved in regard not only to subjective feelings but also to behaviour. A considerable proportion of the returnees take care of their children better than they did before the migration (see table 21). For example, about half of them spend more time assisting their children with education, while a small proportion, 8 per cent, spend less time. After migration, nearly nine out of every ten migrants (88 per cent) developed a greater concern for the future of their children.

Similarly, after returning the migrants had improved relationships with their spouses. Husbands gave more assistance to wives in housework (45 per cent), went out with them more often (39 per cent), discussed housekeeping regularly (62 per cent) and consulted their wives regarding important decisions.

**Table 22.** Behavioural changes toward wife after employment in the Middle East (compared with before)

| Aspects of change | Much more | More | Same | Less | Total |
|---|---|---|---|---|---|
| Helping with household chores | 22 | 120 | 160 | 12 | 314 |
| | (7.0)[a] | (38.2) | (51.0) | (3.8) | (100.0) |
| Going out | 11 | 108 | 149 | 35 | 303 |
| | (3.6) | (35.6) | (49.2) | (11.5) | (100.0) |
| Discussing housekeeping | 21 | 174 | 118 | 3 | 316 |
| | (6.6) | (55.1) | (37.3) | (0.9) | (100.0) |
| Listening | 37 | 137 | 138 | 6 | 318 |
| | (11.6) | (43.1) | (43.4) | (1.9) | (100.0) |

a. Percentages in parentheses.

### Re-employment after Return

The employment situation after return was different for the various categories of workers. Regular workers resumed their employment with the company that transferred them to West Asia; the employment status of this type of worker did not change. The temporary workers were not as fortunate. A large proportion of the temporary workers had voluntarily remained unemployed for more than one week following their return to Korea; nearly 40 per cent were unemployed for over two months. Among those who were unemployed, a significant proportion sought income-earning opportunities, either in wage employment or self-employment. Ill-health was an important factor, forcing many to withdraw temporarily from the workforce. Unemployment related to features of the labour markets was not very important. The nature and characteristics of the behaviour of migrants upon return make it difficult to identify clearly the extent of unemployment. Unemployment in the sense of those seeking actively but unable to find work is not particularly widespread or important. More temporary migrants desire to change occupations after their return, and a large proportion wish to become self-employed. Among those who had been unskilled migrant workers, about three-quarters (76 per cent) were planning to remain as unskilled workers. Of regular workers, about one in ten was considering self-employment. Nevertheless, only half of those who wanted to be self-employed were able to achieve this.

Most returnees who wished to move to regular (permanent) employment with a firm other than the one they worked for while in West Asia were unsuccessful. All unsuccessful ones with a very few exceptions were manual workers. Among those who became self-employed, about two-thirds (63 per cent) had previous experience (37 per cent had done it at some time before, while 26 per cent were self-employed prior to migration). The migration had therefore been an opportunity to resume or strengthen self-employment ventures. Among those who had been self-employed, nearly one-third (31 per cent) had been engaged in ventures related to construction.

Most of the self-employed workers after the Middle East migration are engaged in such traditional industrial sectors as sales and service (44 per cent) and agricul-

**Table 23**. Desired working status after overseas employment by overseas occupational status

| Desired employment | Temporary workers | | | Regular employees | | |
| --- | --- | --- | --- | --- | --- | --- |
| | Unskilled | Skilled | Total | Low-level | High-level | Total |
| Regular employee | 2 | 34 | 36 | 56 | 36 | 92 |
| | (4.8)[a] | (10.2) | (9.6) | (88.9) | (87.8) | (88.5) |
| Temporary worker | 7 | 67 | 74 | — | — | — |
| | (17.1) | (20.0) | (19.7) | | | |
| Working proprietor | 31 | 228 | 259 | 6 | 5 | 11 |
| | (75.6) | (68.1) | (68.9) | (9.5) | (12.2) | (10.6) |
| Others | 1 | 6 | 7 | 1 | — | 1 |
| | (2.4) | (1.8) | (1.9) | (1.6) | | (1.0) |
| Total | 41 | 335 | 376 | 63 | 41 | 104 |
| | (100.0) | (100.0) | (100.0) | (100.0) | (100.0) | (100.0) |

a. Percentages in parentheses.

ture (26 per cent). Only 26 per cent, or 31 persons, of the self-employed run a construction or related business. Most of those self-employed after migration have established or re-established their business without any assistance: only 42 persons, or 35 per cent, of the total 119 working proprietors, received some help from others. Most such helpers are close relatives (43 per cent) or friends (38 per cent). Government organizations and private agencies play almost no role in helping them.

On return many workers changed employers, that is, they found work with a firm different to the one that employed them in West Asia. Most were assisted in their re-employment either by their friends, including those made during the migration (74 per cent), or relatives (22 per cent); none of them got any help from government organizations or private agencies.

A significant proportion of both temporary and regular employees (24 and 35 per cent respectively) had acquired new skills during migration. The use of these skills on their return depended on the occupational category of the workers. More than half (52 per cent) of the regular workers who acquired new skills and experience use them in their current occupation. About one-fifth of the self-employed (19 per cent) and one-quarter (24 per cent) of the temporary workers also used their new skills.

Although a considerable proportion of the returnees who learned new skills in the Middle East do not use them in their current jobs, it does not mean that most of them get jobs not requiring these skills. On the contrary, 75 per cent of them use the same skills that they practised in the Middle East. Among the returnees whose current working status is regular employment, only 7 per cent do not use the same skills, and among the temporarily employed and self-employed the proportion is 10 and 57 per cent respectively. The main reasons for not using the skills in present employment are change in job (56 per cent), dissatisfaction with the skills (21 per cent) and failure to get a job using the skills (11 per cent). The primary reason for

**Table 24.** Actual working status after overseas employment by desired status (percentages)

| Actual status | Regular employment by same co. | Regular employment by other co. | Temporary worker | Working proprietor | Total |
|---|---|---|---|---|---|
| | | Desired status | | | |
| Unemployed | — | 2 (8.3) | 4 (5.4) | 9 (3.3) | 16 (3.3) |
| Regular employment by same company | 95 (91.3) | 1 (4.2) | 1 (1.4) | 14 (5.2) | 114 (23.8) |
| Regular employment by other company | — | 6 (25.0) | 1 (1.4) | 13 (4.8) | 20 (4.2) |
| Temporary worker | 9 (8.7) | 14 (58.3) | 65 (87.8) | 118 (43.9) | 209 (43.5) |
| Working proprietor | — | — | 3 (4.1) | 114 (42.9) | 119 (24.9) |
| Others | — | 1 (4.2) | — | 1 (0.4) | 2 (0.4) |
| Total | 104 (100.0) | 24 (100.0) | 74 (100.0) | 269 (100.0) | 480 (100.0) |

not using skills, for both regular and self-employed workers, was the change in job after migration. The reasons for the temporary workers are more diverse.

## Earnings and Remittances

The average monthly earnings of Korean workers in the Middle East are considerably greater than those of domestic workers in a similar job. While working abroad, temporary workers earn 2.5 times more and the regular workers twice as much as domestic construction workers. Furthermore, additional payments for considerable overtime and other allowances result in doubling of the base wage for most workers. The average monthly earnings of migrant workers vary with skill level and occupation: for unskilled workers it is about 474,000 won (US$817 at the 1980 exchange rate), for skilled workers about 542,000 won ($934), for low-level regular employees about 764,000 won ($1,317), and for high-level non-manual workers about one million won ($1,724).

With additional payments over base wage, a small proportion of those in lower-grade occupations earn more than those in higher grades. More than a quarter (28 per cent) of the unskilled workers had higher average earnings than their skilled counterparts. Meanwhile one in ten high-level regular employees earn less than the average of low-level regular employees. The earnings variation is greatest among the latter: about 15 per cent of them earn less than the average earnings of the skilled workers, while 13 per cent earn as much as the high-level regular employees. This is because among low-level regular employees there are many engineers whose salary is larger than that of some high-level workers.

The total amount of earnings during the Middle East employment varied considerably among four categories of workers (table 25). This is due to differences

**Table 25**. Total earnings from the Middle East by occupational status

| Total earnings (millions of won) | Temporary workers | | Regular employees | |
|---|---|---|---|---|
| | Unskilled | Skilled | Low-level | High-level |
| Less than 5 | 6 | 23 | — | — |
| | (14.6)[a] | (6.9) | | |
| 5–9 | 14 | 99 | 1 | — |
| | (34.1) | (29.6) | (1.6) | |
| 10–14 | 11 | 70 | 4 | 3 |
| | (20.8) | (20.9) | (6.3) | (7.3) |
| 15–19 | 6 | 52 | 13 | 3 |
| | (14.6) | (15.5) | (20.6) | (7.3) |
| 20–24 | 2 | 35 | 5 | 2 |
| | (4.9) | (10.4) | (7.9) | (4.9) |
| 25–29 | 1 | 23 | 11 | 6 |
| | (2.4) | (6.9) | (17.5) | (14.6) |
| 30–34 | 1 | 12 | 10 | 5 |
| | (2.4) | (3.6) | (15.9) | (12.2) |
| 35–39 | — | 10 | 6 | 5 |
| | | (3.0) | (9.5) | (12.2) |
| 40–44 | — | 2 | 6 | 5 |
| | | (0.6) | (9.5) | (12.2) |
| 45–49 | — | 4 | 2 | 4 |
| | | (1.2) | (3.2) | (9.8) |
| 50 or more | — | 5 | 5 | 7 |
| | | (1.5) | (7.9) | (19.5) |
| Total | 41 | 335 | 63 | 40 |
| | (100.0) | (100.0) | (100.0) | (100.0) |

a. Percentages in parentheses.

not only in monthly earnings but also in the duration of overseas employment. The average total earnings for the regular employees (about 33 million won or US$56,000) is as much as twice that for the temporary workers (about 15.5 million won or $27,000). The average total earnings for unskilled workers is estimated at about 11 million won and for skilled workers about 16 million won. The low-level regular workers migrate for a longer period than the high-level regular workers. The difference in the total of the two incomes is reduced owing to this factor. The migration yielded an average income of approximately 30 million won for the lower grade while the higher grade generated 37 million won.

The migrants remit about 90 per cent of their earnings. The proportion is higher for those with higher incomes. One of the important factors influencing such a high rate of remittance is the Korean government stipulation that all migrant workers must remit at least 80 per cent of their earnings via the Korean banking system. This stipulation was designed to serve two purposes: to maximize the country's foreign currency earnings from overseas employment and to allow the workers to save as much as possible. Those who do not meet this requirement get a warning

**Table 26.** Percentage of remittance money to total earnings from the Middle East by occupational status

| Percentage | Temporary workers | | Regular employees | |
|---|---|---|---|---|
| | Unskilled | Skilled | Low-level | High-level |
| Less than 80 | 2 | 19 | 6 | 2 |
| | (2.8)[a] | (5.7) | (19.5) | (4.9) |
| 80–84 | 9 | 44 | 8 | 4 |
| | (22.0) | (13.1) | (12.7) | (9.8) |
| 85–89 | 15 | 111 | 14 | 8 |
| | (36.6) | (33.1) | (22.2) | (19.5) |
| 90–94 | 8 | 96 | 23 | 18 |
| | (19.5) | (28.7) | (36.5) | (43.9) |
| 95–100 | 7 | 65 | 12 | 9 |
| | (17.1) | (19.4) | (19.0) | (22.0) |
| Total | 41 | 335 | 63 | 41 |
| | (100.0) | (100.0) | (100.0) | (100.0) |

a. Percentages in parentheses.

from the Korean councillor in the host country, and may lose the chance to renew their contract, to visit home, or to change location. On the other hand, the workers who remit more than others are often honoured and guaranteed a contract renewal. Another factor influencing high rates of savings and remittance is the very high tax on imported goods. Also, travel and living costs are met by the employer for all grades of workers.

Nearly all the migrants bring a considerable amount of goods home with them, in spite of the tax on imports. Expenditure on goods varies considerably with occupational status: the higher the occupational status the higher the value of imports. Unskilled and skilled workers spent an average of 807,000 won and 944,000 won on goods respectively, while low-level regular workers spent about 1,596,000 won compared with 1,904,000 won for high-level workers. The proportion spent on goods is higher for the low-level workers. Skilled and unskilled workers spent about 7 per cent of earnings on goods, while the low-level workers spent 6 per cent and the high-level regular workers about 5 per cent.

**Use of Remittances**

More than half the migrants planned to invest in a home or in self-employment and had deposited funds in a savings institution or lent money on interest. More than four in every ten migrants (42 per cent) upon return purchased a home, while one quarter invested in self-employment. A small proportion invested in stocks or real estate. Over one-fifth of the migrants (22 per cent) had other sources of income while working abroad and their families did not use remittances. A similar proportion used remittances for the purchase of household goods. A significant proportion of migrant households used funds to settle debts (15 per cent) and assist close

**Table 27.** Percentage of remittance money to total earnings from the Middle East by amount of total earnings

| | Temporary workers | | Regular employees | |
|---|---|---|---|---|
| Percentage | Less than W20 million | W20 million or more | Less than W20 million | W20 million or more |
| Less than 80 | 18 | 3 | — | 8 |
| | (6.4)[a] | (3.2) | | (10.0) |
| 80–89 | 141 | 38 | 11 | 23 |
| | (50.2) | (40.0) | (45.8) | (28.8) |
| 90 or more | 122 | 54 | 13 | 49 |
| | (43.4) | (56.8) | (54.2) | (61.3) |
| Total | 281 | 95 | 23 | 80 |
| | (100.0) | (100.0) | (100.0) | (100.0) |

a. Percentages in parentheses.

relatives (12 per cent). More than one half of the migrant families had spent over 5 million won for household expenses.

The proportion of remittances saved in financial institutions or invested in housing increased with the quantity of remittances. Only a quarter of those who remitted a total of less than 10 million won saved in banks (23 per cent) or invested in a home (27 per cent). The proportions were significantly higher for those who remitted 30 million won; 57 per cent in banks and 74 per cent for the purchase of homes. However, those who remitted less invested a larger proportion on self-employment ventures. This reverse association can be attributed primarily to the fact that most of the higher-earning migrants in the Middle East consist of regular employees who are not interested in opening their own business.

The primary use of funds for both temporary workers and regular employees was for savings or the purchase of a home. However, the proportions of regular employees who had savings or who purchased houses (58 per cent for both) are higher than among the temporary workers (38 and 32 per cent respectively). These differences seem to be due to the latter's inclination to invest in their own business (31 compared with 3 per cent). Although the regular employees are more likely to invest in other items such as stocks and real estate, the proportion who invested in these items is also very low (about 8 per cent). The largest portion of remittances was spent on purchasing homes for both categories of workers; the average spent was 10 million won for temporary workers (141 cases) and about 20 million won for regular employees (60 cases). Investment in the migrants' own business or firm (about 8.8 million won for 117 cases) and savings in banks (about 6.4 million won for 120 cases) were important uses of earnings for the temporary workers. The average savings among the regular employees, who saved or invested about twice as much as the temporary workers, was about 11 million won. This closely related, as expected, to the higher earnings of the former. The migrant workers, both temporary and regular, saved or invested an average of about 62 per cent of their earnings or about 69 per cent of the remittance money. They were able to save or invest such a large portion of the remittance money largely because their earnings

**Table 28a.** Main uses of remittances

| Amount (millions of won) | Savings in bank | Loan for interest | Stocks | Real estate | Own business | Own house |
|---|---|---|---|---|---|---|
| None | 298 (62.3)[a] | 409 (85.4) | 470 (97.9) | 448 (93.7) | 358 (75.1) | 276 (57.9) |
| Less than 5 | 80 (16.7) | 53 (11.1) | 8 (1.7) | 4 (0.8) | 33 (6.9) | 49 (10.3) |
| 5–9 | 50 (10.5) | 11 (2.3) | 1 (0.2) | 13 (2.7) | 51 (10.7) | 30 (6.3) |
| 10–14 | 25 (5.2) | 4 (0.8) | — | 4 (0.8) | 20 (4.2) | 51 (10.7) |
| 15–19 | 8 (1.7) | 1 (0.2) | 1 (0.2) | 3 (0.6) | 6 (1.3) | 28 (5.9) |
| 20–24 | 11 (2.3) | 1 (0.2) | — | 3 (0.6) | 5 (1.0) | 21 (4.4) |
| 25–29 | 2 (0.4) | — | — | 1 (0.2) | 2 (0.4) | 11 (2.3) |
| 30 or more | 4 (0.8) | — | — | 7 (0.4) | 3 (0.4) | 11 (2.3) |
| Total | 478 (100.0) | 479 (100.0) | 480 (100.0) | 478 (100.0) | 477 (100.0) | 477 (100.0) |

a. Percentages in parentheses.

**Table 28b.** Other uses of remittances

| Amount (millions of won) | Private car | Household goods | Support relatives | Donations | Pay back debts | Living expenses |
|---|---|---|---|---|---|---|
| None | 473 (98.5)[a] | 392 (81.8) | 424 (88.3) | 468 (97.9) | 404 (84.5) | 103 (21.5) |
| Less than 1 | — | 31 (6.6) | 7 (1.5) | 5 (1.0) | 10 (2.1) | 33 (6.9) |
| 1–1.9 | 1 (0.2) | 37 (7.7) | 13 (2.7) | 3 (0.6) | 21 (4.4) | 63 (13.2) |
| 2–2.9 | 1 (0.2) | 10 (2.1) | 12 (2.5) | 2 (0.4) | 13 (2.7) | 58 (12.1) |
| 3–3.9 | 1 (0.2) | 4 (0.8) | 8 (1.7) | — | 11 (2.3) | 39 (8.1) |
| 4–4.9 | — | 1 (0.2) | 3 (0.6) | — | 6 (1.3) | 35 (7.3) |
| 5 or more | 4 (0.8) | 4 (0.8) | 13 (2.7) | — | 14 (2.9) | 251 (52.4) |
| Total | 480 (100.0) | 479 (100.0) | 480 (100.0) | 478 (100.0) | 479 (100.0) | 479 (100.0) |

a. Percentages in parentheses.

**Table 29**. Percentages of houses owned, before and after migration, by overseas occupational status

| Period | Temporary workers | | | Regular employees | | |
| --- | --- | --- | --- | --- | --- | --- |
| | Unskilled | Skilled | Total | Low-level | High-level | Total |
| Before migration | 17.1 | 21.6 | 21.0 | 20.6 | 51.2 | 32.7 |
| | (7)[a] | (72) | (79) | (13) | (21) | (34) |
| After migration | 29.3 | 46.3 | 44.4 | 65.1 | 82.9 | 72.1 |
| | (12) | (155) | (167) | (41) | (34) | (75) |

a. Numbers in parentheses indicate number of cases.

were much higher than in Korea, but also because many of them had other sources of income to cover family living expenses during the migration.

The mismanagement of remittances was uncommon. A total of 35 persons or 7 per cent of the total said they had lost over one million won due to misuse. The main reasons for the loss are bad judgement in investment (20 persons) and failure to collect personal loans (12 persons). Most of the victims are temporary workers whose educational level is relatively low. Among the regular employees only two persons misused their remittances, but among the temporary workers 33 persons or 9 per cent of the total lost a considerable amount of the remittances owing to poor judgement.

## Economic Effects of Remittances

As expected, the migration had a substantial impact on family income, consumption, savings, and investment. Not only did consumption increase but the asset position of the household improved as well. However, not all migrant families were able to achieve a higher level of income and consumption compared with the period before migration. Similar proportions of temporary and regular workers (14 and 12 per cent respectively) had reduced incomes after migration. However, about two-thirds (65 per cent) of the temporary workers and more than four-fifths (85 per cent) of the regular workers were earning substantially higher incomes. A greater proportion of the regular employees had an increase in income primarily because of promotion, while decreases were due primarily to the formation of nuclear families. The decline for the temporary workers was related to occupation: these persons had not been able to obtain work comparable to their pre-migration employment. After migration a substantial proportion of migrants invested in homes, increasing the proportion owning homes from 21 to 44 per cent for temporary workers and from 33 to 72 per cent for regular workers. A large proportion of migrants in the higher wage levels (during migration) invested in a home. As expected, the higher-level regular worker migrants tended to own homes before migration. Regular worker migrants were more liable to invest in housing and spent larger sums than the temporary workers. About 70 per cent of migrants (temporary and regular) moved after migration to better homes in better locations,

**Table 30.** Total value of real estate owned, before and after migration, by overseas working status

| Total value (millions of won) | Temporary workers | | Regular employees | |
|---|---|---|---|---|
| | Before | After | Before | After |
| None | 286 | 189 | 67 | 25 |
| | (76.1)[a] | (50.3) | (64.4) | (24.3) |
| Less than 20 | 53 | 76 | 5 | 6 |
| | (14.0) | (20.2) | (4.8) | (5.8) |
| 20–40 | 21 | 71 | 20 | 26 |
| | (5.6) | (18.9) | (19.3) | (25.2) |
| 40 or more | 16 | 40 | 12 | 46 |
| | (4.2) | (10.6) | (11.6) | (44.7) |
| Total | 376 | 376 | 104 | 103 |
| | (100.0) | (100.0) | (100.0) | (100.0) |

a. Percentages in parentheses.

though this included a larger proportion of regular workers than of temporary workers (85 and 64 per cent). These figures include not only the new home-owners but also those who moved to another rental house: many families would have moved to better quality rental homes. At the same time a significant proportion of the temporary worker migrants (18 per cent) had moved from rental homes to poorer quality homes which they purchased on return.

The remittances had a significant impact on the consumption behaviour of migrant households. More than half the migrant families had increased consumption expenditure on food, clothing, and shelter. Meat and milk consumption had increased significantly. Expenditure on the education of children had been increased in one out of every six households (17 per cent), and migration expenditures had increased significantly for housing and health care. Small increases were noted for entertainment, vacations, books, and movies. More than one half of the migrant families had increased their savings.

### Changes in Socio-economic Status and Attitudes

The migration had a significant impact on the socio-economic status of families. The attitudes of the migrant workers towards work and leisure, labour unions and foreigners had changed considerably.

Changes in Socio-economic Status

Migrants in the regular worker category did not desire to change their socio-economic status to the same degree as the temporary workers. The regular workers were generally content to maintain their status while most temporary workers desired to become self-employed proprietors. More than two-thirds (68 per cent) of those who had been self-employed prior to migration remained self-employed after their return. Many regular employee migrants who changed firms on return

**Table 31.** Current levels of consumption and savings compared with levels before migration

| Items | Changes in consumption level | | | | | |
|---|---|---|---|---|---|---|
| | Much more | More | Same | Less | Much less | Total |
| Meat | 29 | 210 | 208 | 22 | 1 | 475 |
| | (6.1)[a] | (44.2) | (43.8) | (4.6) | (0.6) | (100.0) |
| Milk | 24 | 204 | 196 | 10 | 3 | 437 |
| | (5.5) | (46.7) | (44.9) | (2.3) | (0.7) | (100.0) |
| Beverages | 28 | 201 | 200 | 21 | 4 | 454 |
| | (6.2) | (44.3) | (44.1) | (4.6) | (0.8) | (100.0) |
| Coffee and tea | 28 | 186 | 208 | 14 | 4 | 440 |
| | (6.4) | (42.3) | (47.3) | (3.2) | (0.9) | (100.0) |
| Processed food | 10 | 114 | 250 | 6 | 4 | 384 |
| | (2.6) | (29.7) | (65.1) | (1.6) | (1.0) | (100.0) |
| Liquor | 11 | 119 | 276 | 29 | 6 | 441 |
| | (2.5) | (27.0) | (62.6) | (6.6) | (1.4) | (100.0) |
| Education | 35 | 126 | 35 | 3 | 2 | 199 |
| | (17.6) | (63.3) | (17.6) | (1.5) | (1.0) | (100.0) |
| Dwellings | 37 | 262 | 157 | 11 | 2 | 469 |
| | (7.9) | (55.9) | (33.5) | (2.3) | (0.4) | (100.0) |
| Clothes | 14 | 195 | 251 | 15 | 2 | 477 |
| | (2.9) | (40.9) | (52.6) | (3.1) | (0.4) | (100.0) |
| Western medicine | 28 | 121 | 259 | 4 | 3 | 412 |
| | (6.1) | (29.4) | (62.8) | (1.0) | (0.7) | (100.0) |
| Chinese medicine | 13 | 77 | 261 | 4 | 1 | 356 |
| | (3.7) | (21.6) | (73.3) | (1.1) | (0.3) | (100.0) |
| Vacations | 17 | 144 | 233 | 23 | 6 | 423 |
| | (4.0) | (34.0) | (55.1) | (5.4) | (1.4) | (100.0) |
| Books | 9 | 122 | 308 | 6 | 3 | 448 |
| | (2.0) | (27.2) | (68.8) | (1.3) | (0.7) | (100.0) |
| Movies | 6 | 36 | 267 | 33 | 9 | 351 |
| | (1.7) | (10.3) | (76.1) | (9.4) | (2.6) | (100.0) |
| Donations on special occasions | 24 | 202 | 227 | 3 | 2 | 458 |
| | (5.2) | (44.1) | (49.6) | (6.6) | (0.4) | (100.0) |
| Offerings | 6 | 100 | 244 | 2 | 2 | 354 |
| | (1.7) | (28.2) | (68.9) | (0.6) | (0.6) | (100.0) |
| Savings | 27 | 194 | 192 | 26 | 5 | 444 |
| | (6.1) | (41.7) | (43.2) | (5.9) | (1.1) | (100.0) |

a. Percentages in parentheses.

became self-employed or temporary workers; about one-third of such employees had become self-employed. However, this does not necessarily mean that their employment situations were worse than those of other workers.

Changes in social status are assessed in terms of migrant perceptions of social mobility and subjective evaluation of living standards. The two dimensions of status differ from each other, the former reflecting the honour or prestige of the household, which is determined in the context of social relationships or the group, and the latter concerning economic improvement.

**Table 32.** Changes in social status by occupational status in the Middle East

| Change in status | Temporary workers | | | Regular employees | | |
| | Unskilled | Skilled | Total | Low-level | High-level | Total |
|---|---|---|---|---|---|---|
| Upward | 8 | 73 | 81 | 27 | 17 | 44 |
| | (20.0)[a] | (22.2) | (22.0) | (43.5) | (43.6) | (43.6) |
| Same | 31 | 243 | 274 | 34 | 21 | 55 |
| | (77.5) | (73.9) | (74.5) | (54.8) | (52.5) | (54.6) |
| Downward | 1 | 13 | 14 | 1 | 1 | 2 |
| | (2.5) | (3.9) | (3.8) | (1.6) | (2.5) | (2.0) |
| Total | 40 | 329 | 369 | 62 | 39 | 101 |
| | (100.0) | (100.0) | (100.0) | (100.0) | (100.0) | (100.0) |

a. Percentages in parentheses.

**Table 33.** Changes in social status by current working status

| Change in status | Regular employee in same co. | Regular employee in other co. | Temporary worker | Self-employed | Family worker |
|---|---|---|---|---|---|
| Upward | 43 | 8 | 39 | 32 | 1 |
| | (42.2)[a] | (25.8) | (17.6) | (32.7) | (20.0) |
| Same | 58 | 23 | 174 | 61 | 4 |
| | (56.9) | (74.2) | (78.4) | (62.2) | (80.0) |
| Downward | 1 | — | 9 | 5 | — |
| | (1.0) | | (4.1) | (5.1) | |
| Total | 102 | 31 | 222 | 98 | 5 |
| | (100.0) | (100.0) | (100.0) | (100.0) | (100.0) |

a. Percentages in parentheses.

**Table 34.** Changes in economic status (living standard) by occupational status in the Middle East (percentages)

| | Temporary workers | | | Regular employees | | |
| | Unskilled | Skilled | Total | Low-level | High-level | Total |
|---|---|---|---|---|---|---|
| Upward | 117 | 21 | 198 | 34 | 18 | 52 |
| | (52.8) | (51.2) | (52.7) | (54.0) | (43.9) | (50.0) |
| Same | 138 | 17 | 155 | 28 | 22 | 50 |
| | (41.2) | (41.5) | (41.2) | (44.4) | (53.7) | (48.1) |
| Downward | 20 | 3 | 23 | 1 | 1 | 2 |
| | (6.0) | (7.3) | (6.1) | (0.6) | (2.4) | (1.9) |
| Total | 335 | 41 | 376 | 63 | 41 | 104 |
| | (100.0) | (100.0) | (100.0) | (100.0) | (100.0) | (100.0) |

Many of the migrant workers have improved their social status, while a few have experienced downward mobility (table 32). The proportion of regular employees that considered they had achieved upward social mobility was twice as large as that for the temporary workers (44 compared with 22 per cent). The changes in social mobility are closely related to occupation. Less than one-fifth (18 per cent) of those who were temporary workers after migration considered their social status to have improved. While changes in social status are closely related to working and occupational status, changes in economic status, measured in terms of living standards, appear to be closely related to earnings rather than occupational status. Over a half of the migrant workers were able to improve their standard of living, while only a few saw their standard of living worsen (table 34). The living standards of the high-level migrants were higher than those of the rest before migration, and the incremental improvements for this category are therefore more difficult to gauge. The migration did not seem to result in an improvement in social status as perceived by these workers.

Changes in Attitudes toward Work and Labour Unions

Working and living conditions in the Middle East are very different from conditions in Korea. The migrant workers have to work longer and harder under conditions of extreme heat. Migration therefore seems to have resulted in workers becoming more satisfied with their present occupations when compared with what they did

Table 35. Changes in economic status (living standard) by total amount of earnings from the Middle East (percentages)

| Changes in status | Less than 20 million won | 20–39 million won | 40 million won or more |
|---|---|---|---|
| Temporary workers | | | |
| Upward | 124 (45.1) | 61 (72.6) | 13 (76.5) |
| Same | 130 (47.3) | 21 (25.0) | 4 (23.5) |
| Downward | 21 (7.6) | 2 (2.4) | — |
| Total | 275 (100.0) | 84 (100.0) | 17 (100.0) |
| Regular employees | | | |
| Upward | 8 (38.1) | 28 (56.0) | 16 (48.5) |
| Same | 13 (61.9) | 21 (42.0) | 16 (48.5) |
| Downward | — | 1 (2.0) | 1 (3.0) |
| Total | 21 (100.0) | 50 (100.0) | 33 (100.0) |

in the past. The self-employed derived greater job satisfaction than other categories of workers. Stability of employment seems to be an important factor affecting job satisfaction after migration.

Return migrants also showed more keenness than before to develop skills and acquire training. The tendency was stronger among the regular workers, about one-half of whom indicated that they were interested in developing skills or acquiring new ones. The corresponding proportion for the migrants in the temporary worker category was substantially lower (33 per cent). The interest in new skills or developing existing ones depends on the present occupation of the respondent.

**Table 36**. Attitude toward labour union before and after overseas employment by occupational status in the Middle East

| Attitude toward labour union | Temporary workers | | | Regular employees | | |
| | Unskilled | Skilled | Total | Low-level | High-level | Total |
|---|---|---|---|---|---|---|
| *Attitude before overseas employment* | | | | | | |
| Should be far more active | 14 (63.6)[a] | 124 (53.2) | 138 (54.1) | 18 (41.9) | 10 (27.8) | 28 (35.4) |
| Should be more active | 7 (31.8) | 80 (14.3) | 87 (34.1) | 16 (37.2) | 16 (44.4) | 32 (40.5) |
| Satisfied with current state | 1 (4.5) | 26 (11.2) | 27 (10.6) | 8 (18.6) | 9 (25.0) | 17 (21.5) |
| Should be less active | — | 3 (1.3) | 3 (1.2) | 1 (2.3) | 1 (2.8) | 2 (2.5) |
| Total | 22 (100.0) | 233 (100.0) | 255 (100.0) | 43 (100.0) | 36 (100.0) | 79 (100.0) |
| DK/NR (%) | 19 (46.3) | 102 (40.0) | 121 (47.5) | 20 (31.7) | 5 (12.2) | 25 (24.0) |
| *Current attitude* | | | | | | |
| Should be far more active | 21 (60.0) | 162 (58.1) | 183 (58.3) | 26 (49.1) | 13 (36.1) | 39 (43.8) |
| Should be more active | 11 (31.4) | 90 (32.3) | 101 (32.2) | 17 (32.1) | 14 (38.9) | 31 (34.8) |
| Satisfied with current state | 3 (8.6) | 25 (9.0) | 28 (8.9) | 8 (15.1) | 8 (22.2) | 16 (18.0) |
| Should be less active | — | 2 (0.7) | 2 (0.6) | 2 (3.8) | 1 (2.8) | 3 (3.4) |
| Total | 35 (100.0) | 279 (100.0) | 314 (100.0) | 53 (100.0) | 36 (100.0) | 89 (100.0) |
| DK/NR (%) | 6 (14.6) | 56 (16.7) | 62 (14.5) | 10 (15.9) | 5 (12.2) | 15 (14.4) |

a. Percentages in parentheses.

95

Migrant workers had worked very long hours while abroad, and this resulted in a willingness to work longer on return. The self-employed, who have invested in their enterprises and in many cases are in the process of expanding, work longest after return. The regular workers have also increased the number of work hours on return compared with the pre-migration period. However, workers tend to take more leave and devote more time to leisure than before. This tendency is stronger among the regular workers.

After migration interest in organized labour movements became stronger (table 36). About one-fifth of the migrants in the temporary worker category had not been acquainted with organized labour movements. The attitudes of the migrant workers toward the labour union movement are closely related to their occupational position. The lower the occupational status in the Middle East was, the more they tended to have a favourable attitude towards organized labour. Among the un-skilled workers 60 per cent felt the movement should be far more active, compared with 36 per cent of the higher-rank regular employees. The corresponding figures for the skilled workers and the lower-rank regular employees are 58 and 49 per cent respectively. In contrast, the percentage of those who are satisfied with their current state is lower for the lower-status occupations. Attitudes toward labour unions differ not only by occupational status during overseas employment but also by current working status. The proportion of those who think that the movement should be more active is greater among the temporary and self-employed workers than among the regular employees.

## Changes in Attitudes toward Religion and Foreigners

Korea is a multi-religious society, where Buddhism, Catholicism, Protestantism, and many traditional religions co-exist. Islam was introduced to the country after the Middle East migration, but the number of Korean Muslims is negligible. Although there are many religions in the country, over half of all Koreans do not practise a religion.

About three-quarters of the migrants had not attended any religious service before migration (table 37). About one-fifth of migrants were Christians. However, during the stay abroad about one-third (32 per cent) attended religious meetings while almost none of the 7 per cent of Buddhists did so. This breaking-away can be attributed partly to the control over religious activities by the host country: in the work camp there are no officially accepted churches or religious organizations, and all religious activities take place on an informal basis. The data perhaps give an indication of the lack of interest or devoutness of the majority of the migrants.

After the Middle East employment many of the migrants changed their religious affiliation. Of those who had been Christians before migration about 40 per cent no longer practise. Meanwhile, among those who had no religious affiliation 25 persons became Christians and 29 became Buddhists. The proportion of those practising religion after migration declined from 27 to 22 per cent. Based on a score developed from answers to four questions, religiosity before and after migration was measured. These questions were related to the function of religion in individual life, in developing a world-view, in maintaining morality, and in the belief in absolute truth. The results indicate that about 5 per cent of the migrants had become less religious after returning home.

**Table 37.** Participation in religious services before and after employment in the Middle East

| Current | Before employment | | | Total |
|---|---|---|---|---|
| | None | Christian | Buddhist | |
| None | 325 | 35 | 11 | 371 |
| | (93.1)[a] | (36.8) | (30.6) | (77.3) |
| Christian | 18 | 59 | 1 | 78 |
| | (5.2) | (62.1) | (2.8) | (16.3) |
| Buddhist | 6 | 1 | 24 | 31 |
| | (1.7) | (1.1) | (66.7) | (6.5) |
| Total | 349 | 95 | 36 | 480 |
| | (100.0) | (100.0) | (100.0) | (100.0) |

a. Percentages in parentheses.

The migrants, regular as well as temporary workers, came into contact with people from many other countries. The temporary workers were more likely to have met South-East Asians (70 per cent) during the course of their stay; a significant proportion had worked with Arabs, Europeans, Americans, and East Asians. The regular workers had more contact because of the nature of their work with non-South and South-East Asians. The effect on the interest in foreign countries and people was therefore greater for the latter group of migrants.

Although many migrants became more interested in foreign countries through their overseas experience, this does not necessarily mean that their attitudes towards foreigners were positive and favourable. The survey data showed that there were both positive and negative reactions among the migrants, and these varied depending on the nationality. A change of attitude was more likely among workers who had experience of working together with foreigners.

The responses of the migrant workers also tend to reflect less favourable attitudes toward Arabs and South-East Asians than toward Europeans and Americans. Except for their attitude towards the Arabs, the migrants tend on the whole to be more favourable to foreigners than they were before. Most of the migrant workers consider the Korean way of life better than the Arab or South-East Asian ways of life but inferior to the European or American. The responses to Arabs seem to be due largely to the cultural differences between Korea and the host country and to some extent to the fact that most of the Arab workers who have worked with Korean migrants have a relatively poor education. As we have seen above, most migrants leave for the Middle East without an adequate understanding of Arab culture, though they are curious about it. This seems to be also one of the main reasons for the formation of such unfavourable opinions about Arabs.

Very few migrants considered that there was much of value to learn from the Arab and South-East Asian way of life. However, they considered that much of value was to be learnt from the other countries. It was also observed that those who have had the experience of working with foreigners are more likely to think there is something to learn from it than those who have not had such an experience.

# Conclusion

Most of the migrant workers are young adults responsible for their family's well-being. They are not only younger but also more educated than domestic construction workers. Most of the temporarily employed migrants have either received vocational high-school education or work experience for a number of years, while most of the regular employees have received a professional college education in subjects such as engineering and business. Some of the temporary workers were regularly employed or self-employed before migration, and gave up stable jobs for the Middle East employment, but most were previously temporarily employed skilled workers.

For most, the main reason for the migration was economic improvement. Saving to purchase a home, to start or develop an enterprise, and to educate children were prime uses of migration earnings (80 per cent). However, a significant proportion (11 per cent) had migrated to resolve immediately pressing problems such as settlement of debt, unemployment, and other economic difficulties. The economic motives were not as important for the regular workers (33 per cent), who volunteered for assignment to West Asian locations. In their case their long-term career prospects in the firm, as well as short-term monetary gains, may have been important considerations.

Since earnings in the Middle East are considerably greater than in Korea, in some cases their overseas employment was strongly recommended by other persons, mostly by their boss or fellow workers. A significant proportion of the migrants had met with serious objections to the proposed work in West Asia from family members, usually spouses or parents.

Migrants obtain information about application procedures, work and living conditions, and social customs of the host country from recruitment companies, employer representatives, or friends. The information, especially as regards the social customs of the host country, was generally considered to be insufficient by the migrants.

Direct money costs for the Middle East migration have been relatively small. The direct costs and loss of possible income for temporary workers, taken together, totalled about 1.4 million won on average, corresponding to about two months' earnings during migration. Despite such high money costs migration was undertaken because the money returns from the migration are far higher than the costs. Average monthly earnings from the overseas employment are 2.5 times higher for temporary workers, and twice as high for regular employees, as in domestic construction.

Although not measurable in quantitative terms, the psychological and non-material costs to the migrant workers appear to be substantial. Many family members had objected to migration because of their dislike for family separation and because the work was considered hard. As a result there were anxiety and stress before and during migration.

About one-fifth of the migrants had encountered serious problems and violations of contracts; a small proportion of them had been unable to meet the full requirements of the contract. The migrants worked and lived in an environment different from that they were accustomed to. Labour–management relations were considered to be superior to those in Korea by more than a third (38 per cent) of the temporary workers, and relations among workers were also thought to be better. However, because of the authoritarian control and favouritism, there was a significant proportion of temporary workers who were dissatisfied. Korean firms in West Asia are normally expected to set up labour–management councils to resolve disputes, but more than a third of the temporary workers, those in labour grades, expressed dissatisfaction with these councils on the grounds that they were inactive or prejudiced against the workers.

Korean workers in West Asia typically live in one of the work camps established by the Korean companies which hire them. The camp resembles a "total institution," with "house rules" to regulate the workers' conduct, and a system of rewards and punishment to support the rules. The worker's everyday life is tightly scheduled and supervised, so that on working days they have only a few hours of leisure. Sundays are non-working days. Leisure-time activities usually include sports, watching TV, playing cards or oriental chess, or reading newspapers and magazines. The management occasionally provides group recreation and entertainment. Workers expressed satisfaction with the recreation facilities provided by the employers. The camp did not satisfy a significant proportion of the migrants because of inadequate medical care, living conditions, and quality of food, but despite these problems the Korean workers seemed to be generally content with living conditions. The regular employees enjoyed better living conditions than the temporary workers and more expressed satisfaction.

The Korean migrant workers' daily life is confined to the camp and the workplace and their social life is limited accordingly. They make a few friends from Korea and foreign lands. There are also few social clubs and friendship associations in the camp. Even religious activities are limited: they must be informal and kept within the camp. With all this, the only meaningful human relationships the workers can maintain are with family members who are at home. Thus, exchanging letters with family members is one of the most important activities for the migrant workers.

Workers encountered problems in adjusting to the work and living in West Asia. The physical environment presented problems, but these were overcome within a few months. Anxiety about the family and the long hours of work resulting from incentive payments affected workers' health, especially that of the manual workers.

The year-long migration not only created a problem with regard to the readjustment of roles within the family, but also introduced new problems such as taking care of the aged and/or children, ensuring the safety of the family, and conflicts between the spouse and her parents-in-law. Most of the burden usually fell on the worker's spouse, but his children were also affected. However, except for a small proportion of the families, these problems were not very serious. For the large majority, the separation created a strong awareness of family bonds, resulting in a new division of family responsibilities and the strengthening of family relationships.

A significant proportion of migrants suffered from various problems of adjustment after return. The arduous work in an uncongenial environment had adverse effects on their health. While regular employees who were despatched by their employing company retain the same employment status after their return, most of the temporary workers face a period of unemployment immediately following their return, and this is partly attributable to ill-health.

More than two-thirds (69 per cent) of the temporary workers and a significant proportion (11 per cent) of the regular workers want to be self-employed on their return, but only a small proportion achieve this. Previous experience is a critical factor. Most migrants do not receive assistance in finding employment; service organizations and placement offices perform only a very small role in the re-employment of migrants. The migration has a substantial economic impact on the family of the migrant, since migrant earnings are more than double those in similar occupations in Korea. About four-fifths of the earnings are remitted. The migration affects social mobility favourably, and changes attitudes towards work, leisure, and foreign cultures.

The average monthly earnings for unskilled workers very considerably with skill level and occupation, ranging from about 474,000 Korean won ($817 at the 1980 exchange rate) to about one million won ($1,724) for high-level workers. The total earnings and remittance during overseas employment also vary with occupation, not only because of the differences in the monthly earnings but also because the durations of employment differ. The average total earnings, which depend on the duration of employment abroad, ranged from approximately 11 million won for unskilled workers to 37 million for high-level regular employees.

The proportion of earnings remitted for all levels was quite high, in the region of 87 to 90 per cent. The high rates of remittance are attributed partly to the employment benefits and partly to the government stipulation that every migrant must remit over 80 per cent of his earnings to Korea through the Korean banking system. In addition to the remittance the migrants bring back a considerable amount of goods: about 6 per cent of total earnings are spent on goods.

The remittances are generally used as planned. The principal use of funds is for purchase of a home. Investment in self-employment, either a business that had been started before migration or a new one, also account for a significant proportion, especially among the temporary worker migrants. Fifty-nine per cent of the regular workers who had no previous home purchased one on return, compared with 30 per cent of temporary workers. Nearly three-quarters improved housing by upgrading or moving, and household assets in the form of buildings and land increased substantially. Many of the migrant workers not only purchased or improved their homes but also bought more durable household goods, such as suites of furniture and various electric and electronic appliances. The level of consumption, especially of food, clothing, housing services and education, had increased.

Migration resulted in upward social mobility and improvements in occupational status and standards of living. When the current monthly household income of migrants is compared with the income before overseas employment, 65 per cent of temporary workers and 85 per cent of regular employees appear to have had a considerable increment, while only 14 per cent of the former and 12 per cent of the latter have less. A significant proportion changed to better occupations or were promoted. A considerable number of previous temporary workers became self-employed proprietors, and over half of the low-level regular employees were promoted to higher levels. The experience of employment in the Middle East exposed most migrants to a harsh regime of work and severe psychological stresses, all of which resulted in major changes in attitudes and values.

The returnees came to appreciate their current job and working conditions in Korea. Many of them became more interested in labour unions and indicated that the unions should be more active. The lower the occupational status of the migrant workers, the stronger the demand for labour union activity.

In regard to their attitudes to work, migrants showed greater readiness to work long hours, learn new skills, and acquire training, and consequently become more productive in their work. The cultural impact of the migration on the workers surveyed was of a mixed character. There was a discernible decline in the observance of religious practices. The migration exposed the migrants to the external world; working together with foreigners resulted in associations and friendships which changed and influenced their attitudes to foreigners. In an evaluation of the foreign style of living with which they had come in contact, many of them considered the Korean life-style superior to that of the Arabs and South-East Asians, but seemed to favour European and North American life- styles.

In an overall appraisal of the migration, the majority of migrant workers and their families have certainly made economic and non-economic gains which far outweigh the costs and any losses. The remittances they sent home improved the household economy substantially, and through the overseas work experience they accumulated skills and became more productive than before. In addition, many of them improved family ties and relationships with relatives, friends, and neighbours and improved their social standing.

Findings from this study have relevance for national policies relating to the export of labour to the Middle East. The type of labour migration that has been investigated would be more beneficial to both the migrant workers and the national economy if some of the major problems highlighted in the survey were resolved. These occur in all phases of the migration. During pre-migration, they include insufficient preparation for the cultural shock, lack of adequate information on conditions in the host country, and some instances of malpractice, fraud, and delays. During the overseas employment, problems range from breach of contract on the part of employers to an excessively authoritarian work regime, ineffective machinery to deal with labour–management relations and worker grievances, insufficient medical care, and absence of any institutional support to migrants' families in times of need. There were no proper advice or counselling services concerning the efficient use of remittances. The full developmental potential of the migration and its resources cannot be fully realized without more effective national policies to deal with these problems. The labour migration to the Middle East until the early 1980s made a considerable contribution to the national economy. Yet, recently, with the decline in crude oil prices, the opportunities for contract work and employment in the region have dropped sharply, resulting in a considerable decrease in labour migration. The Korean government is concerned about the effects of this, and has implemented measures for the smooth withdrawal of business firms, but little has been done to solve the problem of manpower reallocation.

## Note

1. These rules relate to: (1) misconduct which offends against national dignity or policy; (2) violating the confidentiality of the firm; (3) gambling and other forms of behaviour which affect work; (4) violence, destructive behaviour, and instigation of sabotage; (5) violation of the laws of the host country resulting in diplomatic problems; (6) any conviction during

employment; (7) harmful behaviour against the employer or violation of the employer's rules and contract; (8) disobedience to superiors; (9) physical and mental illness; (10) job transfer without employer's agreement; (11) forgery of documents; and (12) work absenteeism of more than 10 days without permission.

## References

Berouti, L.J. 1976. Employment Promotion Problems in Arab Countries. *International Labour Review*, 114 (2):169–185.

Birks, J.S. and C.A. Sinclair. 1979. *The Kingdom of Saudi Arabia and the Libyan Arab Jamahiriya: The Key Countries of Employment*. ILO, Geneva.

——. 1980. *International Migration and Development in the Arab Region*. ILO, Geneva.

Ecevit, Z.H. 1981. International Labour Migration in the Middle East and North Africa: Trends, Effects, and Policies. *Global Trends in Migration: Theory and Research on International Population Movements*. Centre for Migration Studies, New York.

Park, Rae Young. 1983. Effects of Labour Migration to the Middle East on the Domestic Labour Market. *Overseas Migration of Koreans: A Case of Migration to the Middle East*. Korean National Commission for Unesco and the Population Development Studies Centre, Seoul.

Shaw, R. Paul. 1979. Migration and Employment in the Arab World: Construction as a Key Policy Variable. *International Labour Review*, 118 (5):589–606.

**3**

# ASIAN MIGRATION TO THE GULF REGION: THE PHILIPPINE CASE

F.R. Arcinas

Department of Sociology, University of the Philippines, Quezon City, Philippines

## Introduction

The export of manpower has been a principal feature of the Philippine government's economic plan since the late 1970s. While overseas contract work was initially viewed by the state as a temporary measure for easing the problem of unemployment in the country, it has come to be seen as one of the survival mechanisms for the Philippine economy in the wake of the current balance of payments deficit and the national debt problem.

The state justifies the need actively to sell Filipino labour abroad by citing the benefits the country and the worker can reap from overseas employment. The inflow of remittances from contract workers is said to be an important source of foreign exchange (albeit a short-term one, unless such remittances are channelled into real capital formation). Overseas contract work is also alleged to lead to the acquisition by the guest workers of new skills, apart from its function as a source of relief from unemployment and underemployment. Finally, foreign employment is claimed to improve the general material welfare of the worker, his family, and the larger community.

The state's vigorous promotion of the manpower export programme provides further impetus to a contemporary pattern of Philippine out-migration which emerged from a conjunction of the economic difficulties facing the majority of Filipinos, on the one hand, and the expansion of the overseas market for Philippine labour in the 1970s and 1980s on the other. Poverty and the lack of available or remunerative employment opportunities in the country have impelled many nationals to seek their fortunes abroad. The desire to work overseas, however, is not new. In 1920, some 21,031 Filipinos left for Hawaii to work in agricultural plantations. In the 1960s, thousands of labourers went to Guam to rebuild its typhoon-devastated economy. During the same period, Filipino loggers left in large numbers for Indonesia to work in the logging camp of Kalimantan, while construction labourers worked in military bases in Viet Nam, Thailand, and Guam. Throughout the 1950s, 1960s, and early 1970s, Filipino professionals (e.g. nurses) left in significant numbers for the United States and Canada, initially to work in these countries, though they later settled there. What is unique about the 1970s and 1980s is that there are many more Filipinos who are willing to bear the human costs of overseas employment in exchange for material gains. Moreover, while migrant labourers before the early 1970s went to the countries mentioned above, contract workers in the second half of the 1970s and the 1980s sought employment in other areas where the demand for Filipino labour had just developed: the Middle East, Europe, Hong Kong, Japan, and Singapore.

The Middle East countries, which experienced an economic boom with the worldwide oil price increases of the early 1970s, are by far the largest recruiters of Filipino labour. Workers bound for this region accounted for 87 per cent of the 1981 land-based placements, a proportional increase of 47 per cent over the 1976 figures (Arcinas, 1984). The increasing importance of temporary labour flowing to the Gulf area is reflected in the proliferation of recruitment agencies servicing workers bound for the region and in the long queue of urban and rural residents in search of the opportunity to participate in the "Saudi" labour market. ("Saudi" is a term used colloquially to refer to the entire Gulf region, and to the conservable changes in the assets of rural villagers with at least one member in the Middle East.)

The material gains from Middle East employment, demonstrated by the lifestyles of a number of families linked at one time or another to a contract worker in the region, continue to attract Filipino workers, whether they be professionals or skilled labourers. Accounts of the travails of the migrant workers and the human tragedies which have befallen some of them and their families have had little effect on the aspirants who congregate around the announcement board of the Philippine Overseas Employment Administration (POEA). The queue of workers in search of Middle East employment has not been shortened by newspaper and tabloid accounts of hundreds or, maybe, thousands who have lost their money to illegal recruiters. Nor have they been affected by returnees' stories about the difficulties encountered in the host country or the unfaithfulness of the spouses of some fellow workers. If the human costs seem to have almost no impact on the decision-making process of many Filipinos who are aspiring to leave for the Gulf region, neither does the fact that the outflow of migrant labourers to this area will soon have to thin out as a result of the decline in demand for migrant labourers in many Middle Eastern countries.

Despite the significance of temporary labour emigration to the Gulf region in the minds of policy-makers and Filipino workers, and the need to assess the prevalence of the harrowing incidents printed in newspapers or aired over the radio or television, there has been very little scholarly work done on the topic. The Arcinas' State-of-the-Art Report on Filipino migration to the Gulf region (1984) noted that publications by the Ministry of Labout (e.g. the Institute of Labour and Manpower Studies), a few survey reports, papers, and news and feature articles are among the limited sources of information about overseas employment in the Middle East, particularly as regards the impact of such employment on the workers themselves and the families they leave behind. The study further notes that while employment opportunities in the Gulf region have been contracting as a result of the downtrend in construction activities, there is hardly any research on returnees and their adjustment. And this is in spite of the forecast made by international agencies like the International Labour Organisation (ILO) that there will be millions of families with "returned" workers in the Asian region by the end of the decade.

The dearth of information on the nature and impact of the overseas employment of Filipinos in the Middle East underscores the need to gather primary data that can provide the basis for future studies and comprehensive state programmes and policies. In response to this need, a survey of 536 migrant workers was conducted by members of the Department of Sociology of the University of the Philippines with funds from the United Nations University, in collaboration with researchers from Thailand, the Republic of Korea, India, Sri Lanka, Pakistan, and Bangladesh.

## Objective of the Survey and Methodology

The survey aims to explore and describe the odyssey of Filipino workers to the Gulf region from the pre-migration phase to their return to the Philippines upon completing their contracts. It was conducted among a sample of migrant workers who have returned to the Philippines after their employment in the Gulf region. While reliance on the capacity of the respondents to recall their experiences is a major limitation of the study, the choice of returnees as key informants was guided by the fact that only this group of workers could provide information about the complete cycle of labour migration to the Gulf region, including their adjustment to the home country. Moreover, returnees may have more insightful reflections on overseas employment, since they have established some distance, time-wise, from their stint abroad.

From October 1984 to January 1985, the country research team interviewed 506 workers and professionals who had completed at least one job contract in the Middle East and 30 workers who had returned to the country even before completing a contract. All 536 respondents were in the Philippines for at least three months prior to the interview.

Sampling was done purposively, although an attempt was made to obtain a probability sample in the Metro Manila area on the basis of the arrival forms of returnees which are kept at the Philippine Overseas Employment Administration's research office. The attempt failed, however, because hardly any returnees were found at the address stipulated on the arrival form. Most either gave the address of close relatives in Metro Manila or were temporarily away at the time of the interview.

The criteria for selecting the 506 respondents were: residence in Metro Manila versus provincial residence; and skilled status, as opposed to professional, technical, administrative, or clerical. Sex was also one of the criterion variables. However, the field interviewers found it difficult to meet their quota of female respondents, reflecting the fact that, relative to males, the proportion of females working in the Gulf region is quite insignificant.

About 54 per cent of the sample were interviewed in Metro Manila and 46 per cent in four provinces (Pampanga, Cavite, Bulacan, and Laguna) representing regions known to have the highest concentration of overseas workers in 1981 (Arcinas, 1984). Professional, technical, administrative, or clerical workers made up about 20 per cent of the sample. This proportion is close to that found in Sinay-Aguilar et al.'s 1981 study. In the original sampling design, the number of

**Table 1.** Distribution of respondents by province

| Province | No. |
|---|---|
| Central Luzon | |
| Pampanga | 111 |
| Bulacan | 33 |
| Southern Luzon | |
| Cavite | 71 |
| Laguna | 20 |
| Total provincial respondents | 235 |

**Table 2.** Distribution of survey respondents by occupation and region

| Occupation | Region | | | Total (%) |
|---|---|---|---|---|
| | Metro Manila | Southern Luzon | Central Luzon | |
| Professional/technical/ administrative/clerical | 90 | 9 | 16 | 115 (22%) |
| Skilled worker, including service worker | 181 | 82 | 128 | 319 (78%) |
| Total | 271 (54%) | 91 (18%) | 144 (28%) | 506 (100%) |

professionals coming from Metro Manila and from the provinces were supposed to be equal, but the interviewers found it difficult to meet their quota of professional respondents from the provinces. The final distribution of respondents by province and by occupation and region are presented in tables 1 and 2.

While this report is based on the survey results, the research team deemed it necessary to conduct follow-up unstructured interviews of special cases in order to qualify the generalizations in the chapters. Moreover, a simultaneous survey of farmers in a rice-growing community in Pampanga, where a significant group of returnees or migrant labourers reside, was carried out to generate ideas about the effects of overseas migration on the process of social differentiation in a community. The details of this survey are given in the chapter on the economic impact of overseas employment.

## Limitations of the Study

The study has at least three limitations. First, the one-shot structured interviews on which it relied heavily are an inadequate mode of collecting data on the complex dimensions of the worker's experience. Changes in values, for instance, cannot be inferred primarily from responses to specific or even to open-ended questions. The respondent may merely be forced to provide stock answers to questions he has hardly reflected on. When the questions touch on sensitive issues like marital infidelity, the respondent may even withhold information. It should be noted further that one-shot verbal responses, even to less sensitive questions, may not be completely reliable. Respondents, for instance, may underplay the negative impact of temporary separation on their families to convince themselves and other people, wittingly or unwittingly, that the years spent abroad were worth it.

Reliance on the returnee's capacity to recall his sojourn to the Middle East and the months before his departure is the second limitation of the study. His responses to the questions may, after all, be reinterpretations of his past on the basis of his current frame of mind. Moreover, recall is a poor way of obtaining information about income, savings, and remittances. Thus, the economic figures discussed in this report cannot be treated as precise estimates but only as rough indicators of variations in levels of income, savings, and investments.

Finally, since the sample was selected purposively, generalizations can only be made for the respondents and not for other returnees from the Middle East. However, the insights from the study may very well reflect the experiences of others who are not in the sample.

### Organization of the Report

The substantive discussion of the research findings is organized in seven main sections. The first presents a profile of the workers in the sample, while the second discusses the reasons for migration as well as the pre-migration phase. The third section deals with the migrant in the host country. The fourth section looks into the social and psychological impact of overseas migration on the worker and his family, while the fifth examines the economic impact. The sixth section explores the changes in life-style and values of workers. Finally, the last main section examines the employment of returnees, their adjustment to conditions in the home country, and their future plans. The concluding section summarizes the findings of the study and presents some recommendations for consideration by planners and policy-makers.

### Profile of Migrant Workers

A survey of the literature on migrant workers (Arcinas, 1984) reveals that about 75 per cent are males, between 25 and 50 per cent are in the 25–34 age-group, 40 to 80 per cent completed high school with 20 per cent obtaining college degrees, and 28 per cent are unmarried. Most of the workers are employed in Saudi Arabia. About one in five has a job which falls under the professional or technical category, while four in ten are highly skilled, with construction workers making up the bulk of this group. Although the proportions differ, the characteristics of the migrants in the study are consistent with those of workers in the other studies. This section describes the socio-demographic characteristics of the respondents in the sample, and also discusses findings pertinent to the last overseas employment.

## Socio-demographic Characteristics

### Sex

Consistent with the fact that the greatest demand for labour in the Gulf region is found in the construction sector, about 93 per cent of the Filipino workers in the sample are males. In general, Filipino women worked as household helpers, entertainers, nurses, and professionals in other parts of the world (e.g. Japan, Singapore, Hong Kong, European countries), accounting for the low proportion of this group in the sample.

Most of the female respondents in the sample reside in Metro Manila.

### Age

Contract workers in the sample were mostly at the prime age for the workforce at the time of the study, with those in the 25–34 age bracket making up 43 per cent of the total. This is higher than the country as a whole, where workers in this same age bracket constitute only 25 per cent of the labour force (Philippine Census, 1975). Eight out of ten workers were between the ages of 25 and 44. The oldest respondent in the sample was 62 years old, and the youngest 20. The mean age was 36 years.

Only an insignificant 5 per cent of the workers belonged to the old age category of 50 years and over.

### Marital Status

In the Philippines, where the family is a major source of social security and the prevailing system tends to stress kinship obligations, family members are all expected to pitch in whenever there is a need to do so. Contract workers, regardless of their marital status, for instance, remit money to their families to help defray expenses for the schooling of a sibling or to support ageing parents. But the drive to look for more lucrative jobs abroad is none the less stronger for the married who have the responsibility of being the main or, at times, the sole supporter of the family. It is, therefore, not surprising that three out of four contract workers in the sample were married. This is consistent with the findings of the 1983 Institute of Labour and Manpower Studies (ILMS) survey conducted under the auspices of the International Development Research Centre (IDRC) of Canada.

### Education

That the educational attainment of contract workers, as shown by available literature (Gibson, 1983; Jayme, 1979; ILMS 1981 survey), is way above the Filipino norm is confirmed by data from this study. The previous studies show one in every five contract workers to have completed high school. A high 81 per cent of this study's sample respondents were high-school graduates. Those with some college education constituted 12 per cent, which is about the same as the national figure (Arcinas, 1984). One out of every five contract workers in the sample was a college graduate and 1 per cent reached graduate-school level.

The educational attainment of the respondents varied significantly with their present regional address. Metro Manila, being the educational centre of the country, had the largest share of contract workers who were at least high-school graduates. Metro Manila also vied closely with Southern Luzon for the highest propor-

**Table 3.** Distribution of respondents by marital status

| Marital status | Percentage |
|---|---|
| Single | 21 |
| Married | 77 |
| Divorced/separated | 2 |
| Total | 100 |
| No. | 506 |

tion of contract workers with vocational training. The highest incidence of college graduates, however, was found among the contract workers living in the "Others" category (i.e. those temporarily residing in Metro Manila).

Regional Distribution and Geographical Mobility of Respondents

The distribution of contract workers by region reflects the manner by which the sample for the study was drawn. Because available literature on the subject shows that most of the workers placed in 1981 came from Metro Manila and the surrounding provinces, 54 per cent were interviewed in Manila and the other 46 per cent in the provinces of Pampanga and Bulacan in Central Luzon and in Cavite and Laguna in Southern Luzon.

Looking at the types of communities the contract workers were residing in at the time of the study, the data show that two out of three were living in urbanized areas – cities and municipalities – where there are more placement agencies.

A sizeable number of contract workers were geographically mobile before their overseas employment, with about half of them giving one other previous regional address, 16 per cent giving two other previous regional addresses, and 10 per cent having had a third previous regional address.

That some amount of geographical mobility characterized the contract workers before their overseas employment is supported by the finding that 60 per cent of them had lived in a type of community other than the present one, 17 per cent in two other types of community, and 8 per cent in three other types of community. It should be noted, however, that while some contract workers may have changed residence a number of times before they worked abroad, at the time of the study 66 per cent were living in the same region and type of community that they were born in.

Dependency Burden

At the time of the study, more than half of the contract workers had from one to four children each. About 18 per cent had from five to 16. Since the majority of them are still relatively young (86 per cent are between the ages of 20 and 44), theirs are not completed families. They can, therefore, be expected to have additional children later on.

As expected, more of the contract workers had children who were in school than working at the time of the study. If one considers the ratio of the number of children in school to the sum of the number of working children and at least one parent at work as a rough indicator of the dependency burden, then there is at least one working family member for every one child in school. This underestimates the dependency burden, since migrant workers have children who are not yet of school age. However, if one considers the fact that there may be other household and family members at work apart from the returnee and his working children, then the dependency burden can be assumed to be relatively light.

In terms of the number of working family members, while about four out of ten respondents had only one before their overseas stint, 49 per cent had from two to five family members sharing the burden of supporting the family. After working abroad, the number of respondents who had two to five employed family members decreased slightly to about 45 per cent. Twenty-nine per cent of the respondents reported they had two working members both before and after migration.

### Employment of Other Family Members Overseas

The proportion of households with family members employed in the Middle East after the respondents' overseas sojourn was higher by 18 per cent. One may conclude that the overseas experiences of some contract workers provided other members of their families with an opportunity to become familiar with the whole process of applying for and eventually acquiring overseas employment. As a result, the entire procedure was no longer as intimidating. For some of them, income derived from working abroad came in handy as a source of funds to cover the expenses of other family members.

**Variables Pertinent to Overseas Employment**

### Nature of Last Overseas Employment

Construction had the biggest number of contract workers among the different types of overseas employment in the Middle East. Almost four out of ten workers fell in this category in their last job abroad. The agriculture/mining/sales category had consistently been the smallest.

The nature of the last overseas job varied with age, sex, marital status, educational attainment, and regional address. The craft, transportation, and communications category had the highest proportion of workers in the 40–50 and over age bracket.

Females were concentrated in the professional and technical (57 per cent) as well as in the service sector (35 per cent). The former consisted mostly of nurses, while domestics made up the latter group. Males, on the other hand, were found mostly in the construction sector (40 per cent) and in the communication/transportation/craft sector (30 per cent).

Predictably, the educational attainment of the respondents was significantly associated with their last overseas job. The college graduates among them tended to be in the professional/technical/administrative sector and so did all of those who reached graduate-school level. Half of the respondents with vocational training, on the other hand, were communications, transportation, and craft workers. The construction sector, although a poor second to the professional, technical, administrative, and clerical group in having the next-highest proportion of respondents with vocational training, constituted more than half of the respondents with only an elementary schooling.

Professional, technical, administrative, and clerical workers were more likely to come from Metro Manila and regions other than Southern and Central Luzon. Belonging to this work sector were 45 per cent of contract workers living in the "Others" category (i.e. those residing temporarily in Metro Manila) and 29 per cent of those from Metro Manila. Workers in the communications, transportation, and craft sector, on the other hand, tended to be either from Southern (39 per cent) or Central Luzon (32 per cent). As expected, construction workers came from Central Luzon. Most of them hailed from the province of Pampanga, which produces some of the finest construction workers in the country. Southern Luzon contributed the largest share of contract workers in the service sector.

A significant relationship exists between marital status and last overseas job. The married, being the biggest group, were distributed in all job categories, although a relatively large proportion of them (38 per cent) were in construction. The single ones tended to concentrate in the professional/technical/administrative sectors (35 per cent). Half of the separated were in the service category, while the rest were evenly distributed among the professional, technical or administrative, communication, transportation, craft, and construction sectors. The widowed, on the other hand, were found only in the communication/transportation/craft (25 per cent) and in the service (75 per cent) sectors.

### Country of Employment

Saudi Arabia had the largest share of Filipino overseas workers among the countries of the Middle East. Countries with the fewest were Iran, Syria, Jordan, Lebanon, and Turkey.

### Type of Company Employing Overseas Workers

Contract workers in the Middle East were employed mainly by non-Arab companies. This is hardly surprising considering the deep involvement of multinational corporations in the development and movement of foreign workers at all skill levels, not only in the Middle East but in other parts of the world as well.

### Number of Times Employed in the Middle East

While some overseas workers have been employed in the Middle East up to nine times, two-thirds of these actually worked in the area for the first time. Most of the overseas workers who have had more than one job abroad were actually employed by the same company that had hired them for their previous job.

### Relation of Assigned Task to Nature of Last Job

Tasks assigned to overseas workers were generally related to the jobs for which they were contracted. For the 12 per cent, however, who performed work activities outside the scope of their job descriptions, the assignment of such tasks constituted a hidden form of exploitation.

### Duration of Employment Abroad

Contract workers were employed in the Middle East from one to 13 years, although the majority of them held on to their last overseas job for only one to three years.

Overseas contracts are difficult to come by, so once they are acquired overseas workers are generally determined to hold on to them until they expire. Only 4 per cent of the respondents came home without completing their last overseas con-

**Table 4.** Distribution of respondents by present address (percentages)

| Educational attainment | Present address | | | |
|---|---|---|---|---|
| | M. Manila | S. Luzon | C. Luzon | Others[a] |
| Elementary | 6 | 14 | 38 | 20 |
| High-school | 41 | 61 | 37 | 20 |
| Some college | 17 | 9 | 9 | 12 |
| College graduate | 25 | 6 | 13 | 41 |
| Postgraduate | 2 | 1 | 0 | 3 |
| Vocational | 9 | 9 | 3 | 4 |
| Total | 100 | 100 | 100 | 100 |
| No. | 196 | 89 | 145 | 76 |

a. Interviewed in Metro Manila.

tract, 2 per cent failed to finish their second-to-last contract, and 1 per cent their third-to-last. It should be noted that the workers who did not fulfil their last contract had completed previous contracts – hence their inclusion in the sample.

Where Contracts were Obtained

There is a negligible difference between the number of respondents who obtained their second-to-last or third-to-last contracts in the Middle East and those who acquired theirs in the Philippines. Twelve per cent got their second-to-last contract while they were still in the Middle East and 13 per cent got theirs in the Philippines. Among those who had a third-to-last contract, an equal number acquired them before they left the Middle East for home and when they were already home in the Philippines.

**Summary**

The migrant workers in the sample were mostly males who were at the prime age for the workforce at the time of the study. Slightly more than half were interviewed in Metro Manila, while the rest were from four provinces representing the regions known to have the highest concentration of migrant labourers (Central Luzon and Southern Luzon). A sizeable number of contract workers were geographically mobile before their overseas employment. Nevertheless, almost 273 were living in the same region where they were born at the time of the study.

Three out of four contract workers were married. They were better educated than the general population, with 81 per cent having a high-school diploma. However, compared to other migrant workers who feature in the literature, the proportion of workers in the sample with some college units was closer to the national average. As expected, respondents in Metro Manila were more educated than their counterparts in the other regions. The biggest group of workers in the Middle East were in construction. Only one out of five was a professional, technical, construction, or clerical worker on their last overseas stint. Most of the female, the single, the better-educated, Metro-Manila-based overseas workers fell in this category. The

**Table 5.** Distribution of respondents by last overseas job

| Last overseas job | Percentage |
|---|---|
| Professional/technical/administrative/clerical | 22 |
| Agriculture/mining | 1 |
| Transportation/communication | 16 |
| Craftsmen | 12 |
| Service and related workers | 11 |
| Construction | 37 |
| Others | 1 |
| Total | 100 |
| No. | 506 |

majority of the workers were employed in Saudi Arabia, mostly in non-Arab firms, and most worked for the first time for periods of from one to three years.

On the whole, the socio-demographic characteristics and employment status of the sample workers in the Middle East do not deviate from those of most workers in national and local studies. Having presented a profile of migrant workers, the next section looks back at the initial phase of their odyssey.

## The Pre-migration Phase

The Filipino workers who emigrated to the United States and Canada in the early 1960s sought their fortunes in the lands depicted by the educational system and first-hand accounts of other workers as flowing with milk and honey. Many more of their countrymen in later decades would have chosen the same path, given the images, success stories, myths, and illusions Filipinos in general have of life in the USA and Canada. However, the options have changed for today's workers, because there are many more who aspire to leave the country either temporarily or permanently, but the immigration authorities of the land of their dreams have closed their doors. The expansion of the labour market in the Middle East offered a reprieve from poverty and poor working conditions in the Philippines for many of these workers, but the countries where the jobs are found are hardly comparable to the United States and Canada. Instead of glowing accounts, harrowing stories about employees and the cultural practices of nationals in the host country are passed on to the aspirants. Apart from these stories, fellow workers who have been there gossip about the costs of temporary migration to families left behind. Yet, they patiently fall in line and risk being victimized by the illegal recruiters reported in the dailies and tabloids. What drives them to go, albeit temporarily? What ordeals do they have to go through, if indeed there are ordeals? What recruitment process do they go through to obtain their jobs? The answer to the first question is a reflection of structural problems in the society and elements of the culture. The answers to the second can provide the basis for a closer look at the institutions involved and for policies which, if implemented, could make life easier for those going through the first phase of their odyssey. This section explores

113

**Table 6.** Distribution of respondents by duration of their last overseas job

| No. of years | Percentage |
|---|---|
| 1 | 40 |
| 2 | 43 |
| 3 | 11 |
| 4–6 | 5 |
| 7–13 | 2 |
| Total | 100 |
| No. | 506 |

those factors most significant to the respondent sample's decision to leave home and work in the Middle East. It also describes their preparation for departure.

**Push Factors in Migration**

To the direct question of why they sought employment abroad, most of the respondents answered in the expected and obvious economic terms: in general, that they needed the money and that work abroad simply offered better pay. The motivations that can be inferred from this obvious response relate to what *more money* means or represents to this sample population, for it is equally obvious that leaving home, family, and the familiar, even for a definite contractual period, is no small matter, and that the push of economic reasons would have to be considerable to overcome the pull of other reasons for staying.

The most frequently stated reasons for seeking employment abroad have to do with basic economic needs and survival. The majority (65 per cent) first mentioned the fact that their incomes prior to migration were not sufficient to meet the daily needs of their families. Some (10 per cent) were unemployed or had unstable jobs at the time they sought employment overseas.

Other frequently stated reasons are related to consumption and other such needs. A relatively large proportion of the sample (30 per cent) mentioned, as a second reason for leaving, the desire to accumulate enough savings to acquire goods and properties which reflect a higher standard of living. Ownership of house and lot, car, and consumer durable items household appliances are the main examples.

Another strong second reason was the need to liquidate personal debts (29 per cent). It should be added at this point that, in all likelihood, such indebtedness has mostly occurred in the *process* of applying for a job abroad rather than as a precondition of the process. The costs to the individual applicant, as will be shown in the subsequent discussion of preparations for employment, are forbidding, and it is often a recourse of overseas work applicants to borrow or to mortgage their properties in order to raise the amounts needed to secure a work contract.

Lastly, the need to provide for a better future for their families, either through better and higher education for their children, or through capital accumulation for a business venture, was frequently stated. Better educational opportunities for the

Table 7. Distribution of respondents by reasons for working abroad (percentages)

| Reasons for working | Mention | | | | | | |
|---|---|---|---|---|---|---|---|
| | 1st | 2nd | 3rd | 4th | 5th | 6th | 7th |
| No work in the Philippines | 10 | 1 | — | — | — | — | — |
| Income not enough | 65 | 14 | 1 | — | — | — | — |
| Liquidate debts | 2 | 29 | 7 | 1 | 0.5 | — | — |
| Accumulate savings | 13 | 30 | 23 | 7 | 0.5 | 1 | — |
| Provide better future | 6 | 17 | 30 | 35 | 6 | 1 | — |
| Travel | 1 | 7 | 16 | 30 | 43 | 12 | 16 |
| Accumulate capital | 2 | 4 | 12 | 26 | 50 | 83 | 78 |
| Others | 1 | 1 | 1 | 1 | — | 3 | 4 |
| Total | 100 | 100 | 100 | 100 | 100 | 100 | 100 |
| No. | 506 | 471 | 422 | 337 | 226 | 114 | 18 |

children came in third in 30 per cent and fourth in 35 per cent of the multiple responses to this question. The accumulation of capital to be invested in a business was largely mentioned as a fourth to sixth reason in the sample, from which it can be deduced that the more immediate and shorter-term economic goals have been the prime considerations for the respondents. The desire simply to go abroad and travelling to other places came in largely as a fourth or fifth reason, reflecting an element of adventurism and daring in the decision to work overseas (table 7).

When asked, however, which of these reasons they considered were most important, 35 per cent of the respondents first-ranked providing for a better future for their children in terms of educational opportunities, followed by 30 per cent who considered earning enough money to meet their "families'" daily needs most important. For an almost equal 29 per cent, accumulating enough savings and capital for a higher standard of living was most important. A low 6 per cent held such considerations as travel, liquidation of debts, and other reasons as important.

Analysis of the responses of various groupings from among the sample showed very little difference in their ranking of the most important reasons for working abroad. Groups of respondents by age, sex, marital status, and regional address generally gave similar ratings of importance to their reasons for seeking employment overseas. Nor have such factors as country of work, number of times employed in the Middle East, nature of job obtained, or duration of the last overseas job seemed to have affected the respondents' ratings. Such homogeneity of response suggests that, for the sample group as a whole, the economic considerations have been so strong that they have levelled off major differences in personal circumstances. On only one factor have significant differences been found between groups, and that was in terms of educational attainment. Survey results show that respondents with elementary up to high-school level education tended to rate the accumulation of savings and capital for a higher standard of living as more important, whereas those who have had a college education tended to rate providing for a better education for their children as most important.

### The Recruitment Process

Acquisition of the Last Overseas Job

The majority of the respondents (44 per cent) learned of their last job through friends and through local intermediaries (31 per cent). Only some 21 per cent got their information from advertisements and notices printed in the newspapers. This suggests that information on job availability is still very much part of an informal network circulated among those in the know.

Securing the work contracts was largely done through recruitment agencies (76 per cent), with friends, either abroad or in the Philippines, only assisting in 10 per cent of cases. The least frequent course taken was to send applications directly to the Middle East, which was the case among only 3 per cent of the respondents.

Of the 384 workers who channelled their work applications through a recruitment agency, 79 per cent did so through licensed private agencies and 12 per cent through contracting firms. Only a small proportion of the total sample went to government recruiting channels (8 per cent), and an even smaller proportion (1 per cent) admitted to having gone to an unlicensed private agency. These figures support the findings of other studies on the dominance of private recruitment agencies in the migrant labour market.

More workers who admitted to having been recruited by unlicensed agencies obtained jobs in other Middle East countries outside Saudi Arabia (73 per cent out of 61), whereas all those hired by contracting firms were employed in Saudi Arabia.

A little more than half, or 53 per cent, of the sample respondents spent three months or less waiting time between inquiry about the job and their departure abroad. Of the total sample, a relatively high proportion (21 per cent) only had to wait one month, while 6 per cent had to wait for one-and-a-half years before they were finally able to leave.

More professional, technical, and administrative workers spent less than three months waiting time between inquiry and departure (72 per cent), while the longest waiting time of six months to one year, or more, was spent by proportionately more workers in the construction sector. The moderately long waiting period of three to six months was spent by a higher percentage of those in the service sector.

Related to this is the finding of significant differences between worker groups by educational attainment. College-level workers tended as a whole to spend less waiting time, with 65 per cent out of 164 of them waiting for less than three months. Elementary and high-school-level workers tended to wait longer, with a higher percentage of them waiting from six to twelve months or more.

The Contract

Almost all (98 per cent) of the respondents had an oral or written contract before departure. An almost equal proportion (98 per cent) had committed their signatures to some form of contract prior to their departure and, in 97 per cent of the cases, these were formal contracts with terms and conditions. A very small percentage (3 per cent) left on the strength of letters, informal contracts, and other such arrangements.

The majority of those who listed their provincial address as Metro Manila (98 per cent) did not sign their contracts before they departed abroad, whereas nearly all those from Southern Luzon, Central Luzon, and other places in the country did. This may suggest that the Metro Manilans as a group were so desperate to work overseas that they left without even a contract.

Most of the contracts (70 per cent) were executed in English, with a relatively high proportion in a mix of English and Arabic. Some 10 per cent were in English and Filipino and much smaller proportions of the sample had contracts in Filipino and Arabic. This suggests that in the majority of the cases in the sample, the terms of contract were comprehensible to the workers, since the majority of them can be assumed to understand English. A problem can only exist if the fine print of the contract is in complicated English.

In 70 per cent of the cases, the respondents received advice on their legal rights and obligations prior to signing their contracts. Still, the remaining 30 per cent, a relatively large proportion of the sample, claim not to have had this kind of assistance prior to committing themselves to the terms of their contracts.

Proportionately, more workers in the construction sector received advice on their legal rights and obligations and other terms prior to signing their work contracts than any other type of overseas workers (79 per cent as against an average of 64.8 per cent for all other job categories), while proportionately more in the group of professional, technical, administrative, and clerical workers did not receive such advice (41 compared to an average of 27 per cent for all other work groups).

This seems to be directly related to the finding of significant differences between groups by educational attainment, since, more than any other group, workers of elementary-level schooling received advice on their contract terms, with 81 per cent against the 66.6 per cent of high-school and college-level workers. Also, more college-level workers did *not* receive advice (38 per cent), whereas an average of only 27 per cent of elementary and high-school-level workers admitted to having no advice.

The presumption here being that educational attainment is directly related to job nature (i.e. more elementary-level workers in the professional, technical, and administrative sector), it would appear that greater care is given to advising the less educated and lower-skilled workers, whereas highly educated and skilled workers are less likely to receive advice, probably because they are presumed to be more knowledgeable on such matters.

Among those who received advice, the most common (57 per cent) source was the model contract and other such material made available by both private and government agencies. Friends and relatives made up the next best source at about 15 per cent, while advice received directly from voluntary agencies and special government service centres was obtained by about 28 per cent.

The majority of those who received prior advice (57.4 per cent) claimed this proved adequate and a small proportion (4.7 per cent) said it was inadequate. An even smaller proportion (2.3 per cent) claim to have had misleading advice, in the sense that the contract terms turned out to be so different that the advice became useless.

In a few instances (less than 1 per cent), the terms of the contract had to be explained by friends and outside sources, and this explanation was generally considered adequate.

Almost all the respondents (91 per cent) expressed satisfaction with the contract terms but of the 9 per cent who did not, a little more than half (53 per cent) preferred not to inform the authorities, reasoning that to complain would be useless, the problem was minor, or that sanctions might ensue.

## The Documents for Migration

Of the total sample respondents, 73 per cent had their passports secured by the recruitment agency and 18 per cent by the hiring company. Only 9 per cent had to apply for their passports themselves. About the same proportions were shown in the securing of visas, with 76 per cent secured by the agency, 20 per cent by the hiring company, and 4 per cent by the individual applicant.

Tickets to the country of employment were obtained by the agency 74 per cent of the time, by the company 23 per cent, and by the applicants 3 per cent.

Medical and other clearances were similarly largely obtained by the agencies (51 per cent), but here a relatively larger proportion of the respondents (39 per cent) had to get these documents. The company intervened in 15 per cent of the cases.

Those who dealt with the issuance of their own documents for migration generally took the longest time in securing their passports and visas. Waiting time for these documents was about equal – from two weeks (36–38 per cent) to one month (62–65 per cent) – with a few isolated cases waiting for as long as nine to ten months. Those who secured their passports in a week made up 18 per cent of the sample, while a proportionately larger share (21 per cent) got their visas in this same period. Medical and other documents were easier to obtain, with 67 per cent of the respondents receiving them in one week and 74 per cent within two weeks.

## Pre-departure Expenses

Close to half (48 per cent) of the respondents who obtained their own passports spent from P150 to P500 or US$8.3 to US$22 (P18.00 = US$1.00). This is about the range that could reasonably be expected as the actual costs from official and standard processing fees at the Ministry of Foreign Affairs. A relatively large proportion (26 per cent), however, spent from P1,300 to P2,000 or about US$111 for their passports, as usually happens when the responsibility for obtaining this document is entrusted to travel agents, who are often employees of a licensed travel agency, moonlighting on such work. Based on their knowledge of the official ropes, these agents guarantee the securing of passports in one or two weeks, facilitated of course by additional "fees." The manufacture of fake revenue statements, bank account records, affidavits of employment, and even birth certificates is not uncommon at this stage, and may be thrown in by the "friendly" agent as part of the service fee. Since there are no regulations governing such informal arrangements, the agent can, and often does, charge exorbitant amounts, thus explaining the incidence of two cases in the sample in which as much as P9,000 ($500) was paid by the respondent for passports alone.

Only a very small number of respondents (3, or 0.6 per cent) in the total sample reported having paid anything at all for their visas, and this ranged from as low as P120 ($6.7) to as much as P4,000 ($222). Again, the incidence of such cases, even though quite low, reflects the generally risky conditions in the pre-migration phase, particularly for the unwary and uninformed applicant, since no fees are demanded for the issuance of visas to the Middle East.

Similarly, a very small number, comprising 0.4 per cent of the total sample, reported having paid for their tickets to their country of work, whereas the standard practice is for the hiring company to defray the expenses for the transportation of contract workers to the job site.

Of those respondents who paid for their clearances themselves, the majority (41 per cent) spent from P100 to P200 ($5.55 to $11.00), and nearly all (84 per cent) spent P300 ($16.70) or less for such clearances. The largest amount was paid by one respondent, P3,000 ($166.70).

Asked to sum up their expenses prior to migration, the largest proportion of the sample (39 per cent) comprised those who paid from P2,000 ($111.1) to P6,000 ($333). Still, almost 28 per cent claimed to have spent P1,000 ($55) or less. The largest recorded expense in the sample was by one respondent who spent P75,000 ($4,167).

Proportionately more males spent less before migration than females. Of the 423 male workers, 47 per cent paid P10,000 ($555.6) or less, whereas 46 per cent of the 37 female workers spent between P10,000 and P15,000. There was also a higher incidence of female workers than males who spent between P10,000 and P15,000 and above ($555.6 to $833.3).

As a group, workers who were 50 years old and older tended to spend less on preparations for migration than all other age-groups. The highest incidence of those who paid P10,000 ($555.6) to P15,000 ($833.3) was in the 20–29 age-group.

As a group, workers from Metro Manila tended to spend less on their preparations for migration than those from outside the capital. Of the Metro Manilans, 55 per cent spent P2,000 ($111.1) or less, as against only 40 per cent of workers from elsewhere. The majority of those from Central Luzon paid a higher P2,000 ($111.1) to P5,000 ($277.8), and the highest incidence of those who paid P10,000 ($555.6) to P15,000 ($833.3) and more is in the groups from Central Luzon and outside Luzon.

About equal proportions of those deployed in Saudi and those outside Saudi Arabia spent P2,000 or less, but of those who spent the high amount of P5,000 to P10,000, a higher percentage was among those deployed within Saudi Arabia.

Those who relied on the recruitment agencies for the processing of their documents comprised some 55 per cent of the sample. For these services, almost 37 per cent of the subsample spent from P3,000 to P5,000. The next largest share went to those who paid lesser amounts, ranging from P1,000 to P3,000 (30 per cent). The highest recorded payment to an agency was for P20,000.

In 67.3 per cent of the instances where the respondents paid the agency, the applicants received an itemized report of where the money was to be spent, while the remaining 32 per cent did not.

The bulk of the amounts paid to the recruitment agency presumably went to the processing of travel papers, as this was the expense item first mentioned by 85 per cent of the subsample. Next on the list are the recruitment agency fee and other charges for the services of the agency, followed by the performance bonds on the work contracts. Other expense items in the list were contributions to the welfare fund, job requisites such as uniforms, insurance, and others.

Whether Respondents Paid Other Intermediaries

Only a small proportion of the total sample (8 per cent) made payments to other intermediaries. In 67 per cent of such cases, the amounts were for P1,000 or less, with a few (20.8 per cent) paying between P1,001 and P2,000. One respondent paid as much as P10,000.

## Amount Spent for Personal Effects

Expenditures for personal items prior to departure amounted to P1,000 or less for close to 87 per cent of this subsample of respondents. Most of them spent only P500 or less for their personal effects, but in two or three isolated cases as much as between P4,000 and P7,000 was spent.

## Financing of Overseas Employment

Responses to the question of sources of funds for securing overseas work can be classified in three general categories: savings, loans, and mortgaged properties. Thus categorized, the bulk of the responses fall into two nearly equal proportions, with loans having an edge over savings at about 53 against 41 per cent.

The distribution of the responses suggests that these sources may have been resorted to at various stages of the application process; that is, as one source is exhausted, another is utilized. Thus, savings as a whole were mentioned first by 45 per cent of the respondents and second by only 18 per cent, while interest-free family loans were mentioned first by 36 per cent of the respondents and second by 49 per cent.

Savings consist of personal savings, savings from local employment, and savings from a previous overseas job. The majority (37 per cent) reported having drawn from personal savings much more than from the other two types.

Loans consist of interest-free loans from family relatives and friends, and formal loans without interest, the former making up the large share of the responses in the first and second mention, and the latter in the second and third mention.

The number of respondents who mentioned mortgages of their property as a source of funds was minimal at 3 per cent, suggesting that only a few had such resources available to convert to cash as needed.

Asked as to which source of funds they considered was most important, 39 per cent of the respondents cited interest-free family loans, and a close 37 per cent mentioned personal savings. A relatively large proportion (16 per cent) also mentioned interest loans, but on the whole the respondents appear to consider access to cash and credit on easy terms as most important when applying for overseas work.

A total of 377 respondents, or about 75 per cent of 506 in the sample, reported having borrowed money to finance the process. Of these, 80 per cent had loans which were said to have been interest-free, close to 10 per cent were on interest rates of 10 per cent or less, and 9 per cent on interest rates of 10–20 per cent. Four respondents reported having had loans with an excessive interest rate of 80 per cent. In general, however, the respondents in the sample appear to have availed themselves of loans on friendly terms.

## Pre-departure Testing, Training, and Orientation

Only a little more than half of the sample (54 per cent) underwent some form of examination before being awarded their jobs. In 59 per cent of the cases, the tests were administered by the recruitment agency, while 36 per cent were by the hiring company. Government officers and service agencies had a very minimal 4 per cent participation in this stage of the process. This implies that the level of professional, technical, and other skills of the worker being hired is largely the responsibility of the private sector and is left to their different screening processes, rather than being based on a standardized system of rating.

Only 33 per cent of the respondents attended any training programme prior to migration, and these were mostly job-related, i.e. in preparation for the overseas job, although 17 per cent of the subsample said their programme was for personal and skills improvement. Sponsors of the training programmes consisted largely of the recruitment agencies (53 per cent) and of the hiring company (36 per cent). Again, government offices were reported to have had a very minimal role (4 per cent) in the formal training and preparations for overseas work.

Construction workers showed higher percentages for test-taking (65 per cent) and training programmes attendance (42 per cent) than all other occupational groups, which averaged only 48 per cent for test-taking and 28 per cent for training attendance. Conversely, professional, technical, and administrative workers showed the lowest percentage for undergoing these two procedures. Only 34 per cent of this sector took any tests and 20 per cent any training programmes, whereas all other work groups combined averaged 59 and 37 per cent for testing and training respectively.

It would also appear that the extent of pre-migration testing and training programmes is related to differences in the levels of education of would-be migrants. Elementary and high-school-level workers appear to be more tested and more likely to undergo training prior to migration than college-level workers, with the former having a combined average of 61 per cent for testing against the latter's 43 per cent, and of 39 per cent for training as against 79 per cent for college-level workers.

Since testing and training are two procedures which are usually done ostensibly to screen and standardize the skill level of workers, their relatively low incidence in groups with higher-level education and skill could mean that their local qualifications and skill levels are generally assumed to be standardized. In contrast, the higher incidence of testing and training among the less educated and skilled groups could mean that local qualifications and standards do not suffice as an immediate basis for placement. It is possible that such tests and training programmes have been devised better to meet the standards of the hiring company, based on the recruitment agencies' experience.

Other findings, however, suggest equally plausible reasons for this. In relation to testing and training, it is noteworthy that groups in the construction and service sectors, which were among the more tested and trained, also tended to spend larger amounts prior to migration. Combined, they made up 23 per cent of those who paid P5,000 ($277.8) to P10,000 ($555.6), whereas proportionately a much smaller share of the professional, technical, and administrative workers paid this much. The suggestion here is that, in general, the greater costs shouldered by construction and service workers could have been due in part to the added costs of testing and training, not to mention the "grease money" paid to facilitate the acquisition of jobs for which they were not qualified.

In general, the respondents claim to have been given information on the important aspects of their working stay in a foreign country, consisting of facts about the host country such as climate, laws, and customs, as well as about the legal rights

121

of overseas workers, travel formalities and communication with their families, and, to a lesser extent, about contacts with the Philippine consulate and about the Middle East as a whole. On average, 82 per cent had information on all these aspects. The main source of information of this sort is the recruitment agency, with an average share of 40 per cent, followed by the hiring company at close to 26 per cent. Government agencies and friends, both those who have been employed in the Middle East and local ones, had nearly equal shares of around 6 per cent each. The least mentioned source of information is the printed material, with only 0.2 per cent of the sample claiming to have referred to it.

Generally, the information obtained from all these sources was reported to have been adequate, with the possible exception of information about the Philippine consulate, which was scanty to begin with.

Illegal Recruitment

A relatively large proportion (17 per cent) of the sample admitted to having been victimized through fraudulent practices by agencies and other recruiters. In 33 per cent of these cases, the applicant paid their fees but did not secure employment. Others (25 per cent) were recruited by agencies operating illegally. Still others (21 per cent) had contracts that were not followed once they were working abroad. The smallest number (9 per cent) mentioned the overcharging of fees and payments for services.

Redress was sought by less than half (46 per cent) of the victims. Of those who did, 34 per cent confronted the agency and approximately equal proportions complained to the authorities, sued the agency, or formally lodged complaints with the government offices. These actions, however, were by and large unsuccessful, with only 44 per cent having had redress.

Those who did not seek any redress were influenced by such considerations as: (a) the smallness of the amount of money involved in proportion to the bother of following the matter up (30 per cent); (b) lack of evidence (18 per cent); (c) no legal assistance (12 per cent); (d) the intercession of friends for the agency involved (65 per cent); and other reasons.

**Concluding Notes**

The findings discussed in this section suggest that most of the respondents did not go through the much-publicized difficulties experienced by the migrant labourers at the hands of recruitment agencies and the bureaucracy, not to mention illegal recruiters. The majority found their contracts to be satisfactory. Most of them who obtained their jobs through recruiting agencies did not pay the exorbitant fees which have been reported to be as high as P20,000; they paid between P1,000 and P6,000, which is relatively low compared to the fees workers pay today. While the respondents borrowed money, very few had to pay high interest rates. It is easy to conclude, therefore, that, in general, all is well with the recruitment process and the institutions involved in this phase are functioning efficiently. A closer look at the conditions of the majority, however, helps checks any temptation to reach such a sweeping conclusion. The lowest pre-migration costs were incurred by those who went to the Middle East before the 1980s. During that period, the supply of workers was still relatively low and companies were known even to shoulder the full pre-departure expenses. Workers who last worked overseas in the 1980s had to pay the fees in the upper limit of the range. For many of these workers P3,000 to P6,000 is still a substantial sum, which more than 50 per cent had to borrow. What is perhaps disconcerting is the fact that workers who belong to the majority and who left at about the same time paid different amounts to get to their destinations. Those from the provinces, who were generally of a lower economic status, tended to pay more than those from Metro Manila, many of whom were professional, technical, administrative, or clerical workers. The discrepancies in total amounts paid, and even in fees given to recruitment agencies, reflect the inability of government institutions to implement uniform fees.

An assessment of the pre-departure phase in terms of the financial and human costs involved cannot be based solely on the plight of the majority. For as long as there is a sizeable group of workers who are victimized by illegal recruiters and opportunistic travel agencies or local intermediaries, the institutions involved in the process are still to be held accountable. When almost two out of ten workers become victims, the state needs to work harder to impose sanctions on the recruiters. This becomes imperative when one considers the concrete effects of illegal recruitment on would-be workers. One of the special cases, who used to lease three hectares of ricelands, for instance, has been reduced to a hired farm-hand after losing his land on account of a loan paid to unscrupulous fake recruiters. This is a mild case compared that of the victims described in the tabloids, whose obsession to land an overseas "Saudi" job was transformed into the drive to seek revenge against those who had wronged them.

## The Workers in the Host Country

Almost every Filipino migrant suffers some kind of culture shock when he migrates to the Arab world, a cultural context totally alien to his own. No amount of pre-departure briefing seems adequate to prepare the Filipino contract worker for this. The language barrier appears almost insurmountable, though this is somehow alleviated by the ease with which many Filipinos learn basic Arabic words, and the reciprocal efforts of their local superiors to speak in English. To the language problem must be added the strict local Islamic prohibitions against hard liquor, gambling, and even talking to Arab women. The ascetic environment into which the normally carefree Filipino worker is suddenly thrust creates a highly stressful cultural situation, which is perhaps eased only by the fact that Filipino workers tend to live and work together as a community in or near work sites. Such a situation permits them to go through the process of cultural adjustment and survival as a group. The advantage of this is that adjustment to the alien surroundings is accomplished more rapidly. The drawback is that as they come to live and behave like a ghetto, they can also become easily the object of racist attacks by local inhabitants.

In newspaper accounts and informal discussions, migrant returnees tell harrowing stories of being treated and ordered around like slaves by Arab supervisors and bosses. They talk of being stoned and kicked by local youths who openly manifest their deep resentment and contempt for Asian guest workers. A number of Filipino migrant workers, noticing the favourable manner in which Asian Islamic workers are regarded, have, as a result, embraced Islam in an effort to improve their personal situation in the host country.

The situation of the new Filipino migrant worker in an Arab country is clearly one of profound insecurity. Combined with homesickness and a feeling of isolation, the situation can lead to enormous depression which sometimes results in the worker inflicting injuries on himself. Fortunately, these cases are few. The Filipino contract worker is still widely praised for his resilience and adaptability. Returnees who often go through harrowing experiences of physical deprivation do not hesitate to conclude that, in general, the Filipino is a survivor. Accounts of Filipino workers in Libya and Iraq, escaping from virtual imprisonment in harsh work camps, and helping fellow Filipinos, have become legendary.

## The Respondent upon Arrival in the Host Country

Most workers who were first-time travellers were anxious about what would confront them upon their immediate arrival in the land of alien customs and traditions. However, their initial anxieties were relieved by the fact that almost all the sample respondents (95 per cent) were met at the airport. Of these, the majority (83 per cent) were met by representatives of the hiring company and the rest by Filipinos and others.

Asked whether they encountered any problems in their first few days in the Middle East, only 18 per cent answered yes; the principal problems were usually in the form of homesickness, with the next most common problem being with the accommodation and facilities. A few (12 per cent out of 99) had problems with their travel documents, while relatively few had only minor problems such as difficulties with their baggage and the like. Surprisingly, only one mentioned problems with communication and six with their contracts.

The majority of the respondents (80 per cent) spent one week or less after their arrival waiting to start work, and a relatively large proportion (12 per cent) said they had no such waiting time. Only a few (7 per cent) waited from two weeks to as long as one month.

### The Signing of a Second Contract in the Host Country

Almost one out of five workers in the sample (N=117) reported that they were made to sign a second contract. The terms of this second contract largely covered all the significant aspects of work conditions, compensation, benefits and other privileges; only a few included such details as overtime hours, job descriptions, and insurance benefits.

The highest incidence was among professional, technical, and administrative workers (35 per cent), followed by those in the service category. The smallest number of workers who signed a second contract was in the construction sector.

Many of those who had a second contract had them in Arabic (33 out of 117), some in Arabic with translation (25 per cent) and in English (24 per cent), a few in English with translation (16 per cent), and even one in Filipino. A surprising majority, however, 65 per cent, claimed to have been proficient in the language used.

The second contract was explained to seven out of ten workers, mostly by company representatives and much less frequently by fellow Filipino workers and non-

124

Filipino co-workers. A significant proportion signed the second contract without the benefit of an explanation.

Most of those who had a second contract considered the terms and conditions of both contracts on the whole as equal, with a smaller proportion seeing the first contract as better and a still smaller proportion thinking the first was worse.

Fifteen workers who felt signing a second contract was unfair said that they sought redress, largely by complaining to company officials (7), to the Philippine consulate (3), to the labour office of the host country (2), and to government channels (1). A few (2) refused to work and used other such means. Only three respondents said their actions proved successful. Those who did not seek redress at all (4) but felt uneasy about signing another contract were convinced of the futility of further action, one even mentioning the difficulty of finding witnesses against Arabs.

**Living and Working Conditions in the Host Country**

Type of Living Quarters

The largest group in the sample consisted of those billeted in barracks (41 per cent), followed by those in condominiums (18 per cent). A very few were housed in ships' cabins (3 per cent) and in hotel rooms (5 per cent). In the majority of cases, the company owned the workers' living quarters (97 per cent) which were near the job site (72 per cent).

Number of Persons per Room

Those for whom accommodation meant a room with four persons or less comprised 55 per cent of the sample, while the rest had rooms of five to eight persons. Mostly, these rooms had their own toilet facilities (65 per cent). Almost all respondents (91 per cent) shared their rooms with fellow Filipinos, although some rooms were also shared with foreigners.

Professional, technical, and administrative workers were split into almost exactly equal groups of those who had rooms for one or two persons only (33 per cent) and those who had rooms for five to eight persons (34 per cent). All the other groups were largely housed in rooms for five to eight, with workers in the construction sector showing the highest incidence at 93 per cent.

Conditions of Facilities

On the whole, the facilities, which included air conditioning, water facilities, and electricity, were rated as good (87, 82, and 90 per cent respectively). Those who rated them as adequate made up 7, 12, and 9 per cent, while a few (6, 6, and 1 per cent) thought them poor.

Generally, meals were most often said to be regular and palatable. These were most often taken at mess halls (95 per cent), with only a few having meals at restaurants (3 per cent) and their own rooms (2 per cent).

The majority of workers of all groups thought their meals in the Middle East had been palatable, particularly the construction workers, almost all (91 per cent) of whom said this was so. Of those who did not think the meals were palatable, the proportions were highest among the communications, transport, and craft workers

**Table 8.** Distribution of respondents by frequency of remittances

| Frequency of remittances | Percentage |
|---|---|
| Monthly | 73 |
| Twice a month | 3 |
| Once a month | 8 |
| Once in 3 months | 8 |
| When a Filipino returns | 3 |
| Less than 3 times a year | 2 |
| Others | 3 |
| Total | 100 |
| No. | 473 |

(21 per cent) and workers in the service sector (20 per cent). It would thus appear that construction workers as a group were easiest to please, very likely because in most construction sites where Filipinos predominate, the hiring company engages Filipino cooks to prepare the Filipino workers' meals.

Religious Facilities

To 45 per cent of the respondents, the work site offered no religious facilities of any kind. For 24 per cent, there was mention of a mosque, and for 23 per cent of a chapel or church. A few (6 per cent) mentioned improvised chapels within company premises, and fewer still (2 per cent) mentioned charismatic fellowships. The mention of makeshift chapels and secret charismatic group meetings was most common among the construction workers, who were often placed at work sites where hardly any facilities for community life exist. Communication, transport, and craft workers mentioned mosques most often (28 per cent) as being present at their job sites, whereas highest mention of other religious facilities was by the professional, technical, and administrative workers, who were more likely to be placed at the urban centres, where a greater diversity of forms of religious worship may have been available.

Whether Respondents Read Newspapers

A very high percentage (86.8 per cent) of the respondents said they read the papers while in the host country. Of these, most frequent mention was made of a Philippine daily, the *Bulletin Today*, other Philippine tabloids, and *Malaya* and other opposition tabloids.

Frequency of Leisure Activities

Generally, the pattern of responses on the frequency with which overseas workers engaged in various leisure activities while staying in the Middle East suggests that for the majority of them there were marked changes in the type of activities that they undertook. For many, such activities as going to church, joining picnics, watching movies and sightseeing occurred with much less frequency than at home, whereas listening to the radio and watching television were engaged in more frequently than at home. Only around 15 per cent of the respondents said they engaged in these activities abroad as often as they did at home. Some activities meant greater frequency for some and less for others, like sports, of which 45 per cent said they had more, while 41 per cent said they had less than at home. Similarly, watching television increased for 46 per cent of the respondents, while it decreased for 43 per cent.

Most respondents (76 per cent) watched movies in English and only a few (5) watched Filipino movies. Some 13 per cent watched a mix of English and Filipino movies and only very few (3 per cent) watched Arab ones.

The majority of the respondents (67 per cent) denied having watched X-rated movies while in the Middle East. This may be due to the fact that the interviewers were females and male respondents were inhibited from telling the truth. Not surprisingly, only one of the female respondents admitted to having watched such movies at all, whereas 35 per cent of the males did. By age-groups, more of those in the 20–29 category (44 per cent and in the 50-plus category (32 per cent) admitted to having watched X-rated movies, something which the 30–49 age-groups largely denied.

Conditions of Work v. Expectations

For the majority of the respondents, work conditions (e.g. job, salary, work hours, overtime, home leave, etc.) proved better than they had expected. From 20 to 40 per cent of respondents said conditions were equal to or less than expected. Only 18 of these respondents considered these deviations from expectations as a breach of contract, and, among these, only ten sought redress, mostly through complaints to the Philippine consulate (3), refusal to work (2), direct complaints to the company (2) and to the labour office of the host country (1), legal suit (1), and others. Of these cases, only three were successful in reinstating their rights. Those who preferred not to seek redress did so because they were afraid of the consequences (3), they felt action was useless (1), and other reasons (2).

When asked to assess whether their contracts were better than those of other nationalities, 37 per cent thought Filipino workers had contracts similar to those of other nationalities. A relatively high proportion (26 per cent) even held that Filipinos had better contracts, although a close third (23 per cent) thought foreigners had the better deals. The basis for evaluation was mainly the pay and here it is held by many (24 per cent) that, compared to most Asians, Filipinos were better paid, though a larger number (35 per cent) say that their pay was the same as other foreigners.

**Social Contacts with Other Ethnic Groups and Nationalities**

Workers from Southern Luzon appear to predominate as co-workers among the sample respondents, although a relatively large proportion of the respondents also mentioned workers from Central Luzon. Those from Metro Manila were least often mentioned as co-workers. This may suggest that Metro Manilans were either more dispersed in their countries of work or did not tend to cluster in particular job sites.

As in the job site, workers from Southern Luzon were most often mentioned as sharing the respondents' living quarters, followed by those from Central Luzon. Again, workers from Metro Manila were least often mentioned.

With respect to foreigners, Pakistanis and Indians were most frequently mentioned first by the respondents (28 per cent) as having been co-workers. Americans, Canadians, and Europeans constituted the next most mentioned nationalities by 18 per cent of all respondents, followed by Thais and Indonesians at 10 per cent. Least often mentioned were the Chinese (only 0.3 per cent). Workers from the host country were also seldom mentioned at 8 per cent, even if 53 per cent of respondents had Arabs as co-workers. However, respondents described their relationship with Arabs as good, with only 11 per cent reporting poor relations with workers from the Arab nations.

The majority of respondents (59.2 per cent) did *not* share living quarters with foreigners, but of those that did, the relationship was generally described as good. In only two instances was there mention of negative experiences with foreigners.

Significantly, more workers from Metro Manila (82 per cent) shared rooms with foreigners than all other groups based at provincial addresses. Less often found to have shared quarters with foreigners were those from Central Luzon (33 per cent).

On the whole, the majority of workers did not share their rooms with foreigners, particularly those in the professional, technical, and administrative sector (64 per cent). Workers in the services sector, however, differed from all other groups in that the majority of them (61 per cent) did share their rooms with foreigners, most probably because these workers were placed in highly urbanized areas, where there were hospitals, hotels, and the like.

## Evaluation of the Consulate

The majority of the respondents (79 per cent) contacted the Philippine consulate while in the Middle East, although service workers were less likely to contact it than professional, technical, administrative, communication, and transport workers.

Various reasons were given for such contact, but chief among them were matters related to work (39 per cent), to the renewal of passports (37 per cent), and to taxes (18 per cent). Only once was there mention of getting information on the Philippine political situation.

The majority of those who did not contact the consulate reasoned that they did not have the time (35.2 per cent), that the consulate was inaccessible (26 per cent), and that they felt doing so was futile (12 per cent).

Evaluation of the Philippine consulate in the Middle East was generally positive with regard to the handling of work problems (55 per cent), the social life of migrants (53 per cent), and emergency cases (54 per cent). However, evaluations were mostly negative in two areas: remittance and communication with workers' families (56 and 54 per cent respectively). A few workers who were interviewed claim that they refused to contact the consulate because they had heard that other workers who had appealed for help in work-related problems complained that their pleas had fallen on deaf ears.

While workers generally gathered informally to talk, they met hardly at all to organize themselves. Nearly all the respondents (91 per cent) said they were not allowed to organize. Of the 46 who said they were, the majority were members of an organization. Still, 38 per cent did not join such an organization even when it was allowed.

When asked what migrant workers usually talk about when they gather, the largest number (34 per cent) mentioned family-related topics. Work-related topics followed with 24 per cent of the responses, then conditions in the Philippines with 20 per cent. The least mentioned topic of discussion was the consumption of goods.

## Observations

More than 94 per cent of all respondents said they managed to adjust to the new environment. As for the nature of the exertion required by their overseas jobs, the most universal assessment was that the work was lighter and much easier than that required by jobs in the Philippines. Even physical adjustment seemed easy. Apart from the prevalent complaint about extremes of temperature (too hot during the day and too cold in the evening), the great majority (92 per cent) said they do not remember getting sick more often abroad than in the Philippines.

The absence of pork from the local cuisine and the monotony of having chicken at every meal were disconcerting to many workers, but still the majority of the survey respondents found their meals palatable. This is to be attributed to the fact that in most job sites Filipino cooks were brought in to prepare the food. In the smaller labour-contracting establishments, on the other hand, the workers were usually allowed to cook their own meals.

Living arrangements were also generally found satisfactory, though many have complained about the inadequacy of the sleeping facilities during the first few weeks after their arrival in the host country. About 90 per cent of those interviewed said they shared rooms with other Filipinos, which probably partly explains why adjustment was fairly easy.

Homesickness, however, was never totally overcome. Asked what activities they undertook to ward off homesickness and loneliness, 42 per cent of the returnees interviewed said they watched films on video recorders or else listened to music, 22 per cent said they usually socialized with other Filipinos, and 20 per cent preferred to stay in their rooms to write letters or tape messages to their families.

The first thing that the overseas contract worker worries about as soon as he settles down in his new job is how to send money as quickly as possible to his family back home. In-depth interviews conducted among some respondents revealed that, in a number of instances, workers choose not to wait until they receive their first pay. They take the initiative of borrowing some money from fellow workers to send back to their families during the crucial months. To appreciate this anxiety, we must turn to the circumstances of the family left behind.

## The Migrant and His Family: Problems of Adjustment

The Filipinos who become overseas contract workers in the Gulf region are typically heads of families, mostly young husbands who are often just starting to build a home for their growing families. While the turn-of-the century Filipino migrants to America knew that they might never see their country again, today's overseas workers are conscious that their jobs abroad should not take them away from their families for more than two years at most. This feeling is even more intensely shared by the families who are left behind. The prevailing sense is that the father's (or in some cases, the mother's) absence is nothing more than just a temporary break, and that the bonds of family life must be kept as strong as ever.

The discussion that follows revolves mainly around the situation encountered by the migrant's family at the personal and psycho-social levels during the period of absence, and how they adjust to this new situation.

## Management of the Households

The phenomenon of "single-parenting" has become pervasive in Philippine society since the advent of overseas jobs. The parent who stays home to assume sole responsibility for the whole family may either be the wife or the husband, and, in some instances, even the worker's own parents. Many Filipino women who now work as domestics in Hong Kong, Singapore, Italy, Spain, and other European countries typically leave their children and their homes to their husband. In male-chauvinistic Philippine society, these husbands are sometimes jokingly called *tatay-nanay* (literally, "daddy-mummy"). On the other hand, the vast majority of those who have gone to the Gulf countries (93 per cent) are male Filipinos, and they generally have no hesitation about leaving their homes to the single-handed management of their wives. The latter are also sometimes referred to as *matay*, a combination of *mama* (mother) and *tatay* (father).

As might be expected, more than 72 per cent of the migrants' households were left to the care of the spouses and 24 per cent in the care of parents, while the rest had either a sibling or older children to manage the household in their absence. The majority (75 per cent) of the households of male workers were managed by their wives, while a greater proportion (56 per cent) of those of the female workers was managed by their parents. This simply reflects the fact that most of the males in the sample were married while most of the females were single.

Somewhat more interesting were the leads provided by the in-depth interviews that were conducted with a few of the respondents. For example, it seemed natural to most married respondents who were still staying with their parents prior to their departure abroad to leave their spouse and young children with their parents rather than allow the wife to go back to her own family in the meantime. It is likewise interesting to note that in almost all the instances in which this was the arrangement (i.e. wife living with husband's parents), conflict developed between the wife and the in-laws. In almost all cases, the root of the conflict was the parents' share of their son's income and the almost classic presumption of wifely extravagance.

It is also typical that the running of the households has always been the prerogative of the Filipino wife. Therefore, the husband's departure does not much alter this role. The difference, however, is that major decisions concerning money matters beyond everyday household expenses, which used to belong to the husband, now have to be assumed by the wife. The in-depth interviews conducted not only with the workers but with their families revealed the agonies of housewives who have found themselves having to make such important decisions single-handedly. Most of these decisions usually had to do with how much money was to be set aside as savings, whether to buy appliances or, when remittances were not coming in on time, whether to take out new loans, and for how much.

130

## Remittances to the Family

The financial vulnerability of the families left behind by the migrant workers makes them extremely dependent on remittances. When these do not arrive regularly, the families are forced to borrow short-term cash at very high interest rates. The wives who were interviewed also revealed that such occasions are truly the most difficult times of their lives as single parents. Some Arab or European employers who have local Filipino partners may pay out a portion of their workers' salaries directly to their designated payees (e.g. the wives) on a monthly basis, but such arrangements are still exceptional.

While a high proportion (73 per cent) of the workers interviewed in this study did manage to send money to their families at least once a month, the manner in which remittances are sent has remained unstandardized up to now. At least four methods of sending money were identified: bank-to-bank; direct remittances by the company; hand-carried by Filipino returnees; and other methods (e.g. through black-marketeers linked to recruitment agencies).

These different methods are not mutually exclusive, but respondents were asked which method they most frequently used.

The large percentage (62 per cent) given to the bank-to-bank method is unconvincing, for it is a well-known fact that workers tend to avoid this method because it is cumbersome, slow, and even costly. In all the ten intensive follow-up interviews that the research team undertook in Central Luzon, for instance, not a single one of the housewives interviewed acknowledged receiving remittances through the banks. All of them relied on the *padala* (hand-carried) system. What might account for the large number of responses in favour of the bank-to-bank system is that some workers were anxious to impress upon the interviewers that they were complying with the laws on remittances (i.e. Executive Orders nos. 857 and 935) which are necessarily violated when remittances are sent through returnees.

The survey also asked the respondents in what currency the remitted money was received by their families. About 78 per cent said US dollars, while 16 per cent said Philippine pesos, and 4 per cent said Saudi rials. These responses are revealing in the sense that if the money was received by the majority of the families in US currency, the chances are that it was sent through returnees, rather than through banks, as the findings above seem to suggest. Philippine banks would automatically convert the remittance into Philippine pesos; they would not pay out a telegraphic transfer in any other currency unless the payee had a dollar account with the bank, and it is unlikely that the majority of the overseas contract workers would take the trouble of opening such a foreign currency account, which is usually available only in Metro Manila and major cities. Therefore, it seems unlikely that the majority of the workers' families, if indeed they received the remittances in dollars, would have received them through the banks.

The currency in which the remittances is received would also affect the procedure of its encashment. More than 76 per cent of the respondents said that they dutifully encashed their remittances at the bank, while only 15 per cent admitted that they used the black market. Given the ease with which foreign currency and cheques are traded on the Philippine black market, we must view this finding with scepticism. Foreign currency buyers are known to scour all the communities where there are believed to be many migrant workers, and they usually offer better rates than the banks. Thus, it seems a little unlikely that the migrants' families would forgo the convenience of the black market to satisfy the law.

### Communication between the Migrant Worker and his Family

The typical Filipino overseas contract worker and his spouse are prodigious letter-writers, either sending letters or reciting them before a tape-recorder. The survey findings indicate that 61 per cent of all respondents said they wrote "very often" to their spouses. Our in-depth interviews show this to mean at least once a week. On the other hand, 33 per cent claimed they communicated "often" with their spouses, which probably means once per month at the very least.

Spouses left in the Philippines were slightly more diligent communicators. More than 63 per cent said they wrote to their spouses very often, while 34 per cent said they wrote often. Communication between the migrant worker and the children was not as frequent as that between husband and wife. More than 42 per cent of the respondents said they wrote to their children very often, while 38 per cent said they heard from their children very often. Our guess is that it is very difficult to distinguish between communication with the spouses and communication explicitly with the children. Both communications will tend to be contained in the same letter or cassette tape.

Letters tend to be fairly patterned as regards content. Respondents say their own letters from abroad tend to be "informative," i.e. full of stories about the job, the boss, fellow workers, living conditions, the weather, etc. It was amazing to note in a large number of the interviews with workers' wives how the latter would often speak about their husbands' employers as if they had known them all their lives.

On the other hand, letters received from the spouses tended to be "reassuring" in content, mostly about children and what they want, acknowledgements of remittances received, etc. The majority of the migrant workers in the sample also said that they wrote very long letters to their spouses and vice versa. Interviews with the workers' wives revealed that there was generally an explicit avoidance on their part of communicating too many problems from home.

Our probing interviews also revealed that letters and "voice tapes" were read over and over again, especially by the workers. One carpenter from a Central Luzon town once asked his wife to tape the grunts of his pet pigs as they demanded food, in addition to coloured pictures of his children. Others have been known to have asked for tape-recordings of the local church before dusk when all the children were out playing. Families have been fairly imaginative in this poignant effort to capture a slice of the familiar and somehow preserve it on a cassette tape.

The study tried to establish some correlations between frequency of communication and variables like educational attainment, age, etc. Again, the findings were not particularly surprising. For instance, a higher proportion of college and vocational graduates communicate very often with their spouses, as compared to those with less education. College graduates, those residing in Metro Manila and Luzon, those who have spent one year or less in their jobs, and younger respondents (20–29 years old) were more likely to receive communications from their spouses. Communication with other relatives, however, was not frequent. On the whole, a higher proportion of college graduates, young (20–29), professional, technical, administrative, and service workers, and single migrant workers communicated often with their relatives. In turn, the college graduates and professionals tended to receive more mail from their relatives.

What deserves deeper study is the vicious way in which letters and "voice tapes" are sometimes used to denigrate the wife in the eyes of the husband. Cases of such long-distance intrigue were brought to the attention of the research team in the course of the follow-up interviews. Some of them were shown to us, others were played back on tape. One angry worker had to come home expressly to file criminal charges against one of his neighbours who had been the source of these poisonous communications. The communications are often addressed to the fellow workers of the husband. In whatever form they come, they become durable grist for the gossip mill. They may refer to the wife's profligate spending or, worse, to her regular dates with mysterious men. In a number of instances, of course, they are factual, but the picture that is formed in the mind of the worker 7,000 miles away is a grossly exaggerated one. It haunts him at work, over meals, and in his sleep. The scenario is so typical that one cannot sit in an interview with an ex-Saudi worker who does not have one or two stories of this sort to tell.

**Husband and Wife Problems**

The present survey asked about marital infidelity, without any real expectation that such a touchy issue would elicit any reliable responses at all. Still, to the question "whether respondent thinks the spouse became unfaithful while he was away," 19 (5 per cent) of the 350 workers admitted or claimed that their spouses had been unfaithful. The proportion of workers who entertained thoughts of this nature was very likely greater, but what is interesting is that we should get any admissions at all.

On a separate occasion, the research team managed to secure a long detailed interview with a 30-year-old returnee whose wife had committed suicide two months before he was due on home leave. His wife, who was 22 years old, was left to live with his parents and sisters. His mother wrote to say something awful had happened to his wife, without going into details. When he came home, he was told that his wife had taken her own life by slashing her wrists that same morning. She was seven months pregnant. He said he never found out who was responsible for her pregnancy. He felt that he understood the situation of his wife, and that he must also bear a large measure of the blame for what had happened. This reaction is not exceptional. Similar stories recounted to the team by people who had heard of cases of infidelity indicated that such situations usually led to break-ups, with the man calmly returning to the Middle East as soon as his initial anger had subsided.

The survey data tell no such tales. On the whole, the migrants reported that the spouses who were left behind seemed fully adjusted to their situation and managed well under strain. But then, this is a question that should have been put to the spouses instead, as it in fact was in the in-depth interviews.

All the housewives interviewed indicated that the whole family had to make sacrifices to make the migration appear worthwhile. Everyone said the biggest problem of all was repaying the "5–6 loan" (loan lent by a loanshark or usurer which typically doubles in value every five months) which almost all overseas contract workers obtain to pay the recruiter, as well as to help tide the family over until the first remittance arrives. At the time of the study, the going rate in Central Luzon for a placement fee was P12,000 ($667). Because of the rapidity with which a loan of this nature multiplies (at 20 per cent interest compounded monthly), the concern of the family is to pay the whole principal as early as possible. To fail to do so is to risk having to pay to the usurer all the Saudi earnings of the husband. As things stand, most wives of migrant workers seem resigned to the fact that their husbands' first year's earnings are already earmarked for the usurer who lent them the money to pay the "put" or bribe to the recruiter.

In addition to worrying perpetually about the loan for as long as it is not totally repaid, the other source of anxiety for the wife who stays behind is how to budget the monthly remittance in such a way that some savings can be made. One house-wife explained the situation thus: "You see, of the $300 that he earns every month, he sends me $200, he expects me to be able to repay the loan, to feed and clothe the family, to repair the house, and to buy some appliances and things for the house. Then when he comes home he also expects me to have accumulated some money in the bank. On the other hand, I too expect him to bring home some money. It is difficult, but I try to supplement his earnings by taking in some laundry myself."

**Problems with Children**

Our survey sample consisted of a few unmarried and a large number of fairly young married workers. Only 23 per cent of the respondents had any children of working age. The rest of the children were either infants or in grade school. Thus, it is logical to inquire in a study of this nature about the possible effects of single-parenting on the lives of the children.

These possible effects were to be drawn from answers to questions pertaining to the health of the children, problems encountered in disciplining them, their per-formance at school, signs of withdrawal, etc. On the other hand, the unmarried respondents were asked whether their work stint abroad created any fundamental change in the way they were treated at home in relation to their brothers and sisters.

The research team was a little sceptical about the effectiveness of the survey method in eliciting data of this nature. Like the husband–wife relationship, it was thought that this was perhaps a qualitative issue that was best studied through the case method. In any event, the findings revealed nothing spectacular.

Did the children of migrant workers become unruly? On the whole, the impact of the migrant's absence on child discipline did not seem meaningful. Only 12 per cent of the respondents reported that their children had indeed become unruly during their absence, as against 88 per cent who believed that there was no change in the behaviour of their children as far as this item was concerned.

Did the children become spoiled during this crucial period? Here there was a higher percentage (23 per cent) of respondents who replied in the affirmative. We did not actually know how they understood this word, but our guess is that they equate it with an aggressive demand for toys, expensive shoes, jewellery, and all the things that perhaps their children never even dreamed of before their father went to the Middle East. But still, a good 77 per cent of the respondents thought that their kids had not become spoiled.

**Table 9.** Distribution of respondents by amount earned in last contract

| Amount (pesos) | Percentage |
|---|---|
| Less than 40,000 | 12 |
| 40,001–60,000 | 15 |
| 60,001–80,000 | 16 |
| 80,001–100,000 | 17 |
| Above 100,000 | 40 |
| Total | 100 |
| No. | 500 |

Was the schooling of the children affected? On this item, the scores are similar to those registered for unruliness. The majority (89 per cent) thought that there was no effect on their children's schooling. Only a small minority (11 per cent) believed that their children's education had suffered.

Did the children get sick? Nearly 20 per cent of the respondents believed they did, while 80 per cent thought their absence had no effect on their children's health. Interestingly, perhaps because those with more education are more health-conscious, more workers with college degrees noted that their children got sick while they were away. Similarly, a higher proportion of the workers in the professional and technical categories reported that their children got sick during their absence.

Did the children show any signs of withdrawal as a result of the respondent's absence? The number of respondents claiming that they had detected signs of withdrawal was significantly higher at 34 per cent, although the majority (66 per cent) claimed there were no such signs. Curiously, more high-school (41 per cent) and vocational graduates (52 per cent) reported seeing signs of withdrawal in their children.

Turning to the situation of the unmarried respondents, the expectation was that their status within the family would be bolstered by their having been able to remit some money. Improvement in the status is typically shown in the attention lavished by the parents, notably the mother, on the returnee. The survey results did not show any convincing evidence for this. Only 31 per cent of the unmarried respondents said they noticed that they were being favoured over the other brothers and sisters, while 69 per cent said there was no change in the way they were treated at home.

**Concluding Notes**

It has often been argued that perhaps the greatest cost of overseas contract work is also the least quantifiable because it pertains to the quality of human relationships within the family, something that is not easily accessible to measurement. This difficulty, which is inherent in the nature of the object of analysis, is further compounded by two realities.

First, when it comes to summing-up suggestions, our migrant worker respondents seem almost blindly determined to convince others and, maybe more importantly, themselves that all the sacrifices that went into their "Saudi" experience were not in vain, and that the results have, on the whole, been salutary. The difference in the quality of responses became noticeable when we asked detailed, concrete, and more specific questions that encouraged the worker to tell bits and pieces of his story. Then, the respondent became more decisive, more committed, and a lot more convincing in his replies.

Second, in the course of the interviews with many respondents, it was noticed that they gave stock, unexamined answers, rather than deliberate reflective replies. Was this because most of them have not really had the chance to reflect philosophically on the meaning of their overseas experience? Assuming they have not, perhaps the point is to devise a way of penetrating that experience and allowing it to surface as an object of deep reflection.

## The Migrant and His Family: The Economic Impact of Overseas Migration

The method of assessing the economic impact of overseas migration on workers and their families on the basis of recall information leaves much to be desired. In the absence of hard data prior to migration, the researcher is left with no choice but to accept the respondent's perceptions and memories of life and economic conditions at that time. Moreover, one is unable to study the changes experienced by family members except by way of what the worker perceives the changes to be, since he or she is the main respondent. To provide a better picture of the impact of overseas migration on workers and their households and community, a case-study of farmers in a peasant village in Pampanga, Central Luzon, whose economic situations changed within an eight-year period as a result of overseas employment, will be discussed. The data for the discussion of these farm families are not based on a one-shot survey, but on two surveys taken at the same time as the interviews of the 506 sample respondents. The surveys were also supplemented by interviews with other members of the family and observations before and after migration. The analysis of the survey results focused on household incomes and allocation of household labour. The same sample of 63 out of 82 farmers in the village in 1978 was traced and when possible reinterviewed in 1984. In addition, 30 landless workers and their families were also reinterviewed.

### Income, Remittances, Savings, and Investments of Sample Respondents

Income from Migration

The majority of the workers (60 per cent) earned incomes above P80,000, or about $4,500, for the duration of their stay in the Middle East. The distribution of income is extremely skewed since the highest earnings registered were P650,000 ($36,000), while close to 12 per cent of the sample earned less than P40,000 ($2,200).

The amount earned on the last contract varied with the occupation of the worker, the duration of the contract, and his place of work. As expected, almost eight out of ten professional, technical, administrative, and clerical workers had incomes above P80,000 ($4,500), while only five out of ten workers in the other occupational groups were in this category. On the other hand, respondents who worked in Saudi

Arabia had higher incomes than those whose jobs were in other Middle East countries. The longer the worker stayed in the host country, the higher was his earned income.

## Remittances

The total amount of remittances varied with the nature and duration of the last overseas job. Since they have the highest earnings when compared to other occupational groups, close to half of professional, technical, administrative, and clerical workers sent more than P40,000 ($2,222) as remittances. As expected, a third of those whose last overseas job lasted beyond a year remitted more than P80,000 ($4,444), compared to only 15 per cent of those whose contracts were only for a year. The average amount remitted was P191,000 ($10,611), with a large standard deviation. In the absence of more appropriate means of obtaining information on the amount remitted other than asking the respondent to recall the amount he sent home, one must take this figure with a pinch of salt.

Salaries, which were mostly sent to spouses (73 per cent) or parents (21 per cent), were remitted by the worker himself or his company through banks (62 per cent), through fellow workers (21 per cent), through company salary deductions (11 per cent), through the mail (2 per cent), or through a combination of means. Almost eight out of ten remitted in dollars rather than in the currency of the host country. The money was encashed either in banks or on the black market, with about 15 per cent admitting encashing on the black market.

Sending bank drafts was not popular among the respondents, only 15 per cent making use of this means. The rest were unanimous in saying that, on the basis of the experiences of their fellow workers, bank drafts were sometimes lost in the mail or took a very long time to reach their families.

In general, the majority of the respondents' families (64 per cent) received the remittances from one to four weeks after they were sent. There were seven cases, however, where money sent by the worker was not received because the Filipino who hand-carried the remittances failed to deliver them.

## Savings and Investments

More than half of the respondents, regardless of occupation and socio-demographic characteristics, spent their earnings on consumer durables. The amount spent on these items ranged from P450 ($25) to more than P50,000 ($2,778), with the majority spending less than P15,000 ($833). About half, mostly workers in their thirties and forties, spent their money on improving or constructing their houses. Moreover, a larger proportion of construction workers invested in houses compared to other groups. Seven out of ten workers who invested in a house spent less than P40,000 ($2,222), implying that these were not very expensive homes.

Very few invested in productive assets, only 7 per cent buying machinery and equipment. About 17 per cent bought vehicles; most of those worked in the transportation sector in the host country. Business investments were made by about 10 per cent. Compared to other groups, there were more construction workers who invested in business (40 per cent of all those who invested). The businesses they set up were small-scale, mostly retail stores (known colloquially as sari-sari stores), costing between P5,000 and P10,000 ($278–556) on average. These small-scale investments were not seen to employ more than one or two people. About half of the respondents invested in the education of their children.

Three out of four respondents claimed they did not have any uninvested savings at the time of the interviews. Of the different groups, there were more professional, technical, administrative, and clerical workers with uninvested savings. Those who had such savings planned to use them for business (40 per cent), for the education of their children (10 per cent), for facilitating the acquisition of another overseas job (9 per cent), and for building a house (5 per cent), among other things.

When asked if they received advice regarding the use of their uninvested savings, 47 per cent claimed they did. Three out of four respondents were advised by family members.

## The Economic Impact of Overseas Employment: The Case of Farmers in Bo. Sta Lucia, Pampanga

Apart from the takeover by nine landless workers of nine hectares of ricelands, the more dramatic and significant changes in productive assets, in household incomes, and in household allocation among the farm households in the sample occurred as a result of the famous "Saudi" connection. Within the seven-year period between the 1978 and 1984 surveys, one in three farm households in the sample (30) experienced significant reductions in landholdings. Of this group, a half leased or sold all or part of their ricelands in the covert land market in the process of obtaining Middle East contracts for the head or members of his household. One farmer, who used to have three hectares, became a victim of illegal recruiters, losing his entire farm. He has since joined one of the harvesting groups, occasionally engaging in construction work during the slack season. His family has begun to totter on the brink of subsistence. Except for this victim of illegal recruitment, all households were successful in obtaining overseas employment with remunerations of about P2,500 to P4,500 ($139–250) a month. The willingness to part with the most important means of agricultural production reflects the belief held by most villagers that the gains from hired employment, as demonstrated by those who returned from the Middle East, far outweigh the cost of losing productive assets. It also partly reflects the perceptions of the prospects of agriculture relative to alternative sources of income. The local source of demand for leased land also came from a particular group of villagers. Of the 16 households in the sample who accumulated land, nine did so by taking over part of the unused hacienda and the rest used their Saudi money.

The Saudi connection also accounted for the acquisition of productive assets. Five of the seven households in the sample acquired Japanese irrigation pumping units in the seven-year period, using savings from overseas employment. So did three of 17 households with new land tractors for land preparation and two households which acquired small mechanical threshers.

The significance of remittance from overseas employment becomes more apparent when one analyses the changes in income levels. Of the 30 who registered changes in income levels, more than half had members who either worked in the Middle East in the late 1970s and early 1980s or were still working there at the time

138

of the study. Even those who did not have direct ties with the Middle East were able to accumulate on the basis of zero-interest loans obtained from relatives who worked in the Gulf region.

Households in the 50,000 pesos (US2,778) and above cateogry that had higher annual incomes (1978 as base) in 1984 because of the Saudi connection can be divided into two groups: those who returned from overseas employment before 1984 and those who were still in the Middle East, or who had members abroad, during the study period. The former used their savings to invest in capital goods like hand tractors or threshers, the rental of which provided around 30 per cent of their 1984 household incomes. On average, rice production accounted for 37 per cent, while the share of vegetable production was about 28 per cent for this group. On the other hand, households with members who were still in the Middle East were propelled to higher income groups because of remittances from overseas employment. The share of external funds to total income ranged from 60 to 80 per cent. These households used the extra money to maintain the same level of rice production. Two put up a small retail store, while three engaged in moneylending. Key informants in the village claim that the new moneylenders are more vigilant in collecting payments.

In general, however, a large proportion of external remittances was usually allotted to improving the standard of living of the household while a member was still abroad. Concrete houses replaced huts made of light materials. Consumer durables like stereos and televisions were purchased. The proportion of children in school also increased for this group, reflecting the view that education is considered a mechanism for upward mobility. The returnees who invested in productive assets did so towards the end of their contracts when the prospects of renewal were dim and the possibility of returning to the village became more real.

The Saudi connection also accounted for the increase in income among half of the households below the P50,000 ($2,778) category. Except for two former landless heads who were among the new farmers in the village and one farmer who leased his land to obtain overseas employment, all these households depended on remittances from sons in the Middle East, some of whom had families of their own. However, the share of external remittances constituted only about 21 to 30 per cent of their incomes. These remittances were used to cover the cost of rice and vegetable production, but were not used to purchase agricultural assets.

With respect to changes in labour allocation, members of the households with the Saudi connection who were of school age were no longer assigned to work in the farms, unlike counterparts in a previous period. The children have also imbibed the consumer culture in the form of walkmans and stereos.

**Concluding Comment**

It would seem from the above discussion that while workers benefitted differentially from their overseas employment, most of them became economically better off as a result of their stint abroad. It is not clear, however, whether they can maintain this state. It is important to note that focusing mainly on economic gains can make people ignore the human costs. It is, therefore, important to weigh the economic costs against the social and the psychological.

## The Migrant and His Family: Changes in Life-style and Values

Changes in asset holdings and life-style are the directly observable effects of overseas employment. These changes, which often reflect a marked improvement in the economic life of migrant workers, become symbols of hope to neighbours and friends who aspire to a better life which, given their circumstances, only an overseas job can provide. The more subtle but long-term effects of temporary migration on the workers and their families and communities are usually downplayed. Effects on the values, attitudes, and psychological make-up of workers and the people closest to them are hardly reflected upon. This section looks at the changes in both life-style and values of workers. Given the limitations of the survey method in the study of these dimensions, the discussion barely scratches the surface.

### Changes in Life-style

Contract workers as a category cannot be said to belong to the poorest of the poor in the country. As mentioned in the report, their educational attainment is way above the Filipino norm and a large proportion of them were already employed prior to their overseas stint. It is, therefore, not surprising that 59 per cent of them had their own houses even before working abroad.

Home-ownership before migration is significantly associated with the nature of the last overseas job. The professional, technical, administrative, and clerical category has the lowest proportion of respondents who already owned houses before their overseas job. Working abroad made it possible for a number of those who already had houses prior to migration to make improvements on them. Forty-seven per cent of workers had galvanized iron for their roofing material prior to migration; this increased to 64 per cent after working abroad. While only 27 per cent had concrete walls in the houses they owned before working abroad, this figure went up to 44 per cent after their overseas employment. Likewise, there was an increase in the number of contract workers who could afford to have concrete floors, electricity, and toilet facilities as a result of working in the Gulf region.

Since machines and vehicles were not considered basic necessities, only 10 per cent (N = 481) of the workers owned jeepneys, agricultural equipment, etc., before migration. This figure rose to 17 per cent (N = 465) because of overseas employment. Tricycles (24 respondents), jeepneys (17), and cars (16) were among the vehicles commonly bought.

Middle East employment also made it possible for many contract workers to acquire household items like television sets (46 per cent), stereos (46 per cent), radios (30 per cent), refrigerators (28 per cent), and videos (24 per cent). Other items bought include rice-cookers (19 per cent), sewing machines (11 per cent), freezers (10 per cent) and washing machines (8 per cent). All of these are status symbols and are the outward trappings of success for most of the returning contract workers. Although these items may not seem important to some people, they are priority items to migrant labourers. Acquisition of these consumption goods in fact is among the reasons pushing would-be workers to seek overseas employment.

The consumption of basic food items by the contract workers and their families has not altered drastically, contrary to the findings of earlier studies (Francisco and

Ramos-Jimenez, 1983). The data show that the majority of the contract workers were already regular consumers of meat (97 per cent) (N = 488), dairy products (80 per cent) (N = 486), canned goods (85 per cent) (N = 486), soft drinks (83 per cent) (N = 432), coffee (81 per cent) (N = 477), tea (48 per cent) (N = 477), liquor (56 per cent) (N = 478), and cigarettes (59 per cent) (N = 476) even before they left for abroad, suggesting the lower-middle-class background of most of them. The change that occurred after migration was in the increase in the amount of basic food items consumed rather than a change in the items.

When asked if their consumption of specific food items increased after their overseas employment, 65 per cent said yes for meat, 51 per cent for dairy products, and 47 per cent for canned goods. There was only a very slight increase in the consumption of liquor and tobacco/cigarettes, and no increase in the consumption of soft drinks. There were also more respondents who did not change the amount of tea they drank after migration. This can be interpreted to mean that when family incomes increased as a result of hard-earned overseas wages, the respondents and their families preferred to improve their consumption of essentials rather than items viewed as vices (except for coffee consumption, which increased for 45 per cent of respondents).

In terms of reading materials, newspapers were most popular among overseas workers before migration. Sixty-nine per cent (N = 483) of them bought and read newspapers compared to 57 per cent (N = 478) who read periodicals and 55 per cent (N = 479) who bought and read books. Perhaps, because reading is not a preoccupation among the majority of migrant workers, the number of contract workers who bought newspapers, periodicals, and books after migration did not increase very much. Hence, while there were slightly more respondents whose consumption of books increased after their Middle East connection than those whose consumption remained the same, there were more respondents who did not change their consumption of newspapers and periodicals at all after having come home.

Data from the study do not support the findings of previous researchers (Francisco and Ramos-Jimenez, 1983) that overseas employment led to a change in the kinds of services and the forms of entertainment among migrants. Most of the respondents and their families continued using the same kinds of services and forms of entertainment that they had before their overseas jobs. For instance, 95 per cent (N = 461) of them consulted doctors for medical treatment before they went abroad. After their overseas employment, this figure remained the same.

Because it is the cheapest, watching movies is a popular form of entertainment in the country. Among the contract workers, however, it was not really a favourite occupation, considering that less than half of them (48 per cent) (N = 419) watched movies before migration. This proportion decreased slightly to 47 per cent (N = 420) after working abroad, perhaps because of the acquisition of television and video sets by migrant workers.

The material gains the workers derived from overseas employment likewise provided them and their families with an improved perception of themselves in terms of income and status vis-à-vis their neighbours. Prior to working abroad, 55 per cent (N = 492) of them claimed that they had about the same income as their neighbours, while only 20 per cent said their incomes were higher. After their stint overseas, this distribution changed substantially with 46 per cent (N = 493) now claiming they had higher incomes, while 44 per cent said they were just like their neighbours as regards income.

The shift in respondents' perception of their social status vis-à-vis their neighbours was not as significant. This may be attributed to the data-collection technique used in the study. In the Philippines, where stating that one's social position is higher than that of others may be construed as bragging, there is a tendency to downplay what otherwise is perceived to be a higher status.

### Changes in Values and Attitudes

Asked if there were changes in their values and attitudes as a result of working abroad, 54 per cent said there were none, while 46 per cent admitted changes. Is it because their stint abroad was not long enough? Cross-tabulating this variable with the length of stay abroad gave no definite indicator.

The data, however, reveal that changes in values are significantly associated with the nature of the last overseas job. A higher percentage of service workers, craftsmen, and construction-related workers, 60, 56, and 50 per cent respectively, experienced changes in values, whereas only 31 per cent of the professionals did. It would seem that professionals, placed in an alien cultural setting, are more likely to find that they share many values in common with foreigners around them. Work ethics of professionals, regardless of their cultural setting, are after all not too different from each other.

Of the changed values, adherence to the work ethic ranked first. Other responses included becoming more thrifty, avoiding vices, and a changed outlook in life – with the realization that all things will pass, even the difficult situation in Saudi. All told, the changes cited by the contract workers were generally positive.

In terms of aspirations for children, there was a negligible difference in the number of respondents whose aspirations for their children changed after having worked abroad and those whose aspirations remained the same – 41 against 40 per cent (N = 476). The fact that a majority of the contract workers were motivated to go abroad to assure themselves and their families of a better future suggests that many of them may already have had high aspirations for their children to start with, so working abroad could not possibly result in any higher aspirations. Most of those who claimed changes said they wanted their children to have a better future, which, more often than not, means providing them with educational opportunities, particularly a college education. This indicates the high value which Filipinos place on higher education.

In terms of interest in politics, data on political persuasions show that three respondents out of four (N = 499) were not interested in politics before migration. Only 8 per cent (N = 498) of them had joined political parties before working abroad. Further analysis of data shows that interest in politics prior to migration is significantly related to the nature of the last overseas job. Thirty-five per cent of the professionals expressed interest in politics as against 16 and 14 per cent of craftsmen and service-related workers respectively. While they claim not to be interested in politics, 63 per cent of workers (N = 494) admitted to having discussed politics during their stay abroad. They complained about the relative indifference of some embassy personnel to their plight and government impositions on them,

**Table 10.** Distribution of respondents by amount remitted to family

| Amount (pesos) | Percentage |
|---|---|
| Less than 40,000 | 42 |
| 41,000–60,000 | 18 |
| 61,000–80,000 | 11 |
| 81,000–100,000 | 10 |
| Above 100,000 | 19 |
| Total | 100 |
| No. | 431 |

e.g. forced remittance of 50 to 70 per cent of their earnings through legitimate channels, without which their passports could not be renewed. The stiff fees charged for renewing one's passport abroad, etc., resulted in a large 60 per cent (N = 447) of them saying that their fellow workers did not trust the present government.

In terms of interest in the world situation, half of the contract workers (N = 468) were already interested in their host countries prior to migration, a little more than a third (N = 449) in other countries of the Gulf region, and 48 per cent (N = 473) in world affairs. These figures seem to suggest that many contract workers were aware of the need to know what was going on around them and were conscious of the fact that the fate of nations is closely bound together, even before their departure for employment abroad. For example, some contract workers talked about knowing, long before working abroad, how the oil cartel had catapulted the once-impoverished desert countries to sudden wealth, and how their need to import doctors, engineers, etc., from a third-world country like the Philippines had increased. In general, those interested in news about the host country increased from 50 to 68 per cent, those interested in other Gulf countries from 39 to 61 per cent, and those in world affairs from 48 to 62 per cent. It should be noted that the impact of overseas experience in terms of increasing one's interest in global situations is likely to be felt more by the white-collar worker.

## Concluding Notes

The indicators of changes in life-style among the families of migrant labourers reflect their notion of what it means to move up in society. The improved, beautified homes, the conspicuous consumption of consumer items like electronic gadgets, and the occasional splurge of money for a child's baptism or wedding are among the status symbols to which the workers aspire. There is a tendency among some of the respondents to flaunt what they acquired and to discuss what each has in his home. This is also true among the teenage members of the families with "Saudi" employed heads, whether these teenagers are from the city or the barrio. In one sense, while the workers may have had positive changes in values (e.g. became more thrifty, more appreciative of hard work, more aware of the need to know about global events), the members of their families appear to imbibe a highly materialistic culture. This has led to a hypothesis that needs to be explored about the proletarianization of the worker in the host country and the "bourgeoisification" of the members of his family. The materialistic culture, which prevails among some migrant families, is also being absorbed by members of the community, who hope to land Middle East jobs that could be their passport to a better life.

## The Migrant Worker: Employment, Skill Formation, and Adjustment to the Home Country

Keeping up with improved standards of living and the newly acquired tastes of family members when the overseas employment is over requires income levels not far different from those obtaining in the host country. The contraction of the labour market in the Middle East implies a possible return to lower standards of living if high-paying jobs are not in the offing.

### Employment Situation Prior to Migration

The findings of earlier studies (ILMS, 1979; Eco and Tianzon, 1977; Gibson, 1983) that the majority of the overseas workers were employed before they went to work abroad is supported by data in this study. Eighty-nine per cent of the respondents were employed while 11 per cent were without jobs prior to overseas employment. One implication of this is that the migration of overseas workers has alleviated unemployment problems in the country to a certain extent, although at a tremendous cost in terms of the training of new recruits, the declining productivity of the companies concerned, and the deteriorating quality of their services, among other things. Not only were the vacated jobs filled by new recruits from the ranks of the unemployed, but because the latter did not have the skills of those who left, more replacements were needed to do the same volume of work.

Contract workers who were employed in the Philippines before their departure were not really novices in their jobs. Except for about a fifth of them, who were employed for only a year in their last job before migration, the rest had had from two to twenty years' service. This can be attributed to the fact that foreign recruiting teams carefully monitor the applicant's work history, preferring to hire those with more experience (Arcinas, 1984). Advertisements for employment opportunities abroad published in the local dailies invariably require, among other qualifications, at least five years' experience in the specific job applied for. Overseas employment thus turns out to favour those with relative skills acquired from either formal training or experience. This is further strengthened by the fact that a number of the contract workers had more than one job prior to migration. Thirty-six per cent (N = 450) had had two jobs, and 13 per cent three jobs (N = 450).

For their last employment before working abroad, about one out of four had a professional/technical/administrative/clerical job. The construction workers were, however, the largest category, constituting 28 per cent of all workers. This was to be expected, considering that the second half of the 1970s and early 1980s were periods that witnessed a construction boom; the demand for construction workers was then at its peak. For their second- and third-to-last employment before migration, again the professional/technical/administrative/clerical and construction workers had the greatest number of respondents. However, there were slightly more in the professional/technical/administrative/clerical than in the construction category.

## Consequences of Migration on the Middle East Labour Market as Perceived by Respondents

That there are noticeable changes in the composition of skills in demand by Middle East countries is a perception shared by almost six out of ten contract workers. Seven out of ten workers (N = 821) also perceived that the nationality composition of workers in the Middle East is not what it used to be. Some labour-exporting countries have been able to increase their share of the Middle East labour market, while others are sending fewer workers. Among the different countries in the manpower export business, the Republic of Korea was perceived by most respondents as one that is exporting more workers to the Middle East, while Taiwan was considered as such by the least number of contract workers. Many contract workers have nothing but praise for the intensive efforts of the Korean government to place their contract workers in the Middle East. They regret that "the Philippine government is not doing half as much."

Some countries were also perceived as having a declining share of the Middle East labour market. The Philippines heads the list, with 56 per cent of respondents regarding the country in this way. Only one respondent said there is a decreasing number of workers from Bangladesh and Taiwan in the Middle East.

Fifty-two per cent of respondents (N = 474) think that some host countries already have policies aimed at reducing the number of foreign workers. However, an overwhelming 82 per cent (N = 469) of the respondents believe that there is no real opposition among the host countries in the Middle East to importing foreign labour. Some respondents are under the impression that the contract workers in the Middle East are occupying jobs for which the Arabs do not have the necessary skills or which they (the Arabs) find undesirable.

Asked how they would describe the monthly earnings of contract workers for the same job abroad through the years, about four out of ten workers perceived monthly earnings to be increasing in monetary terms. Only 10 per cent say they are declining in monetary terms, and for this many of them blame the contract workers from Bangladesh, Thailand, Pakistan, and India, who are willing to accept lower wages, thus disrupting the salary scale.

## Skill Formation

Overseas employment has provided the migrant with all sorts of experiences, some of which can directly benefit the home country. More than half the returning overseas workers acquired new skills and learned new techniques with new equipment. Although there have been no serious studies on this matter, it has been commonly observed that a sizeable number of workers, 32 per cent in this case, did not learn anything new. Some claim to have been teaching workers from other countries.

It is also a plus factor for the home country if almost seven out of ten workers say they gained more experience in the old skills they already possessed, thereby becoming more adept in their own line of work.

It is unfortunate that, with all the new skills and techniques acquired by contract workers from their overseas experience, many of them could not put these into use. There were as many respondents who could not use their newly gained skills and techniques now that they were home as there were those who have found them useful.

## Re-employment of Respondents on Return

### Problems of Re-employment

Informal interviews with some migrant workers showed that they generally look forward to the prospect of returning home to work because they want to be with their families. It was, therefore, a big let-down when, upon their return, they had great difficulty getting a job. The data revealed that, at the time of the study, more than half of those who had returned from overseas work had not found local employment; only 42 had been lucky. Again, considering the economic condition that the Philippines has been in for several years, this is not altogether unexpected. It also took those who eventually found jobs from one to 60 months waiting. Although half of them found employment after only six months of waiting, the mean waiting time was 30 months.

The non-availability of jobs and low remuneration were the most common difficulties encountered by the contract workers upon their return. Of the 212 respondents who had problems, 47 per cent could not find jobs, while 36 per cent said the remuneration offered them was much too low. The difficulties associated with finding jobs varied with the nature of the most recent overseas job. The hardest-hit among the respondents were construction workers, with 55 per cent claiming there were no jobs available and 21 per cent complaining that the remuneration offered them was much too low. Twenty-one per cent of those in transportation and communication also deplore the unavailability of jobs. The same proportion of craftsmen, on the other hand, say that remuneration for available jobs is too low. Asked whether they had received any assistance for whatever difficulties they may have encountered in readjusting to the Filipino way of life, a very large 82 per cent said they got none. Of those who received assistance, the majority were helped by their own families. Only three of them were assisted by government agencies and twenty by non-government entities.

### Present Occupation of Returnees

Despite the fact that the construction workers had the highest proportion of returnees who had complained about the non-availability of jobs, they also registered the highest percentage of re-employed returnees. Of the 212 respondents who had jobs at the time of the study, 27 per cent of them were construction workers. The service workers had the lowest percentage of re-employed returnees.

### Job Changes upon Return

Close to about 50 per cent of the more recently employed respondents switched jobs upon their return to the Philippines. Some of them claimed that if they had insisted on doing the same jobs they held abroad, they would be out of work, so they were just being pragmatic. Of the 212 respondents who compared their overseas jobs with their present occupation, the following retained their previous occupational classification: professional/technical/administrative/clerical (47 per cent); agriculture/mining (3 per cent); transportation/communication (57 per cent); craftsmen (68 per cent); service and related workers (62 per cent); and construction (77 per cent).

More of those in agriculture/mining and professional/technical/clerical and transportation/communication sectors changed jobs upon their return to the Philippines. Most respondents, regardless of sector, have held on to only one job since their return; 14 respondents have had two and only one has had three.

Plans for the Future

Contract workers' plans for their future include the following: work abroad again (87 per cent); emigrate (1 per cent); get married (1 per cent); start own business (7 per cent); study (–); and others (4 per cent).

Most of them would like to work abroad again or even emigrate, and this in spite of the fact that more than half (57 per cent) who had found local employment admitted that they were satisfied with the jobs they now held.

Asked directly whether they were again seeking employment abroad, the number of respondents who said they were rose to 91 per cent (N = 478).

Most of the contract workers want to be re-employed abroad because of their insufficient income in the Philippines. In informal conversations with some of the respondents, they decried the sharp rise in the cost of acquiring an overseas job; according to them, the going rate among recruiting agencies is $800 to $1,000. Despite the steep fee, however, many are willing to pay, especially among the professionals and the skilled workers, just to be able to work abroad again – if they remain at home, their "families would go hungry." Already more than half of the contract workers, regardless of work sector, have approached recruitment agencies and made inquiries about possible placements abroad.

**Concluding Observations**

While the Middle East labour market was expanding, migrant workers relished the hope of renewing their contracts abroad and postponing the prospects of going home to an uncertain future in a crisis-ridden nation. However, the contraction of employment opportunities in the Gulf region in the 1980s spells the impending return of many overseas workers on the termination of their contracts. Adjustment to life in the Philippines is difficult, particularly because very few workers have invested their money in income-generating activities, and more than half remain unemployed. Those lucky enough to obtain jobs cannot find the same level of remuneration. Like the workers in the sample, many will attempt to begin another cycle of migration. However, the uncertainty of getting another job can increase anxiety and even postpone adjustment to life in the Philippines. Detailed conversations with unemployed workers reveal their psychological insecurity as they watch their savings slowly diminishing with no prospect of refilling the family coffers. One respondent, who used remittances to send his children to exclusive schools, lamented their demotion to the barrio elementary school. He said he is slowly losing his self-respect, often taking out his frustration on his family. The human costs of migration, therefore, cover not only the pre-migration and migration phases, but the months and years after the contract has terminated when the psychological problems of adjustment arise. A member of the research team conducted a re-study of a subsample of the workers in the study one year after the interview. It is worth noting that her preliminary analysis reveals that most of the workers were still unemployed. As a consequence, assets acquired after migration have been sold. Children sent to college while the worker was abroad had to stop studying, like the younger ones, in order to work and help augment family income. It would be no surprise if these initial findings were replicated for other workers within and outside the sample.

## Conclusions

Except for the unemployment problem among returnees, the findings of the survey generally downplay the human costs of overseas migration. The majority of workers in the sample did not experience the problem of illegal recruitment, nor did they have to pay exorbitant fees to their recruitment agencies. In comparison to the amount of money shelled out by workers today or even by the respondents of in-depth interviews, the pre-departure expenses of the sample workers were relatively low. Furthermore, only 16 per cent incurred loans with interest. The rest borrowed money from relatives or used their savings to finance their overseas venture. While they were not properly oriented to conditions in the host country, their legendary resilience made it easy for the sample workers to adjust to life abroad.

On the basis of the workers' accounts alone, it would seem that loneliness was about the only cost of temporary separation from their families. Husband–wife relations did not seem to have been strained and the children did not seem to suffer as a result of their parents' sojourn in the Middle East. On the contrary, the economic well-being of most families improved, and life-styles changed for the better. The only problem seemingly confronting most of these families is that of maintaining the standard of living they have become accustomed to.

The human costs of overseas migration would seem to have been incurred only by the 17 per cent who became victims of illegal recruitment, by skilled workers whose spouses became unfaithful, and by the unlucky ones who signed a second contract in the Middle East with worse terms than the first contracts signed in the Philippines. However, detailed, follow-up interviews, even of the average worker who forms part of the majority of the sample, eventually revealed social and psychological problems, not to mention economic ones, which did not surface in a one-shot survey. The findings or the study should, therefore, be interpreted with caution. Workers may unwittingly downplay the human costs because they are convinced that all the sacrifices are worth it when seen in the light of the material benefits their families are enjoying. Given the unemployment problems of returnees, the human costs of past and future overseas employment in the consciousness of these workers can outweigh perceived benefits.

The human costs, which a one-shot survey of returnees cannot reveal, need to be identified if comprehensive policies governing the export of manpower are to be formulated.

Since this exploratory study merely scratches the surface, the following recommendations are still incomplete. In the light of the findings of this survey, a number

of points with policy implications raised in the State-of-the art Report need to be reiterated:
- Establish a databank and a more systematic monitoring of migrant workers.
- Carry out more vigorous selective recruitment in the more depressed areas of the country on a regular basis as a matter of policy.
- Consolidate recruitment function in a semi-government body with built-in safeguards against abuse of power.
- The semi-government corporation could provide non-interest-bearing loans to cover all overseas employment-related expenses of workers.
- A more effective information campaign must be organized among workers.
- The proposed semi-government corporation could be assigned the task of protecting workers abroad and the families they leave behind.
- The government should establish a programme for the placement of returnees.

## References

Abella, Manola I. 1979. *Export of Filipino Manpower*. ILMS, Minsitry of Labour, Manila.

Arcinas, F.R. 1984. Asian Migrant Workers to the Gulf Region: The Philippine Case (Report on the State of the Art).

Castillo, G.I. 1977. *Beyond Manila: Philippine Rural Problems in Perspective*. Vol. I, pp. 163–164. University of the Philippines at Los Banos College, Laguna.

Eco, C., and R. Tianzon. 1979. *Manpower Availability Study: 1975–1976*. OEDB, Manila.

Francisco, Josefa S., and Pilar Ramos-Jimenez, eds. 1983. *The Effects of International Contract Labor: Community Studies*. Integrated Research Center, De La Salle University, Philippines.

Gibson, Katherine D. 1983. Contract Labor Migration for the Philippines: Preliminary Field Work Report, 1983. Department of Human Geography, Research School of Pacific Studies, Australian National University.

Hunt et al. 1963. *Sociology in the Philippines Setting*, p. 57. Rev. ed. Phoenix Publishing House, Q.C.

International Labour and Manpower. 1979. Filipino Migrant Workers in Iran (Insights into Temporary Migration). *Philippine Labour Review*, 4(2).

Jayme, Rebecca B. 1979. A Study on the Effects of Temporary Worker Outflow from the Philippines. M.A. thesis. University of the Philippines.

Magno, Carlo M. 1984. Implication of the Export Manpower in the Telephone Industry. Paper presented at the University of the Philippines Seminar on "Manpower Export – Unexplored Issues," Manila.

National Census and Statistics Office. 1975. *Philippine Census*.

Sinay-Aguilar, Virginia, Gloria B. Caromen, Carmelita Baquiran, A. Laqui, M. Luwalhati, Nenita Retiro, and Edna Macarrubo. 1981. Effects of Temporary Employment of Professionals and Skilled Manual Workers in the East on the Labor Market. Paper submitted to the Program in Development Schools, School of Economics, University of the Philippines.

Philippine Overseas and Employment Agency. 1985. *Areas for Possible Legislative Action*.

# 4

# MIGRANT WORKERS TO THE ARAB WORLD: THAILAND

**Amara Pongsapich**

Social Research Institute, Chulalongkorn University, Bangkok, Thailand

## Introduction

### Brief History

Organized labour migration has a long history in Thailand. Prior to the Second World War, it had primarily been in the form of the internal migration of corvée labour. Internal migration had also resulted from the Bowring Treaty, signed in 1855 between Great Britain and Thailand, through which Thailand was opened up to international trade and a rapid growth in commercial production and the export of rice had taken place in the lower part of the central region of the country, leading to substantial internal migration.

International migration, however, is a recent phenomenon, and assumed importance only after the Second World War. As in other parts of South-East Asia, during its first phase international labour migration in Thailand had started with an outflow of skilled labour. Students who had gone for higher training in the professions had remained and been absorbed into the labour force of the host countries – an outflow of skills usually referred to as the "brain drain." The sketchy data that are available indicate that about 400 persons migrated to the US during the years 1966-1971. The annual outflow increased to nearly 3,400 in the five years which followed; however, the Department of Labour estimates that there are approximately 300,000 Thai migrants in the US. During the period 1972–1977 the total annual migration to the United Kingdom was about 1,700.

The second phase of international migration was directed primarily to the countries of oil-rich West Asia. The OPEC oil-price increase of 1973 had prompted the withdrawal of US troops from bases in Thailand, and consequently there had been a significant decline in employment opportunities for Thais. When the West Asian employment market opened, the various recruitment agencies had to offer strong incentives to the potential migrants. The migration flows to the Gulf countries gathered momentum as the Thai economy suffered under the international recession following the oil-price increase and the withdrawal of American troops.

The recruitment of Thai labour for international markets became an official busi-

**Table 1.** Number of migrants requested by Thai construction contractors, 1980–1983

| Country | 1980 | 1981 | 1982 | 1983 |
|---|---|---|---|---|
| Saudi Arabia | 42 | 57 | — | 51 |
| Libya | — | — | — | — |
| Kuwait | — | 23 | 34 | 369 |
| Ethiopia | — | — | — | 35 |
| Malaysia | — | 73 | 150 | 27 |
| Singapore | 532 | 38 | — | 52 |
| Brunei | — | — | — | 104 |
| Japan | — | — | 41 | 137 |
| United Kingdom | — | 4 | — | — |
| Hong Kong | — | 4 | — | — |
| Indonesia | — | 1 | — | — |
| Iraq | 29 | — | — | — |
| Total | 653 | 191 | 225 | 791 |

*Source:* Office of Overseas Labour Management, Department of Labour.

ness enterprise after 1973. First, workers had been sent to Europe. The recruitment of workers to the countries in West Asia officially commenced in 1975. The first group of Thai migrants were skilled workers employed by construction firms; foreign firms who had previous experience with Thai workers turned to the Thai market when they won contracts in the labour-scarce Gulf countries. In some cases, the migrants had worked for the same firm when it operated in Thailand.

Public attention was drawn to the phenomenon of migration to West Asia when increasing numbers of cases of fraud by recruitment agencies, as well as various adjustment problems faced by families, were reported by public agencies such as the Bank of Thailand, the Department of Labour, and the National Economic and Social Development Board.

Among the studies of West Asian labour migration, the Bank of Thailand in 1978 examined and recorded the data for the Department of Labour, reporting on the migration with respect to the migrant's origin, the countries of destination, occupations, wages, and foreign exchange remittances. In 1980, the NESDB studied the demand for skilled labour in the construction industry in Bangkok and for skilled and semi-skilled labour, for example carpenters and masons, within the country. This study examined some of the possible effects on the domestic labour market and the economy of the increased demand and outflow to West Asian countries. The interest in migration deepened as outflows increased and the remittances became significantly large. In 1981 the NESDB carried out a further study related to the decision to migrate. The study was based on workers living in eight provinces. Case-studies on migration and its effects were also undertaken in 1981 by several scholars.

### The Government and the Migration to West Asian Countries

West Asian migration had become so important to the Thai economy by the early 1980s that the Fifth National Development Plan (1981 and 1985) devoted a whole

**Table 2.** Number of Thai migrant labourers approved by the Department of Labour, 1973–1984

| Country | 1973 | 1974 | 1975 | 1976 | 1977 | 1978 | 1979 | 1980 | 1981 | 1982 | 1983 | 1984 |
|---|---|---|---|---|---|---|---|---|---|---|---|---|
| United Kingdom | 293 | — | — | — | — | — | — | — | — | — | — | — |
| Bahrain | — | — | 918 | 960 | 776 | — | 75 | 306 | 380 | 10 | 198 | 970 |
| Saudi Arabia | — | — | 16 | 327 | 2,885 | 8,502 | 7,645 | 9,948 | 9,420 | 88,178 | 51,262 | 48,395 |
| Dubai | — | — | — | — | 239 | — | — | — | — | — | — | — |
| Iran | — | — | — | — | — | 3,199 | — | — | — | — | — | — |
| Kuwait | — | — | — | — | — | 2,176 | 188 | 958 | 608 | 577 | 2,208 | 2,617 |
| United Arab Emirates | — | — | — | — | — | 262 | 146 | 757 | 59 | 310 | 161 | 540 |
| Singapore | — | — | — | — | — | 250 | 660 | 191 | 606 | 1,901 | 1,326 | 2,921 |
| Brunei | — | — | — | — | — | — | — | — | 261 | 960 | 136 | 494 |
| Qatar | — | — | — | — | — | 76 | 165 | 1,071 | 1,538 | 2,825 | 1,020 | 821 |
| Yemen | — | — | — | — | — | — | 6 | 215 | — | 20 | — | 4 |
| Jordan | — | — | — | — | — | — | 100 | — | — | 362 | — | — |
| Israel | — | — | — | — | — | — | 100 | — | — | 362 | — | — |
| Wake Island | — | — | — | — | — | — | 134 | — | — | — | — | — |
| Iraq | — | — | — | — | — | — | — | 959 | 1,823 | 3,140 | 1,472 | 5,090 |
| Libya | — | — | — | — | — | — | — | 6,497 | 10,020 | 9,034 | 5,029 | 7,125 |
| Macau | — | — | — | — | — | — | — | — | 15 | 31 | 7 | 1 |
| Algeria | — | — | — | — | — | — | — | — | — | 150 | 228 | 799 |
| Malaysia | — | — | — | — | — | — | — | — | — | 49 | 943 | 2,214 |
| Oman | — | — | — | — | — | — | — | — | — | — | 109 | 736 |
| Total | 193 | — | 984 | 1,278 | 3,870 | 14,465 | 9,129 | 20,881 | 24,730 | 108,127 | 65,932 | |

*Source:* Office of Overseas Labour Management, Department of Labour.

**Table 3**. Number of migrant workers sent to work abroad by the Department of Labour, 1984

| Country | Sent by Thai broker | Sent by Dept of Labour | Sent by Thai entrepreneur | Total |
|---|---|---|---|---|
| Saudi Arabia | 51,262 | 528 | 51 | 51,851 |
| Libya | 5,029 | 43 | 20 | 5,092 |
| Iraq | 1,472 | — | — | 1,472 |
| Qatar | 1,020 | — | — | 1,021 |
| Bahrain | 198 | — | — | 198 |
| United Arab Emirates | 161 | — | — | 161 |
| Jordan | 1,833 | — | — | 1,833 |
| Kuwait | 2,208 | — | 365 | 2,573 |
| Oman | 109 | — | — | 109 |
| Algeria | 228 | — | — | 228 |
| Ethiopia | — | — | 35 | 35 |
| Indonesia | — | 17 | — | 17 |
| Malaysia | 943 | — | 27 | 970 |
| Singapore | 1,326 | — | 52 | 1,378 |
| Brunei | 136 | — | 104 | 240 |
| Macau | 7 | — | — | 7 |
| Japan | — | — | 137 | 137 |
| Total | 65,972 | 588 | 791 | 67,311 |

*Source:* Office of Overseas Labour Management, Department of Labour.

section to overseas employment. The plan stated that it was the government's policy to export labour to labour-deficient countries. The National Economic and Social Development Board carried out empirical studies to identify the target group in order to give effect to this policy.

However, according to reports by the Department of Labour, the role of the public sector in the West Asian migration was negligible. Government organizations, according to available evidence, had been responsible for only about 5 per cent of the total job placements in West Asian countries.

Present government policies indicate that public agencies will not get directly involved in the export of labour. Instead, the government will promote and facilitate the activities of private agencies, while retaining the role of policing, monitoring, and providing information to potential migrants. Since 1982, the Department of Labour has operated the Office of Overseas Labour Management to maintain records of activities related to overseas labour migration. The office provides data on the number of migrants and remittances, and settles disputes between migrants and recruiting agencies.

Table 5 indicates the total number of migrant workers who were granted permission to migrate by the Department of Labour and the remittances sent to the banks. It is estimated that the amounts presented here are about 70 per cent of the total remittances. Table 6 gives the amount of remittances sent from different countries for the period 1976–1984.

According to the Office of Labour Management, Department of Labour (1985), a total of about 240,000 migrants were working in the West Asian countries. A large

**Table 4.** Number of migrant workers sent to work abroad

| Country | 1978 | 1979 | 1980 | 1981 | 1982 | 1983 |
|---|---|---|---|---|---|---|
| Singapore | 250 | 1,251 | 532 | 959 | 74 | — |
| Saudi Arabia | — | 12 | 42 | 385 | 93 | 528 |
| Iraq | — | 175 | 29 | 156 | — | — |
| Libya | — | — | — | 169 | — | 43 |
| Japan | — | — | — | 150 | — | — |
| Oman | — | — | — | 5 | — | — |
| Indonesia | — | — | — | — | — | 17 |
| Total | 250 | 1,438 | 603 | 1,824 | 167 | 588 |

*Source:* Office of Overseas Labour Management, Department of Labour.

**Table 5.** Number of migrant workers granted permission by the Department of Labour and amount of remittances sent through banks during 1976–1985

| Year | Number of migrants | Amount of remittance sent through bank (millions of baht) |
|---|---|---|
| 1976 | 1,287 | 485.1 |
| 1977 | 3,870 | 911.6 |
| 1978 | 14,715 | 2,111.6 |
| 1979 | 10,567 | 3,818.3 |
| 1980 | 21,484 | 7,703.0 |
| 1981 | 26,740 | 10,428.2 |
| 1982 | 108,519 | 14,221.7 |
| 1983 | 68,484 | 19,457.3 |
| 1984 | 75,021 | 20,951.1 |
| 1985 (Jan. – March) | 16,921 | 5,821.5 |

*Source:* Office of Overseas Labour Management, Department of Labour, 1985.

majority of them, two-thirds, were working in Saudi Arabia. Of the remainder, about 12 per cent worked in Libya and about 10 per cent in Iraq.

About 70 per cent of the workers can be categorized as semi-skilled and engaged in construction work, while about a quarter are unskilled and only about 5 per cent are in the professional and managerial grades.

As the flow of migration increased, the reported cases of fraud also increased. According to available data, in 1983 7,264 such cases were reported, involving sums totalling 260 million baht. About one-fifth of the frauds were estimated to have been committed by illegal recruiting agencies, while the remainder were attributed to brokers. In response to this situation, in June 1984 the Thailand Job Placement Co-operative was formed. It was hoped that the number of frauds would be reduced by about 80 per cent during the first three months of the co-operative's activities. Furthermore, it was expected that, through its operations, the cost of job placements to migrants would be reduced substantially. Usually, brokers engaged in job placements charge about 10,000 to 13,000 baht per person.

**Table 6.** Remittances sent back by Thai migrant workers through banking systems, 1976–1984 (millions of baht)

| Country | 1976 | 1977 | 1978 | 1979 | 1980 | 1981 | 1982 | 1983 | 1984 |
|---|---|---|---|---|---|---|---|---|---|
| Bahrain | — | — | — | 0.4 | 0.1 | — | 17.5 | 28.1 | 25.0 |
| Cyprus | — | — | — | 0.3 | 0.7 | 0.2 | 1.2 | 0.5 | .6 |
| Jordan | — | — | 0.1 | — | 1.6 | 4.3 | 8.7 | 10.3 | 2.7 |
| Kuwait | — | 0.2 | 2.7 | 10.8 | 29.6 | 57.2 | 177.2 | 280.6 | 642.8 |
| Libya | — | — | 0.1 | — | 21.2 | 231.3 | 286.3 | 264.6 | 253.3 |
| Qatar | — | — | 5.8 | 7.1 | 22.2 | 39.9 | 39.5 | 29.7 | 21.2 |
| United Arab Emirates | 0.1 | 2.2 | 16.5 | 5.4 | 14.6 | 10.6 | 20.2 | 26.9 | 37.1 |
| Oman | — | — | 0.9 | 7.6 | 16.2 | 27.7 | 23.4 | 32.2 | 29.7 |
| Egypt | — | — | 0.2 | 2.3 | 3.8 | 9.9 | 7.8 | 5.7 | 9.1 |
| Iran | 3.0 | 9.3 | 16.5 | 36.6 | 8.8 | 0.6 | 0.3 | 1.2 | 2.3 |
| Israel | 0.3 | — | 0.1 | 1.3 | 181.1 | 358.0 | 40.2 | 3.8 | 4.5 |
| Lebanon | — | — | 0.2 | 0.1 | 0.7 | 1.8 | 14.1 | 20.9 | 11.7 |
| Saudi Arabia | 11.6 | 76.0 | 468.4 | 1,212.2 | 3,874.5 | 5,814.4 | 9,243.0 | 14,666.5 | 15,311.5 |
| Syria | — | — | — | 0.3 | 0.1 | — | — | 0.02 | .03 |
| Yemen | — | — | — | — | 11.6 | 7.1 | 3.8 | 0.5 | .2 |
| Iraq | — | — | 0.2 | 11.6 | 47.2 | 190.5 | 443.6 | 175.6 | 121.5 |
| Total Gulf Countries | 15.0 | 87.7 | 511.7 | 1,296.0 | 4,234.0 | 6,753.5 | 10,326.8 | 15,547.1 | 16,473.4 |
| United States | 367.4 | 591.7 | 1,189.0 | 1,842.4 | 2,164.9 | 2,358.5 | 206.7 | 2,071.7 | 2,444.6 |
| Singapore | 8.1 | 12.1 | 25.0 | 37.5 | 107.3 | 111.7 | 211.6 | 380.9 | 9.9 |
| Brunei | — | — | — | — | — | — | 9.9 | 24.6 | 53.4 |
| Federal Republic of Germany | — | — | — | — | — | — | — | — | 234.4 |
| France | — | — | — | — | — | — | — | — | 52.2 |
| Italy | — | — | — | — | — | — | — | — | 34.0 |
| Indonesia | — | — | — | — | — | — | — | — | 22.5 |
| Japan | — | — | — | — | — | — | — | — | 494.0 |
| Others | 94.6 | 220.3 | 385.9 | 642.4 | 1,196.8 | 1,204.5 | 1,466.7 | 1,290.3 | 745.5 |
| Total | 485.1 | 911.6 | 2,111.6 | 3,818.3 | 7,703.0 | 10,428.2 | 14,211.7 | 19,315.0 | 21,117.7 |

*Source:* Bank of Thailand.

The co-operative also expects to assist in the setting up and maintainance of labour standards by testing migrant workers before they leave the country. It is hoped that this will help reduce the incidence of mismatched migrants and jobs. Instances have been reported in which brokers or recruitment agencies have attempted to upgrade migrants by overstating their competence or qualifications to the host countries. Training in various skills, orientation related to camp life in the Gulf countries, cultural orientation, language training and information on local conditions are some of the other services that the co-operative expects to provide.

## Methodology

The study is based on both quantitative and qualitative data. The researchers agreed that the returnees would be the primary focus of the study. The sample therefore did not include those who, for various reasons such as fraud, were unable to migrate. This is a limitation of the study that has to be kept in mind.

In terms of quantitative research methodology, pre-test field surveys were carried out in October 1984 and student enumerators were employed. On the basis of the returns the questionnaires were revised. Actual field-work was carried out during March and April 1985 when the students were on summer vacation.

The draft questionnaire was agreed by the research team which carried out the country studies, and consisted of four parts: (1) personal data; (2) pre-migration data; (3) data during the period of work; and (4) post-migration data.

Statistics from the Labour Department for the year 1983 were used as guidelines for sampling. A list of provinces with the number of migrants was obtained and ranked in descending order. The first ten provinces with the highest number of migrants were identified. These provinces are located in the north-east and northern regions of the country, and were separated into two groups (table 7).

Once the provinces had been selected, the provincial labour officials and district heads were consulted in order to identify clusters from which the return migrants could be selected. In each province, the district with the highest number of returnees was identified. When possible, ten returnees each from five villages in the district were interviewed. However, when the number of returnees in each village

**Table 7.**

| Province | No. of migrants | Region |
|---|---|---|
| 1. Udon Thani | 8,879 | NE |
| 2. Khon Kaen | 4,300 | NE |
| 3. Nakhon Sawan | 4,300 | N |
| 4. Lampang | 4,292 | N |
| 5. Nakhon Ratchasima | 4,066 | NE |
| 6. Buriram | 1,274 | NE |
| 7. Chiang Rai | 2,853 | N |
| 8. Sakon Nakhon | 2,777 | NE |
| 9. Phichit | 2,442 | N |
| 10. Maha Sarakham | 2,069 | NE |

was less than ten, those in other villages were interviewed, making total of 50 returnees per province.

Questionnaires collected during March and April 1985 were coded and computerized using SPSS system analysis. First, frequencies were run to check inconsistencies and then cross-tabulations were made. Results of the analysis were examined carefully and only those tables which were meaningful and provided important information were used in the report. Many of the other tabulations not providing new information were discarded.

Regarding the qualitative research methodology, secondary data and interviews of key informants supplemented the survey information. In addition, case-studies were undertaken at the community level in Sakon Nakhon Province. One was selected from an area where a large irrigation system had been completed and where it was estimated that many opportunities for income-earning and generation for the return migrants existed. The second case-study was a poor community in Nakhon Sawan Province, where the level of government development activity was low. These two cases were expected to provide comparative information on the adjustment of migrants following their return.

## The Pre-migration Phase

### Profile of the Migrants: Demographic Information

According to the survey information, nearly nine out of every ten migrants was a married male (88 per cent), a head of a household (83 per cent), and with elementary education (88 per cent).

The migrants came from a family with an average size of 5.1, with nearly three (2.9) working members.

Those in the age-group 31–40 years made up the largest proportion of the migrants. The number of migratory visits increased with age, indicating that people remained in migratory activities for a long period. Among those who had made three or more visits to the West Asian countries, about two-thirds belonged to the 31–40 age-group.

The data also indicated that age and skill were related. There was a significantly higher concentration of unskilled workers in the lower age-groups. In many instances, the younger migrants seemed to be experiencing their first formal employment.

A large majority of the migrants had been drawn from the agricultural sector (73 per cent), and continued in that sector after their return (69 per cent). The proportion of unemployed among the return migrants seems to be higher than the average for the workforce as a whole. This is an indication of their increased capacity to remain outside the labour force and to search for suitable employment for a longer period of time. It appears from the survey evidence that migration to West Asian countries does not have a significant impact on labour mobility across sectors and occupations.

However, during the period of migration, a large proportion of workers, their previous occupation notwithstanding, were able to move into semi-skilled employment. About 60 per cent of the migrants had worked as semi-skilled workers while 28 per cent had been unskilled. However, on their return, a large proportion had been unable to utilize their skills or continue in occupations similar to the ones they had abroad.

Compared with the younger migrants, the older workers were more likely to obtain semi-skilled employment in spite of their previous employment.

When the employment categories are examined by country of destination, no significant differences were observed in the proportion of workers in each category. However, when we compare the migration to countries in the Asian region with the outflow to other countries, the pattern seems to change, with a greater proportion of workers entering unskilled occupations in the Asian migrant labour market. In Iraq and Libya, which together accounted for a little more than one-fifth of the total migrant labour force from Thailand, a higher proportion of the workers were placed in semi-skilled employment.

It is somewhat difficult to compare the employment categories before and after migration, owing to problems of classification. But, on the basis of available data, about 57 per cent of the farmers had worked in semi-skilled employment, while about one-third had obtained unskilled employment when they migrated. Prior to 1985, however, there was no skill-testing service, and therefore many workers had been placed in jobs for which they had little or no experience or skill. The government is now more concerned to ensure that skills and employment opportunities are better matched.

### Reasons for Seeking Employment Abroad

In the early stage of international migration to West Asia, those who had previous experience in US military bases, or who had worked with foreign firms, had an advantage. To work in foreign countries required a capacity to adjust to unfamiliar conditions. The pioneer migrants proved that the monetary returns from each trip were very attractive and this in turn motivated many others to follow. Estimates of returns on migration are presented in table 8.

Among the principal reasons for migration the following were important:
1. To raise standards of living (given as a primary reason by 28 per cent).
2. The need for additional income (43 per cent).
3. To settle loans and to repay debts (8 per cent).
4. To accumulate savings (29 per cent).
5. For purposes of gaining new experience and other reasons (3 per cent).
Quite clearly, monetary considerations are the most important reason for migration.

### Place of Origin

According to the data for the years 1977 to 1981, there is a noticeable shift in the place of origin of the migrants. In 1977, the provinces and towns close to the US military bases supplied a large and significantly higher proportion of the migrants to West Asia. However, by 1981 the pattern had changed, with a larger proportion of migrants coming from the poorer north-eastern districts as the flows increased. Table 11 shows that in 1977 more than half the migrants were from the central

**Table 8.** Comparing wages earned locally with wages earned in foreign countries

| Position | Foreign wages / Local wages | Present value of net foreign earning | Benefit: cost ratio | Rate of return |
|---|---|---|---|---|
| Labourer | 3.657 | 13,040.4 | 2.34 | 2.794 |
| Cleaner | 3.801 | 22,498.2 | 3.13 | 3.038 |
| Carpenter | 3.257 | 38,033.3 | 2.46 | 2.356 |
| Cement worker | 3.218 | 33,473.1 | 2.61 | 2.280 |
| Ironsmith | 2.770 | 41,231.2 | 2.35 | 1.525 |
| Mechanic | 5.330 | 80,823.4 | 4.41 | 4.008 |
| Welder | 3.512 | 51,315.6 | 2.86 | 2.289 |
| Electrician | 4.334 | 51,285.1 | 3.18 | 3.677 |
| Painter | 4.334 | 47,554.0 | 3.63 | 3.146 |
| Driver | 4.722 | 66,676.5 | 4.09 | 3.091 |
| Cook | 3.195 | 33,574.1 | 2.56 | 2.963 |
| Foreman | 2.607 | 53,411.3 | 4.13 | 1.869 |
| Other | 2.373 | 33,445.0 | 1.80 | 1.979 |
| Average | 3.786 | 41,923.6 | 1.69 | 2.194 |

*Source:* Niphon Phuaphongsakorn, *Thai Workers in Foreign Countries: Causes, Impacts, Problems and Policy* (1982).

region, but in 1981 the trend had shifted towards the north-east and the north. By 1983 about half of the migrants were from the north-east, the poorest region of the country.

As mentioned earlier, a large proportion of migrants were drawn from agriculture, and returned to agriculture following the migration. Many of the non-agricultural workers came from regional centres such as Khon Kaen and Nakhon Sawan, which are centres for the north-eastern and central regions. Self-employment and agricultural wage labour were occupations chosen by a large proportion of the returnees from Khon Kaen and Nakhon Sawan.

According to the survey data, there seems to be a small but detectable shift away from agricultural activities following migration. In the predominantly agricultural area of the north-east, about 80 per cent of the migrants had come from agricultural occupations, but on their return a small proportion were able to move out of this sector. The provinces that showed this tendency were Sakon Nakhon, Buriram, and Nakhon Ratchasima in the north-east and Phichit and Chiang Rai in the north. However, for some of the provinces in the north and north-east, for instance Maha Sarakham and Lampang, the proportion of people in agriculture seemed to have increased following migration. This perhaps might be related to factors other than the migration. The two north-eastern provinces Lampang and Udon Dhani, which had pioneered international migration to West Asia, contained the highest proportions of migrants who had travelled more than three times.

The ratio of skilled to unskilled migrants differed markedly between provinces. Lampang, for example, had no migrants in the unskilled category, Nakhon Sawan had 8 per cent, while Khon Kaen had a little less than one-fifth. The latter two provinces represent those in which a significant proportion of migrants have

**Table 9.** Top ten provinces with high number of Thai workers in Middle East countries, 1977, 1981, and 1983.

| 1977 | | 1981 | | 1983 | |
|---|---|---|---|---|---|
| Province | Percentage of country | Province | Percentage of country | Province | Percentage of country |
| Bangkok | 22.6 | Udon Thani | 20.1 | Udon Thani | 13.2 |
| Udon Thani | 14.5 | Bangkok | 14.8 | Khon Kaen | 6.7 |
| Chonburi | 13.1 | Lampang | 6.9 | Nakhon Sawan | 6.4 |
| Lampang | 12.4 | Nakhon Ratchasima | 5.5 | Lampang | 6.4 |
| Ubon Ratchathani | 5.9 | Chonburi | 3.5 | Nakhon Ratchasima | 6.1 |
| Rayong | 5.4 | Tak | 2.8 | Buriram | 4.9 |
| Nakhon Ratchasima | 3.3 | Khon Kaen | 2.7 | Chiang Rai | 4.2 |
| Samut Prakarn | 2.3 | Nong Khai | 2.6 | Sakon Nakhon | 4.1 |
| Nakhon Pranom | 1.6 | Samut Prakarn | 2.3 | Phichit | 3.6 |
| Nong Khai | 1.6 | Nakhon Sawan | 2.3 | Maha Sarakham | 3.1 |
| Others | 17.3 | Others | 36.5 | Others | 41.3 |
| Total | 100.0 | Total | 100.0 | Total | 100.0 |

*Source:* Department of Labour.

**Table 10.** Percentage distribution of Thai workers in the Middle East by region and province of origin, 1977, 1981 and 1983.

| Region and province | Percentage of region | | | Percentage of country | | |
|---|---|---|---|---|---|---|
| | 1977 | 1981 | 1983 | 1977 | 1981 | 1983 |
| North-east | 100.0 | 100.0 | 100.0 | 30.1 | 39.1 | 50.2 |
| Udon Thani | 48.0 | 50.9 | 26.3 | 14.5 | 20.1 | 13.2 |
| Ubon Ratchathani | 19.7 | — | 5.1 | 5.9 | — | 2.6 |
| Nakhon Ratchasima | 11.0 | 13.8 | 12.1 | 3.3 | 5.5 | 6.1 |
| Nakhon Panom | 5.3 | — | 1.0 | 1.6 | — | 0.5 |
| Khon Kaen | — | 6.3 | 13.4 | — | 2.7 | 6.7 |
| Nong Khai | 5.2 | 6.5 | 1.7 | 1.6 | 2.6 | 0.8 |
| Sakhon Nakhon | 3.9 | 5.3 | 8.2 | 1.2 | 2.1 | 4.1 |
| Chaiyaphum | — | 3.5 | 7.0 | — | 1.4 | 3.5 |
| Maha Sarakham | — | — | 6.1 | — | — | 3.1 |
| Buriram | — | — | 9.7 | — | — | 4.9 |
| Central | 100.0 | 100.0 | 100.0 | 52.2 | 38.0 | 11.9 |
| Bangkok | 43.3 | 39.0 | — | 22.6 | 14.8 | — |
| Samut Prakarn | 4.3 | 6.1 | — | 2.3 | 2.3 | — |
| Nonthaburi | 2.6 | — | — | 1.2 | — | — |
| Singhburi | — | 4.9 | — | — | 1.9 | — |
| Ayutthaya | — | 4.2 | 13.5 | — | 1.6 | 1.6 |
| Rayong | 10.4 | 4.0 | 2.7 | 5.4 | 1.5 | 0.3 |
| Chonburi | 25.1 | 9.2 | — | 13.1 | 3.5 | — |
| North | 100.0 | 100.0 | 100.0 | 17.6 | 22.1 | 31.7 |
| Lampang | 70.4 | 29.8 | 20.1 | 12.4 | 6.6 | 6.4 |
| Tak | — | 12.6 | — | — | 2.8 | — |
| Nakhon Sawan | 8.8 | 10.3 | 20.2 | 1.5 | 2.3 | 6.4 |
| Sukhothai | — | 8.6 | 7.6 | — | 1.9 | 2.4 |
| Khampaeng Phet | — | 6.6 | 4.7 | — | 1.4 | 1.5 |
| Pitsanulok | — | 6.6 | 8.7 | — | 1.4 | 2.8 |
| Chiang Rai | — | — | 13.4 | — | — | 4.2 |
| Phichit | — | — | 11.5 | — | — | 3.6 |
| Other | 20.8 | 25.6 | 13.8 | 3.7 | 5.7 | 4.4 |
| South | 100.0 | — | — | 0.1 | — | 6.1 |

*Sources:* National Economic and Social Development Board; Research Division, Bank of Thailand; Office of Overseas Management, Department of Labour.

shifted out of agricultural occupations on their return. However, in Lampang, as previously mentioned, the proportion of those in agriculture increased following migration, which implies that some of the migrants who originally were not in agriculture entered that sector after their return.

**The Recruitment Process**

The flow of migration to West Asia reached a peak in 1982 and then declined. Because of the importance of migration and its impact on the Thai economy, the government has made substantial efforts to improve the institutional and regula-

**Table 11.** Gross provincial product at current market prices (millions of baht)

|  | 1982 | 1983 | 1984 | 1985 |
|---|---|---|---|---|
| Province |  |  |  |  |
| Udon Thani | 13,115.3 | 13,163.5 | 13,366.5 | 13,625.4 |
| Sakhon Nakhon | 5,856.3 | 6,607.8 | 6,628.1 | 6,819.5 |
| Khon Kaen | 13,169.7 | 15,161.0 | 15,586.4 | 16,155.3 |
| Buriram | 7,736.4 | 8,846.2 | 8,741.2 | 8,818.8 |
| Maha Sarakham | 4,896.2 | 5,743.8 | 5,635.8 | 5,775.6 |
| Nakhon Ratchasima | 18,051.4 | 21,810.1 | 22,485.4 | 23,068.5 |
| Nakhon Sawan | 11,575.0 | 12,352.3 | 12,975.4 | 13,353.0 |
| Phichit | 5,660.3 | 5,941.8 | 6,203.0 | 6,245.4 |
| Lampang | 8,137.0 | 8,847.2 | 9,674.0 | 11,351.7 |
| Chiang Rai | 9,389.0 | 10,694.2 | 10,595.8 | 11,064.8 |
| Region |  |  |  |  |
| North | 110,407.2 | 112,161.8 | 128,080.4 | 135,436.9 |
| North-east | 112,820.8 | 141,190.9 | 141,684.9 | 146,496.3 |
| South | 82,752.9 | 95,360.1 | 99,334.8 | 102,552.8 |
| West | 78,653.8 | 77,131.8 | 82,450.2 | 83,756.4 |
| East | 100,222.0 | 107,691.2 | 115,360.9 | 120,976.8 |
| Central | 54,639.6 | 58,518.8 | 65,476.1 | 69,426.0 |
| Whole country (GDP) | 846,135.4 | 924,254.3 | 991,559.0 | 1,047,562.3 |

*Source:* NESDB, National Income Division, 1985.

tory framework. Significant attempts have been made to prevent and reduce illegal travel and fraud. A counselling service is offered by the Office of Overseas Labour Administration of the Department of Labour, which handles complaints related to overseas migration. In 1985, a security fund was set up with the aid of contracting companies to help those needing special assistance while abroad.

It needs to be kept in mind that the study underrepresents those who have encountered problems such as fraud, because the sample contains only those who have gone through the entire process and have been successful in their migration.

Informal networks seem to have played a dominant role in providing information on migration and conditions of work, as well as on fraudulent operators and brokers. The demonstration effects of returning friends and relatives appear to have played a large part in sponsoring migration in some villages. This was observed, for instance, in Nakhon Sawan, a province near Bangkok, where there is no local broker. The experiences of other migrants helped people avoid fraudulent agents and directed them towards qualified and registered agents. However, this does not imply that the recruitment process is now free of fraud, as there are still cases of reported malpractice. It is evident, though, that many migrants learnt their lesson the hard way and helped others to avoid similar misfortune. More than nine out of every ten migrants had formal contracts and agreements containing definite specifications, either in English or in Thai. About 10 per cent reported having signed contracts written only in Thai, while about a fifth were exclusively in English.

**Table 12.** Duration required and charges classified by types of arrangement (percentages)

| | Immigration clearance | Passport | Visa | Medical clearance | Exchange quota | Air ticket |
|---|---|---|---|---|---|---|
| **Duration (days)** | | | | | | |
| 1–7 | 5.2 | 53.8 | 4.2 | 65.0 | — | 5.6 |
| 8–15 | 7.4 | 19.0 | 8.6 | 3.2 | — | 7.8 |
| 16–30 | 10.0 | 14.2 | 11.0 | 3.2 | — | 9.8 |
| 31–60 | 4.6 | 2.2 | 4.4 | 1.8 | — | 4.0 |
| 61–90 | 1.6 | 0.6 | 1.6 | 0.6 | — | 1.6 |
| 91+ | 1.2 | — | 1.2 | — | — | 1.2 |
| No answer | — | 0.8 | 2.8 | 2.0 | 100.0 | 7.0 |
| Don't know | 70.0 | 9.4 | 66.2 | 24.2 | — | 63.0 |
| **Service charges (baht)** | | | | | | |
| 0 | 100.0 | 12.2 | 100.0 | 33.8 | 100.0 | 97.0 |
| 500–800 | — | 0.8 | — | 30.8 | — | 0.8 |
| 1,000–1,099 | — | 35.2 | — | 32.6 | — | 0.2 |
| 1,100–1,199 | — | 3.6 | — | 1.4 | — | — |
| 1,200–1,299 | — | 4.2 | — | 1.4 | — | — |
| 1,300–1,399 | — | 2.0 | — | — | — | — |
| 1,400–1,499 | — | 1.0 | — | — | — | — |
| 1,500–1,599 | — | 11.4 | — | — | — | — |
| 1,600–1,999 | — | 2.8 | — | — | — | — |
| 2,000–2,499 | — | 11.0 | — | — | — | — |
| 2,500–2,999 | — | 8.2 | — | — | — | 0.2 |
| 3,000–3,999 | — | 5.0 | — | — | — | — |
| 4,000–5,000 | — | 2.6 | — | — | — | — |
| 5,001+ | | | | | | 1.8 |

There was a significant waiting period between the initiation of the process of migration and arrival at the destination. The time required for the application process, from the time of submission of application to the time of job confirmation, took less than two months for about 70 per cent of the returnees. After being informed of the placement, there was another period of about two months before the migrant could leave the country (82 per cent of all cases, excluding Nakhon Ratchasima Province). There were variations in the manner in which the recruitment process was organized. The migrants from Chakarat District, Nakhon Ratchasima Province, differed from the others in that here a large proportion of the recruitment agents were people of the village who themselves had been migrants. After returning, one migrant had started a private company, arranging for relatives and friends living in the neighbouring villages to migrate. Most villagers trusted the firm and there had been no reported fraud. Since the relationships between the agent and the migrants were informal and friendly, migrants were generally contented with the arrangements. However, the migrants in this village had a longer waiting period than those from other provinces, partly because their agent was located in the village and partly owing to a lack of professionalism and organizational skill, which was however compensated for by familiarity and the localized service.

**Table 13.** Comparison of contract agreement and actual condition (percentages)

| Agreement | Contract | | Actual condition of specified cases | | |
|---|---|---|---|---|---|
| | Specified | Not specified | Better | Same | Worse |
| Level and type of work | 88 | 12 | 5 | 88 | 7 |
| Job specification | 80 | 20 | 4 | 89 | 7 |
| Payment | 89 | 11 | 8 | 81 | 11 |
| Working hours | 89 | 11 | 1 | 93 | 5 |
| Overtime pay | 78 | 22 | 4 | 89 | 7 |
| Facilities | 71 | 29 | 6 | 89 | 5 |
| Travel arrangement | 65 | 35 | 2 | 96 | 2 |
| Holidays | 82 | 18 | — | 97 | 3 |
| Food | 76 | 24 | 5 | 85 | 10 |
| Maintenance | 84 | 16 | 4 | 89 | 7 |
| Compensation in case of accident | 79 | 21 | 2 | 92 | 6 |
| Vacation at home | 70 | 29 | 1 | 94 | 5 |
| End of contract | 85 | 15 | 2 | 91 | 7 |
| Return travel | 74 | 26 | — | 95 | 5 |
| End of benefit | 78 | 22 | 1 | 93 | 6 |
| Other | 1 | 99 | — | 100 | — |

About a quarter of the migrants had not received advice about conditions of work, etc., prior to their departure. About one in ten had received such information from relatives and friends. For a majority of migrants (about 60 per cent), advice was provided by the contracting agents.

A majority of the migrants (94 per cent) had contracts that specified durations and other requirements. Only about 4 per cent had informal agreements. However, about four-fifths stated that they had not made any negotiations prior to signing their contract; among those that did, salaries had been the primary concern. For those that did not negotiate, one-third were unaware that it was possible and over a half were satisfied with the terms that were presented.

The contracting agents played an important role during the application process, taking care of most of the activities during this phase. Passport and medical clearance were two of the main items that were processed by the migrants. More than three-quarters had made arrangements for the passports themselves. About one out of every ten return migrants stated that the recruiting agents had made arrangements for their passports, while a similar proportion had been assisted by brokers specifically engaged in obtaining passports. The average waiting time for a passport was between one and three days.

More than half (57 per cent) of the migrants obtained the necessary health certificates on their own. In Nakhon Sawan, brokers played a dominant role. Nearly nine out of every ten migrants had paid an agent for job placement. Nearly eight out of every ten incurred costs for travelling and for travel arrangements, about four out of ten had made financial payments for household arrangements, and nearly six out of ten had incurred other personal expenses.

Each migrant paid an average of 30,000 to 40,000 baht for a trip to the West Asian

**Table 14.** Different forms of entertainment of migrants classified by host country (percentages)

| Entertainment | Saudi Arabia | Iraq | Libya | Other Gulf countries | Asian countries | Total |
|---|---|---|---|---|---|---|
| Television, radio | | | | | | |
| Frequent | 68.1 | 59.5 | 41.2 | 84.8 | 58.1 | 65.2 |
| Infrequent | 24.0 | 28.6 | 35.3 | 12.1 | 27.0 | 20.8 |
| Never | 7.9 | 11.9 | 23.5 | 3.0 | 1.4 | 8.0 |
| Cinema | | | | | | |
| Frequent | 12.9 | 2.4 | 11.8 | 9.1 | 8.1 | 11.0 |
| Infrequent | 13.6 | 21.4 | 20.6 | 12.1 | 31.1 | 17.2 |
| Never | 73.5 | 76.2 | 67.6 | 78.8 | 60.8 | 71.8 |
| Sports | | | | | | |
| Frequent | 30.3 | 33.3 | 44.1 | 45.5 | 14.9 | 30.2 |
| Infrequent | 30.6 | 19.0 | 23.5 | 18.2 | 20.3 | 26.8 |
| Never | 39.1 | 47.6 | 32.4 | 36.4 | 64.9 | 43.0 |
| Picnics/tours | | | | | | |
| Frequent | 28.7 | 35.7 | 23.5 | 27.3 | 28.4 | 28.8 |
| Infrequent | 51.4 | 42.9 | 52.9 | 57.6 | 51.4 | 51.2 |
| Never | 19.9 | 21.4 | 23.5 | 15.2 | 20.3 | 20.0 |
| Total | 100 (317) | 100 (42) | 100 (34) | 100 (33) | 100 (74) | 100 (500) |

countries and between 10,000 and 20,000 baht to go to other Asian countries. Most of the money was channelled through the recruiting agents, who claimed that they had to pay bribes both in Thailand and in the host countries. On the basis of the data, it is not clear why some parts of the preparatory work are handled largely by the migrants themselves while other parts are given over to recruiting agents. It may well be that the information flows on how to get particular services are inadequate and need improvement.

The three most important sources of funds for expenses prior to migration were personal savings, loans from relatives, and loans from friends. More than ten per cent obtained loans from private banks to finance their expenditures prior to departure, while about a quarter of the migrants from the different provinces had used their savings. In two provinces which had a high share of the migrant population, Maha Sarakham and Lampang, significant proportions of the migrants had resorted to selling assets for the trip (44 and 30 per cent respectively).

The migrants expressed a strong desire for greater government participation in the recruitment and placement process. However, the government has taken a policy decision to leave this area in the hands of the private sector.

**Training and Information**

More than 80 per cent of the informants stated that they had received training, organized primarily by the contracting agents. These training sessions provided general information on travel procedures, how to remit earnings, and work conditions in the host countries. More than two-thirds of the informants indicated that they had received sufficient information about living conditions and customs in the

**Table 15.** Migrants' personal relationships with others classified by host country (percentages)

| | Saudi Arabia | Iraq | Libya | Other Gulf countries | Asian countries | Total |
|---|---|---|---|---|---|---|
| **Host** | | | | | | |
| Frequent | 21.5 | 35.7 | 32.4 | 27.3 | 40.5 | 26.6 |
| Infrequent | 31.9 | 31.0 | 23.5 | 36.4 | 27.0 | 30.8 |
| Never | 46.7 | 33.3 | 35.7 | 36.4 | 32.4 | 42.6 |
| **Migrants from home** | | | | | | |
| Frequent | 95.0 | 95.2 | 100 | 91.2 | 98.6 | 95.8 |
| Infrequent | 4.4 | 2.4 | | 3.0 | | 3.2 |
| Never | .6 | 2.4 | | 3.0 | 1.4 | 1.0 |
| **Migrants from other countries** | | | | | | |
| Frequent | 49.2 | 59.5 | 55.9 | 42.4 | 51.4 | 50.4 |
| Infrequent | 36.0 | 31.0 | 23.5 | 33.3 | 24.3 | 32.8 |
| Never | 14.8 | 9.5 | 20.6 | 24.2 | 24.3 | 16.8 |
| **Picnics/tours** | | | | | | |
| Frequent | 28.7 | 35.7 | 23.5 | 27.3 | 28.4 | 28.8 |
| Infrequent | 51.4 | 42.9 | 52.9 | 57.6 | 51.4 | 51.2 |
| Never | 19.9 | 21.4 | 23.5 | 15.2 | 20.3 | 20.0 |
| Total | 100 (317) | 100 (42) | 100 (34) | 100 (33) | 100 (74) | 100 (500) |

host country, while a smaller proportion said they had received adequate information regarding emergency action and regulations.

## The Migration Phase

In this section the situation in the host country and the conditions at home during migration will be discussed. However, the information presented is primarily that given by the migrants themselves, and may be influenced by subjective biases of various types.

### Conditions in the Host Countries

Problems on Arrival

The majority of the migrants did not seem to have encountered difficulties on arrival, primarily because contracts were made through contracting agents prior to departure. Arrangements to settle migrants at work were organized satisfactorily by the agents, and in general the accommodation was considered to be adequate or satisfactory.

A large majority of the migrants, nine out of ten, were satisfied with the contract terms as stipulated. This applied to working hours, travel arrangements, holidays, compensation in case of accidents, vacation at home, termination benefits, and return travel. However, two out of every ten found that the actual conditions and terms were different from the contracted ones. Nevertheless, out of the 20 per cent

**Table 16.** Migrants' community activities and group organization classified by host country (percentages)

| | Saudi Arabia | Iraq | Libya | Other Gulf countries | Asian countries | Total |
|---|---|---|---|---|---|---|
| *Community activities* | | | | | | |
| National festivals | | | | | | |
| Frequent | 23.0 | 40.5 | 38.2 | 70.3 | 32.4 | 27.4 |
| Infrequent | 53.9 | 40.5 | 35.7 | 60.6 | 43.2 | 51.0 |
| Never | 23.0 | 19 | 17.6 | 9.1 | 24.3 | 21.6 |
| Sports events | | | | | | |
| Frequent | 27.1 | 40.5 | 50.0 | 27.3 | 20.3 | 28.8 |
| Infrequent | 37.5 | 35.7 | 23.5 | 36.4 | 21.6 | 34.0 |
| Never | 35.3 | 23.8 | 26.5 | 36.4 | 58.1 | 37.2 |
| Music, drama, etc. | | | | | | |
| Frequent | 8.2 | 9.5 | 23.5 | 9.1 | 13.5 | 10.2 |
| Infrequent | 39.4 | 52.4 | 23.5 | 51.5 | 21.6 | 37.6 |
| Never | 52.4 | 38.1 | 52.9 | 39.4 | 64.9 | 52.2 |
| *Group organization* | | | | | | |
| Active member | 17.0 | 14.3 | 17.6 | 21.2 | 6.8 | 15.6 |
| Regular member | 6.9 | 7.1 | 11.8 | 12.2 | 4.1 | 7.2 |
| Total | 100 (317) | 100 (42) | 100 (34) | 100 (33) | 100 (74) | 100 (500) |

who encountered different conditions, nearly equal proportions had either better or worse conditions. About 15 per cent of the migrants found that food was different from what was stated in the contract, or what was expected. But in general, among those who had specified contractual terms on a wide range of items, a large and significant majority found that the actual conditions were in fact similar to what was stated. Less than 10 per cent of the migrants had encountered actual conditions which were worse than those believed to be stated in the contract. In terms of payment, however, about one out of every ten found that payment was lower than what was stated in the contract.

On arrival a small proportion of the migrants (8 per cent) found that they were not placed in jobs that had been promised. About 1 per cent returned home following non-placement on arrival, though, for those who were not placed, no compensation was paid. A small proportion (5 per cent) had managed to leave Thailand without having secured prospects of a job in the host country, but the majority (92 per cent) left with work permits. Among those who had ventured out without job contracts (5 per cent who had no firm jobs) 2 per cent eventually signed contracts.

About one out of every six returnees was able to obtain a further contract period, and for the majority the contract terms were similar to the previous one. However, nearly 18 per cent who had renewed their contracts were able to obtain better terms, while more than one in every ten returned under poorer conditions and terms. Once again, owing to the nature of the sampling it may well be that the cases which had serious difficulties in the initial stage have been underrepresented.

Upon arrival, most migrants contacted the recruiting agents or friends, while a

**Table 17.** Adjustment problems while abroad classified by host country

| | Saudi Arabia | Iraq | Libya | Other Gulf country | Non-Gulf country | All countries |
|---|---|---|---|---|---|---|
| Living conditions | 64.4 | 78.6 | 55.9 | 69.7 | 56.8 | 64.2 |
| Withdrew, stayed alone | 33.8 | 38.1 | 23.5 | 42.4 | 17.6 | 31.8 |
| Needed friends, became outgoing | 47.6 | 50.0 | 44.1 | 39.4 | 52.7 | 68.2 |
| New habits | | | | | | |
| Reading | 55.8 | 52.4 | 55.9 | 48.5 | 37.8 | 52.4 |
| Watching TV | 38.8 | 42.9 | 32.4 | 51.5 | 48.6 | 41.2 |
| Eating out | 11.7 | 4.8 | 23.5 | 12.1 | 18.9 | 13.0 |
| Smoking | 10.1 | 4.8 | 17.6 | 9.1 | 10.8 | 10.2 |
| Heavy smoking | 22.1 | 23.8 | 32.4 | 18.2 | 17.6 | 22.0 |
| Drinking | 8.8 | 7.1 | 17.6 | 6.1 | 17.6 | 10.4 |
| Heavy drinking | 7.9 | 11.9 | 5.9 | 9.1 | 10.8 | 8.6 |
| Sleeplessness | 71.3 | 66.7 | 61.8 | 39.4 | 52.7 | 65.4 |
| Frequent sickness | 23.7 | 23.8 | 14.7 | 27.3 | 17.6 | 22.4 |
| Health problem due to homesickness | 34.4 | 35.7 | 32.4 | 33.3 | 17.6 | 68.6 |
| Learned household chores | 45.7 | 47.6 | 32.4 | 54.5 | 52.7 | 46.6 |

Table 18. Adjustment problems while abroad classified by province of origin

| | North-east | | | | | | North | | | | |
| --- | --- | --- | --- | --- | --- | --- | --- | --- | --- | --- | --- |
| | Udon Thani | Sakon Nakhon | Khon Kaen | Maha Sarakham | Buriram | Nakhon Ratchasima | Nakhon Sawan | Phichit | Lampang | Chiang Rai | Total |
| Adjustment to new environment | 76 | 62 | 64 | 68 | 54 | 58 | 56 | 64 | 68 | 72 | 64.2 |
| Withdrawn | 42 | 44 | 22 | 22 | 44 | 30 | 30 | 36 | 24 | 18 | 31.2 |
| More outgoing | 50 | 50 | 48 | 60 | 30 | 58 | 48 | 32 | 48 | 46 | 47.0 |
| New habits | | | | | | | | | | | |
| Reading | 40 | 48 | 58 | 58 | 54 | 54 | 52 | 56 | 56 | 48 | 52.4 |
| Watching TV | 48 | 34 | 54 | 56 | 42 | 44 | 26 | 34 | 40 | 34 | 41.2 |
| Eating out | 14 | 6 | 10 | 28 | 18 | 8 | 4 | 10 | 16 | 16 | 13.0 |
| Started smoking | 12 | 20 | 8 | 18 | 18 | 18 | 2 | 4 | — | 2 | 10.2 |
| Became heavy smoker | 22 | 20 | 38 | 30 | 14 | 18 | 30 | 14 | 24 | 18 | 22.8 |
| Started drinking | 10 | 12 | 10 | 30 | 14 | 20 | 2 | 2 | — | 4 | 10.4 |
| Became heavy drinker | 4 | 8 | 16 | 18 | 6 | 12 | 6 | — | 6 | 6 | 8.2 |
| Sleeplessness | 68 | 56 | 62 | 64 | 68 | 62 | 70 | 60 | 82 | 62 | 65.4 |
| Frequent sickness | 20 | 20 | 20 | 32 | 26 | 14 | 28 | 18 | 24 | 22 | 22.4 |
| Homesickness | 34 | 34 | 40 | 30 | 44 | 26 | 26 | 24 | 34 | 22 | 31.4 |

very few contacted the Thai embassy. The embassy had been a rescue station at some point for about one-fifth of the informants. About 4 per cent of the migrants had contacted the embassy upon arrival, while about 14 per cent made contact during their period of stay. Assistance was obtained from the embassy concerning arbitration and contract disputes, contacting families, remittances, social activities, and emergencies.

There is the possibility of an important role for the Thai embassies in the West Asian countries with high Thai migrant labour forces. It would be useful to have a labour attaché primarily to assist the migrant. Even minor problems that are not handled appropriately can have disastrous results. The lack of familiarity with local customs, rules, and forms of justice can have serious adverse consequences for migrants.

Living Conditions in the Host Countries

Most of the migrants found that they had to share accommodation with their countrymen. A large majority thought the housing facilities sufficient or even good. However, about 7 per cent indicated that they were bad, while 5 per cent stated that they were unsatisfactory. Nearly half of the migrants were dissatisfied with their food in some way or other. More than three-quarters obtained their food through their workplace, and about one-fifth did their own cooking. About one in every ten migrants (11 per cent) felt the food to be better than what they were used to.

A predominant form of entertainment for the migrants was listening to the radio and watching television; nearly two-thirds did this on a regular basis. However, about 8 per cent of the migrants claimed that they never watched TV or listened to the radio. This may be related both to illiteracy and to problems with the language.

The migrants had the distinct impression that the host countries discouraged mixing and interacting with the locals.

The migrants tend to live and interact primarily with those from the home country, a tendency that is reinforced by communication problems and by the manner in which the host country accommodates the migrants, though it is not, of course, unique to the West Asian migrant setting. Owing to communication problems, most migrants live with people from the home country, while a few have foreign housemates. Less than 1 per cent live with people of the host country.

Nine out of every ten migrants interacted frequently with people from the home country. Because of the lack of facilities, migrants in West Asian countries were rarely able to observe their religious practices, and only about a fifth took part in some form of religious activity.

The nature of the social activities of Thai migrant workers differed between the West Asian and the South and South-East Asian settings. In South and South-East Asia Thai workers had more opportunities for religious worship, and more contact with people from the host country, and seemed to be better equipped for, and better settled in, that environment.

Opportunities for Thai migrants to organize themselves for various social activities, that is, to form clubs and unions, were severely limited. However, about one in five of the migrants stated that they belonged to some form of organization that had been set up to facilitate sports and social activities; of these, one-third were regular members. The lack of associations and clubs might be partly related to the

**Table 19.** Adjustment problems while abroad classified by skill category

| | Unskilled | Semi-skilled | Foreman | Service | Total |
|---|---|---|---|---|---|
| Adjustment to new environment | 65.2 | 62.6 | 85.7 | 57.4 | 64.2 |
| Withdrawn | 32.9 | 34.3 | 42.9 | 16.2 | 31.2 |
| More outgoing | 4.4 | 43.4 | 50.0 | 52.9 | 47.0 |
| New habits | | | | | |
| Reading | 55.5 | 52.5 | 57.1 | 36.8 | 52.4 |
| Watching TV | 38.9 | 43.4 | 50.0 | 47.1 | 41.2 |
| Eating out | 11.9 | 14.1 | 7.1 | 17.6 | 13.0 |
| Started smoking | 10.0 | 10.1 | 14.3 | 10.3 | 10.2 |
| Became heavy smoker | 21.9 | 27.2 | 28.6 | 19.1 | 22.8 |
| Started drinking | 8.8 | 10.1 | 14.3 | 10.3 | 10.2 |
| Became heavy drinker | 7.2 | 10.1 | 14.3 | 8.8 | 8.2 |
| Sleeplessness | 71.2 | 57.5 | 50.0 | 52.4 | 65.4 |
| Frequently sickness | 23.5 | 22.2 | 21.4 | 17.6 | 22.4 |
| Homesickness | 34.5 | 33.3 | 35.7 | 13.2 | 31.4 |
| Total number | 319 | 99 | 14 | 68 | 500 |

skills and past experience of the migrants themselves. It is not possible with the available data to examine the impediments to association in the host country.

Other forms of social activity and entertainment included national festivals, sports events, music, and drama. More than one-fourth of the migrants reported frequent participation in the first two, and about 10 per cent in music and drama. Significant proportions (21 and 52 per cent), however, said they never enjoyed opportunities to participate in any of these activities.

Only a small proportion of the migrants faced legal problems while working abroad. Half of those that did encountered problems in the workplace, while a smaller proportion was involved in gambling and alcohol-related offences.

Adjustment to the stresses of an unfamiliar environment and separation took different forms among the migrants. For about 30 per cent the response appears to have been one of withdrawal, while in others (about half) it was the opposite – one of seeking company and forming friendships. About 30 per cent expressly stated that they were homesick. Insomnia was reported by a majority of migrants, approximately two-thirds. Part of the process of adjustment resulted in the formation of new habits and addictions – smoking among 10 per cent and drinking alcohol among 8 per cent. Existing addictions – smoking and drinking – became more pronounced for larger proportions of migrants. A significant number (22 per cent) reported frequent ill-health.

## Conditions at Home

The typical migrant left behind two types of responsibilities – first, that of looking after his home and family, and, second, the responsibilities related to agricultural activities.

As mentioned earlier, most of the migrants came from traditional rural backgrounds, where relatives and friends played a significant role in assisting the family of the migrant. The extended family assisted in child care, provided support in times of emergency, co-operated and provided labour for agricultural activities.

The information obtained from the surveys indicates that the incidence of maladjustment in the migrant family was acceptably low (see table 20). In three provinces, Maha Sarakham, Lampang, and Chiang Rai, conditions for the families of migrants seem to have improved whil they were working abroad.

Adjustment to the absence of the household head was not easily made for a significant number of the spouses (about 30 per cent). But more than 40 per cent viewed the new situation as a challenge. The absence of the father had an adverse impact on a large number of the children of migrant worker families, with approximately 40 per cent reporting problems ranging from aggression and uncooperative behaviour to ill-health and withdrawal. The responsibilities and duties of the wives had, therefore, increased in a significant measure.

The separation that resulted from migration had not imposed strains on family relationships for most migrants. A large majority (70 per cent) indicated that relationships had improved during the migration, while they were recorded to have deteriorated in only about 5 per cent of the migrant households. About four in every five migrants of the 80 per cent who were married corresponded with their wives; about one in six corresponded regularly with relatives.

## Remittances

This section deals with the manner in which the earnings of the migrants were transferred to their families. It examines the volume and type of remittances, and the manner in which they were utilized.

### The Transfer of Remittances

The large majority of the migrants used the commercial banking system to transfer funds to their families. Remittances, usually in the form of bank drafts or transfers, were sent to family members, wives (73 per cent), and parents (17 per cent).

Funds were remitted by the migrants at regular intervals. About two-thirds sent money every month, while about 17 per cent did so every two months.

The repayment of loans was an important consideration in the frequency and regularity of remittances. For those migrants who borrowed to make the trip, transfers were made to liquidate outstanding debts as soon as adequate earnings were collected.

A significant proportion of the migrants had been accustomed to dealings with the formal banking sector; about four-fifths had maintained savings accounts before migration. Their remittances were transferred into drafts deposited into these accounts. About three-quarters of the migrants sent drafts while the remainder remitted through bank transfers. All respondents indicated that encashments were made within a day.

The frequency of transfers depended on the country of migration. Migrants in most countries transferred funds either every month or every two months. How-

**Table 20.** General family conditions of migrants before and after migration classified by province

| | North-east | | | | | | North | | | | Total |
|---|---|---|---|---|---|---|---|---|---|---|---|
| | Udon Thani | Sakon Nakhon | Khon Kaen | Maha Sarakham | Buriram | Nakhon Ratchasima | Nakhon Sawan | Phichit | Lampang | Chiang Rai | |
| Much better | 22 | 24 | 6 | 8 | 8 | 10 | 14 | 16 | 26 | 2 | 13.6 |
| Better | 22 | 34 | 52 | 52 | 46 | 40 | 50 | 36 | 42 | 56 | 42.8 |
| Same | 50 | 38 | 38 | 40 | 38 | 48 | 34 | 46 | 32 | 42 | 40.6 |
| Worse | 6 | 4 | 2 | — | 8 | 2 | 2 | 2 | | | 2.6 |
| Much worse | — | — | 2 | — | — | — | — | — | | | .2 |

**Table 21.** Change in behaviour of family members classified by province

| | North-east | | | | | | North | | | | |
| | Udon Thani | Sakon Nakhon | Khon Kaen | Maha Sarakham | Buriram | Nakhon Ratchasima | Nakhon Sawan | Phichit | Lampang | Chiang Rai | Total |
|---|---|---|---|---|---|---|---|---|---|---|---|
| **Children's behaviour** | | | | | | | | | | | |
| Aggressive, mischievous | 14 | 22 | 16 | 20 | 12 | 2 | 18 | 14 | 10 | 10 | 13.8 |
| Uncooperative | 4 | 4 | 8 | 10 | — | — | 6 | — | 2 | 2 | 3.6 |
| Sick | 14 | 18 | 20 | 22 | 12 | — | 22 | 10 | 6 | 2 | 12.6 |
| Withdrawn | 12 | 20 | 22 | 10 | 8 | 6 | 16 | 10 | 2 | 4 | 11.0 |
| **Spouse's behaviour** | | | | | | | | | | | |
| Found experience challenging | 42 | 52 | 48 | 50 | 54 | 28 | 32 | 48 | 40 | 40 | 43.4 |
| Felt stressed | 28 | 34 | 34 | 30 | 38 | 24 | 34 | 44 | 24 | 16 | 30.6 |
| Sick/depressed | 24 | 24 | 18 | 18 | 18 | 4 | 24 | 24 | 10 | 8 | 17.2 |
| Fine | 64 | 68 | 64 | 60 | 66 | 58 | 56 | 66 | 68 | 54 | 62.4 |

**Table 22**. Average first month's income, average first month's expenses, and average monthly savings classified by age-group (baht)

|  | 20–30 | 31–40 | 41–50 | 51–60 |
|---|---|---|---|---|
| Average first month's income[a] | 7,725 | 8,924 | 9,214 | 11,691 |
| Average first month's expenses | 2,167 | 1,242 | 1,160 | 490 |
| Average monthly savings | 8,133 | 9,123 | 9,107 | 10,174 |
| Total cases | 154 | 214 | 114 | 18 |

a. Overtime and other income not included.

ever, those in Libya had difficulty in sending money because of government regulations. In Iraq, bank-to-bank transfer is more popular than in other countries, where drafts are the predominant form of transfer. A large majority of the migrants did not encounter serious difficulties in remitting money, but a small proportion, about 5 per cent, reported that they had been cheated or had lost their drafts in the mail. Therefore the prevailing systems which transfer funds from migrants to their families seem to be working with a high degree of efficiency.

The quantum remitted at any given time varied from a few hundred to about 16,000 baht or more.

### Income, Expenditure, and Savings

The average base pay, excluding overtime and other payments, in the first month of work, seems to vary significantly according to age. Those in the youngest age-group earned an average base income which was considerably lower than that earned by people in the middle age category (see table 22). The relationship between the average monthly incomes is derived from the relationship of skill and income. Those in the higher age-groups were predominantly engaged in semi-skilled and skilled employment, while those in the younger age-group, especially between the ages of 20 and 30, were concentrated in unskilled employment. The data are related to the first month's earnings. It is expected that the earnings will increase with experience. Another factor which explains the higher incomes of older persons, even those in similar occupations, is that of experience.

Expenditure during the first month varied significantly with age: the young had much higher expenditure than the old. The older, more experienced migrants tend to exercise greater restraint in making impulsive purchases and regulating their consumption, while the management of higher incomes is a greater challenge for the younger migrants. Expenditures are expected to be reduced slightly in the later months for most of the migrants.

The migrants were able to earn incomes that were higher than the stipulated base pay. As expected, the base wage differed significantly by level of skill: the unskilled workers earned about 40 per cent less than the semi-skilled/skilled workers (base wage only). The premium of the service personnel was about half as large as that of the skilled migrants. Taken as a group, the semi-skilled/skilled migrants had a higher first-month expenditure than the unskilled workers, while those in the service employment category had the lowest first month's expendi-

**Table 23.** Average first month's income, average first month's expenses, and average monthly savings classified by occupation (baht)

| | Unskilled | Semi-skilled/ skilled | Foreman | Service |
|---|---|---|---|---|
| Average first month's income[a] | 6,739 | 9,575 | 12,777 | 8,162 |
| Average first month's expenses | 1,143 | 1,718 | 1,197 | 1,034 |
| Average monthly savings | 6,756 | 9,650 | 13,290 | 8,867 |
| Total cases | 138 | 304 | 11 | 47 |

a. Overtime and other income not included.

**Table 24.** Average first month's income, average first month's expenses, and average monthly savings classified by host country (baht)

| | Saudi Arabia | Iraq | Libya | Other Gulf countries | Other Asian countries |
|---|---|---|---|---|---|
| Average first month's income | 8,987 | 10,867 | 10,236 | 9,542 | 5,792 |
| Average first month's expenses | 1,165 | 1,304 | 1,363 | 1,401 | 1,244 |
| Average monthly savings | 9,007 | 10,035 | 10,085 | 9,975 | 5,539 |

ture. This may be partly explained by the kind of additional non-monetary benefits obtained by these individuals; for example, those working in hotels and in homes may have received food. Payments in kind, because of their impact on incomes, are, therefore, an important consideration in the manner in which savings and expenditures are made by the migrants.

The skill composition and, consequently, average earnings, expenditure, and savings varied according to the country of destination. Migrants to Iraq and Libya earned higher average incomes during the first month, and in general received about 10 to 15 per cent more than those in other countries. Nevertheless, the difference in expenditure was not as large.

There were no significant differences in expenditure, average monthly savings, and amount of remittance by province. Nor did the amount saved by the migrant's family vary by province.

## Types of Investment

The first thing that most migrant households did upon receiving remittances was to repay debts. Those migrants who were unable to complete their contract encountered great difficulty and ended up losing as much as 50,000 baht on their migratory effort. During the period in which debts had to be repaid, the migrant family saved as much as possible. Once the debts had been repaid, it was noticed

**Table 25.** Types of investments by migrants classified by province of residence (percentages)

| | North-east | | | | | | North | | | | Total |
|---|---|---|---|---|---|---|---|---|---|---|---|
| | Udon Thani | Sakon Nakhon | Khon Kaen | Maha Sarakham | Buriram | Nakhon Ratchasima | Nakhon Sawan | Phichit | Lampang | Chiang Rai | |
| Home | 36.0 | 54.0 | 32.0 | 46.0 | 44.0 | 50.0 | 42.0 | 34.0 | 48.0 | 38.0 | 42.4 |
| Land | 38.0 | 36.0 | 34.0 | 36.0 | 26.0 | 22.0 | 30.0 | 28.0 | 28.0 | 42.0 | 27.0 |
| Equipment | 10.0 | 8.0 | 6.0 | 12.0 | 8.0 | 30.0 | 14.0 | 12.0 | 36.0 | 22.0 | 15.8 |
| Vehicles | 22.0 | 18.0 | 24.0 | 20.0 | 26.0 | 24.0 | 42.0 | 32.0 | 68.0 | 60.0 | 66.4 |
| Other assets | 42.0 | 40.0 | 56.0 | 64.0 | 62.0 | 66.0 | 68.0 | 64.0 | 74.0 | 72.0 | 60.6 |
| Fixed deposits | 22.0 | 30.0 | 30.0 | 36.0 | 22.0 | 28.0 | 48.0 | 20.0 | 28.0 | 26.0 | 71.0 |
| Investments | 6.0 | 8.0 | 6.0 | 6.0 | 10.0 | 2.0 | 10.0 | 8.0 | 2.0 | 10.0 | 6.8 |
| Children's education | 24.0 | 10.0 | 26.0 | 22.0 | 14.0 | 14.0 | 14.0 | 14.0 | 20.0 | 6.0 | 16.4 |
| Pay back debts | 76.0 | 88.0 | 80.0 | 84.0 | 86.0 | 74.0 | 86.0 | 78.0 | 76.0 | 86.0 | 81.0 |
| Social activities, helping relatives | 38.0 | 38.0 | 60.0 | 54.0 | 44.0 | 50.0 | 70.0 | 52.0 | 58.0 | 42.0 | 50.6 |
| Marriages | 32.0 | 26.0 | 30.0 | 34.0 | 34.0 | 42.0 | 8.0 | 6.0 | 10.0 | 10.0 | 23.2 |
| Funerals | 24.0 | 30.0 | 26.0 | 30.0 | 34.0 | 38.0 | 8.0 | 6.0 | 16.0 | 8.0 | 25.0 |
| Medicine | 30.0 | 30.0 | 26.0 | 30.0 | 30.0 | 26.0 | 4.0 | 2.0 | 2.0 | 6.0 | 18.6 |

**Table 26.** Amount of investment in housing classified by age-group

| Amount in baht | Less than 30 | 31–40 | 41–50 | Over 51 | Total |
|---|---|---|---|---|---|
| 1–2,999 | 66.7 | 51.6 | 58.8 | 61.1 | 58.2 |
| 3,000–3,999 | — | — | 1.8 | — | 0.4 |
| 4,000–4,999 | 0.7 | — | — | — | 0.2 |
| 5,000–5,999 | 0.7 | 0.9 | 0.9 | — | 0.8 |
| 6,000–6,999 | 0.7 | 0.5 | 1.8 | — | 0.8 |
| 8,000–8,999 | 1.3 | — | — | — | 0.4 |
| 10,000–10,999 | 2.7 | 0.9 | 1.8 | 5.6 | 1.8 |
| 11,000–11,999 | 0.7 | — | — | — | 0.2 |
| 13,000–13,999 | 0.7 | 0.5 | — | — | 0.4 |
| 15,000–15,999 | — | — | 0.9 | — | 0.2 |
| 16,000 + | 26.0 | 45.6 | 34.2 | 33.3 | 36.6 |
| Total number | 150 | 217 | 114 | 18 | 500 |

**Table 27.** Amount of investment in land classified by age-group

| Amount in baht | Less than 30 | 31–40 | 41–50 | Over 51 | Total |
|---|---|---|---|---|---|
| 1–2,999 | 77.3 | 71.9 | 73.7 | 72.2 | 73.8 |
| 3,000–3,999 | 0.7 | — | — | — | 0.2 |
| 4,000–4,999 | 0.7 | 0.5 | — | — | 0.4 |
| 5,000–5,999 | 0.7 | 0.5 | 0.9 | — | 0.6 |
| 6,000–6,999 | 0.7 | 0.9 | — | 5.6 | 0.8 |
| 7,000–7,999 | 1.3 | 0.9 | — | — | 0.8 |
| 8,000–8,999 | — | 0.5 | — | — | 0.2 |
| 10,000–10,999 | 2.7 | 2.3 | 0.9 | — | 2.0 |
| 12,000–12,999 | — | 0.5 | — | — | 0.2 |
| 14,000–14,999 | 0.7 | — | — | — | 0.2 |
| 15,000–15,999 | 0.7 | 0.5 | 1.7 | — | 0.8 |
| 16,000 + | 14.7 | 21.6 | 22.8 | 22.2 | 20.0 |
| Total number | 150 | 217 | 114 | 18 | 500 |

that the family's consumption increased considerably. Conspicuous and luxury consumption followed the repayment of debts.

Housing and transportation figured prominently among the important planned investments made by the migrants. The amount of expenditure on housing depended on the age and marital status of the migrant. Those who were living with their parents invested in repairs and additions to homes. Those in the age category 31–40 made the highest average investment in housing, with over 45 per cent of them investing more than 16,000 baht (see table 26). However, for all age categories, more than half of the migrants spent less than 3,000 baht on housing investments. The proportion spending this amount or less was significantly higher for migrants who were less than 30 years of age. More than one-third of all the migrants invested about 16,000 baht on housing.

**Table 28.** Amount of investment in equipment classified by age-group

| Amount in baht | Less than 30 | 31–40 | 41–50 | Over 51 | Total |
|---|---|---|---|---|---|
| 1–2,999 | 87.3 | 87.5 | 81.6 | 66.7 | 85.4 |
| 3,000–3,999 | — | 1.3 | — | — | 0.6 |
| 4,000–4,999 | — | 0.5 | 0.9 | — | 0.4 |
| 5,000–5,999 | 0.7 | 0.5 | — | — | 0.4 |
| 6,000–6,999 | 0.7 | 0.5 | — | — | 0.4 |
| 7,000–7,999 | 0.7 | 0.5 | — | 5.6 | 0.6 |
| 8,000–8,999 | 1.3 | 0.5 | 0.9 | — | 0.8 |
| 9,000–9,999 | 0.7 | — | — | — | 0.2 |
| 10,000–10,999 | 0.7 | 0.9 | — | — | 0.6 |
| 11,000–11,999 | — | — | 1.7 | — | 0.4 |
| 14,000–14,999 | — | — | 0.9 | — | 0.2 |
| 15,000–15,999 | 0.7 | 0.5 | 0.9 | 5.6 | 0.8 |
| 16,000 + | 7.3 | 7.3 | 13.1 | 22.2 | 9.2 |
| Total number | 151 | 217 | 114 | 18 | 500 |

About one-fifth of the migrants invested a substantial sum (about 16,000 baht) in the purchase of land. The proportion making large investments in land increased with age. As expected, those in the younger age-groups, under 30 years, invested less, though it has to be borne in mind that total earnings increased with age; therefore the volume or the quantum of investment that was possible was also higher for those who were older. Also, those aged 31 to 40 are expected to have a larger proportion of new and young families. Investment in household and agricultural equipment was significantly higher, in terms of the amount of money expended, for those in the older age-groups, though the proportion of migrants who expended high levels of their earnings on equipment was smaller than for housing and land. The proportion investing substantial amounts (over 16,000 baht) was higher for the 31–50 age-group. In fact, investment in transport equipment was higher than for either agriculture or household items.

## Post-migration Phase

One of the main characteristics of those who had returned after their migration was their indecision regarding the immediate future. A significant proportion were contemplating another episode of migration.

### General Conditions

A significant proportion, 38 per cent, of the migrants were forced to return, regardless of their skills, when their contracts expired. Upon return, the majority resumed their previous agricultural occupations. Those who had been foremen while abroad had a different career pattern to their counterparts who were unskilled, semi-skilled, or in the service sectors; nevertheless, this group is a small component of the total pool of migrants. Those migrants who came from Nakhon Sawan

**Table 29.** Amount of investment in vehicles classified by age-group

| Amount in baht | Less than 30 | 31–40 | 41–50 | Over 51 | Total |
|---|---|---|---|---|---|
| 1–2,999 | 72.7 | 66.8 | 69.3 | 72.2 | 69.4 |
| 3,000–3,999 | — | 0.5 | — | — | 0.2 |
| 4,000–4,999 | 0.7 | 0.5 | — | 5.6 | 0.6 |
| 5,000–5,999 | 2.0 | — | 0.9 | — | 0.8 |
| 6,000–6,999 | 1.3 | — | — | — | 0.4 |
| 7,000–7,999 | — | 0.5 | — | — | 0.2 |
| 8,000–8,999 | 1.3 | 0.9 | — | — | 0.8 |
| 9,000–9,999 | — | 0.5 | — | 5.6 | 0.4 |
| 10,000–10,999 | 0.7 | 2.8 | 0.9 | — | 1.6 |
| 11,000–11,999 | 0.7 | — | — | — | 0.2 |
| 12,000–12,999 | 2.7 | 1.8 | 2.6 | — | 2.2 |
| 13,000–13,999 | 1.3 | 0.9 | 0.9 | — | 1.0 |
| 14,000–14,999 | 0.7 | — | 1.7 | 5.6 | 0.8 |
| 15,000–15,999 | 1.3 | 1.4 | 1.7 | 5.6 | 1.6 |
| 16,000 + | 14.7 | 23.5 | 21.9 | 5.6 | 19.8 |
| Total number | 151 | 217 | 114 | 18 | 500 |

turned to non-agricultural labour, or started working in family enterprises. At present there are no agencies which assist in job placement or counselling for return migrants. Services for returnees are equally lacking in all provinces where interviews were carried out.

The experience gained during the period of migration seems to have encouraged a small proportion of the migrants to embark on various self-employment and private enterprises. About one in ten of the migrants started their own enterprise, even though they received no supportive facilities, information, or advice from financing and related institutions. A large majority of the migrants claimed that they had acquired important technical skills (80 per cent). However, less than half (47 per cent) felt that they had acquired management skills at the same time. Of the migrants who indicated that they had acquired technical skills, less than two-thirds (63 per cent) thought they could use these skills upon return to their home villages. The data indicate that the value of the skills acquired during their stay abroad was less in the poorer villages in the north-eastern province, where migrants had fewer opportunities for using them.

The levels of unemployment of the returnees were not particularly high. About one in ten migrants (10 per cent) claimed that they were out of work, though only 4 per cent were actively engaged in seeking employment. In a rural agricultural setting, seeking employment assumes a different form than in other settings. It is expected that most of the migrants would have been exposed to seasonal unemployment and underemployment. Most were also aware of the declining opportunities in West Asia and the need to seek alternatives. A large majority who had decided to re-migrate had made the necessary arrangements: they had contacted recruiting agencies, prepared their documents, and were awaiting the order for departure. Again, a significant proportion expected to return to West Asia but had not made any plans.

**Table 30.** Post-migration career classified by province of residence

| | Udon Thani | Sakon Nakhon | Khon Kaen | Maha Sarakham | Buriram | Nakhon Ratchasima | Nakhon Sawan | Phichit | Lampang | Chiang Rai | Total |
|---|---|---|---|---|---|---|---|---|---|---|---|
| Unemployed | 9 (18.0)[a] | 13 (26.0) | 8 (16.0) | 1 (2.0) | 5 (10.0) | 5 (10.0) | 8 (16.0) | 1 (2.0) | — | 1 (2.0) | 51 (10.2) |
| Paddy cultivation | 30 (60.0) | 33 (66.0) | 29 (58.0) | 40 (80.0) | 40 (80.0) | 37 (74.0) | 14 (28.0) | 43 (86.0) | 40 (80.0) | 41 (82.0) | 347 (69.4) |
| Trade | 3 (6.0) | 2 (4.0) | 10 (20.0) | 4 (8.0) | — | — | 9 (18.0) | 2 (4.0) | 2 (4.0) | 7 (14.0) | 39 (7.8) |
| On-farm labour | — | — | — | — | — | — | 1 (2.0) | — | — | — | 1 (0.2) |
| Off-farm labour | 4 (8.0) | 2 (4.0) | 1 (2.0) | 2 (4.0) | 3 (6.0) | 3 (6.0) | 11 (22.0) | 2 (4.0) | 4 (8.0) | — | 32 (6.4) |
| Self-employed | 4 (8.0) | — | — | 1 (2.0) | 1 (2.0) | 4 (8.0) | 5 (10.0) | — | 1 (2.0) | — | 16 (3.2) |
| Vacation | — | — | 2 (4.0) | 2 (4.0) | 1 (2.0) | 1 (2.0) | 2 (4.0) | 2 (4.0) | 3 (6.0) | 1 (2.0) | 14 (2.8) |
| Total | 50 (100.0) | 50 (100.0) | 50 (100.0) | 50 (100.0) | 50 (100.0) | 50 (100.0) | 50 (100.0) | 50 (100.0) | 50 (100.0) | 50 (100.0) | 500 (100.0) |

a. Percentages in parentheses.

**Table 31.** Benefits gained from migration classified by province of residence

| Skill | Udon Thani | Sakon Nakhon | Khon Kaen | Maha Sarakham | Buriram | Nakhon Ratchasima | Nakhon Sawan | Phichit | Lampang | Chiang Rai | Total |
|---|---|---|---|---|---|---|---|---|---|---|---|
| Skill | 36 (72.0)[a] | 46 (92.0) | 39 (78.0) | 41 (82.0) | 36 (72.0) | 37 (74.0) | 36 (72.0) | 39 (78.0) | 34 (68.0) | 37 (74.0) | 381 (76.2) |
| Technical knowledge | 32 (64.0) | 44 (88.0) | 38 (76.0) | 36 (72.0) | 35 (70.0) | 41 (82.0) | 34 (68.0) | 35 (70.0) | 34 (80.0) | 34 (68.0) | 363 (72.6) |
| Supervisory | 38 (76.0) | 42 (84.0) | 38 (76.0) | 38 (76.0) | 35 (70.0) | 35 (70.0) | 35 (70.0) | 37 (74.0) | 32 (64.0) | 36 (72.0) | 366 (73.2) |
| Managerial | 23 (46.0) | 25 (50.0) | 32 (64.0) | 28 (56.0) | 24 (48.0) | 22 (44.0) | 23 (46.0) | 23 (46.0) | 22 (44.0) | 14 (28.0) | 236 (47.2) |
| Professional skill | 40 (80.0) | 40 (80.0) | 43 (86.0) | 39 (78.0) | 39 (78.0) | 45 (90.0) | 37 (74.0) | 38 (76.0) | 39 (78.0) | 40 (80.0) | 400 (80.0) |
| Domestic skill | 20 (40.0) | 25 (50.0) | 21 (42.0) | 28 (56.0) | 30 (60.0) | 21 (42.0) | 24 (48.0) | 27 (54.0) | 21 (42.0) | 37 (74.0) | 254 (50.8) |
| Personal/public relations | 22 (44.0) | 23 (46.0) | 28 (56.0) | 30 (60.0) | 26 (52.0) | 21 (42.0) | 21 (42.0) | 20 (40.0) | 20 (40.0) | 25 (50.0) | 236 (50.8) |
| Social skill | 35 (70.0) | 42 (84.0) | 39 (78.0) | 45 (90.0) | 34 (68.0) | 36 (72.0) | 41 (82.0) | 38 (76.0) | 41 (82.0) | 42 (84.0) | 393 (78.6) |
| Improved skill in general | 8 (16.0) | 5 (10.0) | 8 (16.0) | 11 (22.0) | 18 (36.0) | 8 (16.0) | 17 (34.0) | 18 (36.0) | 10 (20.0) | 17 (34.0) | 120 (24.0) |

a. Percentages in parentheses.

**Table 32.** Family assets prior to and after migration (percentages)

| | Pre-migration | Post-migration | | | |
| --- | --- | --- | --- | --- | --- |
| | | Less | Same | More | None |
| Land | | | | | |
| Cultivating land | 75.4 | 0.8 | 57.6 | 20.4 | 21.2 |
| Non-cultivating land | 49.4 | 0.2 | 34.4 | 9.8 | 55.6 |
| Buildings | | | | | |
| Residential construction | 91.8 | 0.2 | 58.4 | 37.0 | 4.4 |
| Non-residential construction | 30.2 | — | 26.0 | 7.6 | 66.4 |
| Farm equipment | | | | | |
| Tractor | 4.6 | 0.2 | 3.4 | 5.0 | 91.4 |
| Water pump | 12.0 | 0.2 | 10.4 | 16.2 | 73.2 |
| Truck | 18.6 | 0.4 | 13.4 | 33.4 | 52.8 |
| Household appliances | | | | | |
| Sitting-room furniture | 29.8 | 0.2 | 19.0 | 32.2 | 48.6 |
| Bedroom furniture | 48.8 | 0.4 | 30.8 | 35.4 | 33.4 |
| Dining-room furniture | 44.0 | 0.4 | 27.0 | 32.0 | 40.6 |
| Kerosene gas stove | 5.8 | 0.2 | 9.6 | 20.0 | 70.2 |
| Air conditioner | 7.0 | — | 5.8 | 8.8 | 85.4 |
| Refrigerator | 10.4 | 0.2 | 9.6 | 20.0 | 70.2 |
| Washing machine | 0.2 | — | 0.2 | 0.6 | 99.2 |
| Vacuum cleaner | 0.6 | 0.2 | 0.4 | 0.6 | 98.8 |
| Electronic equipment | | | | | |
| Radio | 44.8 | — | 27.4 | 56.6 | 16.0 |
| Television | 21.6 | 0.2 | 13.4 | 58.2 | 28.2 |
| Video | 0.8 | — | 0.4 | 8.6 | 91.0 |
| Stereo/tape | 6.4 | 0.2 | 4.0 | 38.0 | 57.8 |

About half the migrants did not respond to the question about planned investments in the future, primarily because many are hoping to leave again. In the absence of clear investment plans, most migrants deposited funds in income-earning financial institutions. However, nearly half (47 per cent) had made definite plans for investing incomes earned abroad, and nearly 10 per cent had made plans to invest in private enterprises.

A large part of migrant earnings seemed to be directed towards consumption and consumer durables. Household assets were increased through investments such as improvements in housing, farm equipment, and household appliances. About three-quarters of the migrants owned cultivated agricultural land, while more than 90 per cent owned houses. A significant proportion of migrant earnings were channelled into housing. The decision to invest in farming equipment seems to have taken lower priority than the acquisition of household appliances and other goods, perhaps partly because the household head was contemplating another episode of migration.

The consumer items that are most popular among migrants are the electronic appliances that can be easily purchased at duty-free shops at the airport. They can also be easily transported and have a ready market in the villages. Meanwhile, the manner in which the villages hold their assets (the traditional means was investing in gold) seems to have undergone significant change. Following migration, various goods and appliances have acquired the characteristics of a store of value. Migration had resulted in an increase in income transfers from migrant households to those who have poor relatives: nearly half (47 per cent) the households indicated that they had increased their assistance to relatives. The data also indicate that expenditure on religious activities had increased significantly for a large proportion of the migrant households.

When we examine the major items in which households invested, we find that consumer items take precedence over others:

1. More than half the migrants purchased radios and televisions.
2. About 30 per cent of the migrants had increased their expenditure on homes, vehicles, and furniture.
3. About one-fifth had increased expenditure on agricultural land, farm equipment, and refrigerators.

Migration has had a substantial impact on the consumption patterns of households. Protein food consumption, clothing, footwear, and private vehicles are among the more popular items which are purchased in greater quantities. In the case of clothing, the migration seemed to have had a significant impact on the choice and type of clothing now used by migrants as well as their families. Expenditure on clothing and footwear seemed to have increased significantly for the households.

The normal pattern of food consumption for most migrant households did not include very much meat or fish; however, following migration, as table 33 illustrates, the consumption of fish and meat increased considerably, as did that of canned and processed food, carbonated drinks, alcohol, and cigarettes.

The expenditure pattern on health care for migrant households seemed to have changed. The proportion seeking government hospital care had increased, while those seeking Western medical treatment increased even more. This implies a shift away from indigenous medicine toward Western medical care.

In rural Thailand, a motor-cycle or a pick-up truck is a popular means of transport, used for both private and commercial purposes. Transportation is a form of self-employment which is popular among young rural Thais and draws significant investment from migrants.

The expenditure pattern of migrant households varied significantly according to the age of the migrant. Those with younger migrants experienced higher increases in expenditure on liquor, cigarettes, clothing, and footwear. However, it is not possible to draw conclusions about the differences in the consumption patterns of households according to the age of the migrant, without reference to the composition and size of the households.

Migrants in the 31–50 age-group have made significant increases in their expenditure on education and health compared with households of other age-groups.

Migrant households of all age-groups have made significant increases in their expenditure on transport, though, of course, the large increase for the younger migrants implies greater movement and mobility for their households.

The increased income obtained from migration resulted in one in every six

**Table 33.** Change in expenditure on comsumables before and after migration

| Expenditure | Pre-migration | | Post-migration | | | |
|---|---|---|---|---|---|---|
| | Same | None | Less | Same | More | None |
| Meat/fish | 95.0 | 5.0 | 1.4 | 60.2 | 31.2 | 13.2 |
| Dairy products | 32.6 | 67.4 | 2.8 | 18.0 | 13.0 | 66.2 |
| Canned and processed food | 44.2 | 55.8 | 2.4 | 33.6 | 9.6 | 52.4 |
| Carbonated drinks | 36.6 | 63.4 | 2.0 | 27.4 | 9.6 | 61.0 |
| Liquor/alcohol | 74.2 | 25.8 | 8.6 | 49.2 | 18.6 | 23.6 |
| Cigarettes/cigars | 75.6 | 24.4 | 9.6 | 50.4 | 17.4 | 22.6 |
| Clothing | 93.8 | 6.2 | 2.0 | 55.2 | 39.6 | 3.2 |
| Footwear | 93.0 | 7.0 | 3.6 | 54.6 | 37.8 | 4.0 |
| Newspapers | 45.2 | 54.8 | 5.0 | 29.6 | 14.4 | 51.0 |
| Govt hospital | 86.4 | 13.6 | 4.8 | 70.2 | 12.4 | 12.6 |
| Private practitioners | 36.4 | 63.6 | 2.2 | 26.6 | 9.8 | 61.4 |
| Indigenous medicine | 30.8 | 69.2 | 3.6 | 24.0 | 2.8 | 69.6 |
| Western medicine | 73.6 | 26.4 | 2.6 | 57.0 | 14.6 | 25.8 |
| Education | 47.6 | 52.4 | 1.2 | 23.2 | 28.6 | 47.0 |
| Cinema/theatre | 44.6 | 55.4 | 7.0 | 29.2 | 9.0 | 54.8 |
| Holiday travel/clubs | 23.0 | 77.0 | 2.6 | 14.8 | 6.6 | 76.0 |
| Public transport | 81.0 | 19.0 | 12.2 | 47.0 | 23.4 | 17.4 |
| Private car | 27.4 | 72.6 | 0.8 | 17.4 | 32.4 | 49.4 |
| Motor-cycle/bicycle | 13.6 | 86.4 | 2.0 | 7.4 | 7.0 | 83.2 |
| Donations, charities, gifts | | | | | | |
|   Religious organizations | 90.2 | 9.6 | 2.8 | 42.0 | 48.2 | 6.8 |
|   Relatives | 77.2 | 22.8 | 2.6 | 33.0 | 46.6 | 17.8 |

households moving from their original place of residence. About 10 per cent moved to different homes within the village.

When housing investments are examined more closely, it appears that about 10 per cent of the migrant households improved the quality of the structure. About three-quarters of the households had occupied permanent homes before migration. The quality of the roof, wall, and floor improved and made the transition from non-permanent to permanent more noticeable. The first important change seems to have concerned the flooring: while one in ten dwellings had a cement floor before migration, the proportion increased to 17 per cent following the increase in income.

More than one-quarter (28 per cent) of the dwellings did not have toilet facilities prior to migration, but following migration the proportion halved to 14 per cent. The large majority of the toilets acquired after migration were latrines. Small increases in the number of households serviced by inside and outside flush toilets were also noted (see table 35).

Nearly 90 per cent of the migrant dwellings had been serviced by public wells. However, following migration, a significant increase in the number of households with piped water is observed. A large majority of households had had electricity prior to migration; the proportion increased by 10 per cent afterwards.

**Table 34.** Percentage increase in household and personal expenses of different age-groups

| Age-group | Protein food | Dairy products | Canned goods | Carbonated drinks, coffee, tea | Liquor | Cigarettes | Clothing | Shoes | Reading matter, newspapers |
|---|---|---|---|---|---|---|---|---|---|
| Under 30 | 29.8 | 11.4 | 8.1 | 10.1 | 23.5 | 20.8 | 50.0 | 47.3 | 13.9 |
| 31–40 | 32.7 | 14.7 | 12.9 | 11.5 | 19.4 | 16.1 | 37.8 | 36.9 | 17.1 |
| 41–50 | 30.7 | 13.2 | 7.0 | 6.1 | 12.3 | 16.7 | 32.5 | 29.8 | 11.4 |
| 51+ | 27.8 | 5.6 | — | 5.6 | 11.1 | 11.1 | 22.2 | 22.2 | 5.6 |
| All age-groups | 31.3 | 13.0 | 9.6 | 9.6 | 18.6 | 17.4 | 39.7 | 37.9 | 14.4 |

| Age-group | Public health facilities | Private health facilities | Traditional medicine | Modern medicine | Education | Cinema | Bar | Public transport | Private transport | Religious | Assisting relatives |
|---|---|---|---|---|---|---|---|---|---|---|---|
| Under 30 | 15.9 | 8.6 | 4.6 | 17.2 | 26.2 | 12.8 | 11.4 | 26.0 | 29.8 | 36.4 | 40.4 |
| 31–40 | 10.6 | 12.9 | 2.8 | 14.7 | 30.0 | 8.8 | 4.6 | 21.7 | 35.0 | 55.3 | 51.2 |
| 41–50 | 12.3 | 7.0 | .9 | 11.4 | 30.7 | 6.1 | 5.3 | 25.4 | 31.6 | 51.8 | 46.5 |
| 51+ | 5.6 | — | — | 11.1 | 22.2 | — | — | 11.1 | 27.8 | 44.4 | 44.4 |
| All age-groups | 21.4 | 9.8 | 2.8 | 14.6 | 28.7 | 9.0 | 6.6 | 23.4 | 32.4 | 48.4 | 46.6 |

**Table 35.** House components before and after migration

| | Before | After |
|---|---|---|
| **Structure** | | |
| Temporary | 10.0 | 4.4 |
| Semi-permanent | 14.0 | 8.4 |
| Permanent | 75.4 | 86.8 |
| **Roof** | | |
| Tin zinc corrugated | 85.4 | 83.6 |
| Tile | 11.2 | 15.0 |
| Thatch | 2.0 | — |
| Other | 1.4 | 1.0 |
| **Wall** | | |
| Wood | 89.6 | 85.8 |
| Cement | 4.0 | 6.4 |
| Bamboo | 2.2 | 0.6 |
| Thatch | 0.8 | 0.6 |
| Wood and cement | 2.8 | 6.0 |
| **Floor** | | |
| Wood | 88.8 | 81.8 |
| Cement | 10.0 | 17.0 |
| Wood and cement | 0.2 | 0.2 |
| Other | 1.0 | 1.0 |
| **Toilet** | | |
| Flush (inside) | 1.8 | 3.8 |
| Flush (outside) | 3.8 | 4.0 |
| Latrine | 65.0 | 77.8 |
| None | 28.4 | 14.0 |
| Other | 0.8 | 0.4 |
| **Water supply** | | |
| Public well | 88.8 | 85.8 |
| Piped | 9.4 | 13.0 |
| River | 1.4 | 0.8 |
| Other | 0.4 | 0.4 |
| **Electricity** | | |
| Yes | 82.4 | 92.6 |
| No | 17.6 | 7.4 |

## Impact of Experience Gained while Working Abroad

Most migrants indicated a sense of fulfilment and achievement following their migration. The discipline, the work situation and the experience gained were considered to have been very valuable. Technical and supervisory skills had been gained by more than 70 per cent of the migrants, and managerial and public relations skills had been acquired by a smaller proportion (about 47 per cent in both cases). It should be borne in mind that these improvements are notional and might not reflect actuality. While about 85 per cent of the migrants felt that they had improved skills and gained experience, less than two-thirds thought their skills would be useful in gaining productive employment. Most informants classified themselves as belonging to the middle class. About two-thirds feel that they have

**Table 36.** Attitude towards aspirations for family and family members

|  | Yes | No | N.a. |
|---|---|---|---|
| Higher educational attainment | 16.2 | 68.4 | 15.4 |
| Higher social status | 14.8 | 69.8 | 15.4 |
| Higher occupational status | 14.6 | 70.3 | 15.4 |
| Give more freedom to children |  |  |  |
| In career | 13.8 | 70.8 | 15.4 |
| In marriage | 13.4 | 71.2 | 14.4 |
| Equal opportunities for daughters and |  |  |  |
| sons in occupation and education | 12.8 | 68.0 | 19.2 |
| Daughter's aspirations should be good |  |  |  |
| marriage and good home | 12.6 | 68.6 | 18.8 |
| No substantial change in attitude |  |  |  |
| toward children | 63.2 | 20.6 | 16.2 |

now acquired social status, which will enable them to be important individuals in their villages, i.e. persons who are sought for advice and financial assistance. However, about one-third of the migrants were aware of increased attention and resultant jealousies because of their new-found incomes and changes in consumption habits. These migrants felt that they would be considered a threat to the community.

The migration seems to have had a noticeable impact on a wide range of attitudes and values, for the individual as well as for the household (table 36). About 15 per cent had higher expectations as regards educational attainment, social status, and occupational status. Meanwhile, a significant proportion (about 13 per cent) had changed their attitude towards opportunities for male and female children, showing a greater willingness to educate female children. Increase in income, even though it may not be sustained at the same levels in the future, has had a noticeable impact on female education, and the consequences of this relationship could be far-reaching.

The migratory episode seems to have strongly affected the manner in which household work and household management are shared between husband and wife. Husbands seem to be spending more time with their families, sharing housework, and generally being supportive of family-planning programmes.

The response to questions regarding the management of household expenditure was rather poor, probably because the questions were not properly understood. Nearly one-quarter (24 per cent) of the migrants indicated their support of wives working to earn extra income to support the family.

There was no detectable difference in attitudes to work for all age-groups following migration. However, it seemed that the older migrants were contemplating withdrawal from the workforce.

**Community Involvement**

In a rural village setting, kinship ties are strong, and therefore the need for formal social occasions and organizations is limited. The manner in which the community participates in various forms of activities is fashioned by the context and circumstances. However, following the episode of migration, the degree of group participation in local and voluntary organizations seems to have increased marginally. Only about 17 per cent of the migrants claim to have participated in this manner.

As a consequence of migration there does not seem to have been a discernible change in attitudes towards politics. The proportion of persons who showed interest had increased marginally from 55 to 62 per cent. However, this interest had not been strong enough to increase membership of political parties or to induce people to become active members of political organizations. Also attitudes to fundamental rights and freedom do not seem to have undergone significant change; views on unions and organization of labour, and freedom and control of the press, seem to become only slightly more liberal. Only about half of the respondents supported organized labour or the freedom of the press; about a third favoured the controlled economy and one-fifth preferred a dictatorial government.

Interest and curiosity in international affairs seem to have increased substantially following migration.

The low level of participation in community and political affairs may be related to the fact that a large proportion of the migrants were contemplating remigrating, or were in the process of doing so. Their not being settled may very well explain their unwillingness or lack of interest in participating in various activities. This indecision is reflected by the fact that almost all migrants had not joined occupational groups or labour organizations, and about eight in every ten had not associated themselves with a sports or recreational club. The proportion of younger rural men participating in voluntary organizations of some kind is generally higher than it is for the migrants.

## International Migration and Community Development

The above discussion clearly indicates that international migration has brought the individuals and their families both economic as well as social benefits. Potential high earnings from work in West Asian countries has attracted a substantial number of rural people to seek such opportunities. In addition to the income, the experience gained has been useful in changing values and attitudes towards sociopolitical conditions, as well as having a significant impact on the manner in which the migrant families organize their lives. In this chapter the impact on the community will be examined in detail, and case-studies will be used to illustrate some of the main features.

### Nakhon Sawan Province

Ban Lao is a typical village in the Phai Salee District. The settlement was formed about 50 years ago, when forest land was cleared by migrants from the north-east. The village contains four small grocery stores, a small rice mill, a primary school, and a temple. Saman was a small farmer operating 15 rai of land obtained through inheritance; he lived with his wife and two young daughters. Among the crops grown in the village are paddy, maize, and cassava. Saman migrated to Saudi

**Table 37.** Attitude toward family life

|  | Yes | No | N.a. |
|---|---|---|---|
| More ready to share housework, child-care, domestic responsibilities with spouse | 39.0 | 48.4 | 12.6 |
| Spend more time with family | 53.4 | 34.0 | 12.6 |
| More supportive of family-planning programme | 23.8 | 63.2 | 13.0 |
| Husband and wife should decide together on family and household affairs | 27.2 | 59.4 | 13.4 |
| Wife should earn extra income to help support family | 24.0 | 62.4 | 13.6 |
| Wife should be in charge of family income and expenditure | 3.0 | 13.0 | 84.0 |
| Husband should be in charge of family income and expenditure | 11.6 | 29.6 | 58.8 |
| Both husband and wife should be in charge of family income and expenditure | 15.8 | 27.0 | 57.2 |

Arabia in 1983 and returned two years later. While he was away, his wife and the two daughters found it beyond their capability to work the land, so they rented it to a distant relative and, with the remittances obtained every month, repaid the loans that were incurred when Saman migrated. With two years of work abroad, this family managed to save about 40,000 baht, which was banked periodically.

Upon his return Saman intended to invest the 40,000 baht on an income-generating activity. He had thought of opening up a store or a rice mill. However, on closer examination he found that the village would not be able to support such a venture, and the income potential from it would be too low. Then he considered the purchase of a truck to transport people to and from the village. Meanwhile, he was contemplating repairing and improving his home by replacing the roof and the walls with better materials. Saman and his wife discussed sending their daughters for secondary education in a nearby town. After some discussion, the family decided to make minor repairs to their home, and to purchase a truck for passenger transport. It seemed that Saman's wife would have to find some work to earn additional income during the initial period of the enterprise, though she would have preferred renting out land as before. She obtained training in sewing in the nearby town and had purchased a machine with a down payment of a 1,000 baht. They were no longer a farm family. The land that they owned had been put up as collateral to obtain a loan to purchase a minibus.

During the six months of readjustment, Saman learnt about government programmes and development activities in the area. The village had a committee consisting of many members and a subdistrict (*tambon*) task force. The *tambon* council had existed when Saman left his village in 1983. At present Saman is not quite certain about the kind of involvement he would like to have in community activities. A young man who was working for a private voluntary organization (PVA) has attempted to promote development activities in the village, and has induced Saman to get involved in some of them, obtaining his services in transporting raw material for a project to construct large jars in which families can store water the year through. The main objective of the project was to provide clean drinking water for the villagers.

There seem to be many other possibilities for Saman's involvement in village activities. He recently met a fellow migrant, Somchai, who had returned the previous year and who was planning to return again to Saudi Arabia. In Somchai's village there are many activities which are promoted through government efforts: a village committee, a subdistrict task force and a subdistrict council had been set up. However, none of these activities seem to have interested him much. Somchai did not save as much money as he had hoped during the last trip, and therefore was thinking of re-migrating. This time he intends to save enough to start a small enterprise.

## Sakon Nakhon

In contrast to Ban Lao, Ban Phung is a village in an irrigated area in the Muang District, in Sakon Nakhon Province.

Taworn had operated a bulldozer, digging fishing ponds for the Fishery Department. He migrated to Saudi Arabia and worked for one-and-a-half years as a heavy vehicle operator. The year before he went abroad, his wife died of cancer; he spent a large sum of money during her illness and for her funeral. He placed his children under his sister's care in the same village before he went abroad. Although his contract was for two years, Taworn and many of his friends returned home when their firm reduced salaries from 15,000 to 9,000 baht per month. When he returned the Nam Oon Irrigation Scheme had been completed and was functioning, and therefore a dry-season crop was possible. Two years ago groundnut was grown during the dry season and a price of 9 baht per kilogram had been obtained, but last year the price fell to 5 baht. This year, the traders returned to purchase groundnuts, but, anticipating a serious decline in prices, many people had not cultivated a second crop.

Taworn sees many possibilities for investment on his land. He intends to ask the Department of Fisheries to help him set up a fish pond, giving an estimated net income after six months of about 5,000 to 15,000 baht per pond. Taworn also sees possibilities in supplying tomatoes to the factory which is to be set up nearby. With water available the year round, he would be able to plant at least one additional crop besides rice. Taworn says he would examine the various opportunities for income and investment before considering another trip. It has to be kept in mind that he has an advantage over other types of migrants in that he has a skill which commands a high wage.

The two case-studies presented are examples of villages where development activities are going on. In the first village the social infrastructure is being set up for development, and in the second the physical infrastructure, in the form of a large irrigation project, has been put in place and many new opportunities for agrobased investments have emerged.

It appears that the return migrants can be motivated to become involved in development activities more readily because of their financial capacity to make investments. The growing unemployment and foreign exchange problems of the country somehow seem to be factors which tend to encourage migration. The

**Table 38.** Attitude toward opportunity to work abroad classified by age-group

|  | −30 | 31−40 | 41−50 | 51+ | All age-groups |
|---|---|---|---|---|---|
| Very valuable experience | 93.4 | 96.3 | 94.7 | 100 | 95.2 |
| Will never do again | 15.3 | 10.1 | 22.8 | 27.8 | 15.2 |
| Has not improved quality of life | 8.0 | 10.6 | 5.3 | 5.6 | 8.4 |
| Has made life more meaningful | 92.7 | 96.8 | 93.9 | 94.4 | 94.8 |
| Negative benefit to family and person | 18.0 | 12.4 | 11.4 | 5.6 | 13.6 |
| Changed attitude toward life, politics, women, children | 32.0 | 33.2 | 33.3 | 16.7 | 32.2 |
| Improved attitudes towards outside world and foreigners | 64.7 | 65.0 | 52.6 | 55.6 | 61.6 |

migration pattern is shifting slightly away from West Asia at the moment, with the various Asian countries, even though they limit the labour influx, drawing the attention of migrants. The government should pay more attention to the absorption of returnees in productive employment; advisory services are urgently needed.

## The Promotion of International Migration

The institutional framework to promote and facilitate international migration is being developed rapidly. The establishment of the Office of Overseas Labour Management, the main duty of which is to facilitate migration, is an indication of the government's concern. The degree of fraud and malpractice appears to have declined after the government's improvement, through various regulations and institutional reforms, of the efficiency of the migratory process. Meanwhile, new regulations from countries such as Saudi Arabia have imposed additional strains on migrants. The requirement of an AIDS test for those travelling for work in Saudi Arabia and the need for health certificates have increased the cost of migration. At present only a very few (about four) government hospitals are entitled to issue health certificates, although many institutions are able to conduct test for AIDS. This has created inconveniences and delays.

The role of the Department of Labour in facilitating migration has expanded. In addition to dealing with labour disputes and welfare within the country, the Department is now involved with labour migration, especially at the pre-migration stage. The Office of Overseas Labour Management has taken over this activity. However, the role of the Department of Labour could be expanded beyond national boundaries. Labour attachés stationed in countries where there are large numbers of migrants from Thailand may become necessary and important. Discussions on establishing a trade attaché post within each embassy, to promote products made in Thailand, are under way. Similar consideration should be given to the role of the Labour Department with regard to international migration: appropriate adjustments should be made in order to deal efficiently with pre-migration activities and to provide services to migrants during their stint abroad.

## Promotion of Income-generating Activities for Returnees

Data presented in the previous section indicate that a large proportion of migrant earnings is devoted to consumption and the purchase of consumer durables. At present there are no organizations or institutions providing information and guidance for those who are particularly interested in starting small business enterprises. This kind of counselling activity is necessary in many of the settings that have been examined. However, it is to be expected that a large proportion of the earnings will be devoted to improvements in the immediate standard of living of the migrant families. Consumer durables, such as radios, televisions, stereo sets, refrigerators and fans, rank high among the items migrant families purchased with their earnings. At the same time, improvements in housing and the purchase and construction of new houses, along with the purchase of land, take up a large part of migrant earnings. Nevertheless, a substantial proportion of those in the middle and the early years of their working life are entrepreneurs and would-be entrepreneurs; it is to this group that programmes and policies should pay special attention.

At present, the government has a range of policies to promote rural industry by encouraging entrepreneurs and commercial firms to initiate industrial development activities. Meanwhile, rural credit and other incentives to promote investment are being developed. The Department of Industrial Promotion has many industrial promotion schemes, including ones for weaving and handicrafts and other home industry activities. But many of these schemes are subject to heavy criticism because they lack imagination, and also because there is insufficient demand, as in the case of handicrafts and weaving. The Department of Industrial Promotion needs to examine different avenues and to find new products and processes to promote. Agro-processing activities are one area where serious promotion should be considered. The case-studies from Sakon Nakhon indicate that even in irrigated areas where water is available for a second crop, farmers lack information regarding possible lucrative crops. If agro-processing plants are built and contract farming encouraged to supply produce to the plants, a higher level of employment could be promoted the year round. Co-operation between the Department of Industrial Promotion and the Ministry of Agriculture is needed to examine the possibilities and to establish agro-processing. Meanwhile, the Department of Labour is in a position to advise and direct the investment interests of return migrants into the appropriate areas.

Much work needs to be done in providing information for prospective entrepreneurs about credit, investment opportunities, and markets for output.

## Conclusion

The evidence points to the fact that international migration has largely positive effects and has been of benefit to individuals and to the country. At the individual and family level the migrants had been able to improve their standard of living. A large majority have increased their consumption of food and clothing, while making substantial improvements to their housing. At the same time, migration has made a significant impact on attitudes and values, changing attitudes towards family planning and female education. At the national level, migration has brought in valuable foreign exchange and temporarily reduced unemployment. Government policy is to promote international migration. The efforts made by the Department of Labour and the Ministry of Foreign Affairs are therefore to be commended. However, a greater effort is needed. In addition to facilitating and making pre-migration as easy as possible, government activities during and after migration need to be strengthened. Furthermore, serious attention needs to be paid to the declining demand for various classes of migrant labour in the West Asian market.

There is an urgent need to set up information, guidance and counselling services for the return migrants who are looking for income-earning opportunities and investments. It is necessary to identify the most likely recipients of such services. Young migrants and those with skills are ideal candidates for small pilot programmes which promote migrant investment and employment. International migration is a one-off activity, an educational experience that is not easily repeated. A greater effort must be made to use the experience and the insights gained by these workers in a new and challenging environment, and to harness their new skills for higher productivity, income, and employment in the home setting.

The survey data indicate the presence of many negative aspects to the migration. Although these do not seem very serious, they could become so if the warning goes unheeded. The negative effects on the family, especially the spouse and children, indicate that there is a need for education and information for the migrant families. One possible role for voluntary organizations is to provide support for the families of migrants through information and counselling.

# 5

# MIGRANT WORKERS TO THE ARAB WORLD: THE EXPERIENCE OF PAKISTAN

**M. Fahim Khan**

International Institute of Islamic Economics, Islamabad, Pakistan

## Introduction

Pakistan is one of seven South Asian countries which encouraged labour to seek contract employment in the capital-rich, yet labour-scarce, Arab countries. The mass migration of Pakistani labour commenced in the late 1960s, before the oil boom. Migration from most other South Asian countries gained momentum only after the oil boom in the early 1970s. Thus, Pakistan has perhaps the largest proportion of expatriate labour in the Arab world.

This study focuses on various aspects of labour migration, with the emphasis more on the attitudinal, behavioural, and institutional aspects than on statistics, such as the total stock of Pakistani emigrants in the Arab world, their outflow and inflow, or the number of returnees. Before this study was conducted, a report was prepared on information already available in the country; the present work attempts mainly to supplement the already available information.

This study is of significance to Pakistan because migrant labour from Pakistan, amounting to about two million, constitutes a very significant part (about 8 to 9 per cent) of the country's entire labour force, and remittances are at the same level as merchandise export earnings, hence constituting about 50 per cent of the annual foreign exchange earnings of the country. However, Pakistan is currently facing a mass return of migrant labour and this inflow of returnees is gaining momentum. The return has social and economic significance for the country, and hence needs to be carefully studied. Though several studies on migration and its implications exist, this is the first serious attempt to study the issues arising from the migrants' return.

In addition, as this chapter forms part of a study of seven South Asian countries exporting labour to the Arab world, it provides an insight into the regional issues arising out of the mass movement of population between two major regions of the world – South Asia and the Arab countries. It also aims to analyse the global impact of migration and the way in which the vastly increased scope for mobility and migration in the modern world brings enhanced awareness of the external world,

**Table 1.**

| Country | Percentage of migrants |
|---|---|
| Saudi Arabia | 46.6 |
| UAE | 14.8 |
| Kuwait | 9.1 |
| Iraq | 8.7 |
| Libya | 6.8 |
| Muscat | 4.4 |
| Other Middle Eastern countries | 9.6 |

creates new forms of international contact and human interactions, and poses new challenges.

The study was conducted on the basis of a sample survey of around 470 migrants who had returned after completing at least one job contract in an Arab country. These migrants were interviewed about all phases of migration, from the pre-migration phase to their final return. The data thus collected through a questionnaire were processed and analysed in the context of the objectives of the study and cover the following aspects of the migration:

1. Socio-economic profile of the migrant and his family.
2. Issues relating to pre-migration phases including the motivation to migrate and the problems involved in the process of migrating.
3. Issues relating to the period when the migrant was abroad, with particular emphasis on:
   - family adjustment problems;
   - economic implications (costs and benefits);
   - social implications; and
   - employment conditions.
4. Issues relating to returnees, particularly socio-economic adjustment and rehabilitation.

The returnees selected for this study were from both rural and urban areas, in almost equal numbers. The composition of the selected sample is given below.

## Country Composition

Migrants returning from countries other than oil-producing Arab countries were excluded from the sample. The composition of migrants was thus obtained according to the country from which they had returned (table 1); this is more or less consistent with the composition of Pakistani migrants to the Arab world as reported by the PIDE-World Bank report (Gilani et al., 1981).

## Return Period

All migrants returning from Arab countries were included in the sample, except those who had returned less than three months previously and were in the process of readjustment. Table 2 shows the composition of migrants in the sample when they returned.

**Table 2**

| Period since returning (months) | Percentage of migrants |
| --- | --- |
| 1–6 | 9.5 |
| 6–12 | 20.8 |
| 12–24 | 26.3 |
| 24–36 | 15.3 |
| 36–60 | 17.6 |
| Above 60 | 10.5 |

**Table 3**

| Occupational classification before going abroad | Percentage of migrants |
| --- | --- |
| Unskilled | 19.9 |
| Semi-skilled | 32.8 |
| Professional | 4.5 |
| Clerical | 4.9 |
| Domestic service workers | 13.1 |
| Sales/business | 10.6 |
| Other | 3.4 |
| Unemployed | 10.8 |

## Occupational Composition

An additional consideration in the selection of the sample was that it should adequately represent all the major occupations of migrants before leaving. It was decided that, after selecting 470 sample points, the occupational composition in the sample would be reviewed and, if certain important occupations were found unrepresented in the sample, another set of around 30 sample points would be selected to make up the deficiency. The review of the 470 selected sample points revealed the occupational composition shown in table 3.

This study deals with three phases of migration, namely, pre-migration, migration, and post-migration.

## The Pre-migration Phase

### Who Migrates: Socio-economic Profile of the Migrants

All migrant labour from Pakistan to the Arab world is predominantly (99 per cent) male and Muslim. Female labour migration is mainly confined to para-medical or teaching professions in a few Arab countries. The reason lies in demand as well as in supply.

Migrants are relatively young at the time of migration. More than 80 per cent were reported to have migrated at the age of under 35 years, two-thirds at less than 30 years and one-third at less than 25 years. The median age is around 26 years.

197

**Table 4.** Distribution of migrants by occupation at the time of their migration

| Profession | Percentage |
|---|---|
| Educated workers | 5.4 |
|   Lecturer/schoolteacher | 2.5 |
|   Qualified engineer | 1.5 |
|   Doctor (physician/surgeon) | 0.7 |
|   Bank manager | 0.7 |
| Semi-educated workers | 5.0 |
|   Clerk/typist | 2.5 |
|   Miscellaneous semi-educated workers | 2.5 |
| Government service | 7.8 |
| Semi-skilled labour | 43.8 |
|   Pipe-fitter/steel-fixer/binder | 8.8 |
|   Driver | 5.6 |
|   Electrician | 4.9 |
|   Mason | 4.2 |
|   Tailor | 3.6 |
|   Motor mechanic | 3.2 |
|   Plumber | 1.7 |
|   Carpenter | 1.7 |
|   Textile machinery worker | 1.7 |
|   Welder | 1.2 |
|   TV/radio mechanic | 1.0 |
|   Air-conditioning/refrigeration mechanic | 1.0 |
|   Lathe operator | 1.0 |
|   Painter | 1.0 |
|   Press man | 0.7 |
|   Plant operator | 0.7 |
|   Miscellaneous semi-skilled labour | 2.0 |
| Service workers (cobbler, barber, cook, etc.) | 1.2 |
| Unskilled labour | 25.0 |
| Unspecified labour | 9.3 |
| Businessmen | 2.5 |
| Total | 100.0 |

Migrants thus spend the best period of their young adulthood away from home, which has several psychological and social implications.

Only 14 per cent of the migrants had more than ten years of school. Nearly 15 per cent were illiterate and a slightly higher proportion (16.2 per cent) had less than 5 years' school. About half had less than eight years of secondary schooling. Only 2.2 per cent of the migrants were recorded as having professional qualifications in engineering or medicine, or a Master's degree in any subject. Rural migrants were obviously less educated than urban migrants. The occupational composition of the migrants is shown in table 4.

**Table 5**. Household size at the time of migration

| Household size | Percentage of migrants |
|---|---|
| Less than 5 | 17.5 |
| 5–9 | 58.3 |
| 10–14 | 21.7 |
| Above 14 | 2.5 |

**Table 6**.

| Dependency ratio | Percentage of migrants' households |
|---|---|
| Less than 3 | 17.8 |
| 3–5 | 35.3 |
| 5–7 | 23.6 |
| 7–9 | 14.2 |
| Above 9 | 9.1 |

The majority of the migrants were employed before migration. Only 10.8 per cent of the migrants were reported as unemployed; half of them were unemployed for less than six months. The migration of the employed meant a loss of income to their family, though this was more than compensated through remittances from abroad.

Only 24 per cent of the migrants were married at the time of migration. However, only 6.6 per cent were reported to be living abroad with their spouses. This extent of detachment from the nucleus of the family is likely to have posed many social and psychological problems.

Migrants have generally come from large families, as shown in table 5.

The average household size of the migrants was about seven. However, about 40 per cent of the households were reported to contain more than one family. Although only 24 per cent were married before the migration, more than 50 per cent of migrants reported that they were heads of households.

Half of the households had only one earning member. Of the average of seven household members, only 1.68 members, on average, were found to be employed. This implies an average dependency ratio of about 4.26 members per earning member in a household. Table 6 shows the distribution of migrants against the dependency ratio.

The migrants belonged principally to the lower-middle economic strata of society. The information relating to economic status of the migrant was obtained by asking a simple question. The respondent was shown a ladder with nine steps, the first rung at the top and the ninth at the bottom. He was told that step 1 shows the place of a household who is the richest or most affluent household in his community, and step 9 shows the place of the poorest household. The respondent was then asked the following two questions:

1. At what step would you place your household before migration?
2. At what step would you place your household now?

The responses to these questions revealed the distribution shown in table 7, con-

**Table 7.** Economic status of migrant's family

| Code for economic status | Before migration (%) | After return (%) |
|---|---|---|
| 1 | 1.1 | 3.9 |
| 2 | 3.7 | 7.1 |
| 3 | 2.8 | 11.4 |
| 4 | 9.3 | 18.5 |
| 5 | 20.9 | 25.6 |
| 6 | 8.5 | 12.1 |
| 7 | 20.7 | 12.2 |
| 8 | 18.1 | 8.6 |
| 9 | 4.9 | 0.4 |

**Table 8.** Social status of migrants' households

| Code for social stratum | Before migration (%) | After return (%) |
|---|---|---|
| 1 | 8.4 | 13.0 |
| 2 | 12.1 | 18.9 |
| 3 | 14.3 | 18.0 |
| 4 | 15.8 | 18.4 |
| 5 | 22.7 | 20.4 |
| 6 | 13.2 | 5.2 |
| 7 | 6.5 | 4.2 |
| 8 | 5.6 | 1.5 |
| 9 | 1.5 | 0.4 |

**Table 9.** Composition of migrants by country of destination and country of return (percentages)

| Country | Migrants | Returnees |
|---|---|---|
| Saudi Arabia | 47.5 | 49.4 |
| UAE | 16.9 | 16.0 |
| Other Arab world | 35.6 | 34.6 |

firming that migrants belonged mostly to the middle and lower-middle class of their community. It seems to indicate that the lower strata seldom have the opportunity to go abroad, in spite of the fact that the bulk of the migrants are unskilled, semi-skilled, or semi-educated.

It is interesting to note that migrants found their economic status significantly higher after return and the proportion of migrants in categories 6 to 9 fell from 62 per cent at the time of migration to 33 per cent after return.

A similar method was used to determine the social strata of returned migrants (table 8). Migrants mostly belong to the middle and upper-middle class in terms of social status, which means that it requires considerable push to get a job abroad.

About half of the Pakistani migrants to the Arab world go to Saudi Arabia (table

9). The next most popular country is the United Arab Emirates, while Kuwait, Iraq, Muscat, and Libya take up most of the remainder.

The predominant position held by Saudi Arabia as a country of destination requires special attention. The behaviour of Saudi Arabian migrants needs to be studied separately because Saudi Arabia is different from other Arab world in its political, social, economic, and religious background. For these reasons the sample ensured that 50 per cent of the returnees interviewed were from Saudi Arabia.

### Reasons for Migration

In the dynamics of the migratory process, the motivation of outgoing migrants is very important. Migration to the Middle East and the other countries from Pakistan obviously revolves around better job opportunities which are not available in the home country. People migrate to these countries to earn sufficient money which they can remit to their families. Only 5 per cent of the migrants reported the desire to visit/travel abroad or to enjoy better living conditions as the main reason. The great majority gave economic reasons such as:
- to raise standard of living;
- to accumulate savings;
- to repay debts;
- to raise money for some specific purpose such as children's education or marriage or constructing own house.

The significance of economic motivation for different economic strata of the migrants is shown in table 10. Tabulation of economic motivation against the social status of migrants revealed similar results (table 11).

In general, neither social status nor economic status at home mattered much. The gap between income earned at home by any social and economic stratum participating in the migration and the earning potential of employment abroad was so large that monetary gain became the predominant motive for all groups.

**Table 10.** Significant economic motivation by economic status of the migrant (percentages)

| Economic status of the household | Reasons for migrating | |
| --- | --- | --- |
| | Economic | Others |
| Upper-income group | 89.7 | 10.3 |
| Middle-income group | 93.0 | 7.0 |
| Lower-income group | 90.7 | 9.3 |

**Table 11.** Significant economic motivation by social status of migrant (percentages)

| Social status | Reasons for migrating | |
| --- | --- | --- |
| | Economic | Others |
| Upper social group | 89.2 | 10.8 |
| Middle social group | 93.4 | 6.6 |
| Lower social group | 91.2 | 8.8 |

It is difficult to identify clearly "push" and "pull" factors from the respondents' answers to the question "Why did you migrate?" A rough classification of their answers can be made as follows:

Push Factors

These include all responses that reflect the following:
– Poor economic living conditions at home.
– Lack of employment opportunities at home.
– Debt burden.
All those "push" reasons are in fact economic reasons.

Pull Factors

These include all responses based on the attractions of living abroad (whether economic or non-economic), such as:
– The desire to visit/travel abroad.
– Better opportunities abroad to earn more income.
– Better living conditions abroad.
Push factors are dominant among all groups of migrants. This seems to imply that the Pakistani migrants expect to return as soon as their objectives are fulfilled and the push factors become less compelling. Since all push is "economic," it probably means that when wages rise and employment opportunities increase at home, or when the migrant has stayed long enough abroad to accumulate the required savings, he will return voluntarily.

**Role of Relations Abroad**

A relation who is already abroad can play a significant role in "pulling" a migrant. About 42 per cent of the migrants covered by the present study had a relative already abroad. It has been observed that about 18.5 per cent of the returned migrants found employment through a relative already working abroad. This implies that about 44 per cent of the migrants who had relations abroad were actually assisted in finding employment. The presence of relatives in the country of destination was evidently an important "pull" factor.

**Recruitment System in Pakistan**

In Pakistan, the legal process of emigration falls under the Emigration Rules, 1979, with the Bureau of Emigration having responsibility for the operation and administration of the policies relating to overseas employment promotion. The Protector of Emigrants controls the whole process of emigration in the private sector, and the Overseas Employment Corporation does so in the public sector. Under these rules of emigration, three types of migration are recognized:
– Emigration through the Overseas Employment Promoters (OEP).
– Emigration on a government-to-government basis.
– Emigration with a direct or individual visa.
Usually recruitment for employment abroad takes place through registered overseas employment promoters in the home country after they have received a re-

quest from a foreign employer who has obtained from his government permission to import labour for a specified number of persons and categories. Names are not mentioned in the permission. Thereafter, the foreign employer issues a power of attorney to a local authorized agent for the import of the manpower. The whole process is completed through a licensed overseas employment promoter.

The Government of Pakistan permits two types of direct employment: employment on an individual visa, and employment on a group visa not exceeding five persons. This is also called *azad* (or free) visa. Direct visas are sent by the employer to the selected person who has found work through his own efforts or the efforts of relatives and friends employed abroad. (The foreign employer makes an application to his government and the government issues a visa.) Direct visas specify the names of the selected persons and their occupations. If the direct visa exceeds five persons in number, it is treated as a group visa and has to be processed by a licensed overseas employment promoter. The holder of the direct employment visa receives a foreign service agreement, contract, or letter of appointment from the employer, attested by the embassy of Pakistan abroad, or the Foreign Ministry of the country of the employer. OEPs do not enter into these transactions. All the formalities and completion of documentation are carried out by the selected persons, including registration and clearance from the Protector of Emigrants.

Some illegal emigration takes place through illegal recruiting agents and/or by sea. The Government of Pakistan has taken positive steps to stamp this out.

**Process of Recruitment**

Getting a job abroad has two distinct stages. The first involves the spadework of locating an opportunity abroad, and the second concerns actual recruitment. The way a migrant completes these two stages determines the nature of the problems that he is likely to face.

The spadework is essentially a matter of acquiring information and getting the required training. The major sources of information are the media. The majority of the migrants are from the rural areas where the rate of illiteracy is high and where access to the media is limited. Therefore, though the percentage of literates among the migrants themselves is relatively high, most of them do not have ready access to the media. Their only source of information is, therefore, informal personal contact.

Only 14 per cent of the migrants have reported that they obtained their information through the media. The remaining 86 per cent of the migrants received it through personal contact with friends or relatives abroad, or through a recruiting agent. Informal personal contact is the most important source of information in rural as well as urban areas: 52 per cent of respondents got their information in this manner.

The dependence on recruiting agents is significantly greater in rural areas (40.3 per cent) than in urban areas (28.1 per cent), with a large number of unscrupulous recruiting agents ready to exploit the less educated rural population. Thus the rural migrant's source of information is not only informal but is likely to be unreliable as well.

Despite a long labour emigration history of at least 15 years, no institution has

**Table 12.** Skill level of migrants by their education level (percentages)

| Skill level | Years of schooling | | |
|---|---|---|---|
| | Below 5 | 6–10 | Above 10 |
| Unskilled | 54.2 | 28.6 | 17.1 |
| Semi-skilled | 39.0 | 59.5 | 48.8 |
| Skilled | 1.0 | 3.6 | 7.3 |
| Non-technical | 6.8 | 8.3 | 26.8 |
| Total | 100.0 | 100.0 | 100.0 |

been set up in the country to serve as a formal, reliable source of information for a potential migrant. The informal sources of information have, on the other hand, increased with time.

After information has been gathered on job opportunities abroad, the next stage for all migrants is to get the training required for the job. The proportion of migrants who do this is, however, relatively small: only 13 per cent indicated that they had undergone some sort of training. This obviously reflects a lack of planning or of opportunities for migrating labour to improve their skills in order to get a better job abroad. Several factors are responsible for this: it may be a lack of education, money, opportunity, or time. A study in late 1980 indicated that 43 per cent of outgoing labour was unskilled. Getting sufficient skill as masons, carpenters, welders, drivers, machine operators, etc., requires only six months' training and a small outlay. Acquiring even modest skill means much in terms of salary and living conditions abroad. A migrant with such semi-skills will also have a better chance of not being repatriated prematurely. Appropriate counselling and availability of modest but widespread training facilities could spare migrants much hardship and misfortune. Yet the proportion of migrants being trained and the facilities available have been declining.

The urban population is more inclined (17.6 per cent, as compared to 7.7 per cent for rural areas) to obtain training before going abroad. This is not only because this population is relatively more educated but also because training opportunities are available only in urban areas. In fact, rural migrants who had trained had done so in towns and cities.

It is of interest that the proportion of the semi-educated (secondary level) inclined to undergo training was smaller, at 4.4 per cent, than that of the less educated (illiterate and primary) at 13.2 per cent, or the higher educated (above matriculation) at 15.5 per cent. This could be due to the fact that the majority of the migrants with schooling at the secondary level had already acquired skills as tailors, masons, welders, etc. (table 12).

On the other hand, people with no education found it worthwhile to acquire some training so as to enhance their chances of foreign employment. Those who had education above the matriculation level were also inclined to seek training, as they had both knowledge and access to the appropriate sources. A constraint all educational levels experience is the short time available for training purposes.

**Table 13**. Channels of employment by education levels of migrants (percentages)

| Educational level | Friends or relatives abroad | Government | Agents | | |
|---|---|---|---|---|---|
| | | | Regular private | Illegal private | Direct recruitment |
| Less than primary | 32.8 | 9.0 | 38.0 | 4.5 | 14.9 |
| Primary to matriculation | 28.9 | 10.0 | 43.8 | 5.4 | 11.9 |
| Above matriculation | 31.6 | 10.4 | 32.6 | 4.1 | 21.3 |

## Channels for Getting a Job Abroad

The survey revealed that recruiting agents and friends of relatives are important channels for employment abroad. It showed that most migrants used these sources to secure employment, whereas the government agency only assisted 10 per cent. It is worth pointing out that a small proportion of migrants admitted to utilizing illegal channels successfully. There will, of course, be a very large number of potential migrants who contact unscrupulous agents and, having paid them all the fees and commissions demanded, end up without employment abroad. They were unable to get either a job agreement or a visa from the host country because they were supplied with illegal documents. As has already been indicated, the number of illegal recruiting agents in the country is several times greater than that of legal agents.

Of those who got a job through a friend or relative, 88 per cent received the preliminary information from them. Direct appointments too have been mainly through friends and relatives. Of such direct appointments, 46 per cent of migrants received their preliminary information through their friends or relatives. Advertisements in the newspapers were also an important source of information for those migrants who got a job through direct contact with the employer.

The educational level of the migrant is another important determinant of the use of different channels for obtaining employment abroad. The more educated migrants, for example, seldom use illegal channels. However, it is of interest that the proportion of migrants using illegal agents is not significantly different for the illiterate and those with one to ten years of schooling. However, migrants with education above matriculation level benefitted more from government channels or from direct contracts with the employer. They also depended least on private recruiting agents. Less educated migrants depended more on friends and private recruiting agents (table 13).

With the passage of time, the effectiveness of friends and relatives abroad in getting a job abroad has been declining. With the increase in regular agents, the role of illegal agents has also increased during the last five years, thus raising the cost of migration, as the latter demand an exorbitant fee (table 14).

Illegal recruiting agents have been able to remit unskilled and semi-skilled labour more successfully than the skilled and non-technical grades, who are served principally by the government agency. Unskilled labour has benefitted least from the government recruiting agency (table 15).

The economic status of the migrant's household and his rural or urban origin are

**Table 14**. Changes in channels of recruitment during the course of time (percentages)

| Channels of recruitment | Before 1970 | 1970–1979 | 1980–1984 |
|---|---|---|---|
| Friends or relatives | 53.4 | 32.3 | 27.4 |
| Government agency | 6.6 | 8.8 | 10.2 |
| Regular private agency (OEP) | 20.0 | 39.8 | 39.8 |
| Illegal private agency | 6.7 | 1.6 | 9.1 |
| Direct employment | 13.3 | 17.1 | 13.4 |

**Table 15**. Skill level of migrants and channels of migration (percentages)

| | | Through agency | | | |
|---|---|---|---|---|---|
| | Direct | | Private | | Private or |
| Skill level | contact | Government | Legal (OEP) | Illegal | relatives |
|---|---|---|---|---|---|
| Unskilled | 14.7 | 3.9 | 42.2 | 4.9 | 34.3 |
| Semi-skilled | 16.0 | 11.5 | 36.5 | 7.0 | 29.0 |
| Skilled | 12.5 | 12.5 | 37.5 | 0.0 | 37.5 |
| Non-technical | 17.5 | 21.0 | 31.6 | 1.8 | 28.1 |

other indicators of the choice of channels of migration. Migrants of rural origin are poorly educated and belong to the lower economic levels. Data clearly indicate the influence of irregular channels among these groups: 50 per cent as against 4 per cent for upper economic groups. Rural migrants depend more on private agents, both regular and irregular. However, urban migrants prefer direct contact with the employer; they registered 22 per cent as against 13 per cent for rural migrants. Recruitment through the government channel is also significant among urban migrants at 11.5 per cent.

### Awareness of Terms and Conditions

About 40 per cent of the migrants reported that they were not fully aware of the terms and conditions of their jobs abroad at the time of their migration. Such cases were reported even among migrants who had a formal job contract. The bulk of these cases (60 per cent) concerned those who did not have a formal job contract. On the social plane, the underprivileged proved less aware than those in the middle and upper social groups. It is, however, of interest that the upper group too was found to show poor awareness (20 per cent) of terms and conditions,.

The channel of employment was also a factor influencing awareness of the terms and conditions applicable. Those who obtained their jobs through informal channels were less aware of the terms of employment than those who migrated through regular channels (table 16).

It is interesting to note that education did not play as significant a role in making migrants aware of terms and conditions as did the channel of employment (table 17).

**Table 16.** Channel of employment and awareness of terms and conditions (percentages)

| Awareness of terms and conditions | Direct recruitment | Through agents | | | Through friends or relatives | Illegal channels |
| | | Government | Private | | | |
| | | | Regular | Irregular | | |
|---|---|---|---|---|---|---|
| Yes | 71.6 | 85.4 | 64.6 | 31.8 | 49.6 | 0.0 |
| No | 28.4 | 14.6 | 35.6 | 68.2 | 50.4 | 100.0 |
| Total | 100.0 | 100.0 | 100.0 | 100.0 | 100.0 | 100.0 |

**Table 17.** Education of migrant and awareness of terms and conditions of employment (percentages)

| Education | Awareness of terms and conditions | | Total |
| | Yes | No | |
|---|---|---|---|
| Less than primary | 52.3 | 47.7 | 100.0 |
| Primary to matriculation | 64.6 | 35.4 | 100.0 |
| Above matriculation | 61.1 | 38.9 | 100.0 |

## Documentation

In theory, the documentation required for emigration is quite simple and neither time-consuming nor expensive. Yet many emigrants still face difficulties in getting their documents completed. A lack of information is the main factor responsible for the inconvenience and hardships faced. The entire process should take less than two months, but several respondents reported taking as much as four months, while about 12 per cent took a year or more. The fact that more than 50 per cent of migrants take more than one month to complete the process is indicative of the substantial suffering that many undergo. The process is also costly for migrants from rural areas, as they have to meet board and lodging expenses or be dependent on, and beholden to, a friend or relative.

It is normally not difficult to get a passport. The procedure is simple: forms are easily available at passport offices, bookshops, law courts, etc., and only need filling in and handing over to the passport office along with the applicant's identity card. It normally takes only a week to get the passport. However, paying three times the normal fee will ensure that one gets the passport on the same day. Only 8 per cent of the migrants, mostly of rural origin, reported difficulties; most others received their passports within a month.

The Bureau of Emigration requires migrants to complete following formalities:

1. To deposit a sum of two thousand rupees with a branch of a scheduled bank, which issues a certificate.
2. To submit a letter of employment or contract to the Protector of Emigrants for scrutiny.
3. To appear before the Protector of Emigrants with the service registration.

**Table 18.** Total costs incurred during the process of migration

| Amount spent (Rs.) | Percentage of migrants |
|---|---|
| Less than 999 | 22.0 |
| 1,000–5,000 | 27.6 |
| 5,000–10,000 | 29.3 |
| Above 10,000 | 21.1 |

4. To endorse the registration number, supported by the official seal and signature of the Protector of Emigrants on the passport.

Less than one-fifth reported clearance from the Bureau to be a difficult procedure.

Only 18 per cent of migrants reported that obtaining visas was a difficult process. Once there is a valid job offer from abroad, getting a visa is not a problem; it may, however, pose problems for those who go through unlicensed agents.

**Financial Cost of Emigration**

Two thousand rupees is the official fee for employment abroad through an authorized agent, but actual expenses are often higher. A survey conducted by PIDE in 1979 showed Rs. 6,000 as the average financial cost of emigration. The present survey shows a 50 per cent increase, raising the cost to Rs. 9,000; in some cases it is as much as Rs. 40,000, which is about one-and-a-half year's average remittance per migrant from abroad. Middlemen and irregular agents are mainly responsible for the higher costs.

It was reported that migrants going abroad on direct recruitment paid an average of Rs. 12,300 average to obtain an employment visa. Of this group 18 per cent paid more than Rs. 25,000. Irregular agents charge more for emigration than regular agents. On the other hand, 90 per cent of those who obtained jobs through the government spent less than Rs. 5,000.

Completion of the documentation and other necessary formalities, clearance from the Bureau of Emigration, travelling expenses within the country, etc., are included in the process of migration. Each step in the process involves additional expenses which are not included in the official fee or in the legal amount paid to the recruiting agent. Half the migrants reported additional expenses of up to Rs. 5,000.

**Source of Financing**

Availability of resources is the most crucial factor in migration, owing to the poor economic background of most migrants. Some prospective migrants collect the required amount from their own savings; this ranged from 20 per cent for urban migrants to 28 per cent for rural ones. But insufficient savings compel the majority, nearly 75 per cent, to acquire the required amount by such means as sale of assets, mortgages of land or house, borrowing from relatives and friends, or even bank loans (table 19). Evidence also showed that in some cases the migrant departed abroad without paying the concerned agent, but with the promise that the amount would be paid from remittances.

**Table 19.** Sources of financing of the cost of migration: rural and urban migrants (percentages)

| | Savings or sale of assets | Borrowing | Savings/ borrowing | Total |
|---|---|---|---|---|
| Rural migrants | 41.8 | 29.3 | 28.9 | 100 |
| Urban migrants | 54.3 | 25.6 | 20.1 | 100 |

## Services for Orientation and Training

The services for migrant orientation and training are negligible. It has been observed that more than half the migrants had had no orientation at all; about one-fifth, however, reported receiving adequate orientation on various aspects of migration. Whatever orientation the migrants received was through informal sources. Only 7.3 per cent obtained some orientation through government agencies, which, in most cases, refers to the Orientation Centre of the Bureau of Emigration.

Most of the migrants reported having no knowledge at all of important matters like customs regulations and getting in touch with their embassy if in difficulty. Half of the migrants had no instructions on the various legal requirements and obligations they had to comply with after landing. About one-third were at first not aware of how they could remit money back home until they learnt from other migrants how it was done. However, about 40 per cent had adequate information on remittances before they migrated. One-third of the migrants did not even have any knowledge of such matters as climate, travel requirements, etc. The only matter on which many migrants (48 per cent) had adequate instruction was on communicating with their families; even here 35 per cent had no knowledge.

Lack of education is one of the principal factors for the failure to receive adequate orientation. It is not enough to establish an Orientation Centre under the supervision of the Bureau of Emigration and leave it to migrants to take the initiative.

What is required is the following:

1. To make it obligatory on the migrants to acquire orientation before migration.
2. To make it obligatory for recruiting agents to provide orientation programmes to their clients.
3. To provide orientation centres at the airport to assist migrants.
4. To provide orientation and information centres in the host country.

## Training

The availability of training services to cater to the needs of the migrant workers is extremely poor. The reason is poor demand, on which provision largely depends: only 12.7 per cent of the migrants reported that they acquired some training for the purpose of getting a job abroad. As competition is increasing in job markets abroad, training is important; yet the statistics indicate that the willingness of the emigrants to seek training is decreasing (table 20).

The urban population is more inclined (17.6 per cent) to obtain training before going abroad than the rural population (7.7 per cent). This is because the urban population is better educated and also because training opportunities are available

**Table 20.** Percentage of migrants who acquired specific training

| Year of migration | Percentage of migrants |
|---|---|
| Before 1970 | 14.3 |
| 1970–1979 | 14.7 |
| 1980–1984 | 8.0 |

only in urban areas. There is virtually no training service in the rural areas from which two-thirds of the migrants go abroad; even in urban areas the training facilities are poor. Most semi-skilled migrants had obtained their skills through informal sources.

Some attempt to provide training has been made in the recent past by the Overseas Pakistanis Foundation, which is an institution that looks after the welfare of overseas Pakistanis and their families, and which is financed by a levy of Rs. 500 from each migrant – a once-for-all-time payment. The foundation has started to establish training centres in various cities, but this effort is very recent and has not yet led to the creation of a network of such institutions throughout the country.

## Adjustments at Home and Abroad after Migration

### Conditions in the Host Country

Data show that one-fourth of the migrants faced one problem or another at the time of entry. Among these problems, passport/visa difficulties are prominent. Though such problems could be solved with the help of the embassy, many migrants do not contact the embassy.

Wrong endorsements in the passport/visa are one such difficulty faced at the time of entry; retention of the passport by the employer or his agent in the host country is another. Thus, even if a migrant finds that the working conditions or living conditions are not acceptable he has no choice but to work for his employer on the employer's terms and conditions.

Non-fulfilment of obligations by the employer is another problem faced at the time of entry. This is common among illegal mirgrants. It has been reported that in some cases the employer did not meet the migrant at the airport; consequently he was detained by the police or other authority. In the sample, 8.4 per cent of the migrants reported problems faced at the time of entry due to the absence of the employer. Educated migrants and those recruited by the government or legal agents with valid contracts seldom face such problems.

Data show that one-fourth of the migrants had no firm offer of a job before landing in the host country. They migrated only on the promise of a friend, relative, agent, or employer to get them a job after arrival. Some of these migrants had to wait up to six months for a job.

Even those migrants who arrived in the host country with the firm offer of a job also faced problems, as the large majority of them had no formal contracts with clearly specified terms and conditions of work. In all about two-thirds of the migrants, including those who had migrated without a firm job offer, reported having left for employment abroad without a formal contract. They were thus exposed to various risks ranging from unsatisfactory terms and conditions of employment to outright failure to obtain employment. This risk was taken by almost all groups of migrants; less educated migrants, however, took it more than the educated migrants.

All migrants who had gone through government channels had formal contracts. The next best recruiting channels in this respect were the regular private agents; they are governed and controlled by government regulations. Direct recruitment is also a satisfactory channel from the point of view of providing a formal contract. Most migrants who secure employment through other channels have to leave home without a formal contract, relying on informal arrangements and placing themselves at the mercy and goodwill of the recruiting agent and employer.

Fraud or breach of agreed conditions were experienced to a greater degree by migrants with informal contracts. In such cases the less educated face the greatest difficulties. About one-fifth of the migrants reported that they experienced some degree of fraud or breach of contract.

The channel for obtaining employment was a significant factor in determining the incidence of the problems relating to contract violations. Of the migrants who went abroad through government agencies, 91 per cent reported adherence to the contract, but 41.7 per cent of those who went abroad through irregular agents reported that they were employed on inferior terms. Of the migrants who went abroad through friends and relatives, 43.7 per cent were not employed according to the terms and conditions that were often agreed upon informally. More than a third of those who secured jobs by direct negotiation also complained of inferior terms. This makes it very clear that migrants obtaining employment through informal sources faced the problem of unsatisfactory conditions of employment more often than migrants contracting through formal and organized channels.

An overwhelming majority (90 per cent) reported that they did not contact any agency in the host country to report violations of contract. Only the better educated apparently took steps to have violations redressed. Urban migrants took such steps more frequently than rural migrants. The migrants who went through government agencies and friends or relatives had more opportunities to obtain redress than those using other channels. It also appeared that migrants using irregular channels usually avoided contacting any official agency and suffered in silence. Lack of information and orientation are the main factors which prevent migrants from contacting the relevant authority and reporting violations.

Of the migrants, 34 per cent reported that their wages were below their expectations. It is a common practice for employers to convert monthly into daily wages, thus depriving the migrant employees of the benefits associated with regular employment. A quarter of the migrants were dissatisfied with housing, food, and leave facilities. Free housing facilities are the responsibility of the employer, but several employers do not fulfil this obligation. The younger migrants were apparently most exploited.

The level of satisfaction with the nature and status of employment was highest among professional and non-technical groups. Here too, 98 per cent of those who went abroad through government agencies reported that the nature and status of employment were in accordance with the agreement, whereas only 42 per cent of migrants selected through irregular channels reported satisfaction with the nature

**Table 21.** Problems relating to terms and conditions faced by the migrants

| Channel of getting job abroad | No problems faced | Problems faced |
|---|---|---|
| Friends/relatives | 43.7 | 56.3 |
| Regular recruiting agents | 87.6 | 12.4 |
| Irregular recruiting agents | 41.7 | 58.3 |
| Government agencies | 90.9 | 8.1 |
| Direct employment | 61.3 | 38.7 |

of their jobs. Dissatisfaction relating to wages and salary was high among the younger age-groups. A positive relationship between educational levels and level of satisfaction relating to salary and wages was observed. Of the illiterate, as many as 45 per cent reported dissatisfaction with their salary and wages; on the other hand, only 22 per cent of those above matriculation level expressed dissatisfaction.

The majority of the migrants were satisfied with their daily working hours, but one-third were not satisfied with overtime compensation. Younger, uneducated, unskilled, rural workers and those who migrated through irregular agents were found generally dissatisfied with their working hours and overtime compensation.

More than 28 per cent of the dissatisfied migrants reported under-payments as the principal breach of contract. About 21 per cent reported violations of contracts but did not give specific details. Generally, breaches of contract occurred in the case of employers in the host country who were not well established. However, the migrants in such situations did not complain to the authorities, nor did they leave the job. About 6 per cent reported that the job was not provided after arrival in the host country and a further 7 per cent were repatriated. The latter may well be illegal migrants or those without any valid contract. A change of occupation or nature of job was experienced by 9 per cent of migrants; these were given a job different to what was agreed to or promised. Occasionally, professionals were required to accept a lower-paid job than their qualifications warranted.

Only 28.7 per cent of the migrants facing fraud or breach of contract approached some authority for redress; the majority, however, continued in their jobs, owing to their ignorance of procedures for redress or unwillingness to antagonize the employer. About 70 per cent of the affected migrants did not seek any redress.

Only 10 per cent of the Pakistanis in the Middle East are working with small enterprises of less than 10 workers, while 60 per cent are attached to large companies of more than 250 workers; the rest of the migrants work with medium-size companies.

An often disputed issue relates to working hours. Forty-eight hours per week is the standard ceiling, but in some cases this is exceeded. Thus, 46 per cent reported working more than eight hours per day. Generally, the small employers require the migrants to work for more than eight hours, and they are not paid any extra remuneration for this overtime work. A migrant working with a shopkeeper or in a restaurant or house may have to work over 12 hours a day for seven days a week. International companies, however, honour the standard ceiling and provide allowances in lieu of overtime. This is an exception.

About 91 per cent of the migrants worked one to four extra hours daily with overtime payments. Migrants opted to do so willingly in order to maximize their earnings. This partly explains why two-thirds of the migrants expressed satisfaction regarding their hours of work, even though they well exceeded eight hours.

## Living Conditions during Stay Abroad

Most migrants live in the host countries separated from their families, because only professionals earning high salaries are allowed the privilege of bringing their family with them. In the sample only 7.6 per cent of the married migrants and 6.6 per cent of all migrants were living abroad with their families. This is a very small percentage; however, an increase has been recorded during the last few years; before 1980 only 4 per cent of migrants were living abroad with their families. There are many reasons for the separation from the family other than restrictions imposed by the host countries, including care of the migrant's ageing parents or of property during his temporary absence from home, the expense of maintaining the family abroad, children's education and adjustment problems for the family in the foreign environment. In cases where migrants have been accompanied by their families, the study showed that about 10 per cent of the wives were also in employment. However, job opportunities for women in the Middle East are limited, save at the lowest levels.

More than 80 per cent of the migrants had reasonably good accommodation. As many as 92 per cent were satisfied with the water and electricity supply at the place of residence. Sanitation facilities, however, were reported unsatisfactory both at the work site and the living quarters. Air conditioning at the place of residence was reported by 33 per cent to be poor. Generally, in the Middle Eastern countries, food was not provided and migrants made their own arrangements. Owing to the absence of the family, the quality and quantity of food were poor and inadequate; migrants seldom had the time for food preparation after a long day's work. Nevertheless, about 85 per cent reported that the food facilities were adequate, while only 14 per cent expressed dissatisfaction. The data show that when living conditions are considered as a whole, about one-fifth of the migrants assessed them as "good" and another two-thirds "adequate." The remaining one-sixth were provided with poor facilities.

## Social Contact

More than half of the migrants reported adequate social contact abroad with other Pakistanis, host nationals, and others. Social contact was, however, strongest with other Pakistanis. The facilities for formal social gatherings and associations, however, were reported as poor by more than 75 per cent. For Pakistanis, the Indians proved to be the best resource for social contact abroad; this is perhaps not only because of their common language and cultural heritage, but also because Indians are among the largest foreign communities in the Middle East. Contact with migrants from Egypt, Bangladesh, and Turkey also found favour.

About 122 of the migrants were convicted by the police during their stay abroad. About half of them accepted that they were guilty; the rest pleaded not guilty even though they were convicted. The data suggest that migrants were convicted mostly for traffic offences. Disputes with the employer or with host nationals or colleagues emerged as the second main cause of conviction. Some migrants re-

**Table 22.** Monthly incomes during first and last years of migration

| Occupational group | Monthly income of migrants during first year of migration | Monthly income of migrants during last year of migration | Percentage change |
|---|---|---|---|
| Unskilled | 3,416 | 4,440 | + 30.2 |
| Semi-skilled | 3,771 | 5,757 | + 52.6 |
| Non-technical | 4,911 | 7,126 | + 45.1 |
| Skilled or professional | 5,563 | 7,561 | + 35.9 |
| Total | 3,984 | 5,894 | + 47.9 |

ported that they had visited other towns to meet friends or relatives without prior permission and were arrested by the police after their return, on the sponsor's complaint. In one-fourth of the cases, the penalty was quite severe and included imprisonment or deportation.

Generally, migrants do not contact their embassy if they are in difficulties. Only 31 per cent contacted the Pakistan embassy in the host country with regard to their problems.

The majority of migrants (85 per cent) reported the availability of bank facilities near the work site. One-fifth, however, had difficulty in opening an account with the bank.

Migrants indicated full satisfaction with the postal facilities available to them abroad.

## Problems of Adjustment for the Migrant and the Family

In general, working and living conditions abroad did not create serious adjustment problems for the migrants. Nevertheless, a significant proportion of the migrants (37 per cent) did experience a sense of loneliness on separation from their family. One-fourth reported that they suffered from sleeplessness in the initial period of their stay abroad. Due to this loneliness and depression, about 16.6 per cent of repondents fell ill more frequently. About 21.4 per cent, however, said that they adjusted easily by involving themselves in household activities.

For the family left behind, the adjustment problem was much easier. Only 32 per cent of families reported some difficulties, generally of a minor nature. Not one family in the sample had experienced adjustment problems which were considered serious.

The economic benefits of migration so overwhelmingly outweigh its costs that the migrants, as well as their families, are quite likely to have ignored the social and psychological problems that they faced.

Adjustment problems arise in two ways. Pakistani society has a clear division of family reponsibilities. Males are responsible for all activities outside the household and females for household activities. With the migration of male members, who in several cases are the heads of households, women are compelled to undertake outside activities too, and to exercise more authority in the economic sphere. Secondly, male members of the family play a special role in the upbringing of children and the exercise of authority, particularly in the case of teenage males. With the departure of male members, the children not only undertake extra activities but are free from paternal controls, which can have adverse consequences. However, on important decisions relating to children's education and marriage, the family is still dependent upon the male members even if they are abroad.

Thus, about one-fourth of the wives left behind by migrants faced heavy psychological strains owing to the absence of their husband. A smaller proportion of respondents reported that their wives had to seek the help of relatives to enable them to deal with routine matters. A little more than half of the migrants (55 per cent) complained of deviant behaviour by their children that had arisen in their absence. About one-fourth of the respondents reported that their children's school performance had deteriorated.

Nearly 12.3 per cent of respondents stated that their children were more prone to illness owing to the lack of supervision and medical care. Many referred to the absence of proper medical facilities in their areas and reported that, in the absence of males, the females could not handle health care satisfactorily. A few respondents (7 per cent) reported that, because of the absence of the father, their children had developed bad habits, such as smoking and gambling, and stated that had male supervision been available this would not have occurred. About 15 per cent of respondents reported that their children felt loneliness and insecurity in the absence of their father.

## Income, Savings, and Investment

### Incomes and Savings

Economic reasons dominate the desire to migrate. The economic motivation becomes decisive only when there are substantial differences between income earned at home and abroad. The statistics show that this is indeed the case. It has been reported that, on average, migrants earned abroad approximately Rs. 4,500 per month in the first year of their migration; this was besides other benefits which included free residence (and in several cases food), free medical treatment, a return ticket to travel home once a year, etc. It has further to include overtime and income from part-time jobs. Most of these migrants (90 per cent) migrated only during the last ten years. Ten years ago the average wage rate in Pakistan was around Rs. 250 a month for unskilled labour and around Rs. 450 for semi-skilled labour (e.g. carpenter or mason). More than 80 per cent of the migrants belong to the unskilled or semi-skilled categories. Since, in most of the cases (particularly in the case of unskilled and semi-skilled labour), residence, food, transport and medical care were provided free of cost, the migrant labourers were able to save a substantial amount of their incomes abroad. During the first year of their migration, they are reported to have saved, on average, Rs. 32,000 – more than five times the per capita annual income of their households at the time of their migration (Rs. 5,800).

Not much difference has been observed in emoluments between various occupational groups. Unskilled labour migrates for a monthly salary or wage of Rs. 3,636, whereas highly skilled or professional workers have a monthly salary of

**Table 23.** Use of remittances for acquisition and improvement of assets

| Use of remittances | Percentage of households |
|---|---|
| Residential house (purchase/repairs) | 47.1 |
| Consumer durables (fridge, TV, etc.) | 30.2 |
| Purchase of land/residential plot | 28.4 |
| Vehicles | 9.3 |
| Business | 6.4 |
| Fixed deposits and savings schemes | 4.3 |

Rs. 6,369. The wage differential in the domestic market is much higher than that recorded for migrant labour working abroad – about 1 to 2 for unskilled labour vis-à-vis semi-skilled. The wage differential for the same occupations abroad is about 1 to 1.13.

Migrants have witnessed a decline in their basic wages and salaries during their stay abroad, reflecting the interaction of demand and supply forces. Ten years ago, when Pakistani labour first entered the Gulf market, competition was almost negligible and the Gulf employers had to import labour from Pakistan by offering high wages and salaries. With the passage of time, the competition increased, both from within Pakistan and, to a large extent, from other South Asian and South-East Asian countries, particularly India, Bangladesh, Sri Lanka, the Philippines, the Republic of Korea, and Thailand. Along with the increasing supply pressures, the declining demand (caused by reduced oil earnings during the last five years) have also been causing a downward pressure on wages and salaries. South Asia and South-East Asia being abundant in unskilled labour, the pressure on wages was highest for this class. Semi-skilled and skilled labour is scarce among South Asian and South-East Asian labour, and hence the supply–demand forces did not put as much downward pressure on their wages.

It is, however, apparent that migrants have made attempts to compensate for declines in their basic wages by working overtime, or by doing additional part-time jobs. This is confirmed by the data on their annual expenditures and savings over the entire period of their employment abroad.

The average annual expenditure plus savings abroad are reported to be approximately Rs. 48,000 during the first year of the migration. This figure had increased to approximately Rs. 70,000 in the last year of migration. All occupational groups reported increases in their total spending and savings abroad, ranging from 30 per cent for unskilled to 52 per cent for semi-skilled. For most migrants this compensated for the total inflation during the period of their stay. The unskilled workers, with only an increase of 30 per cent, may have suffered a loss in real income. As will be noted later, the situation of the unskilled migrants is reflected in their savings performance; they were the only category where average annual remittances declined during their stay abroad.

Compared to the decline in basic wages, the migrants' expenditures abroad did not decline in the same proportions. This is, first, because it is difficult to cut down on a living standard once adopted and, second, because inflation has been continuously rising in the Gulf region. Hence, on average, migrants have reported an increase of about 50 per cent in their expenditure during their stay abroad.

The annual savings of migrants abroad are reported to have increased by about 50 per cent. Again, unskilled labour's savings grew at a slower rate than those of other occupational groups, reflecting the differences in the growth of their incomes.

## Remittances and Transfers from Abroad

Remittances from migration take the following forms:
1. Regular remittances from abroad.
2. Savings in cash and in kind while visiting home periodically.
3. Savings in cash and in kind brought home on final return.

The absolute and relative significance of these kinds of remittances depends both on the incomes earned abroad and the length of stay abroad. The length of stay particularly affects type 3. Migrants keep accumulating some small part of their savings to bring with time when returning home. Hence, the lengthier the stay the larger will be the remittances of type 3.

The remittances of types 1 and 2 mainly depend on the incomes earned abroad.

### Regular Remittances from Abroad

Most of the migrants' savings abroad are remitted home. On average, they remit more than Rs. 27,000 during the first year of their migration compared to savings of Rs. 31,748. Most of the remittances were in the range of Rs. 10,000 to 50,000.

Annual remittances continued increasing over time. At the end of the stay abroad they had reached, on average, Rs. 41,276 – a 5 per cent increase over the remittances made in the first year of migration.

There are wide differences in annual remittances among occupational groups. In the first year of their migration, unskilled labour remitted, on average, Rs. 26,000, semi-skilled labour Rs. 10,000, non-technical labour Rs. 28,000, and skilled/professional groups Rs. 25,000. With the passage of time, remittances increased among all occupations except unskilled labour. During the last year of their migration, unskilled labour is reported to have remitted Rs. 20,000, semi-skilled labour Rs. 36,000, non-technical labour Rs. 46,000, and skilled/professional groups Rs. 45,000. Thus, remittances have recorded the highest increase among the skilled/professional groups. This increase was in the region of 82 per cent; skilled and non-technical labour registered 67.3 per cent and 22.4 per cent increases respectively. Unskilled labour is the only group which registered a decline (21 per cent) in its remittances. This is perhaps the group that witnessed the steepest decline in its real wages/salaries abroad and also did not get enough overtime opportunities to compensate for this decline. The excessive supply of unskilled labour in the Gulf countries is obviously responsible for this state of affairs.

### Savings Brought in Cash and Kind when Visiting Home

These remittances are what migrants bring with them in the form of cash or kind on home visits. They have been reported to have brought, on average, Rs. 10,584 per visit. It has also been reported that they visit home after about eighteen months, which means that the second kind of transfers amount to Rs. 7,000 per annum. Part of these transfers are in the form of gifts for friends and relatives.

## Savings in Cash and Kind Brought Home on Final Return

The average savings in cash brought home by each migrant on the termination of his employment abroad is reported to be about Rs. 44,000. Savings in kind at the time of return have been Rs. 11,872 per migrant. Some migrants bring as much as Rs. 20,000 to 50,000 worth of goods when finally returning home, mostly consumer durables, but occasionally machinery or capital goods.

### Utilization of Remittances at Home

All households use a substantial part of their remittances for regular household consumption; they are treated as supplementary income and are used for items such as food and clothing. There are also occasional consumption expenditures which claim a substantial share of remittances, among them children's education, medical treatment, ceremonial functions – especially weddings – and repayment of debts.

In low-income households, expenditure under these heads rises steeply as soon as supplementary income is available. A substantial portion of the remittances appear to be spent on wedding ceremonies. The next important item is the repayment of loans, which is understandable, as 50 per cent of the migrants had to borrow to finance the expenditure involved in their migration.

In the category of expenditure on the acquisition of assets, various types of expenditure on housing, including repairs and purchase of houses, take precedence over others. Related to this is the purchase of land, mainly for residential purposes. Purchase of consumer durables come after expenditure on housing. If we exclude consumer durables and the repair and renovation of homes, the major proportion of the savings went into real estate – the purchase or construction of houses and buildings, and land.

Table 24 shows the proportion of migrants' households using their remittances for various activities, along with the average amount used in these activities. Only about one-fifth of the migrants were able to make investments of this type.

It is estimated that out of the total remittances of Rs. 217,980 per migrant (Rs. 36,330 per year over six years), about 10 per cent has been invested in the forms

**Table 24**. Remittances used in investment activities

| Investment activity | Proportion of households reported to be making investments out of remittances (%) | Average amount invested (Rs.) |
|---|---|---|
| Real estate | 8.7 | 132,372 |
| Agriculture | 1.7 | 116,875 |
| Business | 6.4 | 48,129 |
| Fixed bank deposit | 1.7 | 51,540 |
| Post Office savings scheme | 2.6 | 65,354 |
| Other investments | 1.9 | 138,712 |

**Table 25**. Investment priorities of migrants' families for investment of remittances

| Investment activity | Proportion of total investment made out of remittances (%) |
| --- | --- |
| Real estate | 52.8 |
| Business | 14.1 |
| Post Office savings schemes and bank deposit | 11.8 |
| Agriculture | 9.1 |
| Other investments (industries, transport, etc.) | 12.1 |

mentioned above. The investment priorities of the migrants, on the basis of the above estimates, are shown in table 25.

## Investment Counselling

Migrants lack the facility of organized counselling to advise them in their investment activities. Only 9 per cent were helped by some formal institution and the remaining 91 per cent either did not seek any advice or went to their friends and relatives for advice.

## Costs and Benefits of Migration

### Migrants' Costs and Benefits

Leaving aside the social and psychological costs (of separation from the family and living in an alien environment) and benefits (of visiting a foreign land), the purely economic costs and benefits to a migrant can be estimated on the basis of the data gathered.

### Costs

The costs incurred are the income at home that the migrant forgoes by migrating and the expenditure incurred on the migration, as well as what he was receiving from the family income. This loss is, however, only for the period of migration. After his return he may be able to earn at least as much as he earned previously, though six years' experience abroad entitles him to a better wage/salary than before migration; also, on his return he brings investible resources which ensure some income. On average, a migrant can be assumed to have forgone about Rs. 9,000 per annum (which is the average income earned by the migrant at home, at the time of his departure). Since wages in the country have been increasing over time at a rate of less than 10 per cent, it can safely be assumed that this loss might have increased to a maximum of Rs. 16,000 in six years, which is the average total stay of a migrant abroad. If it is assumed that wages rose by equal annual increments, the average gross earnings from employment over six years would have been approximately Rs. 75,000. The average cost of financing the migration from various items such as payments to agents, cost of clearance documents, etc., has been estimated at Rs. 9,000, bringing the total of both earnings forgone and actual costs to Rs. 84,000.

219

*Benefits*

The total amount that a migrant spent or saved abroad is approximately Rs. 47,808 in the first year and Rs. 70,733 in the last year. The average gross earnings would be approximately Rs. 355,000. It is estimated that the net amount saved abroad after meeting living and other expenses in the host country was 66 per cent of the total amount received – approximately Rs. 235,000.

The net economic benefits to migrants are thus very high, whether measured in terms of total income and consumption abroad or savings.

Cost–benefit calculations for major occupational groups show that at present unskilled labour is benefitting least, though initially it benefitted more than several other occupational groups. During a stay abroad of approximately six years, unskilled labour is estimated to have registered only a 50 per cent increase in benefits, whereas semi-skilled labour, non-technical labour, and professionals registered an increase of 105 and 230 per cent respectively. It is also estimated that less educated labour is now benefitting much less from migration than the better educated. The benefits to the better educated (with more than ten years of schooling) are more than double those to less educated migrants, though initially it seems that the latter had gained more than the former.

Costs and Benefits for Migrant's Family

*Costs*

The migration of a family member results in the loss of the income that he was contributing to the household. It has been estimated earlier that, on average, the dependency ratio in a household is around 4. In other words, an earning member supports four members of a family. It is hence quite reasonable to assume that a migrant was contributing 75 per cent of his income to the family. If the income is Rs. 750 per month or Rs. 9,000 per year before migration, a family loses Rs. 6,750 per annum if one of its members migrates. This loss increases to Rs. 12,000 with the increase in wages.

*Benefits*

Economic benefits arise in the form of remittances from abroad. It was reported that migrants remitted around Rs. 27,000 in the first year after migration, increasing to more than Rs. 42,000.

*Net benefits*

A migrant family thus gained an average of Rs. 20,350 in the first year of migration of their family member, increasing to Rs. 30,000 per annum by the end of the migrant's stay abroad. The net benefits to the families of unskilled migrants were reported to be highest in the initial period of migration. During the first year, these families reaped a net benefit of Rs. 21,194, which was not very different from the net benefits of the families of semi-skilled and professional workers. Families of all occupational groups, however, gained substantial benefits even in the first year of the migration of their members.

The highest increase in net benefits has been registered by the families of skilled, professional, and non-technical migrants. Families of unskilled labour registered a decline of 39 per cent. The net benefits to the families of semi-skilled labour remained unchanged.

Costs and Benefits to the Economy

In terms of the economy, one needs to distinguish between: direct and indirect costs and benefits; and short-term and long-term costs and benefits.

It is possible to make a broad and simplified analysis of costs and benefits on the basis of the data available in the survey. Here, only direct and short-term costs and benefits will be estimated. Other costs and benefits, indirect and long-term, including numerous externalities, positive and negative, will require a separate study.

Output forgone because of migration is the cost to the economy. Wages that the labour earned at home can be assumed to reflect the domestic value of the output for all such occupations in which the economy has full employment or where the economy has neither an excess supply of labour nor an excess demand for labour. Where the economy has an excess supply, the output forgone can be assumed to be zero, as the migrant labour can easily be replaced. In professions where the economy has no excess supply, but where training and learning is heavily subsidized by the government, the wages/salaries may not reflect the true value of output forgone unless it is appropriately inflated.

Unskilled labour is in excess supply in Pakistan and hence output forgone due to their migration can be considered to be zero. Wages of semi-skilled labour and non-technical labour can be assumed to reflect the contribution of these groups to economic output. Highly skilled and professional emoluments will, however, require to be inflated appropriately in order to make them reflect their output value, as higher education and professional training is heavily subsidized. On the basis of information on training costs, it can safely be assumed that the wages and salaries of skilled and professional groups inflated by 50 per cent will adequately represent the domestic value of output forgone by the migration of this group.

Remittances in foreign exchange from abroad are the main benefit to the economy. Since foreign exchange is scarce, the domestic value of foreign remittances is higher than its value at the official exchange rate. Various studies indicate that a premium of 50 per cent can be applied to the remittances to determine their domestic value. (This premium reflects the incidence of import duties and taxes as well as the profit importers enjoy because of the scarcity of foreign exchange.)

Migration of unskilled labour resulted in the highest net benefits, because the cost of migration of unskilled labour is negligible owing to their excess supply, and because they send the highest remittances. On the other hand, the migration of highly skilled and professional groups brought the least benefit to the economy, because they involve the highest opportunity cost to the economy and because they remit less foreign exchange after migration than unskilled labour. Unskilled labour's net benefits to the economy are three times that of the skilled and professionals. The net benefits of the other two occupational groups, i.e. semi-skilled labour and non-technical labour, were almost the same as that of the unskilled labour. With the passage of time the absolute as well as relative net benefits of different occupational groups are changing, mainly because of changes in remittances.

The annual rate of change of remittances from abroad is shown in table 26.

**Table 26.** Cost–benefit of migration to the economy (rupees)

| | Unskilled labour | Semi-skilled labour | Non-technical labour | Skilled and professional | All workers |
|---|---|---|---|---|---|
| **Costs** | | | | | |
| 1. Wages/salaries at home at the time of migration | 4,700 | 8,000 | 10,000 | 14,500 | 7,733 |
| 2. Correction factor to determine the contribution to the domestic value output | 0 | 1.0 | 1.0 | 1.50 | 0.88 |
| 3. Domestic value of output forgone (1 × 2) | 0 | 8,000 | 10,000 | 21,750 | 6,805 |
| **Benefits** | | | | | |
| 4. Remittances at official exchange rate | 25,894 | 29,858 | 27,578 | 24,911 | 27,000 |
| 5. Correction factor to determine domestic value of foreign exchange | 1.5 | 1.5 | 1.5 | 1.5 | 1.5 |
| 6. Domestic value of remittances | 38,841 | 44,787 | 31,367 | 37,366 | 40,500 |
| **Net benefit** | | | | | |
| 6 minus 3 | 38,841 | 36,781 | 31,367 | 156,616 | 33,695 |

The net benefit to the economy from the migration of unskilled labour will remain positive unless their annual remittances from abroad become zero or the excess supply of unskilled labour vanishes, bringing the domestic wage to a level which exceeds the domestic value of their remittances. Both possibilities are remote and hence the migration of unskilled labour will remain beneficial to the economy in the foreseeable future, even if the rate of decline in remittances is higher than that shown above.

Net benefits to the economy from the migration of semi-skilled labour, non-technical labour, and professionals will continue to be positive and increasing as long as the domestic value of their remittances keeps on increasing at a rate higher than the increase in the domestic value of the output contributed by their counterparts at home. While it seems quite likely that the rate of growth of wages and salaries of semi-skilled labour at home may soon exceed the growth rate of remittances by these categories of migrants, it is very unlikely that such a growth will neutralize the benefits of remittances in the foreseeable future. The same is true for other classes of labour, i.e. non-technical and professional. Hence, there is no likelihood in the near future that the migration of any kind of labour will become an economic liability.

In view of this broad (and simplified) analysis of the costs and benefits of migration, it can be concluded that in economic terms migration will remain of substantial benefit to the economy. Hence, there can be no economic reason for migration to cease unless either restrictions are imposed by the home or host country or the social and psychological costs (not included in the above calculation) come to outweigh the net economic benefits.

The second reason is gaining strength with the passage of time, as wages abroad are coming down and wages at home rising. The marginal utility of addition to income goes on declining, while the social costs of separation from family and the home environment keep increasing.

### Institutional Arrangements in the Host and Home Countries for Utilization of Remittances

Counselling institutions that can provide adequate advice to the migrants on feasible investments are almost non-existent. There is only one institution in the public sector – the OPF. In theory, the Foundation is designed to provide investment counselling to migrants, but in practice not many migrants have benefitted from these services. Three-fourths of the migrants interviewed in the survey were not even aware of its existence, and only 10 per cent have sought advice from it. The situation indicates a lack of confidence in the public organizations and their capacity to respond effectively to the special needs of the migrant.

Private companies providing investment services to migrants were surveyed in the mid-1970s, but most of them proved to be unreliable and seemed to be a device for cheating migrants of their savings. The growth of investment companies in the second half of the 1970s was indicative of the growing demand on the part of migrants and their families for appropriate investment opportunities, but unscrupulous elements used these companies to rob the ignorant. The government, therefore, had to close down all private investment companies. There are now no investment institutions for migrants except the banks and post offices where they can open deposit accounts.

Three-fourths of the migrants indicated that there was a bank near the family residence, but the capacity of the migrants' families to utilize banks for investment was limited, mainly owing to ignorance. The banks, therefore, were used only for interest-bearing deposit accounts.

In summary, the institutional arrangements in host and home countries for profitable utilization of savings are very limited.

## Impact of Migration

### Employment and Skill Formation

Impact of Migration on Labour Market

The sample survey conducted for this study indicated that more than 90 per cent of the emigrants were employed in Pakistan at the time of their migration. This was true even in the case of unskilled labour. Among those who were reported unemployed prior to migration, 76 per cent had been unemployed for four to eight months, and the rest for less than four months. Of course, the vacancies created by the departure of those already employed were readily filled (particularly in the case of unskilled and semi-skilled labour, which constitutes more than 80 per cent of the migrants) by the surplus stock of labour already available. Yet, it can be concluded that emigration is reducing the pool of experienced labour, while the domestic economy has to cope with inexperienced labour.

The impact of emigration on the labour market in Pakistan shows features which cannot easily be explained in terms of economic theories of labour supply and demand. The impact has been in two directions. Firstly, it generated higher unemployment in the economy and, secondly, it raised labour wages in real terms for all occupational groups, including the unskilled.

The unemployment rate quoted in official and unofficial statistics during the 1980s is much higher than that quoted for the 1950s, 1960s, or 1970s. This is because a large part of the stock of human resources that withdrew from the labour force, owing to the lack of employment opportunities, counted itself as part of the labour reservoir looking for a job abroad or filling a vacancy that was expected to be created by outgoing labour. The dynamics of emigration has thus succeeded in mobilizing human resources (previously reported to be out of the labour force), which in turn results in a higher unemployment rate. This does not mean that unemployment has increased. On the contrary, employment at home has improved somewhat since migration began. The data indicate that there were 5.8 per cent of households before migration without a single member in employment; this is now reduced to 4.5 per cent. The average number of employed persons per household is also now higher (after migrants return) than the average before their migration.

The wage increases among scarce skill/professions are obviously the result of emigration, which is further intensifying their scarcity. In these professions emigration is raising the wages by creating demand in excess of supply. But the increase in wages in most of the emigrating occupations cannot be so explained, as more than 80 per cent of emigrating labour is either unskilled or semi-skilled. One explanation for the increase in the wages of these types of labour lies in the fact that remittances from abroad have increased the standard of living of the rural population (from which the labour originates), which in turn has raised the minimum reservation wage of labour. The higher reservation wage or supply price of labour thus raises the wage level of all occupations, whether demand is in excess of supply or not (Khan, 1978).

## Skill Formation

There is substantial evidence of significant skill formation that has taken place abroad – particularly the fact that a large proportion of the 25 per cent of migrants who were employed as unskilled workers do not now report themselves as unskilled. Of these 25 per cent of migrants, only 15.6 per cent report themselves as still unskilled, of the rest (9.4 per cent), some have improved their skill and report themselves as semi-skilled, and others state that they became small businessmen on return. The skills acquired by migrants abroad are generally those of driving, carpentry, or a similar level of craftsmanship. It is generally understood that since these workers had the chance of working abroad with higher technology and sophisticated machinery, they are technically more advanced and are an asset to the nation. More than half the returned migrants confirmed this.

To some extent, migration also contributed to skill formation by compelling migrants to acquire some training before their departure. Such training, however, was of short duration and mostly through informal sources.

## Re-employment Problems of Returnees

Though a large proportion of returnees reported being unemployed after return, most of this unemployment is voluntary. The reason for this is obvious: migrants accustomed to a very high wage rate and much better conditions are not prepared to work in poor conditions and at a low wage. Most of these migrants are, therefore, looking for some business opportunity to set up on their own, while others prefer to live for some time on the income from the assets they built up with their earnings abroad. It is, however, quite possible that all these migrants may, with time, reorient themselves to home realities. After this transition phase, no employment problem is visualized at national level due to the return of migrants. In addition, several migrants look forward to going abroad again and many of them succeed.

## Existing Policies and Institutional Arrangements for the Re-employment of Returnees

No special attention has been paid to formulate policies, or to make institutional arrangements for the re-absorption of the returning migrants. There are several reasons for this. First, the inflow of returning migrants has not yet gained sufficient momentum to pose a national problem. Second, the bulk of the returning migrants do not need immediate re-absorption as they depend for a few months on their savings. Third, for policy-makers, employment on re-entry is perhaps not a serious problem, demanding urgent attention.

The problem posed by returning migrants, however, is likely to gain momentum in the near future. This is not only because the labour market for Pakistani expatriates in the Middle East is shrinking, but also because migrants are returning after fulfilling their objectives. Their migration was temporary and they have already spent more than six years abroad separated from their families. For most of them, the time has come to return home. A large influx is therefore likely to take place. Presently, the annual inflow of returnees is estimated to be 150,000, which is another 25 per cent on top of the natural growth of the domestic labour force. Since the growth in the domestic economy can barely absorb this natural increase, absorption of another 25 per cent or more will obviously place too great a pressure on the economy.

It is also incorrect to assume that returning migrants do not need any special attention and that they can be treated on a par with the domestic labour reservoir in respect of their absorption into the economy. There are several compelling reasons that call for special attention for migrants.

First, the returning migrants have contributed a huge amount of foreign exchange to the economy. Currently, this is more than double the value of exports of manufactured commodities. It is said that all efforts to subsidize industrialists failed to earn as much for the country as the migrant unskilled and skilled labour has been able to do. Returning migrants are aware of this fact and they consider it their right to claim special attention with respect to their re-absorption into the economy. Secondly, the returning migrants possess extra financial resources as well as human capital. All this should not be allowed to go to waste. Institutional arrangements are, therefore, required urgently in the following areas:

1. An institution to monitor constantly the inflow of migrants and keep records of the physical and human capital being repatriated; there is presently no agency in Pakistan which can provide reliable estimates of the number of migrants returning annually, what their occupational background has been and what they intend to do.
2. Placement institutions for the returning migrants to guide them to those sectors and activities in Pakistan where their human capital can best be utilized; this institution should have a list of the projects and employment opportunities in Pakistan where returning migrants can be placed in employment suited to their skills.
3. Investment counselling institutions to advise migrants on the investment of their physical or financial capital; government-sponsored public investment companies are required to utilize the capital repatriated by the migrants.

**Impact on Life-style, Values, and Attitudes**

The effects of migration on the life-styles of migrants have been studied here in respect of: changes in the family structure; changes in the quality of life; sources of household income; changes in attitude and values; and social and economic mobility.

Changes in the Family Structure

Pakistan is one of those traditional countries where the joint family system is still quite common. About half the households in the country are reported to consist of extended families. Emigration from Pakistan, however, has been causing adverse effects on the joint family system. About 49 per cent of the migrants said that they were members of an extended family before their emigration; after their return from abroad, only 39 per cent reported that they belonged to an extended family.

Families, particularly in rural areas, live on a single source of income, i.e. income from land, which is the joint property of all family members. Joint sources of income keep the family together. Emigration of a member of a household provides him with a separate source of income and hence induces him and his nuclear family to separate from the rest of the family.

Cultural and economic homogeneity among members of the family is the basis of family cohesion. Migration disrupts this homogeneity, first by separating the migrant member from the rest of the family, which can cause a loosening of family bonds, and second, and more importantly, by affecting specific inter-family relationships like father and son or brother and brother.

Changes in Quality of Life

Migration has resulted in substantial benefits to the migrants and their families. This is expected to have had some permanent effect on their quality of life. During the migration phase, both migrants and their families certainly enjoyed improved life-styles owing to the inflow of remittances at home. But how far the migrants and their families have been able to sustain an improved quality of life after the final return of migrants is discussed below. For the purpose of this study, quality of life has been investigated in relation to: quality of housing; ownership of residential house; emphasis on consumer durables and modern appliances; expenditure on education of children and medical treatment; and savings.

## Changes in Quality of Housing

To determine the effect and the quality of housing of the migrants, the following aspects were investigated:

MATERIAL USED IN THE STRUCTURE. The housing structure in lower-income groups is of mud or at best bricks. Cement structures can be afforded only by higher-income groups. The quality of housing of migrants has improved substantially. About 40 per cent of the migrants indicated that, before migration, they were living in houses with walls and floors made of mud. After return, however, only about 15 per cent of migrants reported that they were still living in mud houses. The remaining 25 per cent had moved to better accommodation.

NATURE OF TOILETS. The nature of toilets also determines the quality of housing. Toilets having no flush system are obviously primitive and usually of extremely poor quality, particularly from the hygienic point of view. The inclusion of a flush system indicates a higher quality of housing. Bathrooms/toilets attached to bedrooms are indicative of modern living and hence of improved quality of housing.

About 75 per cent of the migrants were living in houses without a flush system before migration, whereas after return only 53 per cent of these are reported to be living in such houses; presently 47 per cent live in houses with flush systems. About 86.3 per cent of the houses of migrants did not have any attached bathroom before migration; now 78.6 per cent of the migrants live in houses without attached baths.

TAP-WATER SUPPLY. A tap-water supply in the house was available to 73.6 per cent of the migrants before migration; it is now available to 83.2 per cent.

ELECTRICITY. This was available in 70 per cent of the houses of migrants before migration; it is now available in 84 per cent of their houses.

## Ownership of Residential House

Ownership of one's residence is an indicator of a higher status in life. In Pakistani society it not only provides a substantial degree of psychological satisfaction, but is also a source of social and economic security for the entire family. Ownership of the house also means that other basic needs are more or less met.

House ownership did not increase very significantly. Before migration, 87 per cent owned their houses; on return, the figure was 91 per cent.

## Emphasis on Consumer Durables and Modern Appliances, etc.

Basically, these reflect conspicuous consumption, as it was observed in several cases that migrant households had electric appliances even in rural areas where there was no electricity. Substantial increases were observed in items which are more related to conspicuous consumption than basic needs. It was noted during the study that expenditure on consumer durables and electric appliances in migrant households has been very high. Migrants had not paid as much attention to improving the quality of their routine consumption or of their housing as they did to purchasing modern appliances. Motor-cycles, refrigerators, air-conditioners, washing machines and household electric goods were some of the popular appliances migrants and their families had obtained.

## Expenditure on Children's Education and Medical Treatment

These two heads of expenditure in the family budget reflect the quality of life of a family. With respect to the families of the returning migrants, it was observed that medical treatment continued to remain almost as neglected as it had been before migration. Three-fourths of the migrants reported no change in the amount of medical care received by their families as compared to that received before migration. Only 11 per cent of migrants indicated an increase in the attention given to the medical needs of their family.

Children's education, however, received much more attention than medical needs. One-third of the migrants reported that expenditure on their children's education had increased after migration.

## Savings

Higher incomes are supposed to increase the capacity to save. But the realization of this potential in actual savings will depend on the life-style of the migrants and their households. If they are inclined to prefer present to future consumption, not much saving will result despite the increased income. Pakistanis generally show little ability to save on household expenditure. This is because most households have too low an income to save. Since remittances provide a substantial increase in income, it is expected that their savings will increase appreciably provided they do not change their life-style very much. In response to the question whether household savings were higher than before migration, only 12 per cent reported that savings had increased moderately, whereas 72 per cent reported no change in the level of savings.

## Sources of Household Income

Sources of income play an important role in determining the life-style of a household. No substantial change was registered here. Self-employment in agriculture and wage labour were the main sources of income of most households before migration and they continued to remain so even after the return of the migrant. Other sources apply to only a small proportion of households. Income from rents (of buildings), however, turned out to be a major new source of income for about 6 per cent of households after migration. This would obviously be true of the 7 per cent of migrant households investing in real estate. The other new sources of income for some of the households were interest on bank savings and returns from investments in business enterprises.

## Changes in Attitudes and Values

Significant liberalization seems to have occurred in the attitudes of returnees consequent on their stay abroad. The returning migrants have admitted to substantial changes in their attitude towards children's education, female participation in the labour force, paying more attention to the family, and sharing domestic responsibilities with household females. The most important change is in attitude towards education. Three-fourths of the returnees indicated that they now understand the importance of educating their children more than before migration. This may signal a significant breakthrough in society's neutral or negative attitude towards education, particularly in rural areas. Despite the spread of educational facilities throughout the country, the literacy rate remains constant at about 25 per cent for the last 35 years. This is because the rural population is not inclined to enrol their children in school. The highly positive attitude of migrant workers towards children's education will not only increase the enrolment of children of migrant workers but will also demonstrate to other families in their community the value of education.

The attitude towards female participation in the labour force also has become more positive, but not as much as the attitude towards children's education. One-fourth of the migrants indicated a positive change in their attitudes after migration. Many factors have contributed to this change. Migrant incomes have led to higher expectations and better standards of living, which seem to encourage the employment of females who can bring additional income to households. The change in attitude among migrant families has a demonstration effect on other non-migrant families and promotes positive changes in the community as a whole.

It was stated by 69 per cent of the returning migrants that they like to spend more time with the family, while 83 per cent reported that they now share responsibilities that were previously regarded as exclusively those of females. This also involves the attitudinal changes favouring female employment outside the home and creates an environment more conducive to such employment.

*The Work Ethic*

Most of the returning migrants reported that they had learnt the value of hard and honest work. Now, after returning from abroad, they report that their work ethics have improved. About 56 per cent of these migrants reported that they were now working more diligently and with a higher sense of duty than before migration. About 45 per cent indicated that they are more punctual than before and do not object to working long hours if work so demands. About the same percentage of migrants reported that they now work with more team spirit and co-operation than before migration. About one-third reported that they now derive more psychological satisfaction from completing the job assigned to them.

*Religious Values*

Emigration had created a substantial interest in religious, political, and international matters. About 70 per cent of migrants reported increased attendance at mosques than before. This is likely to be the result of the emphasis on prayers in the Gulf countries, where it is obligatory to break for prayers during working hours. These observances had probably the effect of strengthening religious values and promoting other virtues such as greater charity towards those in misfortune. There was a discernible increase in gifts, donations, and other expenditure of charitable purposes on the part of migrants. These included contributions to religious institutions, financial assistance to relations and friends, and support of welfare institutions. About 42 per cent of respondents reported that their contributions to religious institutions had increased substantially after return, and about 30 per cent provided greater assistance to relatives and welfare institutions.

*Socio-political Attitudes*

An increased interest in the affairs of host countries, as well as interest in the image of the home country abroad, was reported by nearly half of the migrants. Increased interest in international affairs in general and in the political affairs of Pakistan was indicated by one-third of the returning migrants. These changes were attributed by them to their exposure to the outside world during their employment abroad.

Social and Economic Mobility

*Zat* (or caste) determines social status in rural areas. Many groups like weavers, cobblers, carpenters, and blacksmiths, who are considered of low social status because of the nature of their work, are trying to change their *zat* status. Of course, it is difficult for a group of individuals to change their *zat* entirely and have this socially accepted. There is a tendency, however, to change it irrespective of whether other people recognize their new *zat* or not. The process of *zat* mobility or social mobility is occurring only in the *kammis* group (working class), and not among landowners who are already by tradition of higher social rank. Economic prosperity induces households to move up the social ladder. Remittances, after providing economic security, lead ex-migrants to seek a higher social standing too.

This gives the impression that, along with the upward economic mobility, social mobility is also taking place. In fact, the religious structure in Pakistan does not allow for hierarchy in social status; the vertical hierarchy in Pakistan is the result of the social influence of Hindu culture in pre-partitioned India. Since most of the migrants go to the Muslim countries where social hierarchy is non-existent or very weak, it gives them courage to claim equal status in their own society. The economic strength gained abroad also gives them the strength to seek a higher social status in the society than they enjoyed before. It has been indicated earlier that several migrants have succeeded in raising their social status. Socio-economic mobility is more pronounced in rural than in urban areas: in rural areas 26 per cent of migrants in lower social groups indicated movement to upper groups, whereas in urban areas only 18.1 per cent reported an upward movement.

**Socio-economic Characteristics of Returning Migrants**

Migrants belong to the younger age-groups. They migrate young and, after their stay abroad, averaging around six years, they return young. The average age of those returning is estimated to be about 33. (Another study shows 38 years as the average age of returning migrants, but that study included others from the United Kingdom and other European and American countries where the average stay has been around 20 years.) The data show that half of those returning belong to the 26-35 age-group while only 15 per cent are above 50 years of age.

The data also indicate that 83 per cent of the returning migrants are married. Of those married, 57 per cent were married before going abroad, 24 per cent while in employment abroad, and 2 per cent after returning home. Marriage and the formation of new households obviously played an important role in the migration. Migrants with their high incomes were good prospective husbands. At the same time, the high incomes generated would have enabled households to arrange marriages for other members, particularly the young unmarried females. The relatively high proportion of the remittances spent on weddings has to be perceived in this context.

A decline in the household size of the migrants has been observed. Before migration it was reported to be 8.25, but after return it has declined significantly to 7.36. This is probably because many migrants would have opted to leave the joint family system after their return and set up separate households. Data also show that at present 56 per cent of the returning migrants are heads of households. The average age of returning migrants as reported in the previous section is 33 years. The returning heads of households at this average age show a tendency to move away from the joint family system. The proportion of extended families in the sample had dropped from 49 per cent of the total number to 40 and nuclear families had increased proportionately.

Unemployment appears to be relatively high among the migrants who have returned, 25 per cent of them reporting they were not employed. Most of them had not been home for a full year and were in the process of readjustment. Almost all who described themselves as unemployed were engaged in work of some type and were seeking employment. The data show that 29 per cent of those unemployed ex-migrants are interested in clerical/non-technical work, 28 per cent seek semi-skilled work, 17 per cent are trying to establish their own business, and 13 per cent desire professional jobs. Non-technical/clerical and semi-skilled are sought after most by the unemployed ex-migrants, but this is an area where they face difficulties in finding a suitable job.

The data show a positive effect on the employment status of the family after the return of migrants. Before migration, about 5.8 per cent of households had no individuals employed, but after return this percentage had decreased to 4.5 per cent. On average 1.68 persons per household were working before migration; currently this average has risen to 1.8. The data also show that 28 per cent of the returned migrants' households had at least one other family member currently abroad. Some migrants try to replace themselves with other family members before leaving the host country.

The occupational composition of the 73 per cent who reported themselves as employed reveals some interesting developments. Business is the most popular sector; more than 29 per cent are absorbed into small businesses. The rest became employed in paid jobs, the highest number undertaking semi-skilled work. Next in importance are unskilled jobs and clerical/non-technical jobs.

More than half of the returning migrants have shown a desire to acquire further training for better adjustment to the economy. The lack of training institutions, however, does not allow them to undertake training. About 55 per cent of the migrants reported that they had the opportunity to upgrade their skills abroad, though they are pessimistic about being able to use their upgraded skills after returning home. Only 30 per cent of those who reported such upgrading had found satisfaction in this respect; the large majority (56 per cent) were not satisfied, but hoped to benefit from their upgraded skills sometime in the future. About 14 per cent thought they would not be able to utilize their skills at home.

One of the most significant changes caused by the migration concerns the shifts in occupation and changes in the sectoral composition of employment among the migrants after their return. The data provide very useful information about the occupational change. Self-employment in business is a popular option; about 30 per cent of the migrants have established their own businesses after return, whereas only 11 per cent were business workers before going abroad. Half of those migrants who formerly belonged to the agricultural sector have left this sector after their return. Similarly, a proportion of skilled and clerical workers have now established their own businesses.

The current income of the returned migrants is another important indicator of their re-integration into the economy. It has been estimated that they earned an average of Rs. 900 per month before going abroad; they are now reported to be earning Rs. 2,250 per month. The data show that about half the returned migrants earn Rs. 2,000 to Rs. 3,000 per month, 43 per cent earn up to Rs. 1,000 and 7.8 per cent earn more than Rs. 3,000 per month.

Since, on average, the migrants went abroad six years ago, the inflation during the intervening period can be regarded as being less than the increase recorded in the incomes of migrants after their return. The returnees who have been able to get a job have higher real earnings than they had before their migration. This is mainly because of skill formation abroad and the human capital repatriated by them on their return.

**Reasons for Return**

More than half of the migrants interviewed went abroad first during the period 1976 and 1980, and one-fourth after 1981. Only 15 per cent migrated before 1975. About 60 per cent of them came back in 1983–1984 and 25 per cent in 1980–1981. There were many reasons for their return, which varied from country to country and migrant to migrant. Completion of projects, changes in the economic situation in the Middle East countries, and the policy towards importing manpower are among the important reasons. The returning migrants can be divided into three categories according to their reasons for return:
1. Migrants who came back after achieving their purpose.
2. Migrants who came back due to "push" factors in the host country, such as termination of contract, change in immigration policy, hostile environment, illness, etc.
3. Migrants who came back for domestic reasons.

The data provide useful information on the reasons for return. Only 8 per cent came back after achieving their purpose, while the remaining 92 per cent did not come back of their own volition. Two-thirds specifically mentioned "push" factors as the reason. Termination of contract figured prominently among those factors, because more than one-third reported expiry of contract due to changes in the immigration policies of the host country. Eleven per cent of the returnees reported having come back because they were unable to adjust sufficiently to living and working conditions in the host country. Data also show that more than one-fifth returned for domestic reasons.

Push factors thus predominated as the reasons for both migration and for the return. Pull factors proved to be weak in both movements. Pull factors, however, played a much more significant role in the return of migrants than in their migration. The 21.2 per cent of migrants returning owing to pull factors and another 8.1 per cent returning because they have achieved their objectives are strongly indicative of the temporary nature of the migration. The voluntary return of migrants will further increase as the reasons for staying abroad become weaker with the passage of time.

Fifteen per cent of the migrants report that they still have substantial savings, although they returned more than two years prior to the interview. These migrants still have an average of about Rs. 90,000 of unutilized savings. About 1 per cent have more than Rs. 300,000 each. About half of those with savings plan to use them to establish their own business; they lack, however, guidance and counselling.

A little less than half the migrants in the sample intend to re-migrate if they get the opportunity to do so. Push factors are instrumental in forcing the returnees to look for re-employment in the Middle East. Pull factors are, however, more significant than earlier. One-fourth of the returnees want to go back to the Gulf because of their inability to find suitable employment at home. About 40 per cent of the returnees find their incomes insufficient to satisfy their financial needs; above 10 per cent are attracted back by the better living conditions abroad, while another 15 per cent are attracted by the better economic opportunities. The majority of migrants (a little more than half) do not seek opportunities to re-migrate. For most migrants responding in this manner, this is an indication of their satisfactory adjustment after return; for a few, it signifies that the migration was an unwelcome experience which they do not wish to repeat.

More than half of those desirous of re-migrating are already in touch with recruiting agents, and another 13 per cent are in touch with their relatives or friends abroad for the same purpose. Those looking for opportunities to re-migrate belong principally to unskilled and semi-skilled groups. One-fifth of those intending to re-migrate are looking for an unskilled job abroad, whereas more than 60 per cent are seeking semi-skilled jobs as, for example, drivers, electricians, painters, masons, welders, or tailors. The main preference (two-thirds) by country of destination is Saudi Arabia. About 13 per cent want to go to Kuwait and another 8 per cent to UAE. The rest of the Arab world is of interest to only 4.4 per cent. More than 10 per cent of those wishing to re-migrate want to go to the developed world, i.e. Europe, the United States, or Australia.

**Social Adjustment after Return**

The average response regarding social readjustment after return indicated that migrants did not face problems warranting serious concern. The only problem that they face is that of maintaining the social and economic status that their family had built up with remittances from abroad. By and large, they are satisfied with their ability to re-adjust after return. On average, about 15 per cent of the migrants were maladjusted. Most of the maladjustment and dissatisfaction relate to their concern about their future security, as they do not know how to maintain the standard of living to which their families have become accustomed. The next most important problem of adjustment relates to working and living conditions and the local environment. Obviously, the migrants have enjoyed different life-styles and working conditions, and are taking some time to adjust to working and living conditions at home.

There are, however, several sources of dissatisfaction and concern to which the respondents make reference in their interviews. The majority of them find their current levels of wages and salaries unacceptable. Another disturbing feature of the local environment to which a significant proportion react critically is the poor work ethic of their colleagues at their present workplaces.

The returnees do not report any serious problems of readjustment to the local community, their neighbours, friends and relations. Most find themselves elevated in social status. Forty-six per cent reported that they were treated with respect after their return. This may partly be due to their affluence and partly due to the experience that they acquired abroad. Very few returnees (6 per cent) complained that they had to contend with negative or unfriendly attitudes towards them on the part of the community in which they lived.

### Overall Assessment by the Migrants

Returning migrants were asked to evaluate their experiences abroad, the main problems they face after their return and the measures that the government should take to solve their problems.

The general impression that returning migrants have about their experience abroad is overwhelmingly positive. Eighty-six per cent of returning migrants regarded their experience as very beneficial, mostly on the grounds of earnings and savings made abroad. The rest treated their experience as being of no consequence. Some of the broad assessments made by them are listed below in table 27.

The most important problem facing the returnees and their families is that of economic adjustment. About two-thirds are still worried on this account. Their principal problems are reported to be low income and hence difficulty in maintaining the standard of living previously supported by remittances from abroad (44.3 per cent); unemployment at home (18.1 per cent); and problems in establishing businesses (3.0 per cent).

For 12 per cent of the returnees, economic adjustment is not as much a problem as social adjustment. Eight per cent of these simply find it difficult to compromise with the local environment. Family feuds are one of the main sources of disturbance encountered. For another 4 per cent of returnees children's education is a problem because of the differences in the educational systems at home and abroad.

## Conclusion

### Family-level Benefits

Besides social, psychological or cultural costs resulting from the separation of male members (particularly the head of the household), the family has gained substantial economic benefits from the emigration of family members. A migrant family, on average, gained more than Rs. 20,000 in the first year of the migration; this increased to Rs. 30,000 per annum by the time the migrant had completed his stay abroad. This was more than 300 per cent of what he was contributing to the family when he was in the home country. Initially, unskilled labour contributed the maximum net benefits to their family and professional and skilled labour contributed least. With the passage of time, the benefits of different occupational groups

**Table 27.** Rate of growth of remittances

| Occupational group | Annual rate of growth in remittances during migrant's stay abroad (%) |
| --- | --- |
| Unskilled | − 3.0 |
| Semi-skilled | 3.0 |
| Non-technical | 9.5 |
| Skilled/professional | 10.5 |

changed. Now non-techincal labour is contributing the maximum (Rs. 28,416 per annum) to their family, and unskilled labour the least (Rs. 12,858). The benefit–cost ratio, however, is now estimated to be minimum in the case of highly skilled and professional classes (1.76), whereas it is still highest in the case of unskilled and non-technical labour (2.70).

Hence, the family of the unskilled labourer will be the last to recall their family member from abroad. It looks as though very soon it will be of no benefit to the families of professional and highly skilled labour to keep their member abroad. But this class makes up less than 10 per cent of the total migrants abroad. For them, moreover, families are not a significant pull factor. The bulk of the labour is in the other three categories where the benefit–cost ratio is expected to remain far too high for families to recall their members from abroad.

### Economy-level Benefits

Foreign Exchange Benefit

On average, a migrant worker is contributing net Rs. 33,695 of foreign exchange to the economy. The maximum benefit is contributed by unskilled labour and the minimum by the highly skilled/professional group. The benefit–cost ratio to the economy by occupational groups is: unskilled labour: very, very large; semi-skilled labour: 4.6; non-technical labour: 3.1; and highly skilled/professionals: 0.7.

Sometime, in the near future, it may become economically unfeasible for the economy to send its highly skilled/professional workers abroad and the government may have to think of imposing some restrictions on their migration. The migration of the other occupational groups, however, will continue to remain economically feasible for the foreseeable future.

Employment Benefit

The emigration of unskilled labour is a direct employment benefit to the economy. In the presence of an abundant labour supply, emigration of unskilled labour (as well as semi-skilled labour) is simply a mobilizing of the human resources which have been staying out of the labour force because of the lack of job opportunities in the economy. The fact that 80 per cent of the migrant labour is unskilled and semi-skilled has resulted in emigration being of enormous employment benefit to the economy.

The dynamics of emigration, however, has caused a rise in the unemployment rate as well in wages – a peculiar phenomenon as regards the socio-economic structure of the economy.

**Table 28.** Assessment of the migration by returning migrants

| Benefits of migration | Percentage of positive responses |
|---|---|
| 1. It raises the standard of living | 23.4 |
| 2. It brings wealth and incomes which cannot be otherwise acquired | 18.7 |
| 3. It has benefitted the individual as well as the country | 3.1 |
| 4. At least one experience of living abroad is essential | 6.0 |
| 5. It enables one to experience a better social and religious environment | 5.2 |
| 6. It helps to provide for a better future for the family | 3.4 |
| 7. It helps to perform *haj* (a religious duty) | 2.3 |
| 8. There is no need to go abroad if better jobs are available in the country | 11.2 |
| 9. It is beneficial only for those who have skills | 7.8 |
| 10. It is beneficial only for those who can work hard and honestly | 3.4 |
| 11. The environment in the host country is not congenial | 4.9 |
| 12. It brings no significant benefits | 14 |

Skill Formation

There is substantial evidence of significant skill formation that has taken place abroad. The main evidence of this is that many of the 25 per cent of returnees who reported as having unskilled occupations before migration do not now refer to themselves in this way: only 15.6 per cent still call themselves unskilled, while the remaining 9.4 per cent state that they have become semi-skilled or businessmen after returning from abroad. It is generally believed that since migrant workers have the chance while abroad of working with higher technology and sophisticated machinery, they are an asset to the nation.

Capital Formation

Though the large remittances from abroad have substantial potential as regards investment and capital formation in the economy, the non-availability of proper counselling services and lack of investment opportunities prevents them from being utilized for investment to the largest possible extent. Only 19 per cent of the migrants indicated using their remittances for investment or saving purposes. The bulk, however, went to building up real estate. It is estimated that out of the total remittances from abroad, 10 per cent have been invested in different forms.

Migrants lack organized counselling services to advise them in their investment activities. Considering the analysis of the migration phase, it can be said that migration, in economic terms, has been beneficial at all levels, i.e. to the individuals, to the families left behind, and to the economy, and will continue to be so for the foreseeable future. Hence, there can be no economic reason for migrants to return.

If migrants return, it can be for only two reasons: either they are obliged to return by the host country, or the social and psychological costs (not included in the above calculations) become greater than the positive net economic benefits. Both these reasons are gaining strength with the passage of time.

Migrants on average are returning after a period of six years' stay abroad. There are three types of returnees:

1. Successful migrants who come back after achieving their purpose.
2. "Pushed" back migrants who return because of "push" factors from the host country, such as termination of contract, changes in emigration policy of host country, illness, hostile environment, etc.
3. "Pulled" back migrants who come back for domestic reasons.

Two-thirds of the returnees, so far, are those pushed back, mainly on account of their inability to renew their job contract abroad. A substantial number (11 per cent) were pushed back by the unfavourable environment (mainly the work and living conditions) to which they could not adjust. More than 20 per cent of returnees fall into the category of those pulled back. More than 8 per cent are those who can be termed successful migrants, as they return after achieving the objective for which they migrated. The proportion of return of successful migrants is likely to accelerate with the passage of time.

The rate of return of migrants is likely to gather momentum in the near future. This is not only because the labour market for Pakistani workers in the Middle East is shrinking, but also because the migrants are returning after fulfilling the objectives for which they migrated. Their migration was temporary and they have spent more than six years abroad separated from their family. For most of them the time has come to return home. Presently, the annual inflow of returnees is estimated to be around 150,000, the equivalent of 25 per cent of the normal annual increase. Since the rate of growth in the domestic economy can barely cope with the normal increase in the labour force, the addition of another 25 per cent or more will obviously prove a burden that the economy will find difficult to bear. The returning migrants have extra financial resources as well as human capital with them. They have acquired skills abroad. If the financial and human capital of the returning migrants is not put to immediate productive use, these resources are likely to go to waste. The current estimate of migrants who have returned so far puts the figure at about 700,000. Within the next five years, this figure is likely to rise to 1.5 million. These returning migrants are expected to bring with them more than Rs. 20 billion worth of foreign exchange, along with improved skills. The mobilization of these resources for productive use is essential if the reabsorption and re-integration of migrants into the domestic economy is to be a smooth process. The return migration may otherwise have adverse and far-reaching consequences for social and economic life.

## References

Gilani, Ijaz, M. Fahim Khan, and Munawar Iqbal. 1981. Labour Migration from Pakistan to the Middle East and Its Impact on the Domestic Economy. Pakistan Institute of Development Economics, Research Report Series, nos. 126, 127, and 128.

Khan, M. Fahim. 1978. A Study into the Courses of Fluctuations of Wages in Labour Surplus Economy of Pakistan, Ph.D. thesis. Boston University, Boston, Mass.

**6**

# BANGLADESHI RETURNED MIGRANTS FROM THE MIDDLE EAST: PROCESS, ACHIEVEMENT, AND ADJUSTMENT

**Raisul A. Mahmood**
Bangladesh Institute of Developing Studies, Dhaka, Bangladesh

## Introduction

One of the most important characteristics of the migration to the Middle East is that it is temporary and for a fixed period of time — initially the period is limited to one to two years,[1] at the end of which the migrants must return home. Any exception to this would be through further renewal of the contract.[2] This is true for all migrants, irrespective of skill and nationality. In contrast, migrants to the Western European countries and North America can, under certain conditions, acquire resident status and enjoy the option of staying in the host country indefinitely.[3]

Given this temporary nature, all migrants to the Middle East are destined to return after a fixed period of employment. The exact number of those returning home every year will depend mainly on the demand for expatriate labour in the receiving countries, the migrants' ability to obtain a renewal of the job contract through proven skill and efficiency, and the exporting country's capacity to promote the employment of its nationals abroad. Most important, though, would be the job prospects in the Middle East. Recent experience in the region suggests that the "construction boom" which earlier triggered the process of migration to the region has started tapering off (Birks and Sinclair, 1979, 1980; Shaw, 1979; Antonion, 1978). The decline in the oil revenues of the oil-exporting states, together with the Iran/Iraq war, have sharply reduced the development programme and the investment outlays in the region. The development of the social and economic infrastructure which resulted in the construction of highways, airports, public utilities, hospitals, schools, and large building projects of various types has already reached a stage where it must slow down. At the same time, there has been a growing concern over the presence of a large and growing alien population in the major labour-importing countries — at times even outnumbering the indigenous population. All these factors have led to a sharp contraction of the demand for foreign labour. In this context any major social and political crisis in these countries can result in large-scale deportation of foreign workers. The migration to the Middle East is therefore not only temporary, but there are also built-in risks in the situation that can at any time trigger a mass return migration.

In the event of such a mass return migration taking place, what impact will it have on a labour-exporting economy? How is the economy going to adjust to a sudden shock of this magnitude? What are the areas that would be affected most? What precautions should an economy take to contain and cope with any adverse consequences that may follow?

The purpose of the current study is to underscore the problems and the prospects of reabsorbing the returning migrants. Based on a sample survey on a selected number of migrants who have returned, the study analyses the experience of these people during the preparatory period prior to migration, their stay abroad, and the nature of their readjustment and reassimilation on their return.

## Data Sources and Methodology

Data used in this report come from a sample survey on Bangladeshi returned migrants from the Middle East. In total, 368 returned migrants were interviewed from the districts of Chittagong, Noakhali, Sylhet, and Dhaka. The selection of these districts was purposive; traditionally these four districts together account for a large majority of the migrants to the Middle East.

To identify the individual respondents, a door-to-door survey was conducted in the respective areas, and the returned migrants who were available and willing to give an interview were included in the sample. However, no two individuals from the same family were interviewed, and the selection was made so that no particular skill or occupation was overrepresented.

Apart from the questionnaire survey, additional data were also generated. These included information on the process of migration from the respective areas and changes in socio-economic infrastructure – quality of housing, roads, markets, schools, colleges, availability of electricity, drinking water, etc. Moreover, first-hand information was also gathered on the attitudes and social behaviour of the migrant families and their members.

## Organization of the Report

The report is organized as follows. The first section traces the socio-economic profile of migrants prior to migration. Specific references are made to the migrants' socio-economic status on the eve of migration and the process and cost of migration. The second section deals with the adjustment of migrants in their households during the migrants' stay abroad. The third section deals with the post-migration characteristics of the migrants, their use of remittances, and the process of adjustment and assimilation on their return. The concluding section spotlights some of the specific problems which a country may have to cope with in the event of a mass return migration, and contains a summary and some policy recommendations.

**Table 1.** Distribution of migrants by age and area (percentages)

| Age-group (in years) | Area | | | | | |
|---|---|---|---|---|---|---|
| | Chitta-gong | Noa-khali | Sylbet | Dhaka | Dhaka City | Overall |
| Up to 20 | 8.75 | 5.71 | 7.23 | 4.05 | — | 5.43 |
| 21–25 | 31.25 | 22.86 | 22.89 | 31.08 | 14.74 | 25.00 |
| 26–30 | 22.50 | 42.86 | 28.92 | 28.38 | 52.45 | 33.97 |
| 31–40 | 26.25 | 18.57 | 32.53 | 18.92 | 31.17 | 25.54 |
| 41–50 | 8.75 | 8.57 | 8.43 | 13.51 | 1.64 | 8.42 |
| 51+ | 2.50 | 1.43 | — | 4.05 | — | 1.63 |
| Number of cases | 80 | 70 | 83 | 74 | 61 | 368 |

## Socio-economic Profile and Process of Migration

### Demographic Characteristics of Migrants

Age

Table 1 shows that about one-third of the respondents were 25 years old or less when they migrated abroad; more than 60 per cent were below 30 years of age. Among the different areas both Chittagong and Nobabganj[4] account for a relatively higher proportion of migrants within the age limit of 25 years. In Chittagong, for instance, 40 per cent of the migrants were below 25 years, as compared to the figure of about 30 per cent for this age-group for all areas. In Dhaka City, on the other hand, 52 per cent of the migrants were in the age-group 25–30 years, in constrast to the average of 34 per cent.

Sex

Unlike migrants from other countries,[5] Bangladeshis migrating to the Middle East are almost entirely males. Adherence to Islamic principles, traditions and socio-cultural taboos have accounted for the low participation of women in the labour force, and these same trends have prevailed in regard to labour migration to the Middle East as well. Although no official statistics make reference to the sex composition of Bangladeshis migrating to the Middle East as such, there are a few female migrants. They are mainly professionals such as doctors and teachers who accompanied their husbands, followed by nurses and other paramedical personnel. Very recently, a few women have begun migrating to work as housemaids and unskilled workers in hospitals and clinics.[6] The survey identified two female returned migrants, one from the Nobabganj (Dhaka) area and the other in Dhaka City.

Religion

Bangladesh is predominantly a Muslim state and over 90 per cent of the population are followers of Islam. Most of the migrants interviewed were, therefore, Muslims. However, members of other religions, e.g. Hindus and Christians, were also interviewed. The share of these two religions in the total sample was 2.2 and 3.3 per cent respectively.

**Table 2.** Distribution of migrants by religion

| Religion | Number of cases | Percentage of total |
|---|---|---|
| Muslim | 348 | 94.5 |
| Hindu | 8 | 2.2 |
| Christian | 12 | 3.3 |
| Total | 368 | 100.0 |

**Table 3.** Distribution of migrants by marital status

| Marital status | Number of cases | Percentage of total |
|---|---|---|
| Married | 320 | 87 |
| Unmarried | 48 | 13 |
| Widowed | 0 | — |
| Divorced | 0 | — |
| Total | 368 | 100 |

**Table 4.** Distribution of migrants by number of household members prior to migration

| Number of household members | Number of cases | Percentage of total |
|---|---|---|
| Up to 5 | 92 | 25.00 |
| 6–10 | 190 | 51.63 |
| 11–15 | 58 | 15.76 |
| 16–20 | 19 | 5.16 |
| 21–25 | 4 | 1.09 |
| 26+ | 5 | 1.36 |
| Total | 368 | 100 |

## Marital Status

The marital status of the migrants reported in table 3 refers to their status at the time of the interview. It is most probable that the share of unmarried would have been much higher before migration.

## Family Size

As shown in table 4, about a quarter of the migrant families comprise five members or less, 52 per cent between six and ten members, and 23 per cent more than ten members.

## Multi-family Households

Table 5 shows the distribution of migrants by the number of families within a household. These would include father and mother, son and daughter-in-law, daughter and son-in-law, and other such pairs who are residing together in one household.

At the time of migration most of these households comprised one or two fami-

**Table 5.** Distribution of migrants by number of families within a household prior to migration

| Number of families in household | Number of cases | Percentage of total |
|---|---|---|
| 1 | 176 | 48.62 |
| 2 | 128 | 35.36 |
| 3 | 37 | 10.22 |
| 4 | 10 | 2.77 |
| 5 | 4 | 1.10 |
| 6+ | 7 | 1.93 |
| Total | 362 | 100 |

**Table 6.** Distribution of migrants by education qualification prior to migration and area (percentages)

| Educational qualification | Area | | | | | |
| | Chitta-gong | Noa-khali | Sylhet | Dhaka | Dhaka City | Overall |
|---|---|---|---|---|---|---|
| Sign only | 15.38 | 22.85 | 26.83 | 14.86 | — | 16.80 |
| Up to Class V | 32.05 | 30.00 | 26.83 | 35.14 | 1.70 | 26.17 |
| VI–IX | 39.74 | 35.72 | 29.72 | 29.03 | 6.78 | 28.65 |
| SSC and HSC | 12.82 | 11.43 | 15.86 | 22.97 | 32.20 | 18.46 |
| Subtotal | 100 | 100 | 98.79 | 100 | 40.68 | 90.08 |
| Bachelors and Masters | — | — | 1.21 | — | 6.78 | 1.38 |
| Diploma in Engineering | — | — | — | — | 8.47 | 1.38 |
| MBBS | — | — | — | — | 18.64 | 3.03 |
| B.Sc. in Engineering | — | — | — | — | 23.73 | 3.86 |
| Ph.D | — | — | — | — | 1.70 | 0.28 |
| Number of cases | 78 | 70 | 82 | 74 | 59 | 363 |

lies. This was true for about 84 per cent of the cases. Approximately 16 per cent of the households contained three families or more.

## Education and Training

### Educational Qualifications

The educational level prior to migration was very poor in most of the cases. About 17 per cent of the migrants could only sign their name; about 26 per cent had gone to the fifth grade; another 28 per cent had completed nine grades. Only 18 per cent had a senior or Higher Secondary School Certificate.

The educational level of migrants from all the different areas, except Dhaka City, was uniformly low. Only a few of them have an educational qualification of the

**Table 7.** Vocational and technical training prior to migration

| Nature of training | Number of cases | Percentage of total[a] |
|---|---|---|
| Vocational | 43 | 9.24 |
| Technical | 40 | 10.87 |
| Together | 74 | 20.11 |

a. Percentages are in terms of the total number of cases interviewed, i.e. 368.

**Table 8.** Length of vocational and technical training prior to migration

| Length of training (in months) | Number of cases | Percentage of total |
|---|---|---|
| Up to 3 | 18 | 24.32 |
| 4–6 | 13 | 17.57 |
| 7–12 | 18 | 24.32 |
| 13–24 | 12 | 16.22 |
| 25–36 | 7 | 9.46 |
| 37+ | 6 | 8.11 |
| Total | 74 | 100 |

senior or Higher Secondary level. In Dhaka City, however, about 60 per cent of the respondents had an educational qualification above Higher Secondary level.

## Vocational and Technical Training

Even in terms of the training acquired prior to migration – both vocational and technical – the returned migrants had very little expertise. Out of 368 returned migrants interviewed, only 74 have had any such training: 34 had vocational training and 40 technical training of some kind or other.

Even among those who possessed technical and vocational skills, the quality of the training was quite poor. This is reflected in the length of training prior to migration, which in 70 per cent of cases was one year at most.

## Employment and Occupational Status

### Employment Status

More than four-fifths of those interviewed were employed or self-employed prior to migration. Of the reported cases, some 47 per cent were employed, and 41 per cent self-employed. Only about 7 per cent of the migrants are reported to have been unemployed prior to migration; and 5 per cent were students (table 9).

### Nature of Employment

Among those who are reported to have been employed prior to migration, about 78 per cent had regular employment; the rest were casual wage-earners.

**Table 9.** Employment status prior to migration

| Employment status | Number of cases | Percentage of total |
|---|---|---|
| Employed | 173 | 47.02 |
| Self-employed | 149 | 40.48 |
| Unemployed | 27 | 7.34 |
| Student | 19 | 5.16 |
| Total | 368 | 100 |

**Table 10.** Nature of employment prior to migration

| Nature of employment | Number of cases | Percentage of total |
|---|---|---|
| Regular salaried | 135 | 78.03 |
| Casual wage | 38 | 21.97 |
| Total | 173 | 100 |

**Table 11.** Duration of employment prior to migration

| Duration of employment group (in years) | Percentage of total |
|---|---|
| Up to 1 | 76.33 |
| 1–2 | 16.00 |
| 2–3 | 3.00 |
| 3–5 | 2.33 |
| 5–8 | 2.33 |
| Total | 100 |

Duration of Employment

Among those who were employed prior to migration more than 90 per cent were employed for two years or less. In 76 per cent of cases it was for a maximum of one year.

Employment Status of Family Members

Out of a total of 368 cases, there were only 86 where at least one other family member was employed at the time of migration. The maximum number of family members employed was three.

**Instances of Earlier Migration**

Repeat Migration

Out of a total of 368 returned migrants, 37 cases had had the experience of migrating to the Middle East more than once. Such experiences were more prominent among those interviewed in Chittagong.

**Table 12.** Distribution of migrants by the number of family members employed prior to migration

| Number of members employed | Number of cases | Percentage of total |
|---|---|---|
| 1 | 72 | 83.72 |
| 2 | 8 | 9.30 |
| 3 | 6 | 6.98 |
| Total | 86 | 100 |

**Table 13.** Distribution of migrants by experiences of earlier migration

| Areas | Total number of cases | Mirgrants with earlier experience | |
|---|---|---|---|
| | | Number | Percentage |
| Chittagong | 80 | 14 | 17.50 |
| Noakhali | 70 | 7 | 10.00 |
| Sylhet | 83 | 8 | 9.64 |
| Dhaka | 74 | 5 | 6.76 |
| Dhaka City | 61 | 3 | 4.92 |
| Total | 368 | 37 | 10.05 |

**Table 14.** Distribution of migrants by country of earlier migration

| Country | Number of cases |
|---|---|
| Abu Dhabi | 7 |
| Bahrain | 2 |
| Doha | 4 |
| Dubai | 3 |
| Iraq | 5 |
| Kuwait | 2 |
| Libya | 2 |
| Oman | 1 |
| Qatar | 2 |
| Saudi Arabia | 7 |
| UAE | 2 |
| Total | 37 |

Destination of Previous Migration

Most of the earlier migrations took place to Abu Dhabi and Saudi Arabia, followed by Iraq and Doha.

Family Members in the Middle East

In about 41 cases it was found that some family members were in the Middle East at the time of migration. In Chittagong, for instance, 16 out of 80 cases had some of

**Table 15.** Family members employed in the Middle East prior to migration by area

| Number of family members in the Middle East | Area | | | | | |
| --- | --- | --- | --- | --- | --- | --- |
| | Chitta-gong | Noa-khali | Sylhet | Dhaka | Dhaka City | Overall |
| 1 | 10 | 3 | 10 | 3 | 7 | 33 |
| 2 | 4 | — | — | — | — | 4 |
| 3 | 2 | — | 2 | — | — | 4 |
| Total | 16 | 3 | 12 | 3 | 7 | 41 |

**Table 16.** Distribution of migrants by reasons for migration to the Middle East

| Reason for migration | Most important reason | | Second important reason | |
| --- | --- | --- | --- | --- |
| | Number | Percentage | Number | Percentage |
| Higher income/ saving abroad | 322 | 87.74 | 33 | 8.99 |
| To redeem personal/ family loans | 8 | 2.18 | 22 | 5.99 |
| Suitable employ-ment abroad | 5 | 1.36 | 28 | 7.63 |
| To help family/ relatives | 27 | 7.36 | 243 | 66.21 |
| Better education for children | 5 | 1.36 | 38 | 10.36 |
| Others | — | — | 3 | 0.82 |
| Total | 367 | 100 | 367 | 100 |

their family members already employed in the Middle East, while in both Noakhali and Dhaka only three such cases were reported.

## Process of Migration

### Reasons for Migration

The returned migrants were asked to identify, from among a number of stipulated reasons, the two most important reasons for their migration to the Middle East. The information thus generated is compiled in table 16. The most important reason quoted was the higher income/savings abroad; the income differential between home and abroad and the possibility of accumulating some savings were thus the major motivations for migration (88 per cent). To "help family/relatives" was iden-tified as the second most important reason (66 per cent).

### Source of Information

Information about job prospects in the Middle East and the related benefits was transmitted to the prospective candidates through friends, relatives, and neigh-

**Table 17.** Source of information about job prospects in the Middle East by area (percentages)

| Source of information | Area | | | | | |
| --- | --- | --- | --- | --- | --- | --- |
| | Chitta-gong | Noa-khali | Sylhet | Dhaka | Dhaka City | Overall |
| Friends and relatives already abroad | 77.50 | 62.69 | 68.70 | 72.60 | 26.23 | 63.18 |
| Newspaper | 7.50 | 1.49 | 22.60 | 6.84 | 40.98 | 12.37 |
| Local intermediary | 12.50 | 25.37 | 18.10 | 20.55 | 19.67 | 18.95 |
| Others | 2.50 | 10.45 | 3.69 | — | 13.11 | 5.50 |
| Total number of cases | 80 | 67 | 83 | 73 | 61 | 364 |

**Table 18.** Relative importance of different channels of migration by area (percentages)

| Channel | Area | | | | | |
| --- | --- | --- | --- | --- | --- | --- |
| | Chitta-gong | Noa-khali | Sylhet | Dhaka | Dhaka City | Overall |
| Direct application | 13.75 | 2.94 | 6.10 | 9.46 | 18.97 | 0.95 |
| Government agency | 5.00 | 4.41 | 6.10 | 2.70 | 22.41 | 7.46 |
| Licensed recruiting agency | 12.50 | 26.87 | 12.20 | 39.19 | 13.79 | 20.72 |
| Unlicensed recruiting agency | 3.75 | 4.41 | 10.98 | 10.81 | 15.52 | 8.84 |
| Construction firms | 26.25 | 52.94 | 52.44 | 27.03 | 22.41 | 36.74 |
| Friends and relatives | 32.50 | 7.35 | 4.88 | 9.46 | 1.72 | 11.88 |
| Others | 6.25 | 1.47 | 7.38 | 7.30 | 1.35 | 4.42 |
| Total number of cases | 80 | 68 | 82 | 74 | 58 | 362 |

bours who had already migrated. This was true for more than three-fifths of the respondents. In Chittagong, for instance, more than 75 per cent of the migrants became aware of the job prospects in the Middle East through their friends and relatives already abroad. The situation was similar in Dhaka. In both these places the process of migration to the Middle East had been going on for a long time, and almost every family would have had at least one of their relations or friends already abroad. In the case of professionals and semi-professionals in Dhaka City, the most important source of information was the newspaper. In Noakhali and Dhaka the local intermediaries of the recruiting agents or their subagents played an important role in the process of migration.

Channel of Migration

For the sample cases, as shown in table 18, the single most important channel of migration was the construction firms operating in the Middle Eastern countries. These firms alone would account for more than one-third of the migration reported in the survey. The licensed and unlicensed recruiting agents together were the next

**Table 19.** Distribution of migrants by nature of job contract signed prior to migration and area (percentages)

| Nature of job contract | Area | | | | | |
| --- | --- | --- | --- | --- | --- | --- |
| | Chitta-gong | Noa-khali | Sylhet | Dhaka | Dhaka City | Overall |
| Formal contract | 63.16 | 84.28 | 70.13 | 93.05 | 80.33 | 77.81 |
| Informal arrangement | 30.26 | 12.86 | 24.67 | 5.56 | 13.11 | 17.70 |
| Letter of other com-munication giving some of the main terms and conditions | — | — | 2.60 | — | 6.56 | 1.68 |
| Others | 6.58 | 2.86 | 2.60 | 1.39 | — | 2.81 |
| Total number of cases | 76 | 70 | 77 | 72 | 61 | 356 |

**Table 20.** Distribution of migrants by language of job contract and area (percentages)

| Language of job contract | Area | | | | | |
| --- | --- | --- | --- | --- | --- | --- |
| | Chitta-gong | Noa-khali | Sylhet | Dhaka | Dhaka City | Overall |
| English | 40.85 | 76.12 | 47.06 | 57.97 | 37.70 | 52.08 |
| Arabic | 16.90 | 2.98 | 26.47 | 8.70 | 24.59 | 15.77 |
| Both | 42.25 | 20.90 | 26.47 | 33.33 | 37.70 | 32.14 |
| Total number of cases | 71 | 67 | 68 | 69 | 61 | 336. |

most important channel. In the case of Chittagong, friends and relatives played an important role. The highest relative share of migration through direct application was in Dhaka City (19 per cent); the same applies to migration through government agencies.

Nature of Job Contract

More than three-quarters of the respondents would have signed a formal contract prior to their migration. Informal arrangements such as free visa, no-objection certificate, tourist visa, etc., were reported by another 18 per cent. Such informal arrangements were relatively widespread in Chittagong, followed by Sylhet.

Language of Job Contract

English was the language of the job contracts signed by more than half the respondents. In 32 per cent of the cases it was written in both English and Arabic.

For those migrating through unlicensed recruiting agents, Arabic was almost as important a language for job contracts as English. This was true also for jobs secured through direct application. Among the different occupational groups abroad, job contracts in English were more prominent in the case of unskilled workers, and Arabic in the case of professionals and semi-professionals.

**Table 21.** Distribution of channels of migration by language of job contract (percentages)

| Channel of migration | Language of job contract | | | | Number of cases |
|---|---|---|---|---|---|
| | English | Arabic | Both | Others | |
| Direct application | 34.29 | 25.71 | 37.14 | 2.86 | 35 |
| Government agency | 38.46 | 15.38 | 46.15 | — | 26 |
| Licensed recruiting agent | 64.00 | 6.67 | 29.33 | — | 75 |
| Unlicensed recruiting agent | 38.71 | 35.48 | 25.81 | — | 31 |
| Construction firm | 50.00 | 14.39 | 33.33 | 2.27 | 132 |
| Friends/relatives | 68.75 | 9.37 | 18.75 | 3.12 | 32 |
| Overall | 51.35 | 15.41 | 31.72 | 1.52 | 331 |

**Table 22.** Distribution of language of job contract by occupational groups abroad (percentages)

| Language of job contract | Broad occupational group | | | | All together |
|---|---|---|---|---|---|
| | Professional and semi-professional | Skilled | Semi-skilled | Unskilled | |
| English | 42.55 | 46.55 | 36.27 | 50.09 | 50.88 |
| Arabic | 23.40 | 14.94 | 12.24 | 13.64 | 15.48 |
| Both | 31.91 | 37.93 | 24.49 | 21.12 | 31.85 |
| Others | 2.13 | 0.57 | — | 6.06 | 1.79 |
| Number of cases | 47 | 174 | 49 | 66 | 336 |

**Table 23.** Distribution of migrants by access to advice/counselling prior to signing job contract

| Access to advice/counselling | Percentage of total |
|---|---|
| Yes | 69.57 |
| No | 30.41 |
| Total | 100 |

**Table 24.** Distribution of migrants by adequacy of advice/counselling received prior to migration

| Level of advice/counselling | Percentage of total |
|---|---|
| Adequate | 88.15 |
| Inadequate | 9.76 |
| Misleading | 2.09 |
| Total | 100 |

**Table 25.** Distribution of migrants by source of advice/counselling and area (percentages)

| Source of advice/ counselling | Area | | | | | |
|---|---|---|---|---|---|---|
| | Chitta-gong | Noa-khali | Sylhet | Dhaka | Dhaka City | Overall |
| Friends/relatives | 51.16 | 55.74 | 47.46 | 50.91 | 27.27 | 48.20 |
| Recruiting agents | 20.93 | 27.87 | 27.12 | 27.27 | 21.21 | 25.50 |
| Model contracts and other documentation | 6.97 | 4.92 | 22.03 | 12.73 | 36.36 | 15.14 |
| Previous employer | 11.63 | 1.64 | — | 9.09 | 3.03 | 4.78 |
| Voluntary agencies | 2.33 | 1.64 | — | — | — | 0.80 |
| Special government service centre | 4.65 | 1.64 | 1.69 | — | 9.09 | 2.79 |
| Other | 2.33 | 6.56 | 1.69 | — | 3.03 | 2.79 |
| Total number | 43 | 61 | 59 | 55 | 33 | 251 |

### Advice Counselling prior to Signing Job Contract

Since the job contracts were either in English or Arabic (or both), and the migrants were mostly ill-educated or ill-informed about job conditions abroad, signing a job contract should have been preceded by some advice or counselling about the terms laid down in the contract.

In this regard, about 70 per cent of the respondents had access to some form of advice or counselling prior to signing, implying that the migrants were mostly aware of the terms before they committed themselves. Moreover, in the light of their experiences abroad, about 90 per cent considered that such advice/counselling was quite adequate.

The most important source of such advice or counselling was friends or relatives followed by recruiting agents. It is worth noting here that only 3 per cent of migrants received assistance from the government agencies.

Across the different areas the various sources of advice or counselling differed significantly in terms of their relative importance. In Noakhali, for instance, about half the migrants received some advice from their friends and relatives, whereas the corresponding figure for Dhaka City was 27 per cent. About 36 per cent of the migrants from Dhaka City had an opportunity to consult a model contract and other documents relating to job conditions in the Middle East prior to signing a job contract. For migrants from Noakhali, on the other hand, such opportunities were limited. The educated migrants from Dhaka City received some assistance from special government service centres, as compared to almost none for migrants from other areas.

### Scope for Better Terms of Contract

Table 26 suggests that for 80 per cent of cases there was no scope for bargaining, and the contract was final.

This should not mean, however, that the migrants had to accept whatever terms were offered them. On the contrary, to most of the migrants the terms and condi-

**Table 26.** Scope for bargaining for better terms and conditions

| Scope for bargaining | Number of cases | Percentage of total |
|---|---|---|
| Yes | 70 | 20.11 |
| No | 278 | 70.89 |
| Total | 348 | 100 |

**Table 27.** Training prior to migration

| Prior training | Number of cases | Percentage of total |
|---|---|---|
| Yes | 101 | 28.06 |
| No | 259 | 71.94 |
| Total | 360 | 100 |

**Table 28.** Source of training prior to migration by area (percentages)

| | Area | | | | | |
|---|---|---|---|---|---|---|
| Source | Chitta-gong | Noa-khali | Sylhet | Dhaka | Dhaka City | Overall |
| Government programme | 23.81 | 20.00 | 17.39 | 4.55 | 46.67 | 20.79 |
| Voluntary agency | — | 30.00 | 43.48 | 9.09 | — | 17.82 |
| Recruiting agent | 4.76 | — | 4.35 | 0.09 | 6.67 | 4.95 |
| Private training institute | 38.10 | 20.00 | 8.70 | 27.27 | 40.00 | 25.74 |
| Others | 33.33 | 30.00 | 26.09 | 50.00 | 6.67 | 30.69 |
| Total number of cases | 21 | 20 | 23 | 22 | 15 | 101 |

tions offered were already quite satisfactory. Only in 10 per cent of cases did the migrants state that they were apprehensive of bargaining because of possible reprisals, or loss of the job.

Training Prior to Migration

As table 27 shows, only a little over a quarter of the migrants had some kind of training (relating to the job they were hoping for) prior to their migration. Such training was provided by various organizations, the most important being the private training institutes. The government programme was the most important source of training for migrants from Dhaka City. Voluntary agencies played an important role in Sylhet and Noakhali (see table 28).

It should be noted that the source of training classified under "others" was of great importance. In Dhaka, for instance, half the reported cases received some training from this source, though nothing much is known about its composition.

**Table 29.** Prior knowledge about social and climatic conditions in the host country

| Level of knowledge | Special legal requirements | Social and climatic conditions | | |
| --- | --- | --- | --- | --- |
| | | Social customs | Laws | Climate |
| Adequate | 94.15 | 95.59 | 96.69 | 96.15 |
| Inadequate | 3.34 | 2.48 | 2.20 | 2.75 |
| None | 2.51 | 1.93 | 1.11 | 1.10 |
| Total number of cases | 359 | 363 | 363 | 363 |

**Table 30.** Distribution of migrants by cost of migration

| Cost of migration groups (thousands of taka) | Number of cases | Percentage of total |
| --- | --- | --- |
| 1–10 | 77 | 23.12 |
| 11–20 | 55 | 16.32 |
| 21–30 | 82 | 24.62 |
| 31–40 | 61 | 18.32 |
| 41–50 | 35 | 10.51 |
| 51+ | 23 | 6.91 |
| Total | 333 | 100 |

**Table 31.** Distribution of cost of migrants by area

| Area | Number of cases | Average cost (thousands of taka) |
| --- | --- | --- |
| Chittagong | 67 | 23.69 |
| Noakhali | 62 | 26.58 |
| Sylhet | 78 | 29.78 |
| Dhaka | 71 | 24.39 |
| Dhaka City | 55 | 19.20 |
| Overall | 333 | 25.52 |

Orientation prior to Migration

On the basis of table 29, it would seem that the migrants had adequate knowledge of some of the basic facts pertaining to the conditions in the host country.

**Cost of Migration**

Monetary Cost of Migration

*Cost of Migration*

For a sample of 333 cases,[7] for which complete data are available, the cost of migration varied between 1,000 and 90,000 taka, with an average of 26,000 taka.

**Table 32.** Distribution of cost of migration by broad occupational groups abroad

| Occupational group abroad | Number of cases | Average cost (thousands of taka) |
|---|---|---|
| Professionals and semi-professionals | 46 | 21.93 |
| Skilled | 168 | 23.98 |
| Semi-skilled | 44 | 25.41 |
| Unskilled | 68 | 33.65 |
| Overall | 326 | 25.90 |

**Table 33.** Cost of migration by country of migration

| Country of migration | Number of cases | Average cost (thousands of taka) |
|---|---|---|
| Abu Dhabi | 54 | 23.69 |
| Bahrain | 15 | 21.13 |
| Doha | 5 | 11.60 |
| Dubai | 10 | 14.50 |
| Iran | 5 | 17.00 |
| Iraq | 34 | 22.20 |
| Jordan | 3 | 42.33 |
| Kuwait | 20 | 22.45 |
| Lebanon | 4 | 29.75 |
| Libya | 45 | 24.06 |
| Oman | 8 | 17.25 |
| Qatar | 23 | 32.91 |
| Saudi Arabia | 100 | 30.46 |
| UAE | 4 | 21.50 |
| Overall | 330 | 25.59 |

Dividing the migrants into different cost groups, about a quarter of the sample cases incurred a maximum of 10,000 taka while more than two-fifths spent up to 30,000 taka. Among the different areas, the average cost of migration was lowest in Dhaka City (19,000 taka) and highest in Sylhet (30,000 taka).

According to table 32, the higher the level of skill the lower the cost of migration. The highest average cost of 34,000 taka was incurred by unskilled workers, whereas for professionals and semi-professionals the corresponding figure was 22,000 taka.

Table 33 classifies the cost of migration by country of migration. The costs varied significantly for the different countries, ranging between the lowest average of 12,000 taka for Doha to the highest of 42,000 for the UAE.[8]

*Different Components of Cost*

Table 34 shows the distribution of costs incurred on a stipulated list of items.

The most important cost component comprised payments to the recruiting

**Table 34.** Cost of migration by different components

| Different components of cost | Number of cases | Average cost (thousands of taka) |
|---|---|---|
| NOC/visa | 147 | 20.93 |
| Recruitment agent | 103 | 25.25 |
| Passport | 277 | 0.76 |
| Air ticket | 155 | 8.54 |
| Internal travel/ preparation, etc. | 273 | 4.83 |

**Table 35.** Cost of migration by various sources of financing

| Source of financing | Number of cases | Average cost (thousands of taka) |
|---|---|---|
| Own savings | 165 | 10.34 |
| Friends/relatives | 154 | 15.49 |
| Private moneylenders | 39 | 15.36 |
| Bank loan | 6 | 6.33 |
| Sale of land | 166 | 24.45 |
| Others | 38 | 15.87 |

agent – an average of 25,000 taka. Expenses towards no-objection certificate or visa were the second most important component (21,000 taka), incurred mostly by those who went abroad through individual or private channels.[9]

*Financing the Cost of Migration*

Table 35 shows that the most important means of financing the cost of migration was the sale of land. An average of 24,000 taka was procured by 166 migrants through the sale of land for this purpose. Savings, and loans from friends or relatives, were the other common sources of financing. Private moneylenders contributed significantly towards the cost of migration. Evidently migrants have had recourse to more than one source of financing to raise the required funds.

Non-Monetary Cost of Migration

*Waiting Time*

The waiting time refers here to the length of time a migrant had to wait for the offer of a job after his first enquiry about job prospects in the Middle East, and thereafter the time between the offer and his departure abroad.

From table 36 it can be seen that about a third of the respondents got a job offer in the Middle East within two months of their first enquiry; a half within five months. On the other hand, over one-fifth of the migrants waited for more than a year to get a job offer.

Once a job was offered, the remaining formalities took very little time. In 70 per cent of cases, up to six weeks were needed to arrange all the formalities, such as

**Table 36.** Distribution of migrants by time spent between first enquiry and offer of job

| Time interval (in months) | Number of cases | Percentage of total |
|---|---|---|
| Up to 2 | 104 | 29.46 |
| 3–5 | 73 | 20.68 |
| 6–9 | 58 | 16.43 |
| 10–12 | 39 | 11.05 |
| 12+ | 79 | 22.38 |
| Total | 353 | 100 |

**Table 37.** Time spent between recruitment and migration

| Time interval (in weeks) | Number of cases | Percentage of total |
|---|---|---|
| 0–3 | 153 | 42.77 |
| 4–6 | 99 | 27.34 |
| 7–9 | 44 | 12.15 |
| 10–12 | 33 | 9.12 |
| 12+ | 33 | 9.12 |
| Total | 362 | 100 |

**Table 38.** Victims of fraud prior to migration

| Victim of fraud | Number of cases | Percentage of total |
|---|---|---|
| Yes | 27 | 7.38 |
| No | 339 | 92.62 |
| Total | 366 | 100 |

**Table 39.** Victims of breach of contract

| Breach of contract | Number of cases | Percentage of total |
|---|---|---|
| Yes | 16 | 4.43 |
| No | 345 | 95.57 |
| Total | 361 | 100 |

obtaining a passport, visa, medical certificate, etc. About 90 per cent could migrate within three months.

### Victims of Fraud or Breach of Contract

Among the reported cases, the number who became victims of fraud was quite small. Only 27, or 7.3 per cent, of a sample of 366 had been victimized in this

**Table 40.** Distribution of migrants by time spent between arrival and assumption of duties

| Time interval (in weeks) | Number of cases | Percentage of total |
|---|---|---|
| Up to 1 | 84 | 23.77 |
| 2–3 | 129 | 35.73 |
| 4–5 | 35 | 9.70 |
| 6–7 | 38 | 10.53 |
| 8–9 | 6 | 1.66 |
| 10 + | 69 | 19.11 |
| Total | 361 | 100 |

**Table 41.** Distribution of migrants by second job contract signed/not signed abroad

| Second contract signed abroad | Number of cases | Percentage of total |
|---|---|---|
| Yes | 60 | 16.30 |
| No | 308 | 83.70 |
| Total | 368 | 100 |

**Table 42.** Terms and conditions of second contract compared to first contract

| Second contract compared to first | Percentage of total |
|---|---|
| Better | 30.88 |
| Worse | 19.12 |
| Same | 50.00 |
| Total number of cases | 60 |

manner.[10] Even with regard to breach of contract, only 4 per cent of the returned migrants had had any such experience.

## Overseas Employment: Achievement and Adjustment

### Arrival and Assumption of Duties

Waiting Period

Table 40 shows the distribution of respondents by the length of time they spent between their arrival in the host country and the assumption of duties in the job in which they were placed. It is estimated that about a quarter of them assumed their duties within a week, and nearly 60 per cent within three weeks. On the other end, about one-fifth of them had to wait for more than 10 months before they were eventually employed.[11]

**Table 43**. Distribution of migrants by level of monthly earnings abroad (thousands of taka)

| Different components of earnings | Number of cases | Earnings abroad | |
|---|---|---|---|
| | | Maximum | Average |
| Basic salary | 357 | 70 | 8.54 |
| Overtime allowances | 192 | 40 | 3.41 |
| Other cash allowances | 70 | 21 | 3.26 |
| Other occupations | 20 | 10 | 3.15 |
| Total earnings | 357 | 80 | 10.83 |

**Table 44**. Distribution of migrants by different income groups

| Monthly income groups (thousands of taka) | Number of cases | Percentage of total |
|---|---|---|
| 1–5 | 105 | 29.41 |
| 6–10 | 156 | 43.70 |
| 11–15 | 38 | 10.64 |
| 16–25 | 29 | 8.12 |
| 26–40 | 10 | 2.80 |
| 40 + | 19 | 5.32 |
| Total | 357 | 100 |

## Signing Second Job Contract

In 60 out of 368 cases the migrants signed a second contract on arrival in the host country.

It was found that, in 19 per cent of the cases, the terms and conditions of the second job contract were worse than those of the first contract, in half the cases they were similar to those of the first one, and in the remaining 30 per cent they were even better.

## Earnings, Expenditure, and Savings Abroad

### Earnings Abroad

There are several components of earnings abroad, such as basic salary, overtime allowances, and other monetary benefits. Moreover, nationals may have been engaged in more than one occupation on a part-time or full-time basis. Earnings abroad should accordingly include all these items.

The average monthly earnings were about 11,000 taka, including the average salary of 9,000 taka. The maximum basic salary reported in the survey is 70,000 taka, and the minimum 1,000 taka. Over and above the basic salary, more than half the respondents earned overtime allowances averaging 3,000 taka per month. Only 6 per cent of the respondents were engaged in more than one occupation, enabling them to earn 4,000 taka per month on average.

Combining all the sources of income together, as table 44 shows, about 30 per

**Table 45**. Distribution of monthly income by different broad occupational groups

| Occupational groups | Number of cases | Average monthly earnings (thousands of taka) |
|---|---|---|
| Professional and semi-professional | 50 | 23.66 |
| Skilled | 187 | 9.30 |
| Semi-skilled | 49 | 7.59 |
| Unskilled | 71 | 7.70 |
| Total | 357 | 10.83 |

**Table 46**. Different components of monthly income by occupational groups

| Occupation | Basic salary | Overtime allowances | Other cash allowances | Other occupation | Total earnings |
|---|---|---|---|---|---|
| Professionals and semi-professionals | 18.80 (50)[a] | 5.78 (27) | 5.88 (17) | 4.25 (4) | 23.66 (50) |
| Skilled | 6.98 (185) | 3.15 (117) | 3.50 (26) | 2.91 (11) | 9.30 (185) |
| Semi-skilled | 7.50 (50) | 2.00 (22) | 1.40 (10) | 4.50 (2) | 7.59 (50) |
| Unskilled | 5.97 (71) | 3.27 (26) | 1.35 (17) | 1.67 (3) | 7.70 (71) |
| Overall | 8.54 (356) | 3.41 (192) | 3.26 (70) | 3.15 (20) | 10.76 (356) |

a. Items within parentheses refer to the number of cases on which the respective estimates are based.

**Table 47**. Distribution of monthly income by country of migration

| Country of migration | Number of cases | Average monthly income (thousands of taka) |
|---|---|---|
| Abu Dhabi | 63 | 8.94 |
| Bahrain | 17 | 6.18 |
| Doha | 6 | 7.83 |
| Dubai | 13 | 10.69 |
| Iran | 5 | 11.20 |
| Iraq | 37 | 13.19 |
| Jordan | 3 | 6.67 |
| Kuwait | 20 | 9.35 |
| Lebanon | 4 | 6.25 |
| Libya | 45 | 15.87 |
| Oman | 8 | 6.13 |
| Qatar | 25 | 8.20 |
| Saudi Arabia | 106 | 11.21 |
| UAE | 5 | 17.20 |
| All together | 357 | 10.83 |

cent had a monthly income of between 1,000 and 5,000 taka, about 43 per cent between 5,000 and 10,000 taka, and a little more than one-third more than 10,000 taka.

The distribution of monthly income by broad occupational groups abroad is shown in table 45. As might be expected, the highest average income was earned by the professionals and semi-professionals – about 24,000 taka per month – and the lowest by the semi-skilled and unskilled, both of which earned almost the same average income, around 7,600–7,700 taka.

Table 46 presents the different components of earnings abroad by broad occupational groups. As can be seen from the table, the average monthly basic salary of a professional and semi-professional was more than three times (18,800 taka) that of an unskilled worker (5,970 taka). Moreover, the professionals and semi-professionals also earned twice as much as the others as overtime and cash allowances.

Table 47 gives the distribution of migrants by country of migration and level of monthly income.[12] Bahrain and Oman accounted for the lowest average monthly income (6,000 taka), and UAE for the highest (17,200 taka).

Expenditure Abroad

The components of expenditures abroad are many and an individual may not keep a detailed account of all items. As such, it is not easy to ascertain the pattern of expenditure. However, the following discussion takes account of the expenditure on basic items, such as food, clothing, rent, etc., which provide some indication of the migrant's cost of living.

The major items of expenditure incurred by the migrants abroad were food, rent, and clothing. However, in some cases food and lodging were provided free of cost under the job contract by the employer. Out of a total of 312 respondents (for whom information on expenditure abroad is available), there were 72 cases where food was provided free of cost by the employer, and in 82 cases the employer also provided free lodging.

Migrants spent an average of about 2,000 taka per month on food, 1,500 taka on rent, and 1,300 taka on clothing. The item "Others," comprising expenses on recreation, travel, etc., accounted on an average for about 1,300 taka per month. Taking all the expenses into account, the average expenditure per month abroad came to about 2,300 taka.

Table 49 shows the distribution of respondents by various monthly expenditure groups. More than three-fifths of the respondents had a total monthly expenditure below 2,000 taka, and more than one-third of these spent less than 1,000 taka.[13] The maximum monthly expenditure reported was 8,000 taka. The highest average monthly expenditure incurred was by the professionals and semi-professionals.

Savings Abroad

As table 50 shows, more than half the migrants interviewed had average monthly savings of below 5,000 taka and another 30 per cent between 6,000 and 10,000 taka. For the sample of 365, the average monthly savings were about 8,000 taka.

Among the different occupational groups, the highest average monthly savings of 16,000 taka were among professionals and semi-professionals. For the others the amount varied between 5,000 and 7,000 taka.

**Table 48**. Distribution of monthly expenditure by major items

| Major items of expenditure | Number of cases | Level of monthly expenditure (thousands of taka) | |
|---|---|---|---|
| | | Maximum | Average |
| Food | 207 | 8 | 1,870 |
| Rent | 45 | 4 | 1,550 |
| Clothing | 61 | 5 | 1,310 |
| Others | 234 | 5 | 1,260 |
| Overall | 313 | 8 | 2,330 |

**Table 49**. Distribution of migrants by monthly expenditure abroad

| Monthly expenditure groups (thousands of taka) | Number of cases | Percentage of total |
|---|---|---|
| Less than 1 | 108 | 34.62 |
| 1–2 | 104 | 33.33 |
| 3–4 | 69 | 22.12 |
| 5–6 | 25 | 8.01 |
| 7–8 | 6 | 1.92 |
| Total | 312 | 100 |

**Table 50**. Distribution of migrants by level of savings per month

| Savings groups (thousands of taka) | Number of cases | Percentage of total |
|---|---|---|
| Below 5 | 189 | 51.78 |
| 6–10 | 106 | 29.04 |
| 11–15 | 31 | 8.49 |
| 16–25 | 19 | 5.21 |
| 26 + | 20 | 5.48 |
| Total | 365 | 100 |

**Table 51**. Distribution of monthly savings by broad occupational groups

| Occupational groups | Number of cases | Average monthly savings (thousands of taka) |
|---|---|---|
| Professionals and semi-professionals | 49 | 16.08 |
| Skilled | 185 | 6.94 |
| Semi-skilled | 50 | 6.18 |
| Unskilled | 71 | 5.61 |

**Table 52.** Distribution of migrants by level of remittances (thousands of taka)

| Level of remittances | Number of cases | Percentage of total | Average remittances |
|---|---|---|---|
| Up to 80 | 77 | 21.69 | 46 |
| 81–120 | 59 | 16.62 | 100 |
| 121–200 | 57 | 18.87 | 159 |
| 201–400 | 70 | 19.72 | 295 |
| 401–750 | 51 | 14.37 | 544 |
| 751–25,000 | 31 | 8.73 | 1,212 |
| Total | 355 | 100 | 303 |

**Table 53.** Distribution of migrants by different ways of sending remittances

| Different ways of sending remittances | Number of cases | Average remittances (thousands of taka) |
|---|---|---|
| Cash/draft, etc. | 363 | 271.55 |
| Kind | 314 | 39.77 |
| Sent by employer | 41 | 27.80 |

## Remittances Sent Home

Level of Remittances

Table 52 presents the distribution of respondents by level of remittances during the tenure of employment in the Middle East. This excludes a few cases where no remittances were sent or the figures reported seemed unrealistic.

Average total remittances for more than half of the respondents ranged between 46,000 and 159,000 taka. For 20 per cent they averaged 295,000 taka. The average remittances for the balance of 23 per cent exceeded 500,000 taka. The average for the sample of 355 as a whole was in the region of 303,000 taka.

Of the different means of sending remittances, as shown in table 53 cash transfers were the most common. This includes both cash transfers made through officials/private channels and cash brought into the country by the migrant himself. The average level of cash transfers was found to be 272,000 taka. The average level of remittances in kind (again sent through friends/relatives or brought into the country in person) was 40,000 taka. Finally, a part of the migrants' earnings abroad, averaging 28,000 taka, were sent home directly by the employer. In terms of occupation, the highest average level of remittance sent was by professionals and semi-professionals (612,000 taka), which was about four times that of the unskilled migrants (155,000 taka).

Channel of Transfer of Remittances

As table 55 shows, the most commonly used mode of transferring overseas savings was the bank draft, which was used by about 67 per cent of the respondents. The next important means was middlemen, followed by friends or relatives return-

**Table 54**. Level of remittances by different occupational groups

| Occupational groups | Number of cases | Average remittances (thousands of taka) |
|---|---|---|
| Professionals and semi-professionals | 47 | 611.94 |
| Skilled | 184 | 310.88 |
| Semi-skilled | 48 | 170.75 |
| Unskilled | 69 | 155.20 |
| Total | 348 | |

**Table 55**. Relative importance of different channels for sending remittances by area (percentages)[a]

| Channels for sending remittances | Areas | | | | | |
|---|---|---|---|---|---|---|
| | Chitta-gong | Noa-khali | Sylhet | Dhaka | Dhaka City | Overall |
| Friends/relatives returning home | 25.00 | 6.35 | 11.53 | 6.76 | 3.33 | 9.37 |
| Bank drafts | 82.50 | 85.71 | 75.95 | 89.19 | 68.85 | 67.45 |
| Bank-to-bank transfer | 8.70 | 1.56 | 5.06 | 2.70 | 27.87 | 7.26 |
| Middlemen | 20.00 | 17.46 | 21.52 | 12.16 | 11.48 | 14.05 |
| Other | 1.20 | 3.13 | 3.80 | 1.35 | 1.67 | 1.87 |

a. Percentage figures refer to the relative share of migrants using the respective channels to remit savings.

ing home. Migrants from Dhaka City, who are mostly educated, used primarily the services of the banking system.

Among the migrants from the different districts, the preference in regard to mode of transfer varied widely. For instance, 25 per cent of the migrants from Chittagong reported sending remittances through friends or relatives; the corresponding figure for Dhaka City was only 3 per cent. Middlemen also played an important role in this respect in both Chittagong and Sylhet, but not in the case of Dhaka. The reason for this relative importance of friends or relatives may be the fact that both Chittagong and Sylhet have a long tradition of international migration, and most of the migrant families have friends or relatives already working abroad, making it easier for them to remit their savings in this way. To a great extent this would also help the middlemen to widen their operations within these communities.

The wider use of the banking network to transfer overseas savings was possibly due to the fact that banking and remittances facilities available in the host country were viewed as quite satisfactory. Only 3 per cent of migrants felt that such facilities were inadequate, and another 4 per cent that they were poor.

Moreover, most of these migrant families maintained bank accounts of one kind or another, thus enabling them to take full advantage of the banking channels. For

**Table 56.** Bank account maintained by migrant families

| Whether maintained bank account | Number of cases | Percentage of total |
|---|---|---|
| Yes | 276 | 77.53 |
| No | 80 | 22.47 |
| Total | 356 | 100 |

**Table 57.** Distribution of migrants by mode of sending remittances and area (percentages)

| Mode of sending remittances | Area | | | | | |
|---|---|---|---|---|---|---|
| | Chitta-gong | Noa-khali | Sylhet | Dhaka | Dhaka City | Overall |
| At regular intervals | 47.50 | 41.79 | 51.25 | 72.60 | 57.38 | 54.02 |
| If and when required | 31.30 | 32.84 | 25.00 | 13.70 | 22.95 | 25.21 |
| Regular interval and when required | 21.20 | 14.92 | 20.00 | 12.33 | 16.39 | 17.17 |
| Did not send any remittances | — | 1.49 | 1.25 | 70 | 1.64 | 0.83 |
| Brought savings when coming home | — | 8.69 | 2.50 | 1.37 | 1.64 | 2.77 |
| Total | 100 | 100 | 100 | 100 | 100 | 100 |

instance, taking all the migrants together, more than three-fourths of their families maintained bank accounts. Among the areas, this category accounted for as much as 87 per cent in Dhaka City and 85 per cent in Dhaka.

Mode of Sending Remittances

Over half the migrants sent remittances at regular intervals and another quarter "if and when" money was required by the families back home. This pattern was possibly related to the fact that most of the migrants had no bank account in the Middle East; whatever savings they accumulated, therefore, had to be sent home immediately. Only the professionals maintained bank accounts.[14]

Recipient of Remittances

Taking all cases together, the father of the migrant was found to be the single most important recipient of remittances (38 per cent), followed by the migrant's brother and wife. However, there are noticeable variations between areas. In Noakhali, for instance, the wife was the most important recipient, and in Chittagong the son was a major recipient.

**Table 58.** Distribution of migrants by recipient of remittances and area

| Recipient of remittances | Area | | | | | |
|---|---|---|---|---|---|---|
| | Chittagong | Noakhali | Sylhet | Dhaka | Dhaka City | Overall |
| Father | 42.50 | 25.00 | 44.86 | 40.27 | 32.78 | 37.75 |
| Brother | 17.50 | 21.87 | 34.65 | 16.67 | 26.95 | 22.82 |
| Wife | 17.50 | 28.31 | 6.41 | 22.22 | 25.51 | 20.00 |
| Father-in-Law | 5.00 | 3.13 | 1.27 | 2.78 | 4.92 | 2.25 |
| Son | 17.50 | — | 3.85 | 1.39 | — | 2.25 |
| Other | — | 21.87 | 8.96 | 16.67 | 9.84 | 14.93 |
| Total | 100 | 100 | 100 | 100 | 100 | 100 |

**Table 59.** Terms and conditions offered to sample migrants vis-à-vis other nationals

| Terms and conditions | Number of cases | Percentage of total |
|---|---|---|
| Better | 22 | 6.15 |
| Worse | 87 | 24.30 |
| Same | 249 | 69.55 |
| Total | 358 | 100 |

**Table 60.** Facilities for enquiry and incidence of dispute with employer abroad (percentages)

| Facilities available | Procedure for enquiry/ settlement of disputes | Incidence of dispute with employers |
|---|---|---|
| Yes | 33.80 | 10.47 |
| No | 66.20 | 89.53 |

## Facilities in the Host Country

Facilities Relating to Job Abroad

### Terms and Conditions of Work

Out of a total of 358 migrants, 25 per cent found that the terms and conditions of work offered to them were worse than those offered to their counterparts from other countries. Only 6 per cent found such conditions better. However, a large majority of the migrants (70 per cent) found their terms and conditions to be the same as those offered to other nationals.

### Procedure for Enquiry and Settlement of Grievances

In the opinion of more than two-thirds of the migrants, there was no procedure for looking into complaints. This may be due to an absence of disputes: in the sample, less than one-tenth of the migrants reported having a dispute with their employer.

**Table 61**. Affiliation with trade union in the host country

| Affiliation with trade union | Number of cases | Percentage of total |
|---|---|---|
| Yes | 10 | 2.80 |
| No | 348 | 97.20 |

**Table 62**. Assistance received from Bangladesh embassy

| Nature of problem | Number of cases seeking assistance | Percentage receiving assistance |
|---|---|---|
| Grievance and disputes with employer | 76 | 51.32 |
| Emergency or crisis | 77 | 36.36 |

**Table 63**. Quality of food available via-à-vis expectations (percentages)

| Quality of food | Area | | | | | |
|---|---|---|---|---|---|---|
| | Chittagong | Noakhali | Sylhet | Dhaka | Dhaka City | Overall |
| Good | 49.02 | 47.22 | 64.71 | 72.22 | 62.50 | 59.42 |
| Average | 43.14 | 16.67 | 26.47 | 27.78 | 34.38 | 30.43 |
| Poor | 7.84 | 36.11 | 8.82 | — | 3.12 | 10.14 |

Most of them feared that since legal procedures regarding disputes or grievances were either non-existent or non-operational (especially for foreigners), any dispute with the employer could mean loss of employment.

*Trade Unionism*

There was hardly any opportunity for the migrants to form trade unions. This was reported by about 97 per cent of cases.

*Assistance from the Bangladesh Embassy*

Only a small proportion of the respondents went to the Bangladesh embassies for assistance during their stay abroad. Among those who did, about half received some assistance during grievances and disputes with employers and more than a third during emergencies or crises (table 62).

Facilities relating to Living Conditions Abroad

*Quality of Food*

When asked about the quality of food provided by the employer, as compared to their pre-migration expectations, a great majority of the migrants stated that it was good, and another one-third found it acceptable (table 63). However, a significant

**Table 64**. Availability of cooking facility

| Nature of facility | Number of cases | Percentage of total |
|---|---|---|
| Poor | 27 | 7.34 |
| Good | 225 | 61.14 |
| Adequate | 115 | 31.25 |
| Non-existent | 1 | 0.27 |
| Total | 368 | 100 |

**Table 65**. Nature of facilities in the houses (percentages)

| Type of facilities | Nature of facility | | | |
|---|---|---|---|---|
| | Good | Adequate | Poor | Non-existent |
| Running water | 57.10 | 33.61 | 8.74 | 0.55 |
| Electricity | 59.13 | 35.15 | 5.18 | 0.54 |
| Air conditioning | 44.13 | 34.08 | 7.82 | 13.97 |

proportion (36 per cent) from Noakhali found that the food provided was worse than they had expected. Incidentally, most of them were employed by national (construction) firms working abroad.

One of the reasons that respondents were mostly content with the available food was that cooking facilities were commonly available in the houses in which they lived. They could therefore prepare the kind of food they liked. As table 64 shows, most of the migrants had access to adequate cooking facilities.

*Accommodation*

In terms of the availability of both electricity and running water, most of the migrants classified their accommodation abroad as good.

*Recreation*

Questioned about the availability of recreation facilities in the host country, most of the migrants reported in the affirmative, saying that they considered these adequate.

## Adjustment at Home and Abroad

Prior Awareness of Problems Ahead

As table 67 shows, more than 95 per cent of the respondents were adequately informed about the socio-political conditions in the host country. One implication of this is that they had the necessary mental preparation for the conditions to which they had to adjust, and were therefore better able to cope with the problems they encountered.

In terms of the level of social contact the migrants had with each other, almost all the respondents reported that they had good relations with the nationals from

**Table 66.** Recreation facilities in the place of accommodation

| Level of facilities | Number of cases | Percentage of total |
|---|---|---|
| Good | 210 | 57.69 |
| Adequate | 106 | 29.12 |
| Poor | 33 | 9.07 |
| Non-existent | 15 | 4.12 |

**Table 67.** Prior knowledge of socio-politico-climatic conditions in the host country (percentages)

| Level of knowledge | Information about | | | |
|---|---|---|---|---|
| | Special legal requirements | Social customs | Laws | Climate |
| Adequate | 94.13 | 95.59 | 96.69 | 96.14 |
| Inadequate | 3.34 | 2.48 | 2.20 | 2.75 |
| None | 2.51 | 1.93 | 1.10 | 1.10 |
| Number | (359) | (363) | (363) | (363) |

other countries and with fellow Bangladeshis as well. The majority also reported close relations with other residents in the host country. As would be expected, the contacts were closest with other migrants from Bangladesh.

Overall Adjustment

When the different aspects of adjustment are taken together, almost all the migrants adjusted well while staying abroad.

Adjustments at Home: Responsibility for the Family

In half of a sample of 362 cases, family responsibilities were borne by the parents, especially the father. The brothers and wife of the migrant ranked next, assuming responsibility for an almost equal proportion of households.

Mode of Communication

Postal communication was the most common means used by the migrants. The next most important method, though uncommon until very recently, was the taped conversation, in which migrants record their conversation (or rather a monologue) on a cassette and send it home.[15]

Frequency of Correspondence

The sample migrants sent on average about 30 letters a year to family members. In the case of relations and friends, the figure is about 12. The number of letters received is similar. A fortnightly letter both ways would keep the migrants and the respective families well informed about each other. The regularity of communication would have helped families and migrants to adjust and to sustain their relationships. These figures have to be examined in relation to the levels of education

**Table 68.** Level of social contact with different nationalities (percentages)

| Social contacts | Close | Very close | Distant | None | Number of cases |
|---|---|---|---|---|---|
| Residents in the host country | 81.38 | 5.56 | 11.39 | 1.67 | 360 |
| Migrants from other countries | 84.30 | 4.68 | 9.92 | 1.10 | 363 |
| Migrants from home | 40.71 | 54.92 | 3.55 | 0.82 | 366 |

**Table 69.** Migrants' overall adjustment abroad

| Level of adjustment | Number of cases | Percentage of total |
|---|---|---|
| Very good | 98 | 26.63 |
| Average | 251 | 68.21 |
| Felt lonely | 19 | 5.16 |
| Total | 368 | 100 |

and literacy among the migrants. As many as 62 migrants could only sign their name, and another 95 had only a few years of schooling. It would appear that most migrants and their families at home managed to maintain communication despite their illiteracy and low level of education; friends and relations apparently came to their assistance.

Some Adjustment Problems at Home

As noted earlier, owing to its personal nature, information on the social adjustment problems of migrant families was difficult to collect. Nevertheless, an attempt is made here to cast some light on the various adjustment problems experienced by families.

*Juvenile Delinquency*

The absence of the father, as well as the sudden increase in the level of family income, is likely to have an adverse impact on the behaviour and expectations of the children. Some respondents reported cases where children had developed the habit of smoking, drinking, or extravagant and wasteful expenditure.

*Marital Problems*

The long separation of spouses can result in infidelity and illicit relationships. The sample included a few such cases. In many of these instances the persons involved were close relations and neighbours.

*Illness and Psychological Maladjustment*

There were a few cases of family members, particularly wives, who were physically and psychologically affected by the migration. Sleeplessness and chronic

**Table 70.** Allocation of family responsibilities during migration

| Member assuming responsibilities | Number of cases | Percentage of total |
|---|---|---|
| Wife | 74 | 20.44 |
| Children | 7 | 1.93 |
| Parents | 184 | 50.83 |
| Brothers | 78 | 21.55 |
| Others | 19 | 5.25 |
| Total | 362 | 100 |

**Table 71.** Means of communication between migrants and their families

| Medium of communication[a] | Number of cases | Percentage of total |
|---|---|---|
| Letter | 358 | 97.28 |
| Telephone | 19 | 3.16 |
| Taped conversation | 25 | 6.80 |
| Others | 6 | 1.63 |

a. Since more than one medium could be used at the same time, the sum of the percentages is irrelevant.

**Table 72.** Level of communication by number of letters received and sent

| Correspondent | Received | | Sent | |
|---|---|---|---|---|
| | Number | Average | Number | Average |
| Family members | 360 | 30.09 | 358 | 29.80 |
| Others | 224 | 11.73 | 214 | 11.99 |

headaches were a common manifestation of this. The absence of a family member who had exercised responsibility also ocasionally resulted in family conflicts or the unruly behaviour of children, all of which accentuated the problems for the family member who had assumed responsibility, particularly the wife. But, as will be seen later from the respondents' own evaluation of the adjustment experience, these problems of maladjustment occurred only among a small minority.

*Social Harmony*

From the viewpoint of the migrant family, possibly the most serious adjustment problem is that of maintaining harmonious relations with the community – relations, friends and neighbours. The enhanced economic status following the inflow of overseas remittances often tends to disrupt the social equilibrium of the migrant families. Such a problem may also arise between two migrant families. Actual or presumed, the new socio-economic status may become a source of pride for the family and of jealousy and frustration for others.

In the sample studied, these problems were not pronounced, particularly in communities which contained a large cluster of migrant families. There was a tendency

269

**Table 73.** Overall adjustment of migrant families

| Adjusted | Number of cases | Percentage of total |
|---|---|---|
| Very well | 30 | 8.20 |
| Well | 312 | 85.25 |
| Badly | 23 | 6.28 |
| Very badly | 1 | 0.27 |
| Total | 366 | 100 |

**Table 74.** Distribution of migrants by reasons for returning home

| Reasons for returning home | Number of cases | Percentage |
|---|---|---|
| Complete job contract | 190 | 52.92 |
| Resigned from job | 71 | 19.78 |
| Job terminated | 67 | 18.66 |
| Compulsory repatriation | 14 | 3.90 |
| Domestic/personal | 9 | 2.51 |
| Other | 8 | 2.23 |
| Total | 359 | 100.00 |

for the problem to surface only in communities where participation in the migration was limited to a very few families.

The information in table 73 indicates that despite various adjustment problems, most of the migrants interviewed were of the opinion that their families adjusted well during their absence. Only about 7 per cent of families were reported to have adjusted poorly.

## Return Migration: Achievements and Expectations

### Return Migration

Reasons for Returning Home

More than half the migrants returned home because they had completed their job contracts abroad, and another 20 per cent after having resigned from their job. The numbers of the latter are much higher among respondents from Dhaka City and Noakhali – 30 and 28 per cent respectively.[16]

Job termination is the third important reason for return, accounting for about 30 per cent of returnees in Sylhet. The depressed level of economic activities in the host country and the closure of the firms in which the migrants were working were some of the underlying reasons.

Table 75 shows that the reason for return for the great majority of those who went abroad through direct application, construction firms, and friends or relatives is the completion of job contracts. Instances of resignation from jobs are highest

**Table 75**. Reasons for returning home and channels of migration

| Reasons for returning home | Channels of migration[a] | | | | | |
|---|---|---|---|---|---|---|
| | 1 | 2 | 3 | 4 | 5 | 6 |
| Completed job contract | 62.86 | 48.15 | 50.00 | 36.67 | 58.78 | 55.00 |
| Resigned from job | 11.43 | 23.95 | 17.57 | 36.67 | 20.61 | 15.00 |
| Job terminated | 14.29 | 7.41 | 22.97 | 26.66 | 17.56 | 20.00 |
| Compulsory repatriation | 2.86 | — | 6.67 | 0 | 1.53 | 2.50 |
| Domestic/personal | 5.71 | 11.1 | 1.35 | 0 | 0.76 | 5.00 |
| Others | 2.86 | 7.41 | 1.35 | 0 | 0.76 | 2.50 |
| Total | 100 | 100 | 100 | 100 | 100 | 100 |

a. 1 = direct application; 2 = government agency; 3 = licensed recruiting agency; 4 = unlicensed recruiting agency; 5 = construction firm; 6 = friends and relatives.

**Table 76**. Distribution of migrants by reasons for returning home and broad occupational groups

| Reasons for returning home | Broad occupational group | | | |
|---|---|---|---|---|
| | Professional, semi-professional | Skilled | Semi-skilled | Unskilled |
| Completed job contract | 52.94 | 59.02 | 36.73 | 49.27 |
| Resigned job | 33.33 | 15.85 | 30.61 | 13.45 |
| Job terminated | 7.84 | 16.39 | 26.53 | 26.08 |
| Compulsory repatriation | 1.96 | 4.37 | 2.04 | 5.80 |
| Domestic/personal | — | 2.73 | 4.08 | 1.05 |
| Others | 3.92 | 1.64 | — | 4.35 |
| Total | 100 | 100 | 100 | 100 |

among those who migrated through construction firms – about 37 per cent. This channel also accounts for the highest relative share of those who returned because of job termination. Compulsory repatriation is highest among those who migrated through licensed recruiting agencies.

Comparing the reasons for returning home with the occupational groups, as shown in table 76, the professionals and semi-professionals returned because they had either completed their job contract (53 per cent) or resigned from their job (33 per cent). The incidence of job termination is highest among the semi-skilled, followed by the unskilled. There is a significant proportion of resignations in the sample, which are highest for the professional and semi-professional groups in terms of occupational categories, and for unlicensed recruiting agencies in relation to mode of recruitment. Resignations could be regarded as an indication of the dissatisfaction of the migrants with their terms and conditions of service or their living conditions. As domestic and personal reasons for return have been classified separately, it would be reasonable to conclude that the causes for resignation originated in the conditions in the host country.

**Table 77**. Distribution of migrants by time of return

| Length of time since returning home (in months) | Number of cases | Percentage of total |
|---|---|---|
| Up to 6 | 58 | 15.76 |
| 7–12 | 49 | 13.32 |
| 13–18 | 67 | 18.21 |
| 19–24 | 35 | 9.15 |
| 25–36 | 63 | 17.12 |
| 37–48 | 37 | 10.05 |
| 49 and above | 59 | 16.03 |
| Total | 368 | 100 |

Time of Return

More than half the respondents had returned home during the two years prior to the interview, 29 per cent during the twelve months prior to the interview, and another 27 per cent in the preceding 12 months. On the other hand, about a quarter of the migrants had been in the country for more than three years since their return.

**Use of Remittances**

Overall Pattern of Use of Remittances

Table 78 shows the pattern of use of remittances. Among the uses, the most common are the purchase of land, building of houses, medical treatment of family members, repayment of loans, and financial assistance to friends and relatives. The average level of expenditure on each of these major heads is quite high. For instance, for a sample of 177 returned migrants, the average level of expenditure on the purchase of land is estimated at 114,000 taka, and on the building of houses at 96,000 taka. Investment in trade and business, reported by 56 cases, is on average 111,000 taka, and purchase of vehicles, commercial or otherwise, is 106,000 taka.

The levels of expenditure on the different items vary significantly from area to area. For instance, the average level of expenditure on house-building is the highest in Dhaka City (149,000 taka) and the lowest in Noakhali (28,000 taka). Similarly, the average expenditure on the purchase of land varies between 74,000 taka in Noakhali and 177,000 taka in Dhaka City. The highest average expenditure on the purchase of vehicles is by migrants from Dhaka City (182,000 taka), and on business by migrants from Chittagong (153,000 taka). The pattern of expenditure reflects the relatively higher occupational levels of migrants from Dhaka City and the urban life-style. Dhaka City shows the highest averages for buildings, land, vehicles, and consumer durables.

Table 79 shows the use of remittances on various items by different occupational groups. For almost all items, the higher the level of skill of the migrants, the higher the level of expenditure; and among the skill groups such expenditures vary quite

Table 78. Non-consumption uses of remittances by area

| Heads of expenditure | Chittagong | | Noakhali | | Sylhet | | Dhaka | | Dhaka City | | Overall | |
|---|---|---|---|---|---|---|---|---|---|---|---|---|
| | N | Average | N | Average | N | Average | N | Average | N | Average | N | Average |
| House building | 62 | 115 | 45 | 28 | 37 | 118 | 55 | 84 | 30 | 149 | 229 | 96 |
| Purchase of land | 34 | 120 | 40 | 74 | 25 | 94 | 34 | 94 | 44 | 170 | 177 | 114 |
| Machinery and equipment | — | — | 4 | 80 | — | — | 2 | 13 | 1 | 15 | 7 | 51 |
| Vehicles | 10 | 48 | — | — | 1 | 3 | — | — | 9 | 182 | 20 | 107 |
| Consumer durables | 19 | 22 | 10 | 14 | 12 | 6 | 15 | 10 | 31 | 28 | 87 | 19 |
| Fixed (bank) deposits | 21 | 69 | 3 | 10 | 9 | 52 | 22 | 9 | 27 | 152 | 82 | 76 |
| Business | 14 | 153 | 8 | 56 | 5 | 117 | 10 | 30 | 19 | 130 | 56 | 111 |
| Insurance (premium) | 2 | 3 | — | — | 1 | 11 | 1 | 40 | 4 | 8 | 8 | 10 |
| Children's education | 44 | 12 | 26 | 4 | 36 | 13 | 37 | 10 | 19 | 15 | 162 | 11 |
| Payment of loans and liquidation of debts | 36 | 37 | 17 | 14 | 32 | 48 | 51 | 19 | 25 | 24 | 161 | 29 |
| Gifts, donations, assistance to relatives | 43 | 16 | 34 | 5 | 30 | 12 | 24 | 6 | 26 | 16 | 157 | 11 |
| Weddings | 57 | 43 | 21 | 15 | 29 | 33 | 29 | 37 | 22 | 40 | 158 | 37 |
| Medical treatment | 53 | 13 | 41 | 9 | 34 | 11 | 49 | 14 | 29 | 12 | 206 | 12 |

Table 79. Non-consumption uses of remittances by broad occupational groups (thousands of taka)

| Heads of expenditure | Professional and semi-professional | | Skilled | | Semi-skilled | | Unskilled | | Overall | |
|---|---|---|---|---|---|---|---|---|---|---|
| | N | Average | N | Average | N | Average | N | Average | N | Average |
| House building | 28 | 155 | 136 | 96 | 28 | 78 | 33 | 68 | 225 | 97 |
| Purchase of land | 23 | 175 | 96 | 112 | 23 | 78 | 20 | 52 | 173 | 113 |
| Machinery and equipment | 1 | 15 | 5 | 64 | 1 | 24 | — | — | — | — |
| Vehicles | 8 | 181 | 12 | 55 | — | — | — | — | 20 | 105 |
| Consumer durables | 26 | 29 | 43 | 16 | 10 | 16 | 6 | 9 | 85 | 20 |
| Fixed (bank) deposits | 22 | 170 | 42 | 56 | 6 | 18 | 8 | 58 | 78 | 85 |
| Business | 13 | 126 | 26 | 139 | 7 | 19 | 8 | 27 | 54 | 104 |
| Insurance (premium) | 4 | 8 | 4 | 12 | — | — | — | — | 8 | 10 |
| Children's education | 17 | 15 | 99 | 12 | 19 | 8 | 25 | 7 | 160 | 11 |
| Payment of loans and liquidation of debts | 18 | 24 | 89 | 31 | 22 | 37 | 30 | 21 | 159 | 29 |
| Gifts, donations and assistance to relatives | 28 | 16 | 90 | 12 | 15 | 7 | 21 | 6 | 154 | 11 |
| Weddings | 20 | 52 | 96 | 38 | 16 | 24 | 24 | 24 | 156 | 36 |
| Medical treatment | 26 | 13 | 117 | 13 | 24 | 9 | 34 | 10 | 201 | 12 |

274

**Table 80.** Distribution of migrants by construction/improvement of house since migration by area (percentages)

| Constructed/ improved house | Area | | | | | |
| --- | --- | --- | --- | --- | --- | --- |
| | Chittagong | Noakhali | Sylhet | Dhaka | Dhaka City | Overall |
| Yes | 78.95 | 69.70 | 46.84 | 72.60 | 45.61 | 63.25 |
| No | 21.05 | 30.30 | 53.16 | 27.40 | 54.39 | 36.75 |

significantly. For instance, the average level of expenditure on house-building is 135,000 taka for professionals and semi-professionals, whereas the corresponding figure for an unskilled migrant is 68,000 taka. The only exceptions are in the case of "gifts, donations, and assistance to relatives" and "payment of loans and liquidation of debts." For the former an unskilled migrant spent more than a professional and semi-professional – 21,000 and 16,000 taka respectively. For the latter, a semi-skilled worker spent 37,000 taka as compared to 24,000 taka by a professional and semi-professional.

Construction and Development of Houses

More than two-thirds of the migrants surveyed reported that they had constructed, or at least made improvements to, a house since they had migrated abroad. In Chittagong, for instance, 79 per cent of the migrants constructed or improved a house; the corresponding figure in Dhaka City was 46 per cent (table 80).

One reason for this low percentage with respect to migrants from Dhaka City and Sylhet might be that the construction or improvement of a house in both these places is very expensive. In Dhaka City, for instance, the price of land is extremely high, and the purchase of a piece of land alone would require a high level of savings. Similarly, in Sylhet the kind of house commonly built is very cost-intensive, and unless a migrant has been abroad for a long period he cannot afford to build one.

Purchase of Land

As noted earlier, the average level of investment on land is 114,000 taka. However, a comparison of the landholdings of the sample migrants reveals that average holdings declined after migration (table 81). For instance, the average agricultural landholding of a sample of 252 migrant households was about 0.28 acre prior to migration, but the same after migration stood at 0.25 acre, although the number of landowning households had increased to 262.

Diverse explanations may be offered for this reduction in the average size of landholding after migration. First, to finance the cost of migration several migrants had to sell a part of their agricultural land, or even homestead. At the same time, remittances exert inflationary pressure on land prices, and not all migrants are able to accumulate adequate savings to acquire new land at the higher prices. This is evident from the change in land values during the migration.[17] Second, because of the rising value of agricultural land, migrants prefer to increase the size of the homestead or acquire residential land in the village. This partly explains the fall

**Table 81.** Changes in landholding and land value (thousands of taka)

| Location/ type of land | Before migration | | | After migration | | | Relative change | |
| --- | --- | --- | --- | --- | --- | --- | --- | --- |
| | Number of cases | Average | | Number of cases | Average | | Land- holding | Value |
| | | Land- holding (acres) | Value | | Land- holding (acres) | Value | | |
| *Village* | | | | | | | | |
| Agricultural | 252 | .28 | 92.47 | 252 | .25 | 164.35 | −10.71 | 77.73 |
| Residential/ homestead | 328 | .06 | 35.09 | 330 | .08 | 72.06 | 3.33 | 105.36 |
| Commercial | 7 | .033 | 44.71 | 7 | .043 | 87.85 | 30.30 | 96.49 |
| *Town* | | | | | | | | |
| Residential | 18 | .025 | 1.51 | 46 | .067 | 237.30 | 168.00 | 57.15 |

**Table 82.** Distribution of migrants by acquisition of consumer durables

| Items of consumer durables | Number of items | | Increase | |
| | Before migration | After migration | Number | Percentage |
|---|---|---|---|---|
| Radio | 88 | 180 | 92 | 105 |
| Cassette-player | 37 | 210 | 173 | 468 |
| TV | 21 | 90 | 69 | 329 |
| VCR | 13 | 29 | 16 | 123 |
| Camera | 12 | 70 | 58 | 483 |
| Refrigerator | 8 | 37 | 29 | 363 |
| Deep freezer | 0 | 13 | 13 | — |
| Sewing machine | 12 | 47 | 35 | 292 |

in the size of the average agricultural landholding. Land used for residential/household purposes registered an increase of about 33 per cent in size and more than 100 per cent in value during migration. Finally, the migration has accelerated the formation of new households and families, and this process can lead to the division of landholdings, in which the holdings of individual members are less than that of the joint family.

One more aspect worth nating from table 81 is the fact that the number of migrants having a piece of residential land in town more than doubled during migration, as did the average size of such holdings. For instance, only 18 migrants had some residential land in town before migration, averaging about 0.025 acre; but after migration the corresponding number increased to 46 and the size of the landholding to 0.067 acre.

Consumer Durables

Another important use of remittances is the purchase of consumer durables, such as radios, televisions, cassette-recorders, etc. There are very few migrant families who do not have a radio or a cassette-player. The acquisition of consumer durables is an indicator of the improvement in the quality of life, and of changes in the home environment in regard to information, educational background, and recreation. Expenditure on these items can also become extravagant and wasteful, where ostentation, and the value of these items as status symbols, become the primary motive. On the whole, the data recorded do not reveal wasteful or excessive expenditure of this type. However, the priorities which guided household outlays appear to have neglected essential areas such as farm equipment, as noted below.

Table 82 demonstrates that the most common consumer durables acquired by migrants during their stay abroad are radios, cassette-players, televisions, and cameras.

Machinery and Farm Equipment

The information in table 83 shows that there has been little change in the capital stock of farm and related equipment owned by the migrant families as a result of the migration. Some changes have been observed in terms of irrigation pump and paddy thresher. There has also been some improvement in the number of motor-

**Table 83.** Distribution of machinery and farm equipment owned by the migrant before and after migration

| Machinery and equipment | Number of Items | | Change in number during migration |
|---|---|---|---|
| | Before migration | After migration | |
| Plough | 197 | 199 | 2 |
| Irrigation pumps | 4 | 10 | 6 |
| Power tiller | 1 | 2 | 1 |
| Paddy thresher | 4 | 10 | 6 |
| Tractor | 2 | 1 | −1 |
| Truck | 2 | 4 | 2 |
| Van | 4 | 1 | −3 |
| Motor-cycle Rickshaw | 7 | 11 | 4 |

cycles owned by these families. In the case of tractor and van, the changes have been negative.

A comparison of the data for the different areas reveals that the stock of farm equipment and machinery increased significantly in Chittagong. Here most of the items listed in table 83 registered some improvement after migration. The area alone acquired 5 irrigation pumps after migration compared to none previously, 1 power tiller and 5 paddy threshers. The worst situation is in Sylhet. Here the changes are mostly negative. The only items which experienced some positive change are motor-cycles and rickshaws, from none before to one of each after migration. According to the data in the table, 33 households have invested only 357,000 taka on these items, whereas they have been ready to invest 1,653,000 taka on consumer durables. Choices regarding expenditure and investment would of course have been guided by various considerations – the opportunities for a given type of investment, the scale of the outlay involved as between consumer durables and farm equipment and other related aspects. Nevertheless, it is difficult to avoid the conclusion that in the choice of investment and expenditure, the need to acquire income-earning assets or increase the stock of productive capital does not appear to have been a compelling motivation.

**Post-migration Occupational Status**

Post-migration Employment Status

The process of migration seems to have serious employment implications for the returned migrants. The overall employment situation deteriorated in the post-migration period. Many of those who were employed previously have now become unemployed. For instance, only 7 per cent of the respondents were unemployed prior to migration, but after migration the figure has gone up to 43 per cent. The relative share of self-employed has come down to 34 per cent after migration compared to 42 per cent previously (table 84).

There are wide differences in the employment status of the returned migrants in

**Table 84.** Employment status before and after migration (percentages)

| Nature of employment | Area | | | | | |
|---|---|---|---|---|---|---|
| | Chittagong | Noakhali | Sylhet | Dhaka | Dhaka City | Overall |
| Fully employed | | | | | | |
| Before | 32.50 | 27.14 | 18.07 | 47.30 | 68.85 | 32.23 |
| After | 3.75 | 2.86 | 8.43 | 5.41 | 37.71 | 10.06 |
| Casually employed | | | | | | |
| Before | 6.25 | 25.71 | 8.43 | 4.05 | — | 8.96 |
| After | 8.75 | 17.14 | 21.69 | 6.76 | 1.64 | 11.68 |
| Self-employed | | | | | | |
| Before | 46.25 | 41.43 | 61.45 | 32.43 | 21.31 | 41.85 |
| After | 50.00 | 50.00 | 28.92 | 19.92 | 21.31 | 34.24 |
| Unemployed | | | | | | |
| Before | 7.50 | 4.29 | 3.61 | 13.51 | 8.20 | 7.34 |
| After | 36.25 | 27.14 | 38.55 | 67.57 | 39.34 | 41.85 |
| Student/others | | | | | | |
| Before | 7.50 | 1.43 | 8.43 | 2.70 | 1.64 | 4.62 |
| After | 1.25 | 2.86 | 2.41 | 1.35 | — | 1.63 |
| Number of cases | 80 | 70 | 83 | 74 | 60 | 368 |

the different areas. In Noakhali, for instance, 53 per cent of the respondents were employed prior to migration (inclusive of the casually employed), but the figure has come down to 20 per cent. However, after migration the share of self-employment increased from 41 to 50 per cent. In the face of limited employment opportunities, the returned migrants have occupied themselves with their family business, e.g. farming, trade, etc. The only difference between the currently self-employed and the unemployed is that the former are financially better off than the latter.

The underlying reasons for this high level of post-migration unemployment are many. Many of those who had been employed previously resigned from their jobs before they went abroad. But on their return they were confronted with the difficult job situation in the country. Moreover, many of them would have been reluctant to accept the available jobs given the level of remuneration attached to them. It takes time for them, used as they are to a high income abroad, to accept the realities of the job market at home. Finally, indecision on the part of the returned migrants may also play an important role in their current employment situation. Most of those who were interviewed were interested in independent trade and business, and were, therefore, reluctant to get paid employment.[18] A sense of pride and independence, together with the low wage levels, may underlie such a choice.

Post-migration Level of Income

The low participation of the returned migrants in the labour force seems to have an adverse impact upon their post-migration level of income. As table 85 shows, the average monthly income from salary of a sample of 128 returned migrants has been estimated at 1,800 taka, as against 2,400 taka previously (based on 152 cases) – a net decline of about 25 per cent. Among the other components of income, both

**Table 85**.  Levels of family income from various sources before and after migration

| | Number of cases | | Average monthly income (taka) | |
| --- | --- | --- | --- | --- |
| Source of income | Before migration | After migration | Before migration | After migration |
| Foreign remittances | 25 | 63 | 12,720 | 9,570 |
| Salary/wages | 152 | 128 | 2,370 | 1,770 |
| Rent | 7 | 17 | 2,929 | 906 |
| Interest | 2 | 20 | 2,300 | 1,240 |

rent and interest income too have registered a significant fall; rent income declined by 69 per cent, and interest income by 46 per cent. The remittance incomes of the families with members still abroad have also registered a decline, though the number of "families receiving remittances" has increased significantly.

## Changes in Consumption and Attitudes

Changes in Consumption and Expenditure[19]

Given the four different groups of items, as listed in table 86, the migrants were asked to compare their current level of consumption/expenditure with their previous level. The answers were in the form of "less," "same," "higher," and "much higher." In the case of the selected food items, the post-migration level of consumption is higher for about 60 per cent of the cases. With respect to meat and fish the level of consumption and expenditure is higher in 67 per cent of cases. The situation is similar in regard to expenditure on clothing and footwear. Among the "Others," the items which registered significant positive changes are medical treatment and children's education.

These responses regarding higher levels of consumption among the majority of households do not seem consistent with the data that point to reduction in incomes. The discrepancy may rise both from the fact that the income data cover a much smaller sample, and also from the tendency to understate incomes or to provide vague and unreliable estimates of items of income which are non-cash and for which respondents have to depend on recall.

Changes in Attitude

*Attitude towards Religion*

For the majority of the returned migrants, the attitude towards religion has remained unchanged, and more than a third of the migrants are now more conscious of religion than before.

*Attitude towards Politics*

With regard to the migrants' enhanced interest in politics, local or national, migration seems to have had some positive impact. For all the areas taken together, migrants (and families) are now more interested in politics than before, and a large number of them are actively involved.

**Table 86.** Changes in consumption/expenditure on selected items (percentages)

| Consumption/ expenditure items | Present level compared to pre-migration | | | |
|---|---|---|---|---|
| | Less | Same | Higher | Much higher |
| *Selected food items*[a] | (15.65) | (24.69) | (54.23) | (5.42) |
| Meat/fish | 13.97 | 18.90 | 60.55 | 6.55 |
| Dairy products | 17.26 | 28.77 | 49.32 | 4.66 |
| Tea | 15.73 | 26.40 | 52.81 | 5.06 |
| *Clothing and footwear* | 12.07 | 22.90 | 59.20 | 6.03 |
| *Amusement/recreation* | (22.50) | (32.97) | (41.02) | (3.51) |
| Smoking | 18.37 | 26.20 | 50.90 | 4.52 |
| Newspaper | 19.32 | 36.87 | 39.17 | 4.15 |
| Cinema | 26.07 | 33.46 | 38.13 | 2.33 |
| Travelling | 18.57 | 31.60 | 45.93 | 3.91 |
| Holiday | 29.65 | 36.73 | 30.97 | 2.65 |
| *Others* | (13.91) | (26.72) | (59.87) | (4.53) |
| Rent | 21.48 | 28.86 | 44.30 | 5.37 |
| Donations | 15.83 | 28.78 | 52.16 | 3.24 |
| Medical treatment | 9.35 | 23.80 | 62.61 | 4.30 |
| Education | 8.96 | 25.43 | 60.40 | 5.20 |

a. Items within parentheses refer to the simple average of the component items.

# Conclusion

## Some Macro-economic Implications and Policy Options

The study presented in this chapter investigated the impact of the migration through an intensive survey of a sample of households. It has not attempted to examine the impact at the macro-economic level on such factors as the balance of payments, employment, savings, and investment. It is, however, important to place the data analysed in the macro-economic context when evaluating the socio-economic effects of the migration at the household level. The household data gathered in the survey provide some clues about the proliferation of economic activities that has occurred as a result of the migration and the remittance flows. The displacement of employment opportunities in the event of a large-scale con-traction of employment abroad could be quite extensive.

In 1983, Bangladesh earned a total of 15.7 billion taka from overseas remittances. Of this, the contribution of those working in the Middle East was 12.2 billion taka, i.e. 78 per cent of the total.[20] In the context of Bangladesh, the foreign exchange earned from overseas remittances is used mostly to finance imports under the Bangladesh Wage Earners' Scheme (WES).[21] Between 1977/78 and 1981/82, more than three-quarters of the remittances were used to finance imports under the scheme. Imports under WES were equivalent to about one-tenth of the total imports of the country, and one-quarter of the imports paid for in cash over the same period.

**Table 87.** Distribution of migrants by level of religious consciousness after migration

| Consciousness of religion | Number of cases | Percentage of total |
|---|---|---|
| More | 131 | 35.60 |
| Same | 226 | 61.41 |
| Less | 11 | 2.99 |
| Total | 368 | 100 |

These comprise mostly consumption goods, and raw materials and spare parts for industries producing consumption goods. About a quarter of such imports are capital goods or raw materials for the capital goods industries.

Mass repatriation would result in a massive reduction of the country's foreign exchange earnings. Out of the total foreign exchange receipts of 34,973 million taka in 1983/84 (remittances plus export receipts), for instance, remittances alone accounted for about 42 per cent (14,838 million taka). Between 1980/81 and 1983/84, remittances were equivalent to about 70 per cent of the export earnings; and a mass return migration would imply a reduction in the country's foreign exchange earnings of about 40 per cent.

On the basis of first-hand experience during the field survey, an attempt is made here to identify the areas or sectors that experienced increased job opportunities.[22]

## Job Opportunities in Rural Areas

### Construction

As noted earlier, a substantial proportion of overseas remittances are used by migrant households for the construction and improvement of houses. In all the areas surveyed, construction appears to be the fastest-growing sector. As such, there has been a growing demand for the necessary workforce – unskilled construction workers, bricklayers, carpenters, plumbers, and electricians. Wherever there is a concentration of migrant households, construction activities are thriving. Even in places where migration is a recent phenomenon, the available local supply of labour is unable to cope with the increased demand. This is likely to encourage the migration of different skills from other areas, either from within the same district or from other districts.

### Agriculture

Although a large part of overseas remittances is used to purchase land, there has been little change as regards agricultural activities and the overall employment situation in the sector. However, some changes were quite visible. Employment in agricultural activities shows some decline. Members of migrant households are now less inclined to become directly involved in agricultural activities. The inflow of remittances seems to have changed their attitude towards agriculture, resulting in the search for non-agricultural employment and in the diversification of economic activities.

**Table 88.** Distribution of migrants by interest in politics

| Interest in politics | Number of cases | | Percentage change during migration |
| | Before migration | After migration | |
| --- | --- | --- | --- |
| Not at all | 235 | 238 | 1.28 |
| Little | 22 | 13 | − 40.91 |
| Active | 7 | 10 | 42.86 |

## Services

This includes the services of domestic servants, farm workers, shopkeepers, electricians, and plumbers. In migrant areas demand for domestic servants, both male and female, has increased significantly. The greater the concentration of migrant households, the greater the demand for such services.

Increased job opportunities were also observed for shop workers. The concentration of a large number of migrant households has led to the growth of market-places. There are different types of shops catering to the needs of the migrant households: tea stalls, barber shops, grocers, and in some places jewellery shops, department stores, chemists, bookshops, etc. Most of those who work in these shops are salaried, and they too may come from different districts.

## Manufacturing

The impact is as yet limited, but seems to be growing. This includes small manufacturing activities such as bakeries, furniture-makers, potteries, sawmills, brick-works, rice mills, flour mills, jewellers, etc. These activities flourish more in areas where there is a large concentration of migrant workers, and where the process of migration has been going on for a long time. The owners of these enterprises are mostly migrant households, and in some cases returned migrants themselves. Among the activities listed above, brick manufacturing is very common and provides job opportunities to the local people, as does timber processing in sawmills. In some cases such activities were already there prior to migration, but the inflow of remittances has provided a further stimulus, either by providing the necessary capital input or through increased demand, or both.

## Transport and Communication

Increased demand for transportation to and from nearby town and city centres has been responsible for the growth of the transport network, and the related employment opportunities. The increased mobility of the migrants and their family members has a great impact on the growth of these services.

## Social Infrastructure

This includes bridges, power projects, schools, colleges, madrashas, mosques, orphanages, etc. Donations from migrants and their families have financed the construction of roads and bridges in areas where there is a concentration of migrant households. The resources that have been generated through the migration have also gone to support schools, colleges, and religious institutions.

## Job Opportunities in Urban Areas

Since the pattern of use of remittances by urban migrant households is similar to that in rural areas, the resulting impact on employment will also be similar, varying, if at all, only in degree. In addition, the whole process of migration has promoted the growth of other employment opportunities specific to urban areas, for example recruiting agencies, travel agents, hotels and restaurants, banking facilities, housing societies, health clinics, and transportation enterprises. Overseas remittances have also led to a rapid growth in the country's communication network.

### Travel agents

The number of travel agents providing travel facilities has increased significantly along with the process of migration. This includes both registered and unregistered travel agents scattered all over the country, but mostly in cities like Dhaka, Chittagong, and Sylhet. For instance, in 1977 there were about 50 travel agents in Bangladesh, but by 1983 their number had increased to 400 (Siddiqui, 1983). This rapid growth implies that the corresponding employment opportunities too have increased.

### Air Transport

With an increased flow of nationals going and coming from abroad, the load on passenger carriers has increased many times in a few years. With this, the services of different carriers in Bangladesh have also increased, as has the number of people employed. For instance, the number of outbound (international) passengers increased from 144,525 in 1978 to 285,654 in 1982. In the case of Bangladesh Biman (the national flag-carrier), the number of employees increased by about 25 per cent between 1978/79 and 1982/83, from 3,649 to 4,560.

### Hotels

To accommodate passengers going to and coming from abroad, and also those trying to go abroad, together with their dependents, the number of hotels in major cities such as Dhaka, Chittagong, and Sylhet has also increased. In the case of Dhaka, the number of such hotels, big and small, increased from 12 in 1975 to 79 in 1982. There are similar developments in other major cities. Manning these hotels provides job opportunities for different skills.

### Health Clinics

Since the passengers bound for foreign jobs are required to undergo detailed medical examination, the facilities for such health examinations, such as X-rays, pathological tests, etc., have expanded quite significantly. For example, in 1978, there were about 36 private clinics or hospitals in Bangladesh, but by 1983 the number had increased to 164 – a fivefold increase within five years. If the number of small institutions/laboratories carrying out all different pathological tests are included, the total number of such institutions in the private sector alone is even larger. These employ doctors, nurses, clinical assistants, midwives, and the like.

## Banking Facilities

This is another area which has received a tremendous impetus from the inflow of remittances. Local banks have expanded their services, even in remote areas, where there is a concentration of migrant workers. They maintain deposits from overseas remittances and facilitate their use and transfer. In addition to the normal banking facilities, local banks and even subsidiaries of foreign banks provide facilities to the migrant households. Bangladeshi nationals abroad can and do maintain foreign currency accounts with these banks. Even as early as 1981, the number of such foreign currency accounts with the nationalized banks alone was 145,047 (Siddiqui, 1983). Banks also provide services to the migrants or their nominees concerned with the import of goods from abroad under the Wage Earners' Scheme.

Besides the above list of activities relating to the flow and use of remittances, various other activities have also emerged. There are small institutions providing secretarial facilities to the migrants – typing, translation, and photocopying. Then there are the recruiting agencies mediating job opportunities abroad. There were about 38 such firms in 1976, increasing to 398 in 1982. Also important are the institutions providing potential migrants with technical training in various skills that are in demand abroad, such as driving, catering, lift operation, welding, pipe-fitting, electrical work, plumbing, etc. According to a survey carried out by the Bangladesh Bureau of Manpower, Employment and Training (BMET),[23] there were about 31 such training institutes in the private sector in 1979.

There are other indirect ways in which international migration has created job opportunities. A sizeable proportion of overseas remittances are currently used for the modernization and development of existing industries, the development of new industrial complexes, and the provision to existing as well as new industries of the necessary raw materials and spares. This will increase the level of output and employment in the respective industries. It is widely believed that foreign remittances have been a boon to many of the industries in the private sector.

The migration and its manifold linkages have therefore become a vital part of the economy. A drastic reduction in employment in the Middle East and the consequent drop in remittance flows could result in a severe shock to which the economy would find it difficult to adjust. However, the available policy options are limited. Bangladesh cannot afford to reduce its dependence on the migration flow while it lasts. Policies have to be directed at maximizing the long-term benefits of the migration and directing its income flows to savings investment and growth, so that, increasingly, the resources obtained through the migration expand the production base and stimulate self-generating growth within the Bangladesh economy.

The survey data indicate that in the sample the average total net transfer of income to families at home was approximately 303,000 taka, at a monthly rate of about 9,000 taka over a period of nearly three years. The pattern of non-consumption expenditure indicates that as yet the priority given to production investment and the creation of income-earning assets is quite low.

Since mass return migration will involve an immediate drying up of the foreign exchange from overseas remittances, the present use of remittances should be such that the economy can easily adjust to a sudden loss in such earnings. The present use of remittances should have minimum linkages for the future. For instance, if remittances are used to finance imports that will permanently affect the present pattern of consumption, the demand for such goods will persist even in the absence of remittances, and the government may need to reallocate foreign exchange from other sources to allow for such imports. Such a use of remittances will create a perpetual dependence on imports. On the other hand, if remittances are used to finance capital imports, a sudden discontinuation of the same will curtail the flow of capital goods into the economy, and few linkages will be involved in future.

A greater use of remittances for capital investment based on indigenous technical know-how and raw materials is desirable in order or generate additional employment opportunities to absorb the return migrants. It has been observed in the present study that a majority of the migrants find it difficult to get suitable employment on their return. If opportunities could be created for the migrants to invest their overseas savings more productively, this would provide the return migrants with a means of making a living, thus reducing possible pressure on the job market. The greater the level of such investments, given the rate of return, the higher would be the level of income.

In order to encourage nationals working abroad to invest a greater proportion of their overseas savings in productive sectors, an awareness should be generated among them of the existing opportunities for investment. Moreover, new investment opportunities should be created. At the same time, the use of remittances for non-productive purposes should be discouraged.

To make social readjustment easier for the returning migrants, efforts should be made to enable them, during the tenure of their employment abroad, to maintain better contacts with the society and family back home. Correspondence to and from home should be more frequent. Bangladesh embassies abroad should keep the migrants informed about socio-economic conditions back home, and about the problems that they may encounter when they return. The families left behind could be provided with moral support to help them cope with problems during the absence of the migrant. Following the experience of the Republic of Korea, for instance, migrant family groups could be organized so that the families can support each other in overcoming adjustment problems.

While the demand for expatriate workers in the Middle East is expected to continue for a long time in the future, the possibility of a mass return of Bangladeshis working there may arise in the event of a shift in the socio-political environment in the labour-importing countries. The government should, therefore, constantly monitor the changes that take place in the Middle East in general, and in the major Bangladeshi labour-importing countries in particular. Such a responsibility could be vested upon Bangladesh embassies in the respective countries. They should further see that the nationals working in these countries do not indulge in activities that are against the interests of the community as a whole. Recent experience in the Middle East suggests that the labour-importing countries are very strict about the involvement of expatriate workers in subversive socio-political activities. Any such incidence would initiate mass expulsion of the respective nationals, or a complete ban on further recruitment.

As a precaution against the lack of job opportunities and of means of earning a living, it could be made mandatory that nationals working abroad save a certain percentage of their overseas income with the government on a long-term basis. The return on such savings should be comparable to alternative investment opportunities available in the country. The accumulated savings would be returned to the migrants with due interest on their return home. The government could also sell or allocate houses, flats, land, industrial shares, savings bonds, and other return-bearing assets to the migrants against these savings.

Systematic and co-ordinated efforts have to be made to provide migrants with ready opportunities for small productive investments and self-employment, and to make available to them the required information and know-how. The development banking system would have to be strengthened for this purpose, and a set of initiatives, specially directed at achieving these objectives, would have to be developed. The state would need to play a leading role in such an effort.

## Notes

1. According to a study carried out by Hossain (1984), about 40 per cent of the Bangladeshis migrating to the Middle East had an initial tenure of contract for one year, and another 57 per cent for between one and two years. In other words, for more than 96 per cent of the migrants the initial contract in the Middle East was for two years at most.
2. Apart from the proven skill and efficiency of the individual migrants, the possibility of further renewal of job contract in the Middle East will depend on the nature of the firm/establishment in which the nationals are employed. If they are working for an enterprise that will be in operation only for a short period of time, for example foreign construction firms, further renewal of job contracts is likely only up to the point when the project is completed. If, however, such firms get further contracts for similar projects, there will be a need for workers, and some or all of the old staff may be retained. In the case of established and permanent organizations such as hotels, restaurants, municipalities, and government or private offices, the chances of renewing job contracts seem to be better.
3. For further details see Mahmood (1984) and Plender (1972).
4. Nobabganj is henceforth called Dhaka.
5. In the case of countries such as Sri Lanka and the Philippines, for instance, a large proportion of their nationals working in the Middle East are females.
6. A sizeable proportion of Bangladeshi females working in the Middle Eastern countries, especially among those who have migrated in recent years and are doing menial jobs, are believed to have migrated either through illegal channels or in the guise of housewives. According to reports in the press, there is an organized group of people who are involved in smuggling Bangladeshi females to the Middle Eastern countries via land routes through India and Pakistan.
7. For the remaining 35 cases, either all the costs were paid for by the employer or the information available was too unrealistic to be accepted.
8. The individual countries vary significantly in terms of the number and skill composition of Bangladeshis working there. Any comparison of such countries with respect to the cost of migration should accordingly be made with great caution.
9. In one instance the cost incurred for NOC/visa was reported to be 90,000 taka. This could, however, be due to payments made more than once, in which the migrant was first a victim of fraud, losing his money, before finally succeeding in obtaining his papers.
10. The present study is based on those who had the opportunity to migrate to the Middle East. Therefore, even if they had ever been victims of fraud prior to migration, this did not stop them from going abroad. However, there are cases not covered in this report where

aspirants' hopes and desires were completely shattered through fraud or breach of contact: cases were reported of individuals becoming paupers in their attempt to migrate abroad.

11. The long periods of waiting could be due to those who migrated on so-called Free Visas. Under such an arrangement a migrant goes abroad on the pretext of being a prospective employee of a firm which may not exist at all. On arrival in the host country, therefore, he will start looking for a suitable job, and this may take quite some time.

12. There are certain problems in interpreting income on the basis of the country of migration, as different countries vary in terms of the skill composition of the nationals working there. It is therefore inappropriate to compare the average income levels in different countries without taking into account the skill composition of migrants.

13. The average cost incurred per month could be even lower than 1,000 taka. In the case of those who were provided with food and lodging free of cost by the employer, the other incidental expenses would have been minimal. In the Middle East most food items are highly subsidized, as also are electricity, gas, transportation, etc.

14. It would appear that Bangladeshi migrants in general did not develop the banking habit during their stay in the host country. Language problems and the non-availability of banks in the neighbourhood induce most of the migrants to keep their savings in cash. Once they have accumulated a certain amount of savings, they immediately send it home. Even among the professionals and semi-professionals, the habit of maintaining bank accounts is very rare, except for those who have been living abroad for quite some time. In some cases the latter people will also maintain bank accounts in countries such as the UK and USA and transfer their savings to those accounts.

15. The cassette may be addressed to a number of people, and could be heard collectively or by the respective persons separately. A taped conversation may be quite embarrassing at times. For instance, a message to parents or brothers may be followed by the expression of very personal feelings to the wife. In any case, the recorded messages create occasions for new types of interaction within the family, as they listen to these messages collectively.

16. In the case of migrants from Noakhali, the large number of resignations was mainly due to the fact that most of them were employed by national construction firms working in the Middle East. On arrival in the host countries, most were required to sign a second contract, with terms and conditions worse than those in the contract they had signed before migration. Consequently, these migrants opted to resign and return home. During the field survey many of them complained about their poor level of remuneration and job conditions. The situation was completely different for migrants from Dhaka City. Many of these professionals and semi-professionals were on secondment from the government service for a fixed period of time, at the end of which they had to return to resume their earlier duties. They, therefore, resigned from their jobs abroad and returned home.

17. The value of houses noted in the text is based on the presumed market value for comparable houses. It is possible that the respondents have overestimated the actual value of their houses.

18. Migrants who have labelled themselves as self-employed may not in fact be much different from those who consider themselves unemployed. The only difference might be that the former are not very keen, at least for the time being, to obtain wage employment, as they either have some savings or can afford to depend on their family for their livelihood. In the meantime, they will be exploring the possibility of suitable employment opportunities, or even getting further employment abroad.

19. Collecting information on the family consumption budget poses numerous problems, owing to the very detailed and diverse nature of the information required. It is quite difficult for a migrant to recollect the expenditures incurred on the various items. The details of consumption expenditures were, therefore, avoided.

20. It should be noted here that a part of the non-Middle Eastern remittances is actually the

savings of nationals working in the Middle East, many of whom maintain bank accounts in Western countries, especially the UK. These savings are later transferred to Bangladesh under the name of the country where the bank account is maintained. If such transfers could be identified and added to remittances from the Middle East, its respective share would increase significantly.

21. Under the Bangladesh Wage Earners' Scheme (WES), nationals working abroad are allowed to sell their foreign exchange earnings in the market. They are also allowed to maintain foreign currency accounts. The foreign exchange thus accumulated can be sold in the market or can be used to import certain goods allowable under the scheme. The demand for and supply of foreign exchange (derived from import demands and other international payments) will decide the exchange rate prevailing in the market. Such a rate is normally higher than the official rate of exchange.

22. The following analysis has been adapted from Mahmood (1985). It should be pointed out here that whatever developments have taken place in these individual sectors may not all be related to the process of migration and the use of remittances; the overall development of the economy could also have made a contribution. Nevertheless, migration is assumed to have had the greatest influence on the growth of the various activities mentioned below.

23. For further details, see Siddiqui (1983).

# References

Antonion, J. 1978. Construction in the Middle East. Special Report no. 55. Economist Intelligence Unit, London.

Birks, J.S., and C.A. Sinclair. 1979. *The Kingdom of Saudi Arabia and the Libyan Arab Jamahiriya: The Key Countries of Employment*. ILO, Geneva.

——. 1980. *International Migration and Development in the Arab Region*. ILO, Geneva.

Hossain, A.R.M. Anwar. 1984. *Remittances from International Labour Migration: A Case Study of Bangladesh*. Bangladesh Manpower Centre, Dhaka.

Mahmood, R.A. 1984. Implications of International Movements of Labour for Trade and Development, with Particular Reference to Bangladesh. Ph.D. thesis. University of Sussex, Brighton.

——. 1985. International Migration and the Domestic Economy. Bangladesh: Selected Issues in Employment and Development: A Report Prepared for the Bangladesh Planning Commission. ILO/ARTEP, Bangkok.

Plender, R. 1972. *International Migration Law*. Law and Population Series, no. 2. Sijthoff, Leiden.

Shaw, R.P. 1979. Migration and Development in the Arab World: Construction as a Key Policy Variable. *International Labour Review*, 118 (5).

Siddiqui, A.M.A.H. 1983. Economic and Non-economic Impact of Migration from Bangladesh: An Overview. Paper presented to the East–West Population Institute Conference on Asian Labour Migration to the Middle East, East–West Centre, Honolulu, 19–23 September.

# 7

# SRI LANKA

**Godfrey Gunatilleke**

Marga Institute, Colombo, Sri Lanka

## Introduction

The outmigration of Sri Lankans for employment in the Arab world began around 1975 and increased rapidly, reaching an annual gross inflow of approximately 65,000 during the period 1982–1984. The migration thereafter levelled off, and, with the return of migrants after the completion of their contracts, the net outflow has tended to decline. The adjustments made by the Middle East economies to the fall in their oil revenues and consequent contraction of the demand for foreign labour has had its impact on the Sri Lankan migration, but owing to its special characteristics – the relatively small size of the flow and the type of labour supplied – Sri Lanka has not been affected as adversely as many other Asian countries.

The present migration to the Middle East has very distinctive characteristics which are quite different from those of earlier outflows. In contrast to the earlier migration of professionals and highly skilled personnel, the predominant majority of the migrants to the Middle East are manual workers, most of them in semi-skilled or unskilled grades. Another significant feature is that females outnumber males in the total flow of migrants. The majority are from low-income families to whom the remuneration in the host country is quite attractive, although they are the poorest paid of all migrant employees from all countries. Finally, migration to the Arab World is on contracts of employment for a limited period of time and is therefore temporary in character. The migrants travel alone and are separated from their families during their employment abroad.

The present study has been undertaken to investigate in detail the different phases of the migration process with specific reference to the problems of return migrants. It therefore concentrates on (a) the pre-migration phase, with the objective of assessing the socio-economic status of the migrant prior to departure; (b) the migration phase, for an examination of the conditions of the migrant and the household during this phase at both locations; and (c) the post-migration phase, to evaluate the return and re-entry of the migrant into the workforce.

The field survey for the study was based on a sample of 500 migrants who had

**Table 1**. Sample according to age and sex

| Age-group | Male | Female | Total |
|-----------|------|--------|-------|
| 15–19 | 0 | 6 | 6 |
| 20–24 | 9 | 37 | 46 |
| 25–29 | 37 | 68 | 105 |
| 30–34 | 69 | 88 | 157 |
| 35–39 | 38 | 67 | 105 |
| 40–44 | 21 | 31 | 52 |
| 45–49 | 11 | 14 | 25 |
| 50–54 | 7 | 4 | 11 |
| 55–59 | 1 | 2 | 3 |
| Total | 193 | 317 | 510 |

returned after employment in the Arab countries. In order to obtain a representative sample, the Marga Institute first attempted to identify a minimum population of 5,000 such migrants, as there was no readily available and reliable source of information in any of the government or private agencies dealing with the migration that would enable the Institute to construct the required sample frame. The Institute compiled a list of 5,144 migrants in ten districts, through personal visits and identification. In this initial phase, besides the names and addresses, the returnee's occupation and country, sex, race, and date of return were gathered. The main characteristics of the population so identified – the age and sex composition, the distribution according to district, host country, and skill level – corresponded closely to those identified for the migration as a whole in recent studies. The coverage of districts presented some problems. It was not possible to include those in the northern and eastern provinces owing to the unsettled conditions there. However, the proportions of migrants from these areas are quite small, approximately 5 per cent of the total. The final sample of 500 interviewees was selected from the group of 5,144 migrants. A stratified multi-stage, random sampling technique was adopted, taking into account location, sex, ethnic group, and skills.

## Profile of Migrants

### Age and Gender

Table 1 indicates the distribution of returnees by age and gender. The respondents in the sample fall into a wide age spectrum ranging from 15 to 59 years. The youngest returnee interviewed was 17 and the oldest 55. The 25–39 age-group amounted to 72 per cent of the total sample. The overwhelming majority of the female migrants were in the reproductive age-group of 15–45 years. The sex distribution reflects the proportion in the total sample population. The majority, 62 per cent, are females. This corresponds to the proportions which have been reported for the migration as a whole.

**Table 2.** Ethnic groups by gender

| Ethnic group | Male | Female | Total |
|---|---|---|---|
| Sinhalese | 128 | 243 | 371 |
| Tamil | 8 | 5 | 13 |
| Moor | 42 | 45 | 87 |
| Malay | 12 | 22 | 34 |
| Burgher | 2 | 2 | 4 |
| Indian Tamil | 1 | 0 | 1 |
| Total | 193 | 317 | 510 |

### Ethnicity

Table 2 reflects the sample according to ethnic groups and gender. It is apparent that the percentage of Tamils in the sample is much less than their share in the total population of the country. As stated earlier, this is due to the non-coverage of the northern and eastern districts in the survey for security reasons. On the other hand, Moors, along with Malays, account for 23.73 per cent of the sample. This situation can be probably explained by the fact that migrants who adhere to the Islamic faith are given preference by the Arab countries.

### Occupation

Table 3 gives the ethnic composition of the skill levels. The proportion in the different levels has, of course, been predetermined by the sampling method and corresponds to the national proportions, the high and middle level comprising 4.1 per cent, the skilled 21, and the unskilled 74 per cent. Nevertheless, some inference can be drawn about skill distribution according to ethnic group. The sample for the high-level category being quite small, it is difficult to make any significant observations on it. When the high level and middle level are taken together, the Moors have a somewhat larger proportion (5.7 per cent) than the Sinhalese (3.5 per cent). In the skilled category the proportion in the Sinhalese ethnic group is higher (22.1 per cent) than that of the Moors (18.3 per cent).

### Religion

Distribution of the sample according to religion and gender is given in table 4. For reasons mentioned earlier the Hindus make up only 1.18 per cent and are under-represented. The proportion of Muslims is considerably higher than the national proportion, probably for the reasons mentioned in the observation on the ethnic distribution.

### Marital Status

At time of migration nearly 32 per cent of the total sample were single and 66 per cent married. The other three categories were quite low, with 0.4 per cent divorced, 1.2 per cent separated, and 1.0 per cent widowed. Only a small change in

**Table 3.** Occupation category by ethnic group

| Category | Sinhalese | Tamil | Moor | Malay | Burgher | Others | Total |
|---|---|---|---|---|---|---|---|
| High-level | 4 | — | 2 | — | — | — | 6 |
| Middle-level | 9 | — | 3 | 3 | — | — | 15 |
| Skilled | 82 | 3 | 16 | 5 | 2 | — | 108 |
| Unskilled | 276 | 10 | 66 | 26 | 2 | 1 | 381 |
| Total | 371 | 13 | 87 | 34 | 4 | 1 | 510 |

**Table 4.** Religion by gender

| Religious group | Male | Female | Total |
|---|---|---|---|
| Buddhist | 112 | 220 | 332 |
| Hindu | 4 | 2 | 6 |
| Muslim | 55 | 65 | 120 |
| Roman Catholic | 19 | 21 | 40 |
| Other Christians | 3 | 9 | 12 |
| Total | 193 | 317 | 510 |

**Table 5.** Marital status by gender

| | Single | | Married | | Divorced | | Widowed | | Separated | | Total | |
|---|---|---|---|---|---|---|---|---|---|---|---|---|
| | 1[a] | 2 | 1 | 2 | 1 | 2 | 1 | 2 | 1 | 2 | 1 | 2 |
| Male | 82 | 61 | 111 | 131 | 0 | 1 | 0 | 0 | 0 | 0 | 193 | 193 |
| Female | 78 | 57 | 226 | 243 | 2 | 2 | 5 | 8 | 6 | 7 | 317 | 317 |
| Total | 160 | 118 | 337 | 374 | 2 | 3 | 5 | 8 | 6 | 7 | 510 | 510 |

a. 1 = Before migration; 2 = At time of survey.

marital status is recorded since return. At present, 73 per cent of the total number of returnees interviewed were married, an 11 per cent increase. The number divorced and separated shows only a marginal increase in the new situation, indicating some stability in regard to family and marital relations.

Marital status by sex is given in table 5. The proportion of female migrants who were married at the time of migration was larger than that of males – 71 compared with 57 per cent. A little less than half of the married migrants were below 35. The families without mothers, as well as the very young families, would have been specially vulnerable components among the households who participated in the migration.

**Level of Education**

Table 6 shows the educational status of the migrants by gender. Of the sample, 23.33 per cent have not progressed beyond the primary level while 74.12 per cent

**Table 6.** Level of education by gender

| | At time of migration | | | At present | | | |
|---|---|---|---|---|---|---|---|
| | Male | Female | Total | Male | Female | Total | Percentage |
| Illiterate | 0 | 9 | 9 | 0 | 8 | 8 | 1.5 |
| Primary | 20 | 99 | 119 | 20 | 99 | 119 | 23.3 |
| Secondary | 169 | 209 | 378 | 169 | 210 | 379 | 74.3 |
| University | 4 | 0 | 4 | 4 | 0 | 4 | 0.7 |
| Total | 193 | 317 | 510 | 193 | 317 | 510 | 100 |

**Table 7.** Position in the household by gender

| | Before migration | | | After return | | |
|---|---|---|---|---|---|---|
| Position | M | F | T | M | F | T |
| Head of the household | 76 | 10 | 86 | 86 | 12 | 98 |
| Head of the family | 16 | 4 | 20 | 17 | 4 | 21 |
| Income-earning member | 65 | 49 | 114 | 43 | 36 | 79 |
| Dependants | 36 | 254 | 290 | 63 | 250 | 313 |
| Total | 193 | 317 | 510 | 193 | 317 | 510 |

have reached the secondary level. The majority of the migrants had had between six and ten years of schooling. A noteworthy feature is that only 1.56 per cent of the total sample is classified as illiterate, while 100 per cent of the males and 97.16 per cent of the females are literate. At the other extreme, only 0.78 per cent of the males, and none of the females, record a university-level attainment. In the sample, males are generally of a higher educational level than the females, with 89.64 per cent of males having progressed beyond the primary level. The corresponding percentage for females is 65.93.

Table 7 presents the position of migrants in the household. 16.86 per cent of all migrants were heads of households before migration but since return there has been a shift to 19.22 per cent. The category "head of family" remains approximately the same at both points. A significant phenomenon is the reduction by 30.7 per cent in income-earning members. This does not always signify unemployment: the change in status may be due partly to marriage and voluntary withdrawal from the labour force, particularly in the case of females. Thirteen migrants had assumed positions as heads of household and family after migration. The category which indicates non-employment and absence of income-earning capacity is, however, that of dependents. The increase in this category is 23, nearly 8 per cent.

On a gender basis a high proportion of males – nearly 40 per cent – were heads of households before migration; after return 44.55 per cent fell into this category. Only 3.15 per cent of the females had this function before departure and very little change has taken place since their return. Heads of households and families taken together constituted a little more than one-fifth of the sample. It is in this category

**Table 8.** Distribution of household members according to gender

| Household members | Male | Female | Total | Percentage |
|---|---|---|---|---|
| 1–4 | 37 | 73 | 110 | 21.6 |
| 5–6 | 63 | 125 | 188 | 36.9 |
| 7–8 | 50 | 68 | 118 | 23.1 |
| 9–10 | 21 | 26 | 47 | 9.2 |
| 11–12 | 14 | 17 | 31 | 6.0 |
| 13–22 | 7 | 8 | 15 | 2.9 |
| Over 22 | 1 | 0 | 1 | 0.2 |
| Total | 193 | 317 | 510 | 100 |

of migrants that adjustment problems for households would have been most severe.

## Household Members

The average household in the sample has just under seven members (6.58) which is higher than the national average of 5.23 (according to the Consumer Finance Survey, Sri Lanka, 1981/82). Table 8 presents the distribution of respondents according to household size prior to migration. Households with one to four members make up approximately 21 per cent; the highest proportion of households, 37 per cent, is in the 5–6 member bracket, followed by 23 per cent in the 7–8 bracket. It will be seen that a substantial proportion of both male and female migrants are from households with seven or more members. The majority of migrants, therefore, are from households which are larger in size than the national average, and with a heavier burden of dependence.

In households the number of families varies from one to over seven. The approximate average family size is 4.44 persons. The majority of respondents (70.78 per cent) were from single-family households, followed by 27.65 per cent with two to three families.

## Activity and Employment Status

Table 9 indicates activity status according to gender prior to migration. The respondents' employment status covered a wide spectrum of activities, ranging from the professional and technical to students and pensioners. The majority of the migrants, though belonging to the young adult category, do not have any professional qualification, vocational training, or special skills. The general distribution of activities shows that prior to migration about 24 per cent were unemployed. Both male and female migrants reported approximately similar unemployment numbers (23.32 and 24.29 per cent respectively). Activity status classified according to age-group is given in table 10. Unemployment is highest in the 25–29 age-group which records 28 per cent, followed by the 30–34 age-group.

The job composition of the respondents indicates that prior to migration only

**Table 9.** Activity status before migration by gender

| | Unemployed | Engineers/surveyors | Auditors | Managers | Technicians | Stores and supplies | Carpenters | Masons | Plumbers | Bartenders | Painters | Welders/tinkers | Fitters | Mechanics | Machine operators | Electricians | Drivers/cleaners | Room/bellboys | Cooks/chefs | Dressmakers/tailors | Other skilled workers | Labourers | Male domestic labour | Unspecified | Housemaids | Housewives | Students | Non-earning family workers | Pensioners | Total |
|---|---|---|---|---|---|---|---|---|---|---|---|---|---|---|---|---|---|---|---|---|---|---|---|---|---|---|---|---|---|---|
| Male | 45 | 1 | 6 | 1 | 3 | 3 | 6 | 14 | 7 | 3 | 1 | 1 | 2 | 4 | 2 | 14 | 2 | 4 | 13 | 5 | 3 | 4 | 16 | 5 | 0 | 0 | 10 | 16 | 2 | 193 |
| Female | 77 | 0 | 0 | 0 | 3 | 0 | 0 | 0 | 0 | 0 | 0 | 0 | 0 | 0 | 0 | 0 | 0 | 0 | 0 | 0 | 2 | 0 | 0 | 0 | 7 | 228 | 0 | 0 | 0 | 317 |
| Total | 122 | 1 | 6 | 1 | 6 | 3 | 6 | 14 | 7 | 3 | 1 | 1 | 2 | 4 | 2 | 14 | 2 | 4 | 13 | 5 | 5 | 4 | 16 | 5 | 7 | 228 | 10 | 16 | 2 | 510 |

**Table 10.** Activity status before migration by age-group

| Age group | Unemployed | Engineers/surveyors | Auditors | Managers | Technicians | Stores and supplies | Carpenters | Masons | Plumbers | Bartenders | Painters | Welders/tinkers | Fitters | Mechanics | Machine operators | Electricians | Drivers/cleaners | Room/bellboys | Cooks/chefs | Dressmakers/tailors | Other skilled workers | Labourers | Male domestic labour | Unspecified | Housemaids | Housewives | Students | Non-earning family workers | Pensioners | Total |
|---|---|---|---|---|---|---|---|---|---|---|---|---|---|---|---|---|---|---|---|---|---|---|---|---|---|---|---|---|---|---|
| 15–19 | 5 | 0 | 0 | 0 | 0 | 0 | 0 | 0 | 0 | 0 | 0 | 0 | 0 | 0 | 0 | 0 | 0 | 0 | 0 | 0 | 0 | 0 | 0 | 0 | 0 | 1 | 0 | 0 | 0 | 6 |
| 20–24 | 25 | 0 | 0 | 0 | 0 | 0 | 0 | 0 | 0 | 0 | 0 | 0 | 0 | 0 | 0 | 0 | 0 | 0 | 0 | 0 | 0 | 0 | 1 | 0 | 0 | 9 | 6 | 5 | 0 | 46 |
| 25–29 | 35 | 1 | 4 | 0 | 1 | 0 | 1 | 1 | 0 | 1 | 0 | 1 | 0 | 0 | 0 | 0 | 0 | 1 | 2 | 1 | 0 | 0 | 4 | 0 | 3 | 45 | 3 | 4 | 1 | 105 |
| 30–34 | 30 | 0 | 0 | 0 | 3 | 1 | 2 | 5 | 5 | 2 | 0 | 0 | 1 | 3 | 1 | 6 | 0 | 2 | 4 | 2 | 2 | 0 | 4 | 5 | 1 | 68 | 0 | 6 | 0 | 157 |
| 35–39 | 19 | 0 | 1 | 0 | 1 | 1 | 1 | 5 | 1 | 0 | 0 | 0 | 1 | 0 | 0 | 4 | 2 | 1 | 4 | 2 | 2 | 1 | 4 | 0 | 0 | 54 | 1 | 1 | 0 | 105 |
| 40–44 | 0 | 0 | 0 | 1 | 1 | 1 | 1 | 3 | 1 | 0 | 0 | 0 | 0 | 1 | 1 | 2 | 0 | 0 | 2 | 0 | 1 | 1 | 1 | 0 | 3 | 31 | 0 | 0 | 0 | 52 |
| 45–49 | 7 | 0 | 1 | 0 | 0 | 0 | 1 | 0 | 0 | 0 | 0 | 0 | 0 | 0 | 0 | 2 | 0 | 0 | 0 | 0 | 0 | 1 | 1 | 0 | 0 | 11 | 0 | 0 | 1 | 25 |
| 50–54 | 1 | 0 | 0 | 0 | 0 | 0 | 0 | 0 | 0 | 0 | 1 | 0 | 0 | 0 | 0 | 0 | 0 | 0 | 1 | 0 | 0 | 0 | 1 | 0 | 0 | 7 | 0 | 0 | 0 | 11 |
| 55–59 | 0 | 0 | 0 | 0 | 0 | 0 | 0 | 0 | 0 | 0 | 0 | 0 | 0 | 0 | 0 | 0 | 0 | 0 | 0 | 0 | 0 | 1 | 0 | 0 | 0 | 2 | 0 | 0 | 0 | 3 |
| Total | 122 | 1 | 6 | 1 | 6 | 3 | 6 | 14 | 7 | 3 | 1 | 1 | 2 | 4 | 2 | 14 | 2 | 4 | 13 | 5 | 5 | 4 | 16 | 5 | 7 | 228 | 10 | 16 | 2 | 510 |

**Table 11**. Job composition of migrants prior to departure

| Level | Male | Female | Total |
|---|---|---|---|
| High-level | 8 | 0 | 8 |
| Middle-level | 6 | 3 | 9 |
| Skilled-level | 81 | 2 | 83 |
| Unskilled | 53 | 235 | 288 |
| Unemployed | 45 | 77 | 122 |
| Total | 193 | 317 | 510 |

**Table 12**. Number of times employed in the Gulf countries

| Number of times | Male | Female | Total |
|---|---|---|---|
| 1 | 167 | 255 | 422 |
| 2 | 21 | 57 | 78 |
| 3 | 3 | 4 | 7 |
| 4 | 1 | 1 | 2 |
| 5 | 0 | 0 | 0 |
| 6 | 1 | 0 | 1 |
| Total | 193 | 317 | 510 |

1.57 per cent had any type of high-level employment. The middle-level employment category, too, indicates a low of 1.76 per cent. On the other hand, 16.27 per cent had skilled-level jobs prior to migration. The rest, comprising 56.47 per cent of the total, were in the unskilled category. There were no female migrants in the high-level category, and an insignificant proportion in the middle and skilled levels. Nearly three-quarters of the females were unskilled, but only 27.46 per cent of the males were in this category.

Table 12 reveals the number of times employed in the Gulf countries according to gender. Of the total sample the majority of migrants (82.75 per cent) were "first-timers," having served only once. On a gender basis approximately equal proportions of males (86.5 per cent) and females (80.4 per cent) have had only one contract of employment. In general, only 15.29 per cent have served twice in the Gulf countries. Those who have gone more than twice number a mere 10, which constitutes only 1.96 per cent of the sample.

**Rural and Urban Distribution of Migrants**

The migrants of the sample come from diverse backgrounds, but they can be classified into urban and rural mainly on one factor, location. The term location, in this context, signifies migrant's residence – whether it is in a designated urban area or a rural area. On this basis, 60 per cent of the sample was urban and 40 per cent rural.

**Table 13**. Monthly aggregate income for migrants and their families (286 respondents)

| Income groups (rupees) | Male | Female |
|---|---|---|
| Below 250 | 2 | 2 |
| 251–500 | 18 | 19 |
| 501–1000 | 53 | 89 |
| 1,001 and over | 64 | 39 |
| Total | 137 | 149 |

## Income

For a considerable number of migrants the responses to the questions regarding income were incomplete and the survey data did not provide adequate information on the incomes of all income-earning members of the households and the total household income of the migrant households. Of the 510 migrants only 286 supplied information which was sufficient to make reliable estimates of their household incomes. Table 13 presents the available information. On the whole, a larger proportion of male migrants came from households with income levels above Rs. 1,000 per month – approximately 47 per cent for males compared to 26 per cent for females. The proportion of migrants in households with incomes below Rs. 500 was approximately the same for both male and female migrants, that is, in the region of 15 per cent. For the large majority of households, the regular income they received from household members employed abroad resulted in a sudden and steep increase in the resources available to them. As will be seen later, the capacity to handle this sudden increment varied widely among households.

## The Pre-migration Phase

### Motivation for Migration

The reasons for migration as given by the respondents are classified in table 14, ranked in order of preference. Respondents had to indicate what they considered the most important motivations among several that were listed. Several respondents gave more than one reason for their decision, but the large majority (77.25 per cent) concentrated on their poor income and unsatisfactory living conditions prior to migration. 55.44 per cent of the male migrants and 90 per cent of the females selected this as the most compelling reason for their decision to seek employment abroad. The responses which focused more on achieving a higher standard of living in the future rather than escaping present poverty came next. But the proportion was much smaller – approximately 25 per cent. This would reflect the mix of income levels and the profile of aspirations as regards migration. Only a minority could initially conceive of the migration in a future-oriented perspective, as a clear opportunity to save and raise their level of living.

With the exception of the two motives mentioned, the importance of other reasons varies quite widely with gender. The females showed a distinctly greater

**Table 14.** Reasons for seeking employment abroad

| Reasons | Frequency | |
|---|---|---|
| | Male | Female |
| 1. Income prior to migration insufficient to maintain reasonable standard of living | 107 | 287 |
| 2. To accumulate sufficient savings to reach a high standard of living | 56 | 74 |
| 3. To provide better educational facilities for children | 16 | 96 |
| 4. To recover from serious domestic or personal crisis | 51 | 51 |
| 5. Lack of suitable employment at home | 36 | 62 |
| 6. To liquidate personal debt | 7 | 54 |
| 7. To redeem mortgage on family property | 3 | 8 |
| 8. To travel abroad and experience life in a foreign country | 17 | 11 |

concern for the education of their children, approximately 30.28 per cent, compared to only 8.29 per cent for males. Domestic or personal crises came next in importance. About 26 per cent of the males identified this reason as having significantly influenced their decision. The proportion was lower among females. Lack of suitable employment was a push factor for a larger proportion of females than males. This can be attributed to the increasing participation of the women in the workforce, and the higher rate of female employment in the young age-group compared to males. A more specific reason given by the migrants is the liquidation of debts, including redemption of mortgages on family property. For 72 migrants, mostly female, this reason was important. A small proportion cited reasons which were unrelated to economic motivations, such as the desire to travel and experience life in a foreign country. Personal debts were cited by more females than males: 17.03 compared to only 3.63 per cent. A similar situation is seen with regard to the question of redeeming mortgages on family property. Whether they borrowed specifically to finance their migration abroad is doubtful, for it is evident that the actual cost of migration was quite low.

The pulls and pressures that motivated the respondents, therefore, are endemic to the social layers from which they come. Economically, the majority belong to the disadvantaged class and their aspirations reflect this. This is especially true of the female migrants.

## Source of Information

Getting the necessary initial information and locating a job are two prerequisites prior to initiating action for employment abroad. In Sri Lanka a recognized or organized system of information for potential Arab world migrants does not exist. The agencies, however, have access to information through their own contacts in the Arab world. In almost all cases, whatever information was received by the potential migrant was from informal sources.

Table 15 reveals the three main sources of information. For about half of the migrants, friends and relatives already abroad, or who had been abroad, were the channels through which they obtained information about job opportunities.

300

**Table 15.** Source of information about employment opportunities

| Respondents | Friends/ relatives abroad | Advertisements in newspapers | Local intermediaries | Not specified | Total |
|---|---|---|---|---|---|
| Male | 69 | 55 | 38 | 31 | 193 |
| Female | 191 | 25 | 69 | 32 | 317 |
| Total | 260 | 80 | 107 | 63 | 510 |

Females were more dependent on this source – 60 per cent – than males – 35 per cent.

The next important source is the local intermediary. The middleman may be an accredited agent, a "representative" of an agent, a small-scale businessman with Arab World connections, or even a person carrying out a recruiting business as a sideline or part-time activity. The presence of a large number of middlemen is due to the proliferation of "mushroom" recruiting agencies. These agents or brokers have played quite a significant role, about one-fifth of respondents having obtained information through this source. Newspaper advertisements had relatively less importance, accounting for about 15 per cent. In terms of occupation, it is revealed that the information for more skilled job opportunities was through newspapers but the majority of unskilled jobs, especially those in the housemaids category, were through friends and relations or through local intermediaries.

## Means by which Employment was Secured

Prospective migrants to the Arab world have at least six options to select from in order to secure employment in these countries. But in practice they have a limited choice because of the manner in which the various agencies involved in supplying labour to Arab countries operate.

Table 16 reflects the frequency distribution of respondents, classified according to source of securing employment. The most common type of employment available does not demand direct application to prospective employers. Except for one respondent in the sample, an engineer, who obtained employment through direct application, all others secured their jobs through a third party. It is evident from tables 15 and 16 that, although the majority initially received information about job opportunities abroad through informal sources, such as relatives, friends, and migrants, after they had begun to seek employment the actual recruitment in most cases was through agencies.

A substantially large proportion, 83.53 per cent, indicated employment agencies as their main means of securing placements in the Arab world. These agencies are of two types: first, the licensed agencies, i.e. those registered with the Department of Labour under existing legislation, and, second, the unlicensed agencies, i.e. agencies and individuals not registered with the Labour Department.

Of the total sample, three-quarters (74.90 per cent) secured their job placements through licensed agencies. More males (81.87 per cent) than females (70.66 per

**Table 16.** Means of securing employment by gender

| Means | Male | Female | Total |
|---|---|---|---|
| Direct application | 1 | 0 | 1 |
| Government | 8 | 2 | 10 |
| Licensed recruiting agency | 158 | 224 | 382 |
| Unlicensed recruiting agency | 12 | 32 | 44 |
| Contracting firm | 4 | 4 | 8 |
| Friend/relative | 10 | 55 | 65 |
| Total | 193 | 317 | 510 |

cent) sought their aid to secure jobs. In fact, under the prevailing conditions the respondents had little choice but to approach these agencies, for there is no government-to-government arrangement or agreement between Sri Lanka and the Arab World to process or regulate the recruitment procedure to these countries. Within such a framework the licensed agencies control, to a great degree, the type of jobs available, selection, wages, working conditions, and fees.

Friends and relatives have been instrumental in placing a fair number of respondents in jobs. A total of 12.75 per cent more females (17.35 per cent) than males (5.18 per cent) found placements from this source. The unlicensed agencies come next, with a small share of the recruitments (8.6 per cent). These figures contradict the general impression that the informal sources and unregistered agencies account for the larger proportion of placements. One official report was of the view that the bulk of the placements nevertheless seems to be sponsored by the unlicensed agencies (Ministry of Labour, 1981). However, the data from the sample survey indicate that they play a minor role; the informal sources, including unlicensed agencies, together account for only one-fifth of the recruitments. On the whole this is quite a satisfactory situation, which lends itself to surveillance and regulation and works against widespread irregularity and fraud. However, the number of registered agencies had increased from a few in 1976 to 567 in 1981. Despite registration, "mushroom" organizations can operate for short periods, and control of their activities for the prevention of fraud and of the victimization of migrants becomes a difficult task. The government's contribution has been negligible, a mere 1.96 per cent. In this case too, more males (4.15 per cent) than females (0.63 per cent) have utilized the service.

### Period of Waiting between First Inquiry and Firm Offer

A mere inquiry does not result in a firm offer by the recruiting establishment. Observations indicate that the majority of respondents had to make a number of visits to receive such an offer. Table 17 shows the waiting period of respondents on a gender basis; this varied from 2 to over 25 weeks. But a redeeming feature is that a high proportion, approximately 40 per cent, had a firm offer within a month and another 22 per cent within five to eight weeks. Nearly 10 per cent were less fortunate and had to wait for more than six months.

A firm offer usually connotes a positive result. But there was a time lapse varying

**Table 17**. Waiting period between first inquiry and firm offer by gender

| Sex | Period (weeks) | | | | | Total |
|---|---|---|---|---|---|---|
| | 0–4 | 5–8 | 9–12 | 13–24 | 25 + | |
| Male | 78 | 35 | 33 | 27 | 20 | 193 |
| Female | 122 | 78 | 50 | 39 | 28 | 317 |
| Total | 200 | 112 | 83 | 66 | 48 | 510 |

**Table 18**. Waiting period between recruitment and migration by gender

| Period (weeks) | Male | Female | Total |
|---|---|---|---|
| 0–4 | 147 | 285 | 432 |
| 5–8 | 28 | 18 | 46 |
| 9–12 | 5 | 10 | 15 |
| 13–24 | 8 | 3 | 11 |
| Over 25 | 5 | 1 | 6 |
| Total | 193 | 317 | 510 |

**Table 19**. Type of contract of employment by gender

| Contract type | Male | Female | Total |
|---|---|---|---|
| Formal contract with terms and conditions | 136 | 161 | 297 |
| Letter or other communication | 14 | 12 | 26 |
| Informal arrangement | 43 | 144 | 187 |
| Total | 193 | 317 | 510 |

between 4 and 25 weeks between recruitment and migration. Table 18 indicates this waiting period according to gender. A high proportion of both males (76 per cent) and females (90 per cent) waited less than a month between recruitment and migration and more than three-quarters of both male and female respondents were able to migrate within two months of receiving their appointment papers.

**Contractual Formalities**

Table 19 discloses the type of contract classified according to sex of migrants. More than half the respondents (58.24 per cent) went on some form of formal contract with terms and conditions specified. A substantial number – about 37 per cent – went through informal arrangements and 5.1 per cent had only letters. A larger proportion of males (70 per cent) than females (50 per cent) had formal contracts prior to their departure. It is interesting to note that for every one who migrated through informal arrangements nearly two went with firmer contracts.

**Table 20.** Language of contract by gender

| Language | Male | Female | Total |
|---|---|---|---|
| English (1) | 157 | 275 | 432 |
| Sinhalese (2) | 1 | 13 | 14 |
| Tamil (3) | 0 | 1 | 1 |
| Arabic (4) | 4 | 4 | 8 |
| 1 and 2 | 6 | 12 | 18 |
| 1 and 4 | 24 | 10 | 34 |
| 1, 2, and 3 | 1 | 1 | 2 |
| 1, 2, 3, and 4 | 0 | 1 | 1 |
| Total | 193 | 317 | 510 |

But more female respondents have informal agreements. This is probably due to the nature of their employment, which was mainly as housemaids.

**Contract Language**

Four hundred and thirty-two (85 per cent) of the 510 contracts or letters concerning the arrangements made were in English. A very few contracts were in Sinhalese (14). There were a small proportion (about 32) in two languages. Contracts including the contracts in two languages were available in Sinhalese. Field observations indicate that the large majority of migrants did not have the contracts explained in detail.

It seems doubtful that the legal rights and obligations of employee and employer parties were explained in all their important implications. At the same time the survey data indicate that a fair proportion of males (42 per cent) and a smaller proportion of females (26 per cent) had access to advice or counselling from various sources (table 21).

**Negotiations for Better Terms and Conditions**

Bargaining for better terms and conditions in relation to employment can only be undertaken when the contract offered is read carefully and correctly understood. It is important to note that in most cases the time interval between receipt of contract and departure is very short and provides little opportunity to study the contract. In fact the majority reported that the copy of the contract was handed to them at the airport prior to departure. Even a model contract was available to only 32.75 per cent of the migrants; only a quarter of the females and less than half the males received such a contract. Observations also indicate that a large percentage of migrants had no opportunity to study the contract prior to departure or even later. One of the adverse results of this unsatisfactory situation is the inability of the majority of migrants to bargain for better terms and conditions; less than a quarter (23.33 per cent) were able to bargain for better wages. This group contains more males (61.60 per cent) than females (19.56 per cent) and includes a few migrants in categories such as carpenters and mechanics. Housemaids form the largest category of migrants, but only 18.99 per cent had tried to obtain better wages, although

**Table 21.** From whom advice taken, by gender

| Advisor | Male | Female | Total |
|---|---|---|---|
| Friends (1) | 29 | 21 | 50 |
| Relations (2) | 6 | 29 | 35 |
| Previous employer (3) | 2 | 1 | 3 |
| Voluntary agency (4) | 10 | 9 | 19 |
| Govt Servicing Centre (5) | 2 | 1 | 3 |
| Other (6) | 29 | 17 | 46 |
| 1 + 2 | 2 | 4 | 6 |
| 1 + 2 + 6 | 1 | 0 | 1 |
| Not sought | 112 | 235 | 347 |
| Total | 193 | 317 | 510 |

Sri Lankan housemaids are the lowest paid of all the migrant workers in the Arab countries. A similar situation was observed in regard to other benefits and working conditions. Less than a quarter of males and a mere 13.56 per cent of females have attempted to bargain for other benefits and better working conditions.

### Time Spent and Cost Incurred to Obtain Documents and Clearance

Prior to the reorganization of the passport office the issue of passports to migrants was subject to considerable delay. It is during this period that most of the migrants in the sample went abroad for employment. Even under these conditions the majority of the migrants obtained their passports within four weeks, though a small proportion had to wait for periods ranging from three to six months. A mean of 6.1 weeks for males and 7.0 for females was observed. It must also be emphasized that even 57.41 per cent of the housemaids, the least qualified, obtained their passports in four weeks. This clearly reveals a situation contrary to what is generally considered as having prevailed at that time. It was observed that the agents or middlemen, in most cases, gave a "package" deal inclusive of passport.

Obtaining visas was no problem. For the majority of migrants this took between 14 and 28 days; only a very small minority had to wait for between two and three months. The ease with which these were obtained is due to the personal handling of this aspect by the agents. Health clearance too created no problems; almost all obtained clearance within two weeks.

### Costs of Migration

Under normal conditions the total costs of migration are limited to the approved fees of agents, the cost of travel within the country for interviews, and the fees for obtaining passports, visas, and health clearance. All these expenses amount to a modest sum. The agency may charge a nominal fee of Rs. 150 as stipulated by government. The air tickets are sent from the host country. Substantial revenue accrues to the local agencies as commissions from their foreign counterparts. Field investigations, however, indicate that migrants are at times required to pay far in excess of the normal charges and agency fees, and that agencies, both registered

**Table 22.** Time spent in obtaining passport by gender

| Gender | Weeks | | | | | Total |
|--------|-----|-----|------|-------|-----|-------|
|        | 0–4 | 5–8 | 9–12 | 13–14 | 25 + | |
| Male   | 131 | 25  | 23   | 9     | 5   | 193 |
| Female | 185 | 75  | 27   | 18    | 12  | 317 |
| Total  | 316 | 100 | 50   | 27    | 17  | 510 |

**Table 23.** Mean, minimum, and maximum cost of migration according to occupation

| Item | Mean | Minimum | Maximum |
|------|------|---------|---------|
| Male (high-level) | | | |
| Travel documents and related items | 487.00 | 100.00 | 950.00 |
| Agents | 7,975.00 | 3,000.00 | 15,500.00 |
| Male (middle-level) | | | |
| Travel documents and related items | 463.50 | — | 1,410.00 |
| Agents | 8,457.50 | — | 30,900.00 |
| Male (skilled-level) | | | |
| Travel documents and related items | 566.00 | — | 10,310.00 |
| Agents | 4,593.00 | — | 3,300.00 |
| Male (unskilled-level) | | | |
| Travel documents and related items | 574.06 | — | 8,650.00 |
| Agents | 4,570.00 | — | 20,400.00 |
| Female (domestic workers) | | | |
| Travel documents and related items | 473.22 | — | 5,500.00 |
| Agents | 2,155.32 | — | 12,500.00 |
| Female (other occupational) | | | |
| Travel documents and related items | 335.00 | 100.00 | 525.00 |
| Agents | 2,679.60 | — | 7,500.00 |

and unregistered, often determine the levels of payment in relation to income earned abroad, regardless of the officially stipulated limits.

The cost incurred in obtaining passports varied between Rs. 100 and over Rs. 3,000, with a mean of Rs. 208.8. Table 23 indicates cost distribution according to occupation. It is evident that more than half the migrants (55.69 per cent), comprising a wide spectrum of occupations, spent only the minimum stamp fee of Rs. 100 (presently it is Rs. 200). This situation applied especially to the skilled personnel, although lower grades too have benefitted. Quite a large number of housemaids (42.44 per cent) spent between Rs. 100 and Rs. 500 and another 1.29 per cent spent over Rs. 1,000. This distribution is based on the responses given by the migrants.

Health examination is costly because of the need for clinical tests. Consequently, 54.71 per cent of the migrants spent between Rs. 500 and Rs. 2,000, with 1 per cent paying over Rs. 2,000. Air tickets did not cost the migrants anything and were received in two weeks.

There are three major items of cost incurred by migrants. These are payments made to the various agencies and authorities, such as the fees to the recruiting agencies, and cost of passport, visa, and health clearance; cost of domestic travel and incidental expenses during the period of preparation and costs incurred in making domestic arrangements for the migration; and purchase of clothing, travel equipment, and other related items. Although exact amounts incurred have not been reported, the mean cost for male migrants appears to have been in the region of Rs. 3,500, with a minimum of Rs. 400 and a maximum of Rs. 15,000. For females the mean cost was about Rs. 1,500, with a maximum of Rs. 6,500 and a minimum of no payment. There is also a close relationship between the mean cost and occupation type, ranging from comparatively lower costs in the domestic worker group to a high in the middle-level category. This could mean that the higher the salaries or wages the higher the costs, especially the payments to recruiting agencies. However, the mean cost for the high-level group was lower than that for the middle-level but higher than that for the skilled-level group. This situation may be due to the fact that those with higher or specialized training and qualifications are in a better position to bargain with the agents and protect their rights.

The money paid to recruiting agencies varied between Rs. 1,000 and 22,000. According to the responses, the majority of migrants (52.0 per cent) had not paid the agencies any money; as a whole, 20 per cent of the migrants had paid sums between Rs. 1,001 and Rs. 5,000. A small proportion, about 5 per cent, paid sums ranging between Rs. 7,500 and Rs. 10,000. In general, more males than females have paid large amounts to the agencies. For example, 28 per cent have paid sums ranging between Rs. 2,501 and Rs. 12,500, compared with 16 per cent of females in the same range. This may be because payments vary according to occupation and income earned abroad. The majority of females have secured unskilled jobs with low pay, hence the lower amounts paid by the female migrants. On the other hand, a fair number of males were placed in skilled jobs carrying higher wages, on which higher payments are demanded by the agents. For example, a foreman paid between Rs. 20,001 and Rs. 22,500, and some of the electricians between Rs. 5,001 and Rs. 15,000. The clerk/steno category paid between Rs. 7,501 and Rs. 10,000.

Table 24 indicates other payments and costs according to gender. It is significant that, with the exception of a small minority (5 per cent), migrants have not paid any money to intermediaries (five migrants paid between Rs. 500 and Rs. 6,000). Domestic arrangements did not pose serious problems, for there was no cost for over three-quarters of the respondents; however, about 25 per cent spent sums ranging from below Rs. 500 to Rs. 6,000. The low cost of domestic arrangements is understandable, as in most cases the family members left behind managed for themselves, with the spouse or an elder assuming the responsibilities of the migrant.

The expenditure on preparation for travel was a more significant item. While a third of the migrants reported no new expenditure for this purpose, at least a quarter of the migrants spent between Rs. 501 and Rs. 1,500. Thirty-seven per cent spent less than Rs. 500 for the same purpose. The outlay on clothing, etc., was also minimal, with more than half the respondents (50.39 per cent) not spending any money for this. Twenty-seven per cent of migrants spent less than Rs. 500 and 18 per cent between Rs. 501 and Rs. 1,500. Only 3 per cent spent between Rs. 1,501 and Rs. 3,000, with one male migrant spending Rs. 3,001–4,000.

**Table 24.** Other costs and payments by gender (rupees)

| Gender | No payment | 1–500 | 501–1,500 | 1,501–3,000 | 3,001–4,000 | 4,001–6,000 | Total |
|---|---|---|---|---|---|---|---|
| **Payment to intermediaries** | | | | | | | |
| Male | 186 | 3 | 1 | 0 | 0 | 3 | 193 |
| Female | 296 | 2 | 9 | 10 | 0 | 0 | 317 |
| Total | 482 | 5 | 10 | 10 | 0 | 3 | 510 |
| **Cost of domestic arrangements** | | | | | | | |
| Male | 142 | 11 | 21 | 14 | 1 | 4 | 193 |
| Female | 261 | 19 | 24 | 12 | 0 | 1 | 317 |
| Total | 403 | 30 | 45 | 26 | 1 | 5 | 510 |
| **Money spent on preparation for travel** | | | | | | | |
| Male | 49 | 78 | 51 | 10 | 5 | 0 | 193 |
| Female | 115 | 111 | 73 | 13 | 4 | 1 | 317 |
| Total | 164 | 189 | 124 | 23 | 9 | 1 | 510 |

**Financing of Migration**

There have been at least eight sources available for the potential migrant worker to finance the entire process of leaving the country. For convenience these sources can be divided into two groups: first, personal savings, gifts, mortgage, and sale of goods and property, and, second, borrowing.

The amount of personal savings utilized varied from zero to Rs. 20,000, with a mean of Rs. 4,075 for males and Rs. 1,857 for females. It is significant that 35.6 per cent of the total sample used their own savings for this purpose. More than half the males (53.8 per cent) and about a quarter (24.6 per cent) of the females were able to finance the whole or part of the total cost with their savings.

As a source of finance for the migration process the contribution of gifts is quite insignificant: only 1.57 per cent gave positive responses, all of which fall into the less than Rs. 2,000 slot. The third source, mortgages, sales, etc., is also insignificant, for only 7.84 per cent of the returnees utilized this source to finance their pre-migration preparations. Yet the amounts obtained were quite substantial, ranging from Rs. 5,001 to Rs. 30,000.

Borrowing is classified under three heads. The most popular source was borrowing from relatives. Of the total sample, about 25 per cent had obtained loans in this way. Although in absolute terms the number utilizing this source may be small, the quantum of money involved is quite high, ranging up to Rs. 20,000. Next in order of popularity was the moneylender, used by 20 per cent of the sample.

Friends came next as a source of borrowing (17.25 per cent of the sample); more females (18.93 per cent) than males sought help from friends. The sums borrowed ranged from Rs. 1,000 to Rs. 10,000. One male respondent was able to borrow Rs. 16,000 from friends. Banks as usual are conservative, and it is extremely difficult for migrants with no special credentials or collateral to obtain loans from such institutions. None of the men, therefore, had approached banks to finance their migration. Only three females gave positive responses; these had obtained loans of between Rs. 1,001 and Rs. 5,000.

## Training for Employment in the Arab World

During the period in which the migrants in the sample sought employment abroad, there were no recognized programmes or organizations (government, voluntary, or others) providing training to prospective migrants on a significant scale. According to the information gathered in the survey, 24 per cent of the male respondents and 7.5 per cent of the females had received some formal training at the time of migration. The skilled and semi-skilled migrants, who are comparatively few in number, had different levels of training and work experience, depending on the type of work. Electricians, welders, mechanics, nurses, and the few professionals had had training in institutes. The majority of the masons and carpenters, on the other hand, reported having some informal training through work or informal apprenticeship. Only two were trained under a government programme as supervisors.

During this period there was no effort to provide training to other types of workers, such as domestic aides. These workers might have been able to command better terms if they had been given basic training in the use of modern appliances, cooking, home management and child care, and other activities to improve their ability to cope with the miscellaneous range of duties in middle-class and upper-class homes.

## Orientation, Basic Information, and Arrangements

Orientation in the present context connotes not only the familiarization of an individual with the formalities and procedures associated with the entire migration process, but also the preparation of the individual to face new situations and circumstances in a given environment. Orientation programmes could give the migrant a certain degree of confidence to make the necessary basic arrangements for both departure from the home country and the stay in the host country. Only a small proportion of migrants (13.3 per cent) had received orientation of any kind. The rest migrated without any formal preparation. None of the females had gone to a government source for orientation, though two female respondents had followed programmes in voluntary institutions. On the other hand, 12.35 per cent had obtained some assistance in this direction from friends, relatives, and schoolteachers.

While there had been very little formal orientation, it is evident that a fair majority had obtained basic information in essential items prior to migration. Only 27 per cent of the respondents, comprising more males (43.52 per cent) than females (16.72 per cent), had acquired beforehand the necessary information regarding travellers' cheques. On the other hand, the majority – about 68 per cent, comprising 75 per cent males and 63 per cent females – were conversant with the procedure required to remit money home. A similar response was given to questions regarding "communication" with family. In this aspect 82 per cent of the migrants

**Table 25.** Acquisition of basic information and knowledge regarding living conditions in the host country (percentages)

| Sex | Adequate | Inadequate | None | Total |
|---|---|---|---|---|
| Knowledge of climate | | | | |
| Male | 41.95 | 30.05 | 28.00 | 100.00 |
| Female | 25.25 | 21.45 | 53.30 | 100.00 |
| Total | 31.56 | 24.71 | 43.75 | 100.00 |
| Knowledge of laws | | | | |
| Male | 41.97 | 23.31 | 34.72 | 100.00 |
| Female | 24.29 | 16.40 | 59.31 | 100.00 |
| Total | 30.98 | 19.02 | 50.00 | 100.00 |
| Knowledge of customs | | | | |
| Male | 36.79 | 24.87 | 38.34 | 100.00 |
| Female | 26.81 | 12.62 | 60.57 | 100.00 |
| Total | 30.59 | 17.25 | 52.16 | 100.00 |
| Knowledge regarding action in an emergency | | | | |
| Male | 41.97 | 18.13 | 39.90 | 100.00 |
| Female | 23.03 | 13.56 | 63.41 | 100.00 |
| Total | 30.20 | 15.29 | 54.51 | 100.00 |

had full knowledge of the ways and means of communicating with their relatives and friends. But few (31 per cent) had contacts with embassies or consulates. This may be attributed to their lack of knowledge of the duties and functions of such services. At present, the government has diplomatic missions in Saudi Arabia, Kuwait, and the UAE, which are the countries with the largest concentrations of migrant workers from Sri Lanka. These missions also play a welfare role, as a large number of workers are from the rural sector and need greater care and attention.

### Basic Information and Knowledge of Host Country

Information and knowledge of the country's customs, traditions, and cultural norms is of vital importance. Without such preparedness, the psychological impact on the migrant can be quite a shock. Whether the migrants were adequately prepared is doubtful, judging from table 25. The majority of the migrants appear to have left the country without adequate information or knowledge of the host country: its climatic conditions, laws, customs, and traditions.

### Victims of Fraud and Malpractice

Considering the types of migrants and the circumstances under which the majority left, there is a likelihood of fraud occurring at both ends – in the home country and the host country. Furthermore, accounts in the news media suggest that these migrant workers were subject to fraud almost at every step. But the responses obtained do not give such a gloomy picture. (It must, however, be noted that the survey sample only includes those who migrated successfully. Those who became victims may not be adequately represented in such a sample.) On the basis of responses given it is evident that about one-fifth (19.80 per cent) of the total sample were victims of malpractice by agencies and intermediaries. A little more than a quarter reported that there had been violations of contracts. Although a significant proportion reported "malpractices" and breaches of contract, only a very small number attempted to obtain redress – a mere 2.35 per cent. While the sample was generally co-operative and willingly volunteered most of the information sought, in regard to malpractices and redress they did not appear to be ready to divulge information. Many of them probably felt that they would have to use the same channels if they sought re-employment, and preferred to be discreet. Some of the migrants felt that the entire process of seeking redress was too costly in terms of both time and money.

## Working Conditions in the Host Country

### Problems on Arrival in the Host Country

Theoretically, there should not be any problems when the process of recruitment and placement has been legally completed. If the procedure had been normal, the migrant would have examined the agreement or contract, and verified and understood all terms and conditions prior to accepting the offer. Hence, there is no reason for difficulties on arrival in the host country. Problems, however, may arise if the migrant left the country illegally or without a visa or work permit. Other problems may appear if the migrants were not given the opportunity or adequate time to study the contract prior to departure. In spite of conditions described in the preceding section – absence of formal contracts for a large proportion of migrants, the lack of opportunity to study the contract documents where contracts were available – no serious problems were encountered by the migrants on arrival even in regard to entry and placement. Only 18 out of 510 migrants faced passport, visa, work permit or related problems. Visa problems rank first among the difficulties these migrants had deal with. This problem has partly arisen from the lack of diplomatic representation of the host countries in Sri Lanka. Saudi Arabia, which takes in the majority of Sri Lankan migrants, is one such example; the visas to these countries have to be obtained by the migrants in India or elsewhere. This, of course, adds to the cost of processing the travel documents. All the 13 female migrants who faced problems on arrival in the host country belong to the employment category of housemaids. Their low level of education and lack of experience may have compounded the difficulties. The large majority of migrants were met by the employer or his representative; only 10 per cent had difficulties in contacting their employer. Most of these persons contacted friends and relatives or their employers with the assistance of Sri Lankans.

**Table 26.** Knowledge of specific terms and conditions of contract prior to migration by gender

| Terms and conditions | Male | | Female | |
|---|---|---|---|---|
| | Knowledge | No knowledge | Knowledge | No knowledge |
| Level and type of occupation | 130 | 63 | 151 | 166 |
| Job description | 112 | 81 | 100 | 217 |
| Salary and allowances | 139 | 54 | 180 | 137 |
| Hours of work | 122 | 71 | 74 | 243 |
| Overtime | 94 | 99 | 45 | 272 |
| Living conditions | 121 | 72 | 144 | 173 |
| Travel facilities | 100 | 93 | 103 | 214 |
| Leave facilities | 121 | 72 | 101 | 216 |
| Food | 114 | 79 | 148 | 169 |
| Medical facilities | 110 | 83 | 131 | 186 |
| Accident compensation | 75 | 118 | 48 | 269 |
| Home leave | 74 | 119 | 58 | 259 |
| Termination of contract | 121 | 72 | 144 | 173 |
| Return travel | 108 | 85 | 115 | 202 |
| Termination benefits | 37 | 156 | 12 | 305 |

## Migrant Workers who Arrived in Host Country without Contract

Undoubtedly, almost all the problems associated with migrant workers affect those who have left Sri Lanka without formal contracts or letters. There were 187 such migrants. Of these, 85 did not have work permits. It was also observed that the majority of them (77 per cent) were females and unskilled. Of the 187 who had gone to the host country without signing a formal contract of employment, only three used their own funds to finance the passage. Nearly three-quarters of these migrants were financed by their employer/agent.

## Signing of Second Contract in Host Country

Of the total sample, 199 migrants (39 per cent), comprising 28 per cent males and 45 per cent females, have revealed that they signed a second contract after their arrival in the host country. All the females (144) who went through informal arrangements signed a second contract at that end. The majority of both males and females (80 per cent) stated that the contract was in English. Almost all of them reported that they were not proficient in the language in which the contract was drafted and could not therefore understand its contents. The survey was therefore unable to elicit detailed information regarding the nature of this second document.

Table 26 contains information regarding the knowledge of specific terms and conditions of work that migrants had acquired prior to migration.

About one-third of the males (32 per cent) and over half the females (52 per cent) in the sample migrated without full knowledge of the level and type of occupation they had accepted. Even the exact wages and salaries were known only to 72 per

**Table 27**. Actual terms and conditions of contract in relation to expectations by gender

| Terms and conditions | As expected | | Lower | | Higher | |
|---|---|---|---|---|---|---|
| | Male | Female | Male | Female | Male | Female |
| Level and type of occupation | 119 | 146 | 69 | 166 | 5 | 5 |
| Job description | 100 | 95 | 78 | 190 | 15 | 32 |
| Salary and allowances | 118 | 139 | 70 | 176 | 5 | 2 |
| Hours of work | 101 | 68 | 64 | 209 | 28 | 40 |
| Overtime | 75 | 58 | 106 | 243 | 12 | 16 |
| Living conditions | 105 | 122 | 77 | 182 | 11 | 13 |
| Travel facilities | 107 | 97 | 85 | 215 | 1 | 5 |
| Leave facilities | 101 | 81 | 90 | 234 | 2 | 2 |
| Food | 109 | 127 | 76 | 179 | 8 | 11 |
| Medical facilities | 106 | 115 | 83 | 198 | 4 | 4 |
| Accident compensation | 81 | 59 | 110 | 257 | 2 | 1 |
| Home leave | 78 | 69 | 114 | 241 | 1 | 7 |
| Termination of contract | 114 | 124 | 78 | 192 | 1 | 1 |
| Expenses of return travel | 111 | 110 | 79 | 203 | 3 | 4 |
| Termination benefits | 58 | 95 | 134 | 210 | 1 | 12 |

cent of the males and 56 per cent of the females. The situation was worse in regard to hours of work, particularly for the females, most of whom were housemaids and stated that very frequently they got only a few hours' sleep. A significant proportion were ignorant of such basic conditions as leave entitlement, conditions pertaining to board and lodging, travel arrangements on return, termination benefits, and medical facilities.

Table 27 compares the expectations entertained by migrants with their actual terms and conditions of employment. On the main items of type of occupation and salaries and allowances approximately half the migrants found that what they received was the same as what they had expected. A very small proportion (7 to 10 migrants in all) did better than expected. For the rest the job was below their expectations. On other items the situation is less favourable: large numbers of migrants found conditions below their expectations in regard to home leave, hours of work, travel, food, and medical facilities. Female migrants appear to have fared worse than males: a large proportion of them considered the terms and conditions they received worse than expected. For example, 52 per cent of the females were of the view that the level and type of occupation were below their expectations, in comparison to 35 per cent of males.

## Comparison of Contracts with those of Migrants from Other Countries

In comparing their terms and conditions of work with migrants from other countries more than half (53 per cent) were of the opinion that there were no significant differences. The majority of those who reported that the contracts were similar were females (63 per cent). But only 36 per cent of males gave a positive response to this question. A major reason for the high percentage of females responding in

**Table 28**. Meals provided to the migrant

| Meals | Positive response | | | Negative response | | |
|---|---|---|---|---|---|---|
| | Male | Female | Total | Male | Female | Total |
| Were the meals given regularly and at the correct time? | 168 | 284 | 452 | 25 | 33 | 58 |
| Was the food clean and tasty? | 148 | 249 | 397 | 45 | 68 | 113 |
| Was the food same as the food usually cooked at home? | 129 | 264 | 393 | 64 | 53 | 117 |
| Was the quantity of food adequate? | 164 | 250 | 414 | 29 | 67 | 96 |
| Were the meals generally obtained from restaurants? | 19 | 10 | 29 | 174 | 307 | 481 |

this fashion may be their lack of opportunity to compare conditions with other migrants. This applies particularly to those in domestic employment. The sample, however, included cases where Sri Lankan maids worked with domestic aides from other countries. A significant proportion, comprising 41 per cent of the total, reported that their own contracts were worse, while a very small proportion (6 per cent) stated that they were better.

Among imported labour in the Arab countries, wage scales for Sri Lankan migrants, particularly those in domestic service, appear to be among the lowest offered for similar occupations. The United Arab Emirates (UAE) Ministry of Labour and Social Affairs Study, for example, classifies Asian housemaids into three categories – Sri Lankan, Indian, and Filipino. The Sri Lankan migrants, comprising 67 per cent of all housemaids, are the lowest paid at US$100 per month; Indian maids, on the other hand, are paid US$130 per month and the Filipino maids even more. The level of wages or remuneration appears to be based not only on differences in skill and experience, but also on the country of origin or differences in standard of living.

### Living Conditions in the Host Country

Accommodation

The majority of migrants (93.53 per cent) were quite satisfied with the accommodation provided them. In this connection more females (70.73 per cent) than males (29.38 per cent) reported the accommodation facilities as very good. The very wide variation in the responses is due mainly to the difference in the type of employment. All females who responded with this assessment were housemaids who lived in, and were, therefore, comfortably placed. In the case of the males, the majority were associated with work sites, and accommodation was provided in camp dormitories. It is, however, a redeeming feature that, of the total number of males, 90 per cent were provided with accommodation which can be classified as satisfactory and adequate. A similarly high proportion of 95 per cent for females is reported. The 10 per cent of males who reported unsatisfactory accommodation may be due to adverse conditions on the work sites, but an explanation was not offered for the 4 per cent of females who had been given unsatisfactory accom-

**Table 29.** Entertainment and recreation

| Facility | Male | Female | Total |
|---|---|---|---|
| Nil (0) | 8 | 180 | 188 |
| Watching television (1) | 104 | 46 | 150 |
| Listening to radio (2) | 15 | 45 | 60 |
| Picnics and tours (3) | 0 | 35 | 35 |
| 1 + 2 | 65 | 10 | 75 |
| 1 + 3 | 0 | 1 | 1 |
| 1 + 2 + 3 | 1 | 0 | 1 |
| Total | 193 | 317 | 510 |

modation. Almost all the migrants had facilities and amenities which they would never have had in Sri Lanka. Unlike in Sri Lanka, air conditioning, running water, and electricity are standard facilities in average homes and offices in the Arab world. Ninety-four per cent of the migrants had accommodation equipped with air conditioning, electricity, and water on tap. Running water and electricity minus air conditioning was available to the balance of 6 per cent.

Meals

Most of the migrants recorded their general satisfaction with the quality of the meals.

Entertainment and Recreation

Entertainment and recreation facilities for the migrants were quite limited. Watching television and listening to radio were the most popular methods of recreation, according to the responses given.

The majority of females (56 per cent), however, reported that they were denied any form of entertainment, compared with only 4 per cent males. These were the housemaids, whose hours of work were not specified and who enjoyed no regular rest time. The information gathered in the survey indicated that quite a high proportion of housemaids had to be available at all times to attend to household work as it arose and were denied even the basic forms of entertainment. A few males who did not enjoy adequate recreation facilities owing to the special demands of their work were, according to information gathered in the field, adequately compensated with other benefits such as higher wages, better overtime payment, and better gratuity and home leave facilities.

Males were in a better position in regard to entertainment and recreation than females, as the majority of male workers enjoyed fixed hours of work and were on their own after the working day was over. An interesting feature is that 11.04 per cent of the females indicated their participation in picnics and tours. As domestic aides the females had the opportunity to travel in the country, and even outside it, in the company of the families for which they worked. Migrants were also asked to compare the opportunities they enjoyed for watching TV or listening to the radio with those they enjoyed at home. Seventy per cent of the migrants reported that they watched TV more often than they did at home, while 50 per cent listened to the radio more often than at home. This has to be seen in a context in which other

**Table 30.** Social contact maintained by migrants

| Contact | With local residents | | | With migrants from Sri Lanka | | |
|---|---|---|---|---|---|---|
| | Male | Female | Total | Male | Female | Total |
| Very close | 13 | 3 | 16 | 67 | 17 | 84 |
| Close | 46 | 28 | 74 | 84 | 89 | 173 |
| Distant | 100 | 127 | 227 | 24 | 105 | 129 |
| None | 34 | 159 | 193 | 18 | 106 | 124 |
| Total | 193 | 317 | 510 | 193 | 317 | 510 |

forms of entertainment were severely limited and, in the case of housemaids, restrictions were placed on outside social contacts.

## Facilities for Religious Observances

Only one-third of the sample reported the availability of facilities for religious observances. It is most likely that almost all of them belonged to the Islamic faith. As against this, the majority of the migrant workers, being Buddhists who were employed in a completely non-Buddhist environment, could not expect such facilities. It must also be noted that the schedule of holidays in the Arab world is arranged, as might be expected, to cater to the Muslims and not to others.

## Social Contact Maintained by Migrants

Social contact with local residents or compatriots outside the workplace was restricted. Approximately half the migrants reported that they were able to maintain close or very close relations with other Sri Lankans. About three-fourths of the males and one-third of the females fell into this category. The females, the majority of whom were housemaids, had little opportunity to meet their compatriots. Relationships with local residents were either distant or non-existent. This is understandable, as the language barrier between migrants and local residents would be a serious obstacle to any close social contact. The responses regarding contacts with local residents generally referred to social contacts outside the workplace and those with the employer. The housemaids, of course, lived in Arab households and came into daily contact with the family members, particularly the mistress and children. Some of them report that they had formed relationships in which they had earned the confidence and trust of the families for whom they worked, and a few were able to maintain contact with their employers after their return.

## Participation in Social and Other Activities by Migrants

Only 14 per cent of the sample, comprising 27 per cent of males and 6 per cent of females, reported that there were opportunities for them as migrants to organize social activities, including entertainment. These included their own national festivals, sports, and musical and variety entertainments.

The large majority had no opportunity to participate in any social activity. In the small group that participated males outnumbered the females by about three to one. Forming of clubs and associations was minimal. Only seven migrants (1.37

per cent of the sample) reported that they were allowed to form themselves into clubs or associations.

## Adjustment Problems for Migrant and Family

This section attempts to examine problems of adjustment for the migrant and the family. It will include the responses to questions regarding the migrant's adjustment in the host country, the problems experienced by the family at home, the manner in which the spouse and children adjusted to the migration and the additional household responsibilities, the role of women, the care of children, and the psycho-social problems (if any) created by the migration, such as separation and loneliness.

### Delegation of Household Responsibilities on Migration

The problems of delegating responsibility for the household and its management were most serious for migrants who were heads of households and families. This group comprised approximately one-fifth of the sample. The other households facing problems were those of married migrants taken together – approximately 337, of whom 226 were females. In the majority of these cases, the spouse left behind a husband or wife who assumed the main responsibility for the household. Nearly 40 per cent of the migrants delegated responsibility in this manner. The parents of the migrant or spouse were the next choice, with one-third of the migrants opting for this arrangement. A few relied on elderly relatives and close friends. Where the migrant was an unmarried dependent prior to migration, his or her migration did not cause any major problems of adjustment for the household. The prevailing household arrangements and division of responsibilities continued without change.

The survey data indicate that the majority of migrants did not have to make special arrangements for the care of the children left behind. Again the problems would have been acute only for young families where mothers migrated, and to a lesser extent for families with growing children where the authority of the head of the household was removed. Again, only about 32 per cent of the migrants could have been considered to have young families. Of these, families where young mothers were the migrants formed the larger proportion. Altogether, 145 households, or 28 per cent of the sample, reported that they had to make special arrangements for pre-school children; a slightly smaller proportion made special arrangements for schoolgoing children. Many of these families fell into both categories. Responsibility for the children in most of these cases (60–65 per cent) was assumed by the spouse left behind. The rest depended mainly on their parents, especially the mother of the migrant.

In the majority of cases the responsibility for receiving and using the remittances was entrusted to the spouse. This was the situation for 310 of the 337 married migrants. One hundred and twenty-four of the balance entrusted the responsibility to parents, and a very small proportion to relatives and elder children. Approximately 10 per cent, probably single unmarried migrants with few family responsibilities, made no special arrangements.

317

**Table 31.** Arrangements made for the care of dependents, children, etc.

| Persons responsible | Male | Female | Total |
|---|---|---|---|
| Pre-school children | | | |
| Husband/wife | 43 | 51 | 94 |
| Parents | 2 | 8 | 10 |
| Relatives | 6 | 9 | 15 |
| Mother | 3 | 21 | 24 |
| Elder children | 0 | 2 | 2 |
| No arrangements | 137 | 226 | 368 |
| Total | 191 | 317 | 508 |
| Schoolgoing children | | | |
| Husband/wife | 31 | 60 | 91 |
| Parents | 2 | 6 | 8 |
| Relatives | 4 | 4 | 8 |
| Mother | 4 | 13 | 17 |
| Elder children | 1 | 2 | 3 |
| No arrangements | 151 | 227 | 378 |
| Total | 193 | 312 | 505 |
| Agricultural land | | | |
| Husband/wife | 76 | 37 | 113 |
| Parents | 66 | 68 | 134 |
| Relatives | 10 | 68 | 98 |
| Mother | 6 | 67 | 73 |
| Elder children | 14 | 31 | 45 |
| Others | 1 | 14 | 15 |
| No arrangements | — | 6 | 6 |
| Total | 173 | 311 | 484 |
| Remittances | | | |
| Husband/wife | 94 | 216 | 310 |
| Parents | 35 | 49 | 84 |
| Relatives | 4 | 17 | 21 |
| Mother | 16 | 24 | 40 |
| Elder children | 2 | 1 | 3 |
| Others | 3 | 4 | 7 |
| No arrangements | 39 | 6 | 45 |
| Total | 193 | 317 | 510 |

## Assistance to the Family during Migrant's Absence

Neither government institutions nor private institutions were of any assistance to the family in the absence of the migrant. On the other hand, neighbours, relatives, and friends were quite helpful. Of these, migrants identified neighbours as having been most helpful to families – their help included care of children when needed, writing and reading of letters, encashing and deposit of remittances, occasional financial assistance, and help in times of crisis. About 90 per cent of the migrants reported help from neighbours at one time or another on any one of these items. Friends and relatives were much less in evidence.

## Remittance of Money to Family

More than 90 per cent of the migrants reported that remittances were sent to their families regularly. Seventy per cent sent their remittances monthly, the rest once in two months. A small proportion – probably migrants whose responsibilities for their families at home were minimal – remitted money at much longer intervals.

## Remittances Sent to Whom and Means of Sending and Encashment

In sending remittances, the migrants had a number of choices. The majority – 57 per cent – utilized the mail transfer system, followed by 27.23 per cent using bank drafts. Only a very small proportion remitted through cheques on respondents' foreign accounts or through bank-to-bank transfer to a home account.

Encashment of remittances was not a problem for the majority, who used banks for this purpose. Sixteen per cent reported that the remittances were deposited in relatives'/guardians' bank accounts. Only about 15 per cent stated that they had their own bank accounts into which the remittances were deposited. The data indicate that there is considerable scope for promoting the banking habit and encouraging interest-earning savings quite early in the migrant's stay abroad.

## Overall Adjustment to Separation by Family and Migrant

The respondents were required to make an assessment of the overall adjustment made by family and migrants to the separation caused by the migration. On a scale of four assessments, nearly one-third of the respondents were of the view that they were able to adjust very well. Another 42 per cent thought that they had adjusted well. In all 75 per cent of all the migrants, according to their own perceptions, coped with their adjustment problems well or very well, both at home and abroad. A very small proportion – 13 migrants in all – said that they could not adjust to the separation, while for nearly one-fifth the separation did not create a situation which called for significant adjustments.

The response to inquiries regarding the adjustment problems of children revealed a similar situation. The large majority of migrants with children reported that they had no problems which deserved mention. Approximately one-fifth of these families reported cases of unruly behaviour, poor performance in school, increased proneness to illness, and signs of deep grief and withdrawal. In general, it would appear that the migration of parents had very little significant adverse effects on the children. This is quite contrary to some of the prevailing ideas and conclusions. The situation, according to our sample, indicates that the majority of the children were well looked after in the absence of the mother or father and there was no reason for insecurity in the majority of children. It must, however, be stressed that any overt manifestation in children cannot be correlated from the findings of a single interview survey. This aspect needs a close study over a period of time.

## Spouses' Responsibilities and Adjustments

The inquiry into the reactions and adjustment of the spouses to the new situation in which husband or wife had migrated revealed that 95 per cent of respondent spouses had no problems in accepting greater responsibility. In fact, half the migrants who responded indicated that their spouses had carried on work as usual, and the other half stated that the spouses had faced up to the challenge quite well with no adverse effects. Approximately equal proportions of males and females revealed that their spouses were quite capable of taking on added responsibilities by acquiring new capabilities and skills, especially as regards household work, shopping on their own, looking after the finances of the home, dealing with children's schooling, and travelling, and that they "carried on as usual" despite the extra load of work and responsibility entrusted to them. Contrary to prevailing opinion, the sample revealed that only about 3 per cent, or 14 spouses, broke down under the strain of their new responsibilities.

## Effect of Migration on Marital and Family Relations

In assessing the effect of migration on marital and family relations, greater sharing of responsibilities between spouses was given quite a high rating by both married males (99 per cent) and female migrants (92 per cent). Similarly, the strengthening of family bonds got a high rating by married respondents. In this connection, 97 per cent of the married males and 92 per cent of married female migrants gave positive responses. Only 15 per cent of the single males and 18 per cent of single female migrants reported that there was a strengthening of family bonds. Loss of affection between spouse, respondent and children was reported by only 1.8 per cent of the married males and 5 per cent of married female respondents. Contrary to prevailing opinion, infidelity or other marital problems were insignificant, with 1.8 per cent (n = 2) of married males and 1.32 per cent (n = 3) married females reporting this. Breakdown of family relations too is reported only in a very small number of cases (8). The distribution according to our sample, therefore, indicates that the adverse effect of migration on marital and family relations was minimal, and that, on the contrary, the migration was seen as strengthening family relations.

## Migrants' Behaviour

Migrants' behaviour pattern in the host country was quite normal for the overwhelming majority, who reported that they were able to adjust to the environment satisfactorily. Those who reported signs of maladjustment to the new conditions were few – about 16 per cent. But even among them many have reported that they were able to adjust satisfactorily.

Some of the migrants had cultivated or intensified certain habits and addictions to varying degrees. Thirty per cent of the males reported "heavy smoking" and a little more than a quarter of the males stated that they increased their consumption of liquor. Around 10 per cent of the migrants said they suffered from sleeplessness and an equal number that they became more prone to illness or that their existing ailments became intensified. The conditions that were reported on the whole were

**Table 32.** Overall adjustment to separation by family and migrants according to age

| Age-group | Adjusted very well | | Adjusted well | | No change | | Could not adjust at all | | Total | |
|---|---|---|---|---|---|---|---|---|---|---|
| | Male | Female | Male | Female | Male | Female | Male | Female | Male | Female |
| 15–19 | 0 | 1 | 0 | 2 | 0 | 3 | 0 | 0 | 0 | 6 |
| 20–24 | 0 | 8 | 4 | 11 | 3 | 8 | 0 | 1 | 7 | 28 |
| 25–29 | 11 | 11 | 13 | 27 | 9 | 17 | 0 | 3 | 33 | 58 |
| 30–34 | 23 | 23 | 22 | 44 | 18 | 11 | 0 | 3 | 63 | 81 |
| 35–39 | 19 | 18 | 11 | 22 | 3 | 20 | 1 | 3 | 34 | 63 |
| 40–44 | 7 | 8 | 9 | 15 | 3 | 5 | 0 | 1 | 19 | 29 |
| 45–49 | 3 | 4 | 6 | 3 | 1 | 4 | 0 | 1 | 10 | 12 |
| 50–54 | 6 | 2 | 1 | 0 | 0 | 1 | 0 | 0 | 7 | 3 |
| 55–50 | 0 | 0 | 0 | 0 | 0 | 2 | 0 | 0 | 0 | 2 |
| Total | 69 | 75 | 66 | 124 | 37 | 71 | 1 | 12 | 173 | 282 |

not of a magnitude or intensity to alter the overall impression of a tolerably smooth process of adjustment to the new environment.

### Communication between Respondents and Family, Relatives, etc.

The information gathered in the survey indicates that almost all migrants maintained regular and frequent contact with their families. For nearly 90 per cent the only means of communication was by letters. About 10 per cent were able to maintain contact by telephone as well. A small proportion – eight migrants – reported use of cassettes. The frequency of communication is an indicator of the concern of both parties for each other's welfare. Weekly communication with husbands and wives was quite common – this was the case for 60 per cent of males and about 43 per cent of female migrants. A slightly smaller proportion communicated once a fortnight. Two hundred and seventy-nine migrants also reported keeping in contact with their children by letter. Given the fact that the married migrants numbered 337 and of these not all would have had children in the age-group that could correspond or receive letters, the proportion in frequent communication with their children is quite high. Relatives and friends received much less attention. What was noteworthy was the place taken by parents in the case of female migrants: nearly one-third of them communicated with their parents once a month. This was not the case with male migrants. The survey data indicate that on the whole frequent contact and communication with relations and parents must have played an important part in giving emotional and psychological support to migrants and families.

### Personal and Family Problems and Crises

A significant proportion of migrants and their families had to cope with personal and family problems of a serious kind. Serious illness or death of a family member affected about 94 families. Two or three other families reported violent disputes with neighbours and marital problems. Although 80 per cent of the sample had gone through the period of migration without a serious crisis of any kind, the fact that about one in five did have serious problems suggests that these are contingencies which migrants must take into account and provide for, and that support should be available to such migrants on a more organized basis through government and voluntary agencies where necessary or feasible.

## Income, Expenditure, and Savings

The survey encountered the usual problems of recall in regard to the data on income and expenditure. The respondents did not appear to have detailed accounts of their earnings and disbursements and were able to provide the information only in approximate estimates and round sums. Investigators also reported that they observed some degree of reluctance on the part of the respondents to give details of income earned, assets acquired, and savings that had been accumulated and brought back. This applied particularly to current incomes and wealth, which was relevant with regard to both the food stamp scheme and personal income tax.

**Table 33**. Migrants' behaviour

| Behaviour pattern | Male | | | Female | | |
|---|---|---|---|---|---|---|
| | Yes | No | Total | Yes | No | Total |
| Adustment to environment | 183 | 9 | 192 | 299 | 18 | 317 |
| Withdrawal from society | 10 | 182 | 192 | 72 | 245 | 317 |
| Seeking company or becoming more extrovert | 29 | 163 | 192 | 6 | 311 | 317 |

Subject to these qualifications, the survey data provide estimates which are sufficient for the purpose of ascertaining the average levels of income earned and the behaviour of migrants in regard to expenditure, savings, and investments. It has also to be noted that the income and expenditure data have been expressed in terms of Sri Lankan rupees. These figures will reflect the changes in the value of the rupee in relation to the foreign currency in which the incomes were earned. During the period 1980–1985, the Sri Lankan rupee depreciated by approximately 54 per cent against the US dollar. The rupee value of the US dollar, for example, was Rs. 16.53 in 1980, increasing to Rs. 26.28 by the end of 1984. These variations had to be kept in mind when examining the data gathered in the survey.

**Income and Expenditure Abroad**

Tables 34 to 39 show the aggregate data relating to income, expenditure and savings for six categories of migrant. The average monthly incomes earned by migrants range from Rs. 2,600 for the lowest-paid migrants, that is domestic workers and housemaids, to Rs. 11,000 for workers in the high-level category who receive the highest remuneration (table 34). There was, however, considerable variation in the incomes earned within each category.

The monthly expenses of the employees in the different categories varied widely. The professional and middle-level categories incurred approximately Rs. 2,000 per month on living and other expenses, leaving a net average monthly income of about Rs. 9,300 and Rs. 5,300 respectively. But in the case of the skilled and unskilled workers, the expenses were lower – Rs. 1,415 for the skilled and Rs. 1,200 for the unskilled (table 35). The housemaids had the lowest level of living expenses as both the cost of board and lodging, as well as various items of personal expenditure, were borne by the employer. The average monthly expenses abroad of those who reported expenditure were only about Rs. 400. A comparison of the net income after deduction of living expenses is given in table 34. The ratio of average monthly income of the lowest-paid category with that of the highest-paid category is 1:3.6.

The entire population in the sample had earned approximately Rs. 41 million on their employment contracts, which averaged a period of 24 months. The average earnings per employee in the total sample was therefore in the region of Rs. 80,000 for the entire period of the contract. The earnings of the professionals amounted to approximately Rs. 322,000, while the average for the housemaids was approximately Rs. 50,000.

**Table 34.** Net monthly earnings of migrants by category (rupees)

| Category | Monthly salary | Other cash benefits | Living expenses abroad | Other expenses | Net monthly earnings |
|---|---|---|---|---|---|
| Female domestic workers | 2,609 | 152 | 57 | 22 | 2,583 |
| Male skilled workers | 6,832 | 997 | 1,415 | 131 | 6,282 |
| Male unskilled workers | 4,379 | 799 | 1,216 | 60 | 3,902 |
| Male middle-level workers | 5,895 | 1,687 | 2,103 | 110 | 5,369 |
| Male high-level workers | 10,500 | 1,000 | 1,566 | 500 | 9,334 |
| Female other occupational group | 3,750 | 666 | 383 | — | 4,033 |

**Table 35.** Monthly living expenses by category (rupees)

| Category | Monthly living expenses |
|---|---|
| Female domestic workers | 400.00 |
| Male skilled workers | 1,400.00 |
| Male unskilled workers | 1,200.00 |
| Male middle-level workers | 2,100.00 |
| Male high-level workers | 7,700.00 |
| Other female workers | 1,150.00 |

**Table 36.** Income, expenditure, and transfers from employment abroad

| Item | Total | Mean |
|---|---|---|
| 1. Income by the first contract (monthly salary) | 2,016,900 | 4,009 |
| 2. Total for the period the contract is valid | 37,125,000 | 73,807 |
| 3. Other cash benefits/earnings (total) | 3,902,200 | 32,249 |
| | | (7,757) |
| 4. Expenditure: living expenses abroad (total) | 5,324,800 | 10,586 |
| | | (23,985) |
| 5. Expenditure: money sent for expenditure back home (total) | 16,152,600 | 32,112 |
| | | (39,492) |
| 6. Other expenses (total) | 709,800 | 1,411 |
| | | (12,905) |
| 7. Savings: money brought home | 10,318,800 | 20,514 |
| | | (24,165) |
| 8. Transfer in kind | 4,907,600 | 9,756 |
| | | (12,147) |
| 9. Total earnings (2 + 3) | 41,027,200 | 81,565 |
| 10. Total expenditure (4 + 6) | 6,034,600 | 11,991 |
| 11. Total savings abroad | 34,992,600 | 69,567 |
| 12. 11 as percentage of 9 | 85 | |
| 13. Total transferred (5 + 7 + 8) | 31,379,000 | 62,383 |
| 14. 13 as percentage of 12 | 76 | |

Table 36 presents the total net earnings for each category of employees after deducting both the foreign and local expenditure incurred by them, as well as the income forgone by those employees who were gainfully employed prior to the migration. For the purpose of this calculation, it has been assumed that these employees would have continued in employment and earned the same income had they not migrated and that the situation for the other employees would not have changed had they remained in the country. The total net benefit accruing to the 510 employees in the sample was approximately Rs. 31 million. It has to be noted here that the earnings of the high-level group do not seem to be quite representative of the incomes earned abroad by this category. Information available from sources other than from the survey indicates that the average earnings of professionals, such as accountants and engineers, are considerably higher than the average reported by the individuals who were included in the sample survey. However, this category comprises a very small share of the migrants. If we assume that the net average earnings of this group are double what has been recorded in the survey, the total net earnings would have risen by about 3.0 per cent.

The large majority of the migrants who were female domestic workers made average earnings which would have normally taken them about 15 years to earn on the salaries they could have expected as domestic aides in middle-class Sri Lankan homes. The next largest group, the male skilled workers, would have taken at least six to seven years to earn the amount they accumulated as net earnings, working regularly and receiving monthly gross wages of about Rs. 11,500. For the male unskilled group, the third largest in the sample, the corresponding figures for the period of employment required in Sri Lanka to accumulate the net income earned abroad would have been in the same range. Domestic earnings at this income level, however, would have gone almost entirely into the current consumption of households, and left little or no surplus for the acquisition of assets and for investment. These figures provide a broad measurement of the extent to which migrants have benefitted from their employment abroad.

For the high-level employees the monthly salaries earned abroad approximate about three times what they might have earned in Sri Lanka. This, however, is subject to the qualification made earlier regarding the incomes recorded for this category in the sample survey. For female domestic workers, the average monthly salary earned abroad is the equivalent of ten times what they could have normally earned in domestic service in Sri Lanka. The male skilled employees enjoyed wages abroad which were about five to six times what they could have earned had they been able to secure continuous employment at the prevailing market wage rates. The same would be true of the unskilled workers.

The survey data reveal that all categories of employees remitted a very large proportion of the incomes that were earned – approximately 76 per cent. In all categories, the average amount remitted to Sri Lanka in cash and kind exceeded 70 per cent of the total earned. In the case of housemaids, out of a total income of Rs. 15.4 million for 311 employees, the remittances in cash and kind and savings brought back with them when they returned home amounted to Rs. 13 million. For the skilled workers, who numbered 124 in the sample, out of a total income of Rs. 17.6 million remittances in cash and kind amounted to Rs. 12.4 million. The bulk of the money was sent as remittances in regular instalments for the expenditure of the households in Sri Lanka. This was particularly true of the migrants in unskilled categories and the housemaids. In the case of the housemaids, Rs. 8 million out of a total of Rs. 13 million transferred were in the form of regular remittances. For skilled employees, Rs. 5.4 million out of a total of Rs. 10.3 transferred fell into this category, and for unskilled workers Rs. 1.4 million out of a total of Rs. 2.5 million.

The pattern of remittances was significantly different for the middle and high-level categories, where the regular remittances were less than half of the total money remitted. Although regular remittances formed the larger share of the money transferred to Sri Lanka, it appears that substantial sums of money were accumulated by migrants and retained until their return. In the case of the female domestic workers, the savings brought home on their return averaged Rs. 10,000. This amounts to a total of Rs. 3.1 million out of transfers totalling Rs. 13 million, that is, about 24 per cent. In the case of the next largest category of skilled workers, the savings accumulated and brought back on their return amounted to as much as Rs. 15 million, i.e. nearly 40 per cent of the total transferred. This phenomenon deserves some comment.

The inducements for migrant employees to send back as much of their earnings as possible and hold them in interst-bearing accounts in local banks do not appear to have been entirely effective. While employees in almost all categories brought back between 70 and 83 per cent of their income, they appear to be retaining considerable sums with them until they terminate their contract and return. This behaviour may be motivated by a variety of reasons, including a desire to hold the income in convertible currencies until the employment is terminated, the need to have ready access to funds in the event of an emergency, or to regulate the expenditure back at home and make sure that the income earned is not spent wastefully. While there is some loss to the national economy as well as to individual migrants as a result of the retention of funds abroad, it seems unlikely that migrants will change their responses and significantly reduce the sums they retain.

Transfers in kind also account for a significant proportion of the income and assets brought back by migrants. In the case of female domestic workers this came to approximately 12 per cent of the total income earned. For skilled workers, the proportion is also around 12 per cent. In the other categories, the proportions varied from 8 per cent for females in other occupational groups to around 12 per cent for high-level categories. It would, therefore, seem that the expenditure of migrants on various assets such as consumer durables, which they transfer to Sri Lanka, is in the range of 10 to 15 per cent of their income, which, although significant, does not suggest an extravagant pattern of expenditure.

## Household Consumption and Expenditure

The survey data help us to draw some broad conclusions regarding the levels of consumption enjoyed by the households of migrants during the period the migrants were employed abroad. To be able to assess the impact of the remittances of migrants on household consumption during the migration, we need to have firm data on the household incomes and the incomes of spending units prior to the migration. The data that the survey had been able to gather do not enable us to obtain a well defined profile of incomes of migrant households prior to the migration. There are several problems in interpreting the data. First, the period covering the migration witnessed a rapid and continuing rate of inflation. Money incomes rose steeply. For example, according to Central Bank surveys, the average household incomes for the fourth income decile rose from Rs. 523 in 1978/79 to Rs. 856 in 1981/82. The value of the rupee also depreciated steadily, as mentioned earlier. Therefore, the increases in consumption that took place in real terms during the period remittances were being received by households were considerably less than what is observed in terms of money incomes. The survey was also unable to obtain complete responses regarding household incomes from all the respondents. This is partly explained by the fact that migrant respondents were unable to provide detailed information on the income obtained by other members of the household or the income and expenditure of the spending units where a single household contained several.

However, from the responses received regarding incomes earned by migrants prior to the migration, it is possible to determine broadly the level of income enjoyed by households before the migrants left for employment abroad. The second section of this study analysed these data in some detail. On the basis of the available data it would appear that the average income enjoyed by the migrants at the time of migration would have been in the region of Rs. 700 for the female domestic workers, and of Rs. 1,000 to Rs. 1,500 for male skilled workers – the two largest categories. Household incomes have been higher, but these do not correctly represent the incomes available for spending by the migrants' families as separate spending units in the household.

The monthly remittances that were sent by the migrant workers were much higher than the income that had been enjoyed by the families prior to the migration. This would initially suggest that households were able to raise considerably their level of current consumption. It could be argued that the migration resulted in a sudden elevation in the standard of living of households which they would not be able to sustain after the migration unless they had prudently managed their consumption and investment during this period. The monthly remittances, however, did not go entirely to finance consumption. When we make allowance for savings from monthly remittances in the case of female domestic workers, estimates indicate that household consumption would have increased by more than two-and-a-half times. On average, current expenditure by families of migrants would have reached approximately Rs. 1,800 per month for those who received regular remittances from migrant members employed abroad. In the case of the skilled workers, who on average sent Rs. 5,000 a month, the expenditure incurred on consumption would have been in the region of Rs. 2,500 per month. It would therefore seem that the substantial increases in income did result in a sudden increase in consumption and standards of living. This aspect will be examined in further detail when we deal with the adjustments households had to make when migrants returned and when the same levels of regular incomes were not sustained.

On the whole, however, the patterns of expenditure do not suggest extravagant spending or wasteful consumption. The average expenditure on consumer durables for almost all groups amounted to about two months' income. This was highest for the skilled level category, averaging about Rs. 14,500 per migrant for the households reporting expenditure on this item, as against a monthly income of approximately Rs. 7,000. In the case of female domestic workers, the average expenditure amounted to approximately Rs. 6,404, which was more than two months' income. Of course, these averages do not accurately reflect the proportions of income spent on consumer durables. There was a significant number who did not acquire consumer durables.

Most of the consumer durables would have been acquired abroad and included in the transfers in kind. The figures, however, indicate that a substantial portion of the transfers in kind would have also gone into consumption expenditure and would have included items such as food and clothing.

Another item which enables us to assess the quality of spending on investments in the money spent on jewellery. The expenditure as a proportion of savings in income was highest for the category of high-level employees. Since the number

**Table 37**. Net earnings of migrants by category

| Category | Total earnings abroad | Total expenditure | Local expenditure | Total expenditure | Total net earnings | Total earnings mean | Total net earnings mean |
|---|---|---|---|---|---|---|---|
| Female domestic workers | 15,433,000 | 331,000 | 774,000 | 1,105,000 | 14,328,000 | 50,000 | 46,000 |
| Male skilled-level group | 17,656,000 | 3,084,000 | 605,000 | 3,689,000 | 13,967,000 | 142,000 | 113,000 |
| Male unskilled level group | 3,756,000 | 614,000 | 233,000 | 847,000 | 2,909,000 | 78,000 | 61,000 |
| Male middle-level group | 2,357,000 | 484,000 | 138,000 | 622,000 | 1,735,000 | 139,000 | 102,000 |
| Male high-level group | 1,288,000 | 307,000 | 34,000 | 341,000 | 947,000 | 322,000 | 237,000 |
| Female other occupation group | 539,000 | 47,000 | 15,000 | 62,000 | 477,000 | 90,000 | 80,000 |
| Total | 41,029,000 | 4,867,000 | 1,799,000 | 6,666,000 | 34,363,000 | | |
| Net income from domestic employment forgone | | | | | 3,546,000 | | |
| Total net surplus | | | | | 30,817,000 | | |

involved, however, is only four, it would be unwise to regard this as being representative of the expenditure of this category. Skilled-level groups invested approximately 2.6 per cent of their total savings on jewellery, while female domestic workers invested 4.4 per cent. These, however, are not large proportions and it appears that on average migrants did not indulge in extravagant spending on gold and jewellery.

Yet another item of expenditure that would be indicative of ostentatious spending would be expenditure on ceremonies such as weddings and funerals. This item has been recorded inclusive of expenditure on illness. Even so, the entire item has only absorbed a small proportion of the savings. In the case of female domestic workers, it amounted to 4.07 per cent of the total amount transferred; the corresponding figure for skilled male workers was 3.02 per cent. The data in the survey in regard to these items, however, have to be related to the relevant changes that have occurred in the status of households. Given the fact that most married migrants had young families, the opportunity to spend on occasions such as weddings would have been limited.

The income and expenditure data also throw some light on the state of indebtedness of the migrants and the efforts they have made to repay their debts. The analysis in the third section indicated that the cost of the migration to the large majority of the migrants was surprisingly low. In the case of female domestic workers, the large majority of them did not incur expenditure on agency fees. The cost of internal travel and domestic arrangements during the sojourn abroad were all contained at very moderate levels. There is no evidence that migrants are compelled to incur large debts in order to secure employment or to make the necessary preparation for migration. The item on repayment of debts, therefore, would largely cover debts incurred by the households for causes other than the migration. In the case of the female domestic workers, repayment of loans and debts amounted on average to approximately Rs. 5,500 – a little more than two months' income abroad. In the case of male skilled workers, the corresponding figure was a little more than one month's income. Assuming that these migrants were able to liquidate their debts fully, it would appear that the debt situation for the sample as a whole, as well as for indebted households, was not particularly grave. Relative to income earned prior to departure, debts may have amounted to about a year's total earnings. In the sample as a whole there were 219 households which reported repayment of debts, indicating that at least 43 per cent of the households had been indebted prior to migration. The migration has helped these indebted households to move out of the situation of indebtedness and acquire new assets, improving their general financial position and creditworthiness.

Another item indicative of the pattern of expenditure and investments is education. As in the case of expenditure on marriages and funerals, expenditure on education would depend on the age structure of the household and the presence of children of schoolgoing age. In all, 107 households or 21 per cent of the sample incurred some expenditure on education, the average ranging from Rs. 8,000 for the high-level professional category to Rs. 1,200 for the skilled level. Female domestic employees and unskilled workers spent on average less than skilled workers, suggesting that educational aspirations for children bear some relation to levels of income and skill.

**Savings**

The data gathered in the survey provide information on the pattern of savings made by the households of the migrants (tables 38 and 39). In all categories, the level of savings was quite high. The aggregate savings for the sample as a whole was approximately 50.4 per cent. In the case of the female domestic workers, the savings, excluding repayment of debts and consumer durables, amounted to as much as 30.6 per cent of the total earned. When the repayment of loans and debts is accounted as savings, the total goes up to 36 per cent. If consumer durables are added it rises to 42 per cent. In the case of next largest category, the skilled workers, the corresponding proportions were 44 and 49 per cent respectively.

The largest investments made by the migrants were on homes. The female domestic workers spent approximately Rs. 2.4 million (38 per cent) of their investments on improvements to and construction of homes. The male skilled workers spent Rs. 2.6 million (30 per cent) on similar investments, the middle-level category 37 per cent, and male unskilled workers 31 per cent. The changes in housing conditions and what it denotes for improvements in the living conditions of migrants are examined in the section that follows. What is relevant at this point is to note that although housing investment was the single largest investment for most groups, once again it has not resulted in highly extravagant forms of house construction. The maximum spent on housing for the different groups is in the range of Rs. 300,000 to Rs. 100,000. The highest investment – Rs. 300,000 – made on housing is by a migrant in the male skilled category. In the case of female domestic workers, the highest investment was Rs. 100,000, and for male unskilled workers it was Rs. 170,000.

The next highest investment in all categories was the amount placed in fixed deposits in banks. This was highest for the skilled workers: those who held such deposits had an average of Rs. 50,000 in them. The deposits amounted to a total of Rs. 1.8 million, or 20.8 per cent of the investments made out of their savings. In the case of female domestic workers it was 15.4 per cent.

The analysis of the data in each category indicates that the savings performance varied very widely within each category. Only about 26 per cent of the migrants in the sample, or 134 migrants in all, had fixed deposits to their credit after return: 68 of the 311 female migrants and 66 of the 153 male migrants. The monthly household incomes from fixed deposits ranged in the case of females from Rs. 500 to smaller sums in the region of Rs. 50 and Rs. 75. In the case of male migrants, incomes from fixed deposits were higher, one-third earning more than Rs. 500 per month. There were a few who were earning income as interest from fixed deposits of between Rs. 1,000 and Rs. 3,000. One reported an income of Rs. 7,500 per month.

The investments on land ranged from a low 5.6 per cent of the total investments for female domestic workers, and 7 per cent for unskilled workers, to a high 27 per cent in the case of the male high-level group. Male skilled workers invested 10 per cent of their savings on land. Agricultural land did not figure prominently in the pattern of investment. The proportion of the migrants investing in land was in the region of 11 per cent of the total number.

The cases where savings were invested in business are few. The group which

Table 38. Use of savings, excluding current household consumption

| Item | Female domestic workers and other female workers (311) | | | Male unskilled workers (48) | | |
|---|---|---|---|---|---|---|
| | No. of positive responses | Total (rupees) | Mean | No. of positive responses | Total (rupees) | Mean |
| 1. House | 169 | 2,433,600 | 14,400 | 18 | 414,000 | 23,000 |
| 2. Land | 23 | 355,500 | 15,500 | 4 | 93,000 | 23,000 |
| 3. Machinery and equipment | 21 | 160,000 | 7,600 | 6 | 5,400 | 900 |
| 4. Vehicles | 3 | 64,000 | 21,300 | 3 | 26,000 | 9,000 |
| 5. Consumer durables | 126 | 807,000 | 6,400 | 14 | 133,000 | 10,000 |
| 6. Fixed deposits | 66 | 968,600 | 14,600 | 11 | 205,000 | 19,000 |
| 7. Business | 11 | 88,000 | 8,000 | 6 | 225,000 | 38,000 |
| 8. Education of children | 65 | 172,700 | 2,600 | 8 | 27,000 | 3,000 |
| 9. Jewellery | 106 | 684,000 | 6,400 | 10 | 52,000 | 5,000 |
| 10. Repayment of loans and debts | 135 | 750,000 | 5,500 | 16 | 119,000 | 7,000 |
| 11. Gifts, donations, assistance to elders | 90 | 272,500 | 3,000 | 16 | 59,000 | 4,000 |
| 12. Weddings, funerals, illness, medical and other | 89 | 526,000 | 6,000 | 12 | 126,000 | 11,000 |
| 13. Total | | 7,282,500 | | | 1,484,900 | |
| 14. 13 as percentage of total earnings | | 47 | — | | 40 | — |
| 15. Items 1–7, 9, 10 as percentage of total earnings | | 40 | — | | 34 | — |
| 16. Items 1–4, 6, 7, 9, 10 as percentage of total | | 35 | — | | 30 | — |

**Table 39.** Use of savings, excluding current household consumption

| Item | Male skilled workers (124) | | | Male middle-level workers (17) | | |
|---|---|---|---|---|---|---|
| | No. of positive responses | Total (rupees) | Mean | No. of positive responses | Total (rupees) | Mean |
| 1. House | 72 | 2,637,500 | 36,600 | 17 | 373,00 | 22,000 |
| 2. Land | 19 | 903,000 | 47,500 | 17 | 115,000 | 6,800 |
| 3. Machinery and equipment | 12 | 197,800 | 16,500 | 17 | 14,000 | 800 |
| 4. Vehicles | 20 | 879,800 | 44,000 | 17 | 90,000 | 5,300 |
| 5. Consumer durables | 56 | 804,500 | 14,500 | 17 | 74,400 | 4,400 |
| 6. Fixed deposits | 36 | 1,812,000 | 50,300 | 17 | 198,000 | 11,600 |
| 7. Business | 19 | 673,000 | 35,400 | 17 | 40,000 | 2,350 |
| 8. Education of children | 15 | 102,500 | 6,800 | 17 | 20,000 | 1,200 |
| 9. Jewellery | 40 | 372,300 | 9,300 | 17 | 29,500 | 1,750 |
| 10. Repayment of loans and debts | 49 | 419,700 | 8,500 | 17 | 65,800 | 3,900 |
| 11. Gifts, donations, assistance to elders | 47 | 514,500 | 10,900 | 17 | 35,000 | 2,000 |
| 12. Weddings, funerals, illness, medical and other | 35 | 378,600 | 10,800 | 17 | 36,000 | 2,100 |
| 13. Total | | 9,695,200 | | | 1,090,700 | |
| 14. 13 as percentage of total earnings | | 55 | | | 46 | |
| 15. Items 1–7, 9, 10 as percentage of total earnings | | 49 | — | | 42 | — |
| 16. Items 1–4, 6, 7, 9, 10 as percentage of total earnings | | 45 | — | | 39 | — |

shows the highest propensity for this kind of investment is that of male unskilled workers, which invested approximately Rs. 225,000, or 17 per cent of their total savings, in business. The male skilled workers come next with Rs. 673,000 or 7.7 per cent. There were in all 36 migrants who had invested in business, and their investments ranged from small sums in the region of Rs. 2,000 to Rs. 5,000 to more substantial amounts of between Rs. 50,000 and Rs. 200,000. In many cases the businesses were grocery stores and self-employed transport activities. In the latter case, migrants had purchased vehicles which they used for the transport of passengers or goods. In the entire sample of migrants, the proportion of those investing in business and capable of entrepreneurship of any type is not likely to be larger than the proportion that might be found in the country as a whole. They are, as a group, both in respect of skills and attitude, oriented towards wage employment, and entrepreneurial types are likely to be somewhat rare in these categories. Nevertheless, the survey indicates that as much as 7 per cent of migrants attempted to set themselves up in some type of business. Other investments made out of savings include vehicles, machinery and equipment, and jewellery. The highest investment in jewellery is to be found among the female domestic workers, who invested approximately Rs. 264,000, or 4.5 per cent of their total savings abroad, on this item.

The savings performance also points to another feature which is common to all the categories. The monthly remittances sent by the various categories range from Rs. 5,000 sent by male skilled workers to Rs. 2,000 sent by female domestic workers. In each case it would seem that households received an average remittance considerably higher than the income they had enjoyed prior to the migration. The evidence available regarding expenditure and savings, however, reveals that a considerable part of the money that had been remitted was saved. In the case of the female domestic workers, for instance, the money sent back in the form of regular remittances amounted to approximately Rs. 8 million. Transfers in kind and money investments, including repayment of debts and consumer durables, amounted to Rs. 6.3 million. It would therefore appear that at least 17.5 per cent of the money that had been sent regularly had been saved and contributed to financing various forms of investment. A similar pattern can be observed for the skilled workers, who brought back Rs. 4.9 million and transferred in kind Rs. 2.1 million, but whose total investments amounted to Rs. 8.6 million.

The performance on savings, both in terms of proportion saved and the use of savings, varies widely within each category (table 40). These data are examined in greater detail in the analysis provided under different categories of migrants later in this section. If investments on consumer durables, housing, and fixed deposits are taken as indicators of the number who made significant savings out of their earnings, it would appear that, in the aggregate, of the 510 migrants in the sample, the largest number, 284 or 55 per cent, have invested in housing – a fairly reliable indicator of the number who have succeeded in accumulating savings. Two hundred and sixteen, or 42 per cent, have invested in consumer durables and 134, or 26 per cent, in fixed deposits. Another 13 per cent reported that they had substantial savings which they had not yet used and which they planned to invest in fixed deposits, business, land, and housing, among other investments. Not all those who invested in consumer durables and fixed deposits would have invested in housing or had the opportunity to do so; the number who have effected savings

**Table 40.** Composition of investments and percentage share of total by main categories of migrants

| Item | Female domestic workers | Female other occupational group | Male high-level | Male middle-level | Male skilled-level | Male unskilled level |
|---|---|---|---|---|---|---|
| House | 38.76 | 51.50 | 24.40 | 37.30 | 30.30 | 31.30 |
| Land | 5.66 | 9.47 | 27.10 | 11.50 | 10.37 | 7.04 |
| Machinery and equipment | 2.55 | 0.00 | 0.00 | 1.40 | 2.77 | 4.08 |
| Vehicles | 1.02 | 9.47 | 0.00 | 9.00 | 10.10 | 1.97 |
| Consumer durables | 12.85 | 0.00 | 9.76 | 7.40 | 9.30 | 10.06 |
| Fixed deposits | 15.42 | 22.73 | 28.49 | 19.80 | 20.80 | 15.50 |
| Business | 1.40 | 0.00 | 0.00 | 4.00 | 7.70 | 17.03 |
| Jewellery | 10.89 | 1.50 | 10.17 | 2.95 | 4.27 | 3.97 |
| Repayment of loans and debts | 11.94 | 5.30 | 0.00 | 6.58 | 4.81 | 9.00 |

would have been more than the number reflected in the housing investments. It is therefore reasonable to conclude that not less than two-thirds of the migrants have been able to save and invest in some type of assets. This would, however, mean that for about one-third of the migrants, their employment abroad did not bring them any significant savings and new assets.

Another interesting feature revealed in the survey is that the key variables of educational levels and marital status do not appear to have any significant differential impact within each category in regard to savings and pattern of investments.

The survey revealed that there had been hardly any systematic effort by government of non-governmental agencies to provide assistance and service to returning migrants to help them adjust and re-enter the workforce. The responses showed little evidence of any counselling of migrants or assistance in prudently investing their savings. Neither was there any formal or organized effort to identify return migrants, to help them to obtain re-employment, or to assist them to establish themselves in self-employment. The migrants' responses indicated that there was a significant proportion who were seeking means of self-employment. A number of initiatives taken by the government to reach return migrants and to cater to their needs had not yet had time to show results by the time of the survey.

## Socio-economic Improvements, Adjustments, and Attitudinal Changes

On the socio-economic conditions of households, the survey encountered the usual problems of obtaining accurate information on current incomes and wealth. In the majority of cases firm conclusions regarding post-migration adjustments are not warranted, as migrants had returned recently and sufficient time had not elapsed to indicate how they had adjusted. We will see that this applies particularly to activity status and employment of migrants after their return. A significant number of migrants were awaiting employment and, in all likelihood, would re-enter the workforce after a brief interval. In the case of several other migrants, income from investments recently made in business and returns have not yet begun to accrue. As many as 35 of the male and 33 of the female migrants indicated that they had substantial savings which they had not yet invested. They were planning to make various income-generating investments with these savings, including types of self-employment (table 41).

A more reliable indicator of the changes in living standards in the households of migrants would be the improvements that have been reported in the cost of housing, the type of furniture, and other consumer durables in use before and after migration, and the perceptions of the migrant households themselves regarding increases in their normal consumption.

### Unemployment

The data indicated that the employment situation among return migrants had deteriorated after their return in comparison with the situation prior to migration. In the case of male migrants, there were in all 73 who were not gainfully employed prior to migration, including 45 migrants who were openly unemployed, 10 students, 16 non-earning families, and two pensioners. The situation after migration

**Table 41**. Unemployment time period since arrival by gender

| Period (months) | Male | Female |
|---|---|---|
| Less than 3 | 20 | 12 |
| 4–6 | 14 | 19 |
| 7–9 | 14 | 10 |
| 10–12 | 23 | 8 |
| 13–18 | 23 | 17 |
| 19–24 | 22 | 11 |
| 25–30 | 10 | 5 |
| 31–36 | 4 | 2 |
| 37–42 | 3 | 3 |
| 43–48 | 4 | 1 |
| 49–54 | 3 | 1 |
| 55–60 | 2 | 0 |
| Over 60 | 1 | 0 |

had changed significantly. The category of those not gainfully employed had increased to 143. Eighty-nine of the 124 skilled employees who had returned after employment abroad declared themselves unemployed. A considerable number of them (51) had not returned to their previous occupations. In addition there were 14 employees in the category of male domestic labour who had migrated for employment but had failed to secure employment on their return. Table 42 provides information regarding the period of waiting of these unemployed workers. Of the 143 male migrants who reported that they were unemployed, there were 20 whose stay in Sri Lanka after their return had been less than three months at the time of the survey; 71 had been there less than a year. However, 49 had periods of waiting in excess of two years. In the majority of cases, where the periods of waiting are short and where the migrants possess skills in demand, it can be assumed that they are likely to find employment. Some of the migrants who have been categorized as unemployed are likely to be seeking opportunities for self-employment with the savings they have obtained. It also appears that several migrants who responded to the question assumed that they were unemployed if they did not hold a job which provided a regular wage or salary. For example, of the 143 who stated that they were not employed, 23 reported that they had invested in businesses. Their condition of unemployment has also to be seen in the light of other income-earning investments they have made. Twenty reported substantial investments on vehicles; 49 had fixed deposits averaging Rs. 50,000, which at the time of the survey would have yielded about Rs. 800 per month.

The sample of migrants surveyed included approximately 48 unskilled workers, of whom 28 were unemployed prior to migration. The number reporting themselves as unemployed at the time of the survey was 39. The data indicate that 11 unskilled workers who were unemployed have been able to accumulate savings and invest in fixed deposits which averaged Rs. 18,600 per migrant; six have made investments in businesses.

The survey data concerning the male migrants, therefore, present a mixed picture. Although the unemployment situation has worsened in terms of numbers, it

**Table 42.** Income, expenditure, and savings of unemployed return migrants

| Item | Female workers (89) | | Male skilled (89) | | Male unskilled (39) | | Male middle-level (12) | |
|---|---|---|---|---|---|---|---|---|
| | Number who have invested | Average investment | Number who have invested | Average investment | Number who have invested | Average investment | Number who have invested | Average investment |
| House | 56 | 6,300 | 51 | 37,000 | 12 | 26,750 | 8 | 40,000 |
| Land | 10 | 5,300 | 15 | 34,200 | 4 | 23,250 | 2 | 57,500 |
| Machinery and equipment | 12 | 0 | 8 | 21,600 | 6 | 9,000 | 0 | 0 |
| Vehicles | 1 | 0 | 16 | 42,700 | 3 | 8,700 | 1 | 20,000 |
| Consumer durables | 38 | 2,600 | 43 | 13,700 | 12 | 10,300 | 5 | 8,500 |
| Fixed deposits | 42 | 8,700 | 29 | 49,900 | 11 | 10,700 | 6 | 23,800 |
| Business | 5 | 3,300 | 15 | 40,000 | 6 | 37,000 | 2 | 20,000 |
| Education of children | 41 | 1,200 | 11 | 8,700 | 6 | 3,000 | 2 | 10,000 |
| Jewellery | 22 | 6,400 | 34 | 9,400 | 7 | 5,500 | 3 | 9,800 |
| Repayment of loans and debts | 25 | 3,400 | 37 | 8,200 | 12 | 7,300 | 5 | 13,100 |
| Gifts, donations, assistance to elders | 18 | 5,100 | 47 | 9,900 | 14 | 4,000 | 3 | 7,000 |
| Weddings, funerals, illness, medical and other | 20 | 6,800 | 28 | 10,000 | 9 | 13,000 | 3 | 3,700 |

is difficult to conclude that this situation will continue in the case of most of the skilled employees. The data, however, suggest that migrant workers are not being readily absorbed into the workforce on their return. As many as 49, i.e. 25 per cent of all male migrants, had been unemployed for periods exceeding 24 months after return. A significant number among the unemployed had acquired resources which enabled them to secure income opportunities of various kinds, including self-employment. The skills and other benefits of the migration have not markedly improved their position in the labour market. In reply to the question of whether they had acquired new skills and capacities which improved their employability, only 31 male employees answered in the affirmative.

There is another important factor which has to be taken into account in assessing the unemployment situation. A large number of them were seeking opportunities for re-employment abroad; consequently it is likely that initially they remained voluntarily unemployed in the expectation of securing employment abroad. Of the 193 male migrants, 130 were either seeking or planning to seek re-employment abroad. These responses indicated that the majority of migrants were not fully adjusted to the prospect of remaining permanently in the country. Only about one-third of the male migrants had decided not to look for employment abroad and were presumably satisfied that what they had been able to earn and save was adequate to organize their lives at home.

The position in regard to the female migrants was significantly different from that of the males. For them the unemployment situation had not deteriorated seriously; 77 had reported themselves as unemployed prior to migration, while the figure after migration was 89. A large majority of females prior to migration were housewives – 228 out of 317. Two hundred and five of the migrants had returned to this position. Of the female migrants, 161 reported that they were seeking re-employment abroad, most of them as housemaids. Nearly half of the female workers appeared to have regarded their employment abroad as a once-and-for-all effort to accumulate some savings and then return to their previous household responsibilities. In regard to skill formation and acquisition of new competence, most employees in these categories appear to have regarded their work experience as being satisfactory in equipping them with new skills for housework. The survey did not investigate further into this aspect. It would be useful to examine how the work experience of these females has influenced their behaviour and skill as housewives and providers of home care. This will have to be part of a later study.

**Quality of Housing**

It was observed in the previous section that 284 households, or 55 per cent of the sample, had invested in housing. The average investment per household varied from a high of Rs. 36,000 for the male skilled group to a low of Rs. 7,825 for female domestic workers. The unskilled workers had an average of Rs. 23,000. The average sums invested by households indicate that the majority of the housing investments undertaken were small and comprised improvements to existing houses, cementing of floors, tiling of roofs, and increases in the covered area. These improvements, however, indicate the nature of the changes that have taken place in regard to the physical quality of life enjoyed by the households before and after migration. There have been few households that have increased the area of their

**Table 43**. Building materials and toilet facilities

| | Before migration | | | After migration | | |
|---|---|---|---|---|---|---|
| | Male | Female | Total | Male | Female | Total |
| *Walling materials* | | | | | | |
| Brick | 121 | 129 | 250 | 126 | 128 | 254 |
| Plank | 8 | 116 | 124 | 10 | 118 | 128 |
| Zinc sheets | 16 | 3 | 19 | 0 | 4 | 4 |
| Wattle and daub | 7 | 11 | 18 | 9 | 5 | 14 |
| Cabook | 1 | 18 | 19 | 8 | 22 | 30 |
| Total | 153 | 277 | 430 | 153 | 277 | 430 |
| *Roofing materials* | | | | | | |
| Tile | 98 | 138 | 236 | 101 | 143 | 244 |
| Zinc sheets | 23 | 54 | 77 | 21 | 55 | 76 |
| Asbestos | 15 | 23 | 38 | 21 | 33 | 54 |
| Cadjan | 10 | 50 | 60 | 4 | 32 | 36 |
| Concrete | 3 | 11 | 14 | 3 | 12 | 15 |
| Tile and zinc sheets | 1 | — | 1 | 1 | — | 1 |
| Tile and asbestos | 3 | — | 3 | 2 | — | 2 |
| Zinc sheets and cadjan | — | 1 | 1 | — | 2 | 2 |
| Total | 153 | 277 | 430 | 153 | 277 | 430 |
| *Flooring materials* | | | | | | |
| Mud | 19 | 83 | 102 | 7 | 75 | 82 |
| Cement | 126 | 97 | 223 | 141 | 99 | 240 |
| Terrazzo | 3 | 9 | 12 | — | 3 | 3 |
| Plank | — | 24 | 24 | — | 36 | 36 |
| Brick | — | — | — | — | 50 | 50 |
| Others | — | — | — | — | 19 | 19 |
| Total | 148 | 213 | 361 | 148 | 282 | 430 |
| *Toilet facilities* | | | | | | |
| Water-seal and flush toilets | 103 | 126 | 229 | 109 | 174 | 283 |
| Pit and bucket latrines | 40 | 81 | 121 | 34 | 37 | 71 |
| Without toilet facilities | 8 | 23 | 51 | 8 | 39 | 47 |
| Total | 151 | 250 | 401 | 151 | 250 | 401 |

houses. Therefore, in terms of space, the sample surveyed does not indicate any major change. While housing investments have taken place in more than half the households, clearly visible changes in the structural quality were revealed in the survey for only a small proportion; there has been no significant improvement for the majority. Most of the investments had evidently gone into improvements such as additional rooms and structural changes in a few housing units, as revealed in the survey, as well as repairs and renovations, which would have improved the

**Table 44.** Consumer durables: household furniture

| Type of furniture | Before migration | | | After migration | | |
|---|---|---|---|---|---|---|
| | Male | Female | Total | Male | Female | Total |
| Sitting-room | 14 | 29 | 43 | 18 | 49 | 67 |
| Bedroom | 4 | 6 | 10 | 5 | 5 | 10 |
| Dining-room | — | — | — | — | 1 | 1 |
| Sitting-room and bedroom | 6 | 10 | 16 | 14 | 54 | 68 |
| Sitting-room and dining-room | 3 | 2 | 5 | 6 | 3 | 9 |
| Bedroom and dining-room | 6 | 4 | 10 | 12 | 7 | 19 |
| Sitting-room, bedroom, and dining-room | 46 | 31 | 77 | 66 | 56 | 122 |
| Not applicable | 114 | 235 | 349 | 72 | 142 | 214 |
| Total | 193 | 317 | 510 | 193 | 317 | 510 |

housing quality though they would not be manifest as structural changes and improvements in terms of the specific characteristics researched in the survey.

Among the females, 50 migrants had houses with cadjan roofs before migration. The number after migration had fallen to 32. Proportionate increases were observed for roofs with tiles and asbestos. Houses with wattle and daub walls had fallen from 11 to 5, and those with cabook or laterite blocks had increased from 16 to 22. Similarly, the number of mud floors had dropped from 83 to 75. In the case of male employees the majority of roofs had been built with permanent materials even prior to the migration. However, there had been visible improvement in the poorest category; houses with thatched roofs had dropped from 10 to 4, mud floors from 19 to 7 and mud walls from 16 to 9. The housing conditions of this category of employees appear to have been at a higher level than those of female domestic employees prior to migration. Nevertheless, 90 of the 193 households in the two categories, male skilled and unskilled, had invested substantially in housing out of their savings abroad.

The improvements observed in water and sanitation covered a considerable number of houses. The reduction in the number of pit latrines and "other types" reflects this upgrading. For the entire sample the number in these two categories fell from 121 before migration to 71 at the time of the survey. Water seal and flush toilets had increased from 229 to 283. Houses with piped water increased from 145 to 157. In regard to lighting and fuel significant improvements were noted. Before migration 118 households were using wood as the main source of fuel; after migration the number had dropped to 75; the balance had diversified their sources of fuel to include gas and kerosene.

**Furniture and Equipment**

The majority of migrant households have invested in equipment for their homes. The one indicator of the changes in modes of living and life-styles is the interior of the households – the availability of furniture and household appliances. The

**Table 45**. Consumer durables

| Item | Before migration | | | After migration | | |
|---|---|---|---|---|---|---|
| | Male | Female | Total | Male | Female | Total |
| Sewing machine | 56 | 52 | 108 | 88 | 90 | 178 |
| Kerosene/gas/electric cooker | 14 | 12 | 26 | 45 | 42 | 87 |
| Refrigerator | 6 | 5 | 11 | 54 | 24 | 78 |
| Deep-freezer | 5 | 1 | 6 | 11 | 3 | 14 |
| Radio | 76 | 75 | 151 | 108 | 152 | 260 |
| Television | 10 | 6 | 16 | 99 | 92 | 191 |
| Video | 1 | 1 | 2 | 31 | 7 | 38 |
| Stereo | 4 | 1 | 5 | 32 | 26 | 58 |
| Washing machine | — | — | — | 2 | 3 | 5 |
| Dishwasher | — | — | — | 1 | 1 | 2 |
| Vacuum cleaner | — | — | — | 17 | 7 | 24 |
| Fan | 5 | 5 | 10 | 37 | 54 | 91 |
| None | 98 | 221 | 315 | 42 | 103 | 145 |

poorest households in Sri Lanka would have very few items of household furniture; living space would seldom be sufficient to provide separate furniture for the sitting-rooms, bedrooms and dining-rooms. Among the female workers, there were only 82 households who stated that they had separate furniture for dining, sleeping, or sitting before the migration. After migration there were 175 households who had acquired this range of furniture for their homes. Whereas only 31 had possessed the combination of all three, 66 had acquired the combination after the migration. If we take the possession of a combination of these types of furniture as an indicator of the specialized use of space and an enhancement of the quality of life in the home, 20 per cent of the households in the sample had a combination of two of the three types of furniture in their homes, and manifested a visible improvement in their quality of life.

The position regarding consumer durables was even better. The acquisitions made by households are set out in table 45. The radio, which is a very common item even among relatively poor households, was possessed only by 83 households prior to migration. After migration, 191 households among the female workers had acquired a radio; 84 of them had television sets, as against four prior to the migration; and 28 acquired refrigerators as against 5 before migration. Only a few households have gone in for sophisticated equipment that would seem to be above their level of living. Only four had deep-freezers and five had acquired video sets; seven had vacuum cleaners, and 13 stereo sets.

In the case of male employees, the number of households with furniture of all three functional types had increased from 46 before migration to 83 at the time of the survey. As indicated in table 45, there were 98 households of male migrants that did not possess any items of consumer durables that have been listed before they migrated for employment abroad. Only 15 of these households had a combination of three of these items. After the migration, the number of households which did not have any of the items had dropped to 42 and the number possessing three or more had increased to 104. Whereas only seven households had possessed TV sets prior to migration, 92 owned them at the time of the survey. Similarly, six households had possessed refrigerators prior to the migration; 92 had acquired them after employment abroad.

## Patterns of Consumption and Savings

The survey gathered data on the levels of consumption of households after the return of migrants. These levels of consumption would obviously be related to resources currently available to households, both in terms of accumulated savings which now go to finance consumption as well as incomes which they are presently earning. A large number of households were in a situation which could be regarded as transitional, where they had not fully adjusted to conditions following the return. Therefore many households would have been using their accumulated savings in order to finance current consumption.

Nevertheless, the responses that were given indicated that, in the majority of households, there was no significant variation in regard to major items of consumption. This applied to items of food, tobacco, liquor, and clothing, as well as to services such as health, education, and entertainment, and donations to charity. In the case of milk foods, only about 16 per cent of the households of male migrants and 12 per cent of the households of female migrants stated that they were consuming more of these items than before migration. On items such as cool drinks, the proportions that were consuming more were in the region of 30 per cent for males and 13 per cent for females. Only a small proportion of both male and female migrants reported increases in the consumption of alcohol and tobacco.

In regard to clothing, the proportion of households with high levels of consumption after migration was larger than for all other consumer items. This applied both to female members and male members of the households of all migrants. The figures ranged between approximately 31 per cent for males and 26 per cent for females. In the case of footwear, the proportions of households which had increased their consumption was lower – approximately 20 per cent for both males and females.

The situation in regard to expenditure on entertainment had changed very little. Visits to cinemas recorded an increase in the case of about 8 per cent of female migrants, but correspondingly there was a decrease reported in approximately 35 of the households. In the case of the males, the increase was slightly larger both for films and plays.

There was, therefore, no evidence of a major change in the levels of current consumption and their patterns. A small proportion, 20 to 30 per cent, of households recorded improvements. The large majority appear to have resumed consumption patterns not very different from what they were accustomed to prior to migration.

## Perception of Social and Economic Status

The survey attempted to find out how the households themselves perceived their place in the social and economic hierarchy, both before and after the migration, in order to assess whether in the judgement of the migrants themselves there had been some upward social mobility. Migrants were asked to respond to two ques-

**Table 46**. Economic level

| Level | Before migration | | | After migration | | |
|---|---|---|---|---|---|---|
| | Male | Female | Total | Male | Female | Total |
| Upper class | 0 | 0 | 0 | 0 | 0 | 0 |
| Upper-middle class | 5 | 0 | 5 | 7 | 0 | 7 |
| Middle class | 76 | 76 | 152 | 82 | 76 | 158 |
| Lower-middle class | 62 | 116 | 188 | 71 | 126 | 197 |
| Lower class | 50 | 125 | 165 | 33 | 115 | 148 |

tions: first, how they perceived their economic status in terms of wealth and in-come on a scale of five, ranging from upper to lower. The second question inquired how they assessed their social status, the assumption being that social status may not entirely coincide with economic status and may be influenced by factors such as family, caste, and occupation. In regard to economic status, the households that regarded themselves as belonging to the lower-middle and the lower categories made up the larger share. Their perception of alteration in their economic status after migration was marginal. In the case of females, 10 households in the lower class had moved up to the lower-middle. Upward mobility in the case of males was greater; 17 families in all had moved to a higher class after migration.

The situation regarding social status, however, was quite different. A significant number of households seem to have drawn a clear distinction between their eco-nomic status and their social status. For a variety of reasons they appear to have concluded that even though in terms of wealth and income they have not im-proved their status in a significant manner, socially, in terms of their standing in the community, they have benefitted significantly, particularly the households of female migrants. Twenty-seven of these felt that they had graduated into the upper part of the scale, whereas only one household had ranked itself in this part prior to the migration. The households that regarded themselves as in the upper-middle category had increased from 6 to 59, while those in the lower-middle and lower had dropped by approximately 40 per cent.

In the case of the male employees, 18 migrants thought their households had moved from the lowest to the lower-middle category, 13 from the lower-middle to the middle category and 6 to the other two higher categories. In contrast to the female migrants, the changes in social status of the households of male migrants are not significantly different from those perceived in relation to economic status.

A significant number of households, approximately 77 per cent for females and 36 per cent for males, was of the opinion that the attitudes of the community to-wards them had undergone some change as a result of the migration. The others either perceived no change or were not certain of the community's responses. The change in the community's attitudes included both positive as well as negative elements. In the case of males the majority of the migrants reported that the com-munity was more ready to seek their assistance and advice in community affairs. In the case of the female migrants, the proportion was much smaller, approximately 15 per cent. Similarly, nearly one-third of the male migrants reported that the com-munity expected them to assume leadership and play active roles in community affairs. Again the proportion is much smaller in the case of females – approximately 12 per cent. The tendency for members of the community to go to migrants for help, both in money and kind, was reported by approximately half the male migrants and one-fourth of the females. The proportion of households that had experienced negative reactions from the community formed a fairly significant component among the female migrants – 66 out of 317 or a little more than 20 per cent. These households detected an attitude of envy towards the newly acquired wealth and assets. Among the male migrants, however, the proportion was quite small – approximately 6 per cent. Resentment on the part of the community at changes in life-style was noted by only an insignificant number of households – 12 in the case of females and 6 in the case of males. Similarly, only a very few households felt that they experienced a sense of alienation or distancing from the community in which they lived as a result of the migration.

On the whole, therefore, the evidence available from the survey does not suggest any serious dislocation in community relationships resulting from the migration. On the other hand, a significant proportion of households, particularly among the male migrants, have been able to participate in the community more actively and assume more positive roles. In evaluating these data, it has to be noted that the capacity and motivation to take part in community affairs and assume leadership roles is generally limited to a minority. The fact that the proportion of migrants who report that the community has sought their leadership and participation is as high as revealed in the survey is worthy of special note. It would certainly suggest that the improvement in social and economic conditions associated with the migration contributed to the perceptions of both the community as well as of the migrants.

**Attitudinal Change relating to Education, Occupation, and Marriage of Children**

The survey sought information from households regarding their aspirations for their children and their attitude on crucial matters relating to higher education, jobs, and the choices made by children in employment and marriage. In answering the question, the respondents were required to indicate whether their attitudes had changed after the migration. As might be expected, a large majority of both male and female migrants wanted their children to obtain a higher education, achieve a better status than their parents, and secure more remunerative jobs than the parents. Those who expressed the view that they did not expressly desire an improvement in the status of their children over that of the parents were very few – only one in the case of male migrants and between four and nine for each of the questions in the case of the females. There was, however, a large number of households that did not make any definite response, presumably for the reason that the questions may have been regarded as either speculative or unrealistic, or because the respondents felt they had not given adequate thought to this subject. On the question of choice of employment and marriage, the changes in attitude were quite significant. Those who stated that they would give freedom of choice to their children in regard to employment had increased by 120 (36 per cent) in the case of females, and 132 (65 per cent) in the case of males.

Another sensitive question addressed to the migrants related to their attitude to the differences in their aspirations for sons and daughters. Again, a large proportion of the households of the migrants reported shifts in attitude; they were now of the view that sons and daughters should do equally well in regard to career, employment and well-being. Some caution, however, should be exercised in interpreting these general responses. Although the questions were posed in specific terms and migrants were asked distinctly whether they had entertained similar views and attitudes prior to migration, there may have been instances where households did not pay close attention to the differences and changes in attitude which the survey was seeking to elicit. It was also assumed that the changes were primarily caused by the migration and the exposure of migrants to the new experience of living and working abroad. The data available relate to changes that have occurred over a short period, and therefore the effect of other intervening factors would have been marginal. The survey indicates that the exposure of the migration has certainly resulted in greater liberality and openness in regard to migrants' relations with their children and decisions concerning their future.

## Changes in Religious Beliefs, Values, and Practices

The survey went on to elicit information on the changes that have taken place in regard to religious beliefs, values, and practices. The preponderant majority of those who responded reported that there had been no change in observance and belief.

## Political Ideology

The survey attempted to uncover the shifts that had occurred in political ideology, participation in political life, and membership of political parties. A large majority of both male and female migrants stated that they had no interest in politics both before and after the migration. The changes, if at all, were marginal and do not suggest any impact on the political behaviour of the migrants. Membership of political parties had declined for both males and females, for females from 65 before migration to 26 afterwards and for males from 70 to 69. There were a very few migrants who had been participating actively in politics before migration: 8 in the case of females, declining to 2 after migration, and 13 for males, declining to 11 after migration. In regard to both membership and political participation, it has to be noted that many of these migrants have returned only recently and have had little opportunity to re-enter or participate anew in political activities.

The survey went on to obtain responses from migrants in regard to the views and attitudes held by them on important political issues such as the need for a democratically elected government, and the need for a free press.

An interesting pattern emerges from the responses given by female migrants. It would appear that, for a significant proportion of females, political views have hardened, taking them in the direction of authoritarian government. A small proportion of them – approximately 8 per cent – have expressed their preference for an extreme left ideology. Prior to the migration there were only two female migrants in this category; the number had increased to 26 after migration. The position of the males, however, showed little change – approximately 80 per cent of the male migrants showed preference for a democratic system both before and after migration. In the case of both males and females, the category which did not give any

**Table 47.** Social level

| Level | Before migration | | | After migration | | |
|---|---|---|---|---|---|---|
| | Male | Female | Total | Male | Female | Total |
| Upper class | 0 | 1 | 1 | 0 | 27 | 27 |
| Upper-middle class | 4 | 6 | 10 | 7 | 59 | 66 |
| Middle class | 81 | 73 | 154 | 85 | 85 | 170 |
| Lower-middle class | 62 | 131 | 193 | 68 | 89 | 157 |
| Lower class | 46 | 106 | 152 | 33 | 57 | 90 |

definite response had increased and the number that had indicated their political alignment had declined. As a result, the number that had declared themselves to be left, centre, or right had all dropped quite substantially. The figure seems to indicate a growing lack of interest in political activity, particularly in the partisan and committed political activity which calls for alignment on party lines. It is difficult to say whether this is a temporary manifestation affecting only recently returned migrants. It may also derive from a growing awareness that the economic opportunities they enjoyed had little to do with political patronage.

## Impact on the Work Ethic

The survey also examined the attitudes of migrants to several issues relating to the work ethic and the desire for improvement of skills and training. The responses have to be viewed in the light of what was stated earlier regarding the recent return of migrants as well as the situation of unemployment in which a large number find themselves. Some of the questions, however, continue to have relevance to the work situation of migrants, including that of female domestic workers. There was a marked increase in the willingness to work longer hours; as many as 83 migrants, or 27 per cent, of females said they were prepared to do this. About 33 per cent of the males fall into the same category. Some of the other questions were aimed at obtaining the respondent's attitude to job satisfaction, and to determine his keenness to perform well in a job and to obtain the approval of his superiors. For females, the proportions responding positively to these questions ranged from 27 to 30 per cent, and for males from 23 to 31 per cent. More than 25 per cent of the males reported that they were pursuing further training. In the case of females, nearly 20 per cent fell into this category. The responses indicate that between 25 and 30 per cent of migrants acquired a more positive attitude to work after their migration experience.

## Attitudes to International Affairs and Foreigners

The survey gathered data on the impact that the migration has had on migrants' perceptions of international affairs and their relationships with foreigners they had met abroad. There was a positive response to the question about the impact of the migration on international awareness. More than 50 per cent of the females and nearly two-thirds of the males reported that they had become more interested in international affairs after the migration. More than one-third of the females stated that they continued to maintain the friendships which they had made abroad. The figure was much smaller for the males – approximately 18 per cent. The large majority of migrants, approximately three-fifths of them, had become more sensitive to the international image of their country and were concerned with the way in which the behaviour of nationals abroad would affect this image. Approximately one-third of the female migrants and about 40 per cent of the males reported that they were more receptive to foreigners and ready to enter into and maintain relationships with them. There was a small proportion, however, who appeared to have reacted adversely to their experience and stated they were less inclined to deal with foreigners and were cautious in their relationships with them. On the whole, however, the responses indicated that the experience of the migration had influenced a sizeable proportion of the migrants to be more open to foreigners and to take a greater interest in what happens in the world outside as well as in relationships with the international community.

## Overall Evaluation and Conclusions

In the final part of the survey an attempt was made to gather information about the migrants' impressions of the current trends in the Gulf countries as regards the migration as well as their overall assessment of the impact of the migration on their own lives. Nearly 80 per cent of the migrants, or about 400, considered the migration an experience of great value: 342 rated it as "very valuable"; the balance regarded it as "valuable." Similar proportions stated that they would accept a second term of employment in those countries. A small proportion, 26 out of 510, stated they would not migrate again given the opportunity. The majority of the female migrants stated that the migration had had a major impact on their lives. Of the male migrants, approximately half agreed with this view, while the other half denied that the migration had been a significant influence.

In response to the question of whether the material benefits from the migration were regarded by them as substantial, about 40 per cent answered in the affirmative, 32 per cent of females in the negative and 50 per cent of males in the affirmative. These proportions broadly correspond with the conclusions that have been drawn from the analyses of the survey data. In examining the situation of migrants and the durable benefits that have accrued to them in terms of income-generating assets, such as fixed deposits, investment in businesses, etc., the survey reveals that about 28 per cent had fixed deposits that were yielding regular incomes ranging from small amounts to in excess of Rs. 500 a month. About one-third of the households have liquidated their debts. Another 12 per cent reported substantial savings which had not yet been used, and which they planned to invest in fixed deposits, housing, small businesses, and other investments. About 10 per cent had already invested in businesses and a slightly larger proportion had acquired machinery, equipment, and vehicles, which do not appear to have had any significant differential impact on the behaviour of migrants in each occupational category. The income ranges and the savings investments cut across these variables and appear to be distributed without significant variations arising from marital status, age, and educational level. The profile that emerges indicates that more than half of the migrants have improved their financial status and have acquired, or plan to acquire, some income-earning assets, but that these investments alone often provide insufficient income to sustain a household. They do, however, provide supplementary sources of income. The proportion who have succeeded in making substantial improvements probably are no more than the 40 per cent who reported substantial benefits from the migration.

The durable impact which the migration has had on the quality of life of the migrants and their households is also discernible in the improvements that have taken place in the quality of housing, the ownership of furniture and equipment, and the pattern of consumption and expenditure. The survey reveals that approximately two-thirds of the migrants have made investments in housing; however, improvements in structural quality and space are confined to a much smaller proportion. The survey reveals that in the case of a few households, investments have resulted in the replacement of temporary roofs with permanent roofing, mud walls with permanent brick walls, and mud floors with cement floors. Apart from these visible improvements, investments would have be used for repairs and renovations and upgrading of the house with minor improvements which are not reflected in the major structural changes recorded in the survey. There have also been significant improvements in sanitation and in the quality and availability of toilet facilities.

The most obvious improvement is in the acquisition of furniture and household appliances. Nearly 21 per cent of households had newly acquired combinations of furniture, which indicated that there was a definite improvement in the quality of accommodation and housing. Similarly, nearly 34 per cent of households that previously had no equipment, such as radios, television sets, sewing machines and so on, had invested in some consumer durables after the migration. The total picture that emerges is one in which approximately 30 per cent of the households indicate a significant improvement in the quality of their homes. If we take this figure as a measure of the benefits of the migration, it would seem that for as many as 70 per cent of the migrants improvements in life-style and in the interior of the home were negligible.

Only around 30 per cent have been able to acquire assets and improve their houses to the extent that the migration has made some impact on the quality of their life. At the other end, about one-third of the households show significant change neither in their income and asset position nor in the quality of their homes.

The large majority of migrants, both male and female, were clearly of the view that the migration had no disruptive or negative impact on their personal and family life. This is substantiated by the fact that the migrants have reported only one separation. The proportions confessing to a negative impact were about 10 per cent among males and 15 per cent among females. On the other hand, there was evidence that for the large majority the migration was a positive experience; they showed greater concern for family relationships and were willing to share responsibility for household activities. A greater degree of joint decision-making on financial and other matters was also evident. The survey indicated that the migration has influenced attitudes to children. A significant proportion recognized changes in their attitudes to children. They were more desirous of a higher status and better occupation for their children than what they themselves enjoyed. They were more willing to allow their children to choose their partners in marriage and decide on their own careers.

In the overall assessment the majority of migrants did not identify any significant impact on religious beliefs, values, observances, and practices, indicating that on the whole the experience of the migration and the exposure it provided did not result in any serious erosion of the accepted value systems or disturbance of accepted moral and social norms. In regard to political attitudes, the only unusual feature was the hardening of attitudes among female migrants, where there was a significant minority which had shifted from a democratic viewpoint to a more authoritarian approach. As a whole, the sample showed little interest in political activity, both before and after migration. The number reporting lack of involvement in political activity had in fact increased after the migration.

In regard to the assessment of their relationship with their community, the large majority of households felt that the migration had not caused any serious strains on that relationship. They did not observe any negative reaction on the part of the community, or any ill-will or envy at the opportunities and benefits the emigrants had enjoyed or the wealth they had acquired. Only a small minority – 6 per cent of males and 20 per cent of females – reported that they observed such negative reactions and experienced a distancing from the community, a sense of alienation on account of their own new attitudes and values. A significant number of households – nearly one-third of males and 15 per cent of females – stated that the community turned more frequently to them for assistance in regard to community activities and were ready to give them an active role, or even one of leadership, in community affairs.

As might be expected, the migration appears to have had a decisive impact on the knowledge and awareness of international affairs and the world outside. More than 60 per cent of the migrants gave positive responses to the relevant questions. Nearly 35 per cent also indicated that they were now inclined to have more contacts and relationships with friendly foreigners.

Approximately 30 per cent of the migrants indicated that the migration had had a positive impact on their attitude to working longer hours, and that they had greater work satisfaction, were desirous of more training, and were concerned with performance in order to win approbation. The responses to the inquiry as to whether they had acquired new skills and training was less definite. Few migrants were able to claim that they had acquired any specific new skills or had received training and experience in higher or upgraded skills in their occupational field. But the majority, including female domestic workers, referred to work experience which had enhanced their competence. The precise quality of skill upgrading and enhancement of human capital that has taken place in terms of knowledge, attitudes, and competence could not be captured in the survey, although the responses hinted at them. This would require a study in greater depth than was possible through the interviews in the survey.

## Some Policy Implications

On the basis of the data obtained in the survey it has been estimated that, of those who participated in the migration, about 40 per cent of households have derived benefits of a substantial nature and have raised their income-earning capacity to a significant extent. This cannot be regarded as a satisfactory performance for the migration as a whole. The data draw attention to two disturbing features in the outcome of the migration.

First, there is evidently a vulnerable group of significant proportions for whom the existing system does not work satisfactorily. These are migrants for whom the financial costs of migration far exceeded the average, as well as those who had to use recruitment channels which proved unreliable on a host of matters, including the contractual arrangements that were made. Although the system worked satisfactorily for most of the migrants, this vulnerable minority cannot be neglected. There have been various institutional improvements for the management and regulation of the migration, which had only recently been introduced and were not in place when the migrants in the sample migrated. The Foreign Employment Bureau now co-ordinates and monitors the migration in all its phases more effectively and more closely than was possible before its establishment. In these conditions it should be possible to make a special effort to identify the minority which is vulnerable at present to various forms of exploitation and victimization and which is therefore deprived of the full benefits of the migration. This requires, on the one hand, further action to close the loopholes and correct the deficiencies in the regulation of the recruiting process and the monitoring of recruitment channels; on the other, it needs what is tantamount to an extension effort to reach the migrants during the period of preparation, particularly those who are most vulnerable, and to provide the necessary guidance and assistance for them to manage efficiently the recruitment phase and their contractual arrangements.

A more disturbing feature, however, is the large gap that exists between the actual performance and the potential benefits of migration. A close examination of the successes and failures indicate that they occur more or less randomly, irrespective of occupation, level of income, educational level, or level of earnings abroad. There are instances where a housemaid earning a low wage has managed the new resources prudently, contained the consumption levels of the household within reasonable limits, maintained stable family relationships, made sufficient savings to invest in a few basic improvements in the home, and invested a small sum in an interest-earning bank deposit which yielded a supplementary source of income to the household. On the other hand, a skilled employee with a much higher level of earnings may have been unable to mobilize the necessary household support to husband the new resources and frittered away his much more substantial earnings on increases in consumption and risky ventures. There is therefore considerable scope for improving the performance of migrants and households in the management of their newly acquired resources. Migrants who have well-defined goals and specific objectives in seeking employment abroad are obviously better motivated to plan for the future and to involve the household in decision-making processes directed towards the achievement of the objectives.

There are two phases of decision-making and adjustment that are crucial to a successful performance by the migrant. At the time of migration the migrant has to be goal-oriented and have the motivation and capacity to plan, even in a rudimentary way, for the appropriate use of his future income. What he does after his return will depend, however, on how he manages his resources during his employment abroad and how he plans for his future. On his return, he should be able to identify and have access to situations and income-earning opportunities in which he can put his resources, both human and financial, to maximum use.

There are various programmes that have been implemented to deal with the problems of the adjustment and reabsorption of migrants after their return. These include training schemes and entrepreneurial development for self-employment and small enterprises. Government agencies and banking institutions are being mobilized for this purpose. These programmes have to be greatly strengthened and extended to reach the majority of return migrants. On the other hand, goal orientation, and the preparation of migrants and households to help them better to plan and manage their new resources, are areas in which much more systematic work needs to be done.

## Reference

Ministry of Labour/Asian Regional Team for Employment Promotion. 1981. Project on Impact of Out and Return Migration on Domestic Employment in Sri Lanka.